Cowboys and Samurai

Cowboys and Samurai

*Why the United States
Is Losing the Industrial Battle
and Why It Matters*

Stephen D. Cohen

HarperBusiness
A Division of HarperCollins*Publishers*

Library of Congress Cataloging-in-Publication Data

Cohen, Stephen D.
    Cowboys and samurai : why the United States is losing the
industrial battle and why it matters / Stephen D. Cohen
        p.   cm.
    Includes bibliographical references and index.
    ISBN 0-88730-416-8 :
    1. United States—Commerce—Japan.   2. Japan—Commerce—
United States.   3. United States—Economic policy—1981-
4. Japan—Economic policy—1989- 5. Competition, International.
I. Title.
382'.0973052—dc20   90-29161
                                                              CIP

International Standard Book Number: 0-88730-416-8

Library of Congress Catalog Card Number: 90-29161

Printed in the United States of America

91 92 93 94 CC/HC 9 8 7 6 5 4 3 2

For Linda,
Sondra, and Marc

Contents

Preface and Acknowledgments

Writing this book has been an extraordinary experience that mirrors the extraordinary degree of change in its subject matter. The book was originally conceived as a second edition straightforwardly updating my 1985 book *Uneasy Partnership*. However, I soon found that I encountered the experience noted by the late Edwin O. Reischauer in the preface of the 1988 update of his book *The Japanese:* he wrote that it quickly became evident that a few alterations and the addition of materials on events that had occurred since the previous edition would not be adequate. So much about Japan's role in the world economy has changed in recent years and so much more is now known about Japanese economic practices that I, like Professor Reischauer, had to produce what is for all practical purposes an entirely new book.

The basic hypotheses of my original work have been verified by subsequent events: a systemic problem exists and will not be cured as long as both countries continue to ignore the need to address causes rather than symptoms; both countries do little more than go through the motions of securing adjustment in the bilateral trade imbalance because both have largely achieved what they most wanted; and both countries are responsible for the escalating trade frictions and continuing disequilibrium. Perhaps the greatest shortcoming of the first edition was inadequate pessimism. Unfortunately the basic conclusions have not changed. But the supporting evidence and argumentation do need extensive augmentation, especially with regard to the more disquieting trend lines. The research and writing of this edition unexpectedly sensitized me to just how much the relative competitive position of the United States has deteriorated since the early 1980s and how slight is the prospect for a quick turnaround.

The new version of my analysis of bilateral economic relations suffers from the many limitations of the first. The really important questions transcend the empirical arithmetic of trade balances; they are highly subjective, often controversial, and emotionally charged issues that cannot be diagnosed and resolved through the use of some foolproof scientific methodology. U.S.–Japanese economic relations are simply too complicated and too tied in to value judgments to allow for definitive conclusions. Mine is an effort by a reasonably well-informed and more-objective-than-most observer of bilateral relations. The failure of any reviewer (at least in the English language) of the first edition to complain that it was too pro-Japanese or too pro-American seems to me significant, for this is a subject increasingly burdened by emotional, polarized debate.

This book is an attempt to bridge a communication gap that remains as wide as the Pacific Ocean. It is an effort to put bilateral trade relations in their broadest context, one encompassing several social science disciplines. It is also an effort to synthesize the two countries' vastly different perceptions of bilateral problems. I am hopeful this approach can fill gaps in the literature of international economic relations and in policy recommendations that will induce an economically efficient adjustment process.

Once again, I wish to disclaim any notion that I speak as a bona fide expert on Japan. Such a status is unattainable without, at least, Japanese language capability and extended residence in the country. What I lack in expertise, I have tried to remedy through scholarly detachment. I have also tried to offset some of my shortcomings by imposing on friends and associates to read parts of my manuscript. The final product is at least a little better and more accurate thanks to the helpful comments of Edward J. Lincoln, Warren Farb, Tom Howell, and Masaru Tamamoto. A formal expression of appreciation is also extended to Kenneth Flamm and Sheridan Tatsuno for their helpful comments on the chapter dealing with the semiconductor agreement. In all cases, I assume full responsibility for any errors of fact and for all interpretations and recommendations.

I wish also to extend my deep thanks for the research funding received from the O'Melveny & Myers Centennial Grant and the MITI Research Institute in partial support of my study of the causes and resolution of the semiconductor dispute.

A very special expression of appreciation goes to Frederick A. Williams, my graduate assistant during the 1989–90 academic year, for his extensive and invaluable assistance throughout the long research and editing that went into the preparation of this book. Thanks also go to Anita G. Lundry for her prompt and cheerful secretarial support and to Michael Hannan for his assistance in the final editing phase. Finally, I need to express thanks for the patience of my wife, Linda, and my children, Sondra and Marc, while I toiled away in splendid isolation at the family computer.

Stephen D. Cohen
Washington, D.C.
September 1990

CHAPTER 1

The Nature and Causes of the Structural Problem in U.S.–Japanese Trade Relations

The Hare, one day, laughed at the Tortoise for his short feet, slowness and awkwardness.

"Though you may be swift as the wind," replied the Tortoise good-naturedly, "I can beat you in a race. . . ."

The rivals started, and the Hare, of course, soon left the Tortoise far behind. Having reached midway to the goal, she began to play about, nibble the young herbage, and amuse herself in many ways. The day being warm, she even thought she would take a little nap in a shady spot, for she thought that if the Tortoise should pass her while she slept, she could easily overtake him again before he reached the end.

The Tortoise meanwhile plodded on, unwavering and unresting, straight towards the goal.

The Hare, having overslept herself, started up from her nap, and was surprised to find that the Tortoise was nowhere in sight. Off she went at full speed, but on reaching the winning-post, found that the Tortoise was already there, waiting for her arrival.

—Aesop's Fables

The modern international political order is in an unprecedented situation: a cooperative mood exists among all of the great powers. The world order has effectively discarded the adversarial system dominated by power struggles over territory, spheres of influence, and political ideology. Now that the rules of the cold war have been discarded, it is unclear what foreign policy concerns, goals, and standards of behavior will shape relations among the major countries. One thing is certain: economic forces have become the pivotal link between the outgoing and the incoming order in contemporary international relations.

The ideological struggle between Marxism-Leninism and capitalism is rapidly dissipating into the universal question of how best to manage the

1

market mechanism. The Soviet military threat to the United States and its allies is ebbing as Moscow turns its priorities to remedying the internal contradictions of its poorly functioning, mismanaged economy. The once tightly controlled Soviet empire has been effectively jettisoned because the financial burden became too big.

Stockpiles of military weaponry are becoming decreasingly important factors in the determination of national power and influence. As we move into the twenty-first century, power and influence will most likely be determined by a country's export capabilities and its possession of investment capital and of advanced technology. The United States can claim victory in the cold war, but it is steadily losing ground in the arguably more important struggle for global economic leadership. Of course the United States will continue to play a key role in the balance of international power, but the odds are mounting against its status as a clear-cut superpower in a new world order that may eventually rank economic power as number one.

The decline in relative American economic strength indicates that the United States is in the early phase of losing a strategically important international struggle. Simple extrapolations are notoriously inaccurate, but Japan, the most dynamic foreign competitor of the United States, clearly has the potential to become the world's leading financial center and primary source of new technology. Should this happen, the main reasons will be misplaced American priorities and forward-looking Japanese ambitions. The relationship between national priorities and national ambitions in the context of economic relations between the United States and Japan is the main topic of this book.

The economic relationship between Japan and the United States is of extraordinary importance to the future of both countries. With economic factors becoming increasingly important in determining a country's international power, this is a particularly inopportune time for the United States to remain oblivious to the possibility that Japan will replace it as the world's strongest economy. What Americans do not know about Japan can and does hurt their economy. Rising dependence on Japan for advanced electronics components and investment capital already is limiting U.S. independence of action.

Relative successes and failures in the economic competition between the United States and Japan, especially in the high-technology industries of the future, will be a critical factor in determining the future global status of these two countries and the shape of the international economic order. The impending economic integration of the West European market is important in commercial terms, but market size does not necessarily determine a country's ability to be the most competitive in the most important technologies.

It is for these reasons that the United States and Japan account for the most important bilateral relationship in the world. Unfortunately, the economic friction that has dogged their relationship for more than twenty years is more likely to grow than to abate. The failure to ease this friction is caused by the inability of either side to properly diagnose the systemic cause of what is by now a long standing economic problem: the success of the Japanese economy relative to the economic performance of the United States.

This is not a minor commercial squabble; the stakes are enormous. International flows of goods, services, and capital are steadily rising determinants of a country's economic vigor and standard of living. An advanced industrial country capable of generating a trade surplus on the basis of technologically advanced goods can expect a strong currency and a growing international creditor status. If the United States does not respond effectively to external economic challenges—primarily from Japan—it will continue to experience a declining role in international economic relations, further weakening of the dollar, smaller increases in real wages, and additional increases in its international debt.

MANIFESTATIONS OF U.S.–JAPANESE TRADE PROBLEMS

The economic relationship between the United States and Japan, which has become tightly intertwined out of mutual need, can be compared to a stormy marriage to which the two partners bring complementary neuroses, along with irreplaceable benefits. The United States as a whole maximizes consumption and recreation, pursues instant gratification, extols the spirit of the individual, and adheres to a belief in the glory of the free market. Japan as a whole opts to work, to save, to sublimate the self to the interests of a larger group, to plan and to sacrifice for the long run, and to adhere to an economic system based primarily on enhancing the size and power of entrenched domestic interests.

The United States is winning the consumption war while Japan is winning the production war. Selecting the real victor in bilateral economic competition presupposes knowing whether the primary purpose of economic activity is to allow for consumption or to give a greater sense of purpose to the human experience.

The rewards of bilateral economic relations differ greatly in the United States and Japan. The Japanese can point proudly to annual trade surpluses with the United States in the $50 billion range and to the decimation by imports of entire industries in the United States. The United States can point proudly to receiving the benefits of importing vast amounts (on a net basis) of real economic resources from Japan in exchange for paper currency that periodically depreciates in value against the yen and is constantly returned to the United States by Japanese investors. These capital flows partially finance the U.S. federal budget and private investment.

Virtually every Western economic theorist subscribing to neoclassical tenets would argue that the United States is thereby conning the Japanese. The Japanese are subsidizing the U.S. standard of living at the expense of gain in their own material wealth. But a nontheorist would point to the dangers of continued dependence on Japan for high-technology goods and of the decline in U.S. living standards if the United States loses its competitiveness in the production of sophisticated capital and consumer goods.

After 1969, paternalistic American feelings toward post-World War II Japan were replaced by a continuous series of economic shocks, threats, tensions, insults, confrontational negotiations, and mutual accusations. Subsequently, it was only during the oil crises of 1973–74 and 1979–80, that a period of economic tranquility existed between the United States and Japan.

The bitter feelings on each side would be less significant if it were not for the fact that so much is at stake. Together, the United States and Japan produce more than one-third of the world's total output of goods and services. Two-way trade between these countries now exceeds $135 billion annually. The United States buys 30 to 40 percent of Japan's annual exports. Japan provides the largest single source of the capital flows needed by the U.S. economy to finance its large current account deficit and to offset its inadequate domestic savings. Important sectors of both economies are heavily influenced by—if not mutually dependent on—the two-way exchange of goods and capital. Both countries share a belief in democracy and capitalism. There is little philosophical disagreement as to what type of global order is desirable.

These common interests notwithstanding, the friendship between Japan and the United States is not secure. Despite a patchwork of trade agreements and Japanese concessions, bilateral discord seems to be at a record high. The gulf in communication widens despite years of effort at mutual understanding. The odds overwhelmingly favor further confrontations rather than reconciliation because neither side has yet identified the real causes of the problem, accepted appropriate responsibility, or undertaken effective remedial actions. While a total breakdown in relations between the United States and Japan remains unlikely, a danger exists in each country that the popular view of the other will become more one of menace than of political and economic partnership.

Over the past two decades, Japan has acquired the reputation among its trading partners for being an unfair or even adversarial trader that often violates the accepted rules of international trade. Complaints against Japan are aimed both at its import and export practices. The benefits in the United States to consumers of Japanese-made goods and to exporters to Japan have been large, but not large enough to prevent an escalation of suspicion and the desire for stronger anti-Japanese policies.

Within Japan, its trading partners in the United States, Western Europe, and elsewhere have acquired the reputation of being complainers and also-rans. Most Japanese observers say that these countries would be better off if they channeled the energy they expend whining and making demands on Japan into making greater efforts to produce goods more efficiently and to understand the Japanese market. The Japanese see themselves being punished for hard work and well-deserved success. As their self-confidence rises, their toleration for economic advice and demands from the United States declines. Although most economic policy officials and business executives in Japan are aware that its trading partners have legitimate claims against Japanese export and import practices, they must be dismayed that the United States seemingly turns a blind eye to the comparably large trade surpluses being recorded by West Germany.

The most visible rallying point for U.S. economic unhappiness with Japan is the persistence of large bilateral trade deficits. The United States's deficit jumped from an average of about $20 billion in the early 1980s to about $53 billion in the late 1980s (imports measured on the customs value basis). Because the trade deficit with Japan in the late 1980s held relatively steady at a time when the U.S. multilateral trade deficit was declining, Japan's share has risen, reaching a significant 45 percent of the total trade deficit in 1989. Also contributing to U.S. discomfort was the fact that the large raw materials component of U.S. exports to Japan caused the trade balance in the economically significant manufacturing sector to exceed $70 billion annually throughout the late 1980s.

Many economists assert that the imbalance in bilateral trade does not necessarily prove that an *economic* problem exists. The cause of the imbalance may be of genuine economic significance, however, especially if the deficit is relatively large. In any event, a serious and continuing problem exists because many business and government leaders in both countries are unhappy with the trade policies of the other. They strongly and sincerely perceive the bilateral trade situation to be in disarray. A *political* problem therefore exists, even if one does not believe that the bilateral deficits constitute a legitimate economic problem, no matter how large or how caused. Legitimate concerns present an underlying threat to what is arguably the world's most important economic relationship.

The United States has been disoriented by the speed, breadth, and intensity of Japanese industrial success. It has watched its former pupil outperform it in one industry after another. There is voluminous evidence demonstrating the extraordinary difficulties encountered by the majority of U.S. companies in penetrating the Japanese market. The modern relationship between the two countries has evolved from the United States being an occupying power, through its demands for "voluntary" Japanese export restraints, to its current efforts to open the Japanese market. The bilateral relationship at the beginning of the 1990s has reached a new and far more important plateau: an intensifying Japanese challenge to U.S. leadership in the critically important high technology sector.

Perceptions of a lack of fairness and reciprocity are increasingly dominating U.S. thinking about the implications of Japan's growing economic strength. According to some public opinion polls many Americans now believe that Japan's economic strength has become a greater long-term threat to U.S. national security than the Soviet Union's military might.[1] Nevertheless, the U.S. response is still based only on lip service and marginal change. U.S. economic policy still has not solved the twin dilemmas of how to revitalize its industrial base or how to restrict imports from Japan without hurting its own domestic economy. The growing dependence of the United States on a vast number of Japanese products suggests that the imposition of import restrictions probably would not be cost-effective (as seen, for example, in escalating automobile prices after restrictions on Japanese exports took effect in 1981).

For an increasing number of Americans, the situation has gone from bad to worse to intolerable. The trade numbers feed a triad of suspicions: that something is radically wrong with U.S. industry's international competitiveness, that Japan's export zeal is extraordinarily voracious, and that the Japanese market for manufactured goods is virtually impenetrable by foreign exporters. The result has been an escalating movement in Washington for imposing retaliatory measures. The most recent efforts have focused on a "results-oriented" approach, presenting Japan with a quantitative goal, say for an increased amount of imports, along with the demand that the Japanese government and business sectors act for themselves to figure out how to comply with the U.S. request. Proof of compliance would come in the trade statistics.

Japan, in the meantime, has been troubled, perplexed, and angered by the substance and implications of the techniques employed by the United States in seeking to alleviate its grievances. The U.S. government is seen as advocating irrelevant actions, damning Japanese strengths instead of remedying U.S. failures, and adopting insulting, arm-twisting tactics. The argument that U.S. pressure is necessary to engender liberalization of the Japanese market is overwhelmed by *perceptions* of a serious abuse of Japanese dignity and sovereignty by the haughty, never-ending trade demands of the United States. Most Japanese are unsympathetic to what they view as the hypocritical and false assertions that the United States is the world's most open market and that Japan's economic structure is playing unfairly and is structured differently from Western industrial countries. Japanese thinking is dominated by the desire to minimize foreign economic intervention and by the knowledge that its series of unilateral import liberalization measures taken over the past twenty-five years is far in excess of any other country's concessions.

If an overt trade war ever were to erupt between these two economic giants, the international economic order would be devastated by the widespread adoption of protectionist measures by smaller economies and a disruption in international capital flows. A U.S.–Japanese trade war also would put at risk cooperative military efforts in the East Asian–Western

Pacific region and would alter Japanese-Soviet relations. But as in any stormy marriage, emotions might someday overwhelm rational consideration of the consequences of divorce.

To a large extent, a smoothly functioning international economic system depends on maintaining compatible domestic economic policies, but there is no adjustment mechanism in today's world to compensate for the major differences in individual domestic economic performances. Major differences in trade performances among industrial countries are inevitable given differences in such factors as inflation rates, productivity increases, savings rates, investment outlays, and government regulation. Neither floating exchange rates nor unilateral trade liberalization measures can offset the effects of different economic policies and priorities in Japan, the United States, and other countries. These differences explain why a big borrower such as South Korea does not have an external debt problem, while all of the big Latin American countries do. The "international" economic order, in some respects at least, is principally the agglomeration of the domestic policies of individual countries.

The U.S. and Japanese economics remain significantly out of sync with each other. Differences in values, priorities, and goals have resulted in equally sharp differences in economic policies and performances. Since foreign trade performance, at least in the manufacturing sector, is primarily shaped by domestic considerations, not vice versa, structural trade problems between the United States and Japan are inevitable.

A BASIC HYPOTHESIS ABOUT THE CAUSE OF THE PROBLEM

Logical diagnosis and recommendations concerning bilateral trade relations will flow from the manner in which the "problem" is defined— assuming that a problem in fact exists. One could argue that there can be no meaningful significance in any bilateral trade balance or one could argue that there is nothing wrong with the United States importing low-cost, high-quality goods paid for in domestically printed currency, much of which is then reinvested by the Japanese in the United States in U.S. Treasury debt instruments, real estate, and the like. This study assumes that there is a problem, that it is important, and that it appears to be getting more serious.

Many previous discussions of U.S.–Japanese trade frictions suffered from the tendency to selectively assemble a limited amount of data. The diverse terms of reference utilized over the years by many commentators to explain bilateral relations have produced a body of literature characterized by conflicting assessments and, hence, contradictory prescriptions for change. Analyses are colored by underlying assumptions, whether of a Japanese economic conspiracy or sour grapes by a jealous, fading superpower. Any useful exploration of the bilateral trade problem must start with a dispassionate, clearly focused definition of what is wrong and why.

The central, integrating hypothesis of this book is that virtually everyone on both sides has historically underestimated and continues to underestimate the degree and impact of the deeply rooted structural differences between the "cowboy" and "samurai" approaches to capitalism. To suggest that the Japanese economy performs differently in many ways from the U.S. economy is neither racist nor "Japan bashing." (In fact, it might more accurately be called "America bashing" because many of the differences we will discuss are to Japan's credit and U.S. embarrassment.) More important is that slogans not cloud the fact that a long-standing *systemic* problem exists in U.S.–Japanese economic relations.

More than any collection of economic indicators, a country's value system sets the tone and direction of the national economy. The gulf between Japanese and U.S. values ensures a gulf in the yin and yang of domestic economic performance with resulting economic frictions between the countries and a nearly insurmountable communications gap. Up to now, U.S. economists have assumed that neoclassical economic theory can be extrapolated without modification to Japan and all other countries. While there are obvious basic similarities in the ways U.S. and Japanese goods, labor, and financial markets function, there are also important differences, both at the core and at the periphery. More than most of their Western contemporaries, U.S. economists have unquestioningly accepted the concept that free market prices and the bottom line of profitability or loss are the ultimate, if cold-hearted determinants of efficiency. In the 1960s, U.S. political scientists learned from the emerging Sino-Soviet dispute that communism is not monolithic. In the 1990s, a third consecutive decade of U.S.–Japanese trade frictions may finally convince the majority of U.S. economists that capitalism is not monolithic.

A different kind of efficiency seems to have been perfected in post–World War II Japan, deriving perhaps most importantly from a historical determination to minimize dependence on and subordination to foreigners. Japanese industrial efficiency is driven by never being satisfied with existing levels of productivity or levels of service to customers, even if shareholders are happy; and by the belief that long-term market share is more important than short-term profits. It is based on thorough homework—from reading technical journals to collecting commercial intelligence on one's competitors' current products and future development plans. On the dark side, Japan's industrial efficiency depends on what most Americans regard as exploitation of labor and of consumers through inadequate wages and excessive domestic prices.

For Americans, Japan is an oversize case study suggesting that what the economic data show to be "normal" in one society is not necessarily normal in another. Japan's competitive edge is not a matter of efficiency in the market "allocative" sense used in the West. Undoubtedly, many

Japanese practices—such as the wage structure set by lifetime employment and seniority systems and oligopolistic collusion aided and abetted by governmental industrial policy—"involve allocative inefficiencies on a grand scale." However, the presumed economic costs of such practices are more than offset "by the fact that all these social arrangements—the compromises made in favour of people who would lose out from the free working of market forces, the mobilizing of a sense of obligation and personal commitment in employment relations and 'customer market' relations—generate a sense of fairness which enables people to work cooperatively, conscientiously and with a will."[2] In sum, when the overwhelming number of Japanese citizens practice a cultural credo of "do your best at all times" for the sake of spiritual fulfillment more than financial enrichment, they have less need for greed or the cold inflexibility of free market pricing as the overriding guidelines for their economy. Japan's cooperative "we" version of capitalism was superbly suited to the successful achievement of the industrial goals sought by a broadly based national consensus.

Many of the strengths (and some of the shortcomings) of the Japanese system can be related to the ethos of the samurai warriors of their past, with fierce loyalty to group institutions and self-identity derived through participation in group activities. This minimization of both divisiveness and interest group politics was an ideal strategy for rebuilding the strong industrial base after World War II, facilitating a harmonious pursuit of a larger economic pie by the business, government, and labor sectors.

In contrast, the U.S. economic performance, especially in the years between 1969 and 1989 has been defined by self-expressiveness, self-interest, and minimal governmental interference in individual risk taking and the pursuit of personal achievement. Social divisiveness and interest group politics caused a preoccupation with redistributing the existing national economic pie throughout the 1970s.

Hostile take-overs, mergers, acquisitions, and leveraged buy-outs became the driving forces in the 1980s for a continued concern with reslicing rather than enlarging the national economic pie.

On a more specific level, the systemic sources of bilateral economic strains in the 1969–89 period can be seen as a result of the trans-Pacific interplay of this policy and attitudinal mismatch in which:

1. The Japanese consciously adopted a mutually reinforcing mix of official economic policies, business strategies, and innovations in production technology. When this mix was combined with preexisting, supportive social values, the result was extraordinary success in translating into reality the sequential objectives of industrial recovery, industrial leadership, and technological self-sufficiency. All of these attributes were strengthened by the total, unequivocal national priority to achieve international commercial success. The seemingly

economically perverse effort to restrict foreign competition and participation amidst this pursuit of global industrial dominance has actually been a source of strength: intense rivalry among domestic corporations more than offset limited foreign competition.

2. The United States unconsciously maintained a relatively debilitating mix of official economic policies, business strategies, predilections for consumption, and social priorities that prevented the U.S. industrial sector from mounting a credible response to the twin challenges of Japan's export offensive and its inhospitable home market for manufactured goods. The seemingly economically rational efforts to allow consumers to buy everything at the cheapest possible price and to emphasize short-term corporate profits became sources of weakness in terms of preserving the international competitiveness of U.S. industry in the face of the globalization of world markets. All of these shortcomings were magnified by the U.S. government's subordination of international commerce to the political struggle against the Soviet bloc.

If this antithetical policy mix is not made more consistent and compatible, there probably will be a steadily growing divergence in the relative industrial competitiveness of the two countries as well as a further escalation of frustration, mistrust, and acrimony on both sides. When the potential acceleration of Japan's leadership in key high technology sectors is added to this equation, a clear and present danger exists to bilateral political harmony and economic stability. The many forces contributing to the growing potential for a loss of friendship and patience in conflict management are at the heart of the bilateral problem. So, too, is continuous low level conflict which burdens and sours relations while distracting and sapping efforts at positive cooperation and collaboration.

The problem is more than the numbers of a secular bilateral trade disequilibrium. It is more than the jealousy of the wounded ego of an allegedly fading superpower. It is more than an allegedly closed Japanese market. The common denominator lies in the systemic imbalance in the relative abilities of the two countries to sell manufactured goods in the other's market. Thus two distinct problems require correction:

1. The inability of U.S. industry as a whole to remain competitive with Japanese industry, either in third countries or in the U.S. home market;

2. Continuing problems of access to the Japanese market, the result of formal barriers, business and social practices, and attitudes about things foreign.

While the United States must be held responsible for the first problem, the second is due to Japan. The economic and cultural factors that underlie Japan's successful export effort also thwart the admittedly inadequate U.S. efforts to pierce Japanese defenses against imports of manufactured goods, services, and processed raw materials. This situation will continue in the 1990s without fundamental changes in at least one of the two countries; to date, neither government has moved beyond modifying symptoms to alter causes.

That U.S. economic power was unsustainably disproportionate in the aftermath of World War II has now been proven by the worldwide erosion of U.S. competitiveness. In some respects, Japan is merely at the top of the list of many countries giving U.S. industry a run for its money, but other circumstances point to Japan's competitiveness being extraordinary. First, most of Japan's other trading partners echo the complaints and failures of the United States. Second, there is little reason to believe that any overall reduction in the U.S. trade deficit would include a proportional reduction in the deficit with Japan.

A third, perhaps more important substantiation to the claim that Japan, not the United States, is the independent variable is the divergence for more than twenty years of Japanese trade patterns from Western norms. Traditional Western economic tools seem unable to neutralize the nonprice characteristics of the Japanese market. The appreciation of the yen relative to the dollar since 1985 has not altered underlying relationships. Exchange rate changes have been especially inadequate in stimulating Japanese demand for U.S.–made manufactured goods. Repeated import liberalization programs by the Japanese have resulted in little impact outside of the agricultural sector, and even the relatively high rates of real GNP growth experienced by Japan toward the end of the 1980s failed to trigger an appreciable increase in its imports of U.S. manufactured goods relative to increases in Japanese exports. It seems unlikely that the answer lies wholly in the ineptness of U.S. exporters.

Japan's market profile for imports of manufactured goods will be discussed in detail in Chapters 6 and 9. By any measurement, there has for decades been a curious paucity of manufactured goods imported into Japan. Japan's extraordinarily poor record of intra-industry trade, that is, minimal imports of goods which it exports, is but one example. A second is the two-tiered pricing system in which Japanese goods tend to be sold at lower prices outside of Japan. What is remarkable here may be less the absence of a consumer revolt than the absence of arbitrage marketing efforts to re-export Japanese goods back into that country. Can anyone doubt that U.S. entrepreneurs would quickly detect and exploit the opportunity to reintroduce cheaper U.S.–made exports (or any foreign-made good) back into the U.S. market whenever the opportunity to make a quick profit presented itself? Here again we come up against evidence of a systemic problem.

It is all well and good to point to the causal effect of the U.S. budget deficit and low U.S. savings on the multilateral trade deficit; to the fact that many U.S. companies do make money in Japan; and to the failure of most U.S. companies to go all out in their marketing efforts in Japan. These arguments seem compelling, but ignore that larger truth that Japanese market dynamics fail to mesh with those of the United States; differences, I will argue, that are based on cultural values and priorities. Hence, we see a bilateral trade disequilibrium that is seemingly impervious to traditional adjustment measures.

Thus, the arithmetic of the bilateral trade imbalance per se is not the proper measure or characterization of the trade problem, though it does evidence the problem's existence. The contributory reasons for the deficit are greater cause for concern than its size.

Ignorance has fostered sloganeering. The Japanese downplay bilateral trade balances in favor of multilateral balances and disparage the quality of U.S. goods and its export efforts while Americans fixate on Japanese duplicity, with wishful thinking about the impending erosion of the Japanese economic miracle. Neither country has yet learned much about resolving continuing frictions that in fact manifest the unrecognized central problem. Failure to use a systemic definition of the problem is largely responsible for the fact that virtually all predictions made since 1969 concerning the evolution of U.S.–Japanese trade flows have been far off the mark. Failure to appreciate the deeply rooted cause of the problem is also responsible for the embarrassing repetition of official expressions of confidence that long-term economic harmony is at hand. Failing to define the problem structurally, neither country considers policies that would reverse underlying causes. Both sides seem as surprised by the evolution of their own foreign trade performance as by that of the other, and as the disparities grow, so too do the economic tensions.

Japan's relative lack of close international political ties, its geographic isolation, and its ethnic distinctiveness created a high degree of foreign sensitivity to its expanding economic strength. The economic hegemony of the United States in the fifteen-year period following World War II was far more dramatic than the international economic power currently possessed by Japan. U.S. hegemony raised few disputes or jealousies among noncommunist countries, however. The United States became a natural and benevolent international economic leader. It literally encouraged discrimination against its exports by Western Europe (such as by the structure of European Payments Union) and Japan. The large U.S. trade surpluses after World War II had nothing to do with a national bias against imports and were quickly overshadowed by a massive capital outflow, much of it in foreign aid outlays and a growing overseas military presence.

If there is an international vision or political mission beyond simple mercantilism (the quest for export maximization) driving Japanese trade policies, it remains invisible to virtually all foreigners, and Japan seems intent on keeping foreign peoples and ideas at arm's length. The Japanese export neither ideology, religion, or life-style. Unlike Great Britain and the United States when they each in turn took on the mantle of international economic leadership, Japan makes it nearly impossible for foreign countries to acquire its currency. Yet, Japan's industrial success, not the U.S. inability to keep pace with it, is the unique factor in the events that have unfolded. The United States is only one member of a very large club composed of countries unable to compete fully with Japanese export strengths. The United States is too big, strong, and dynamic for anyone to conclude that it could not have responded to its flagging bilateral trade fortunes with Japan in a more forceful or positive fashion. Japan utilized a favorable set of circumstances, not miracles. Neither this fact, nor the fact that failure of the United States to keep up with Japan's economic upsurge put it in step with the rest of the world, has brought any comfort to Americans. Trade surpluses maintained with other countries have been irrelevant to a generation of Americans accustomed to the role of world leadership, not that of economic runner-up to a militarily defeated Asian society. (A hint of racism has always existed on the fringe of U.S. attitudes toward Japan.)

The unique nature of Japan's trade position is further suggested by the fact that the relatively anemic success of U.S. industry in exporting to Japan is not widely duplicated in other foreign markets: Japan's contention that the U.S. industrial sector as a whole is a listless, ineffective exporter is not a criticism made by other countries. U.S. complaints about foreign barriers to its goods in countries other than Japan have been directed mainly at the agricultural sector, while complaints about the adverse impact of rising imports from Japan have been far more extensive than any other country.

The negative trade experiences of the United States with Japan since the beginning of the 1970s have not been duplicated elsewhere, but Japan's experiences in its U.S. trade relationship have been repeated with most of its other trading partners. Large bilateral trade surpluses in manufactured goods with other countries—even the newly industrialized economies of Southeast Asia—are as common as foreign complaints about shortfalls in Japanese fairness and reciprocity. Nor has Japan been able to convince any of its trading partners that the principle of comparative advantage justifies recurring record-shattering multilateral trade surpluses in manufactured goods, averaging upwards of $170 billion in the late 1980s.

APPROACH AND METHODOLOGY

The contemporary U.S.–Japanese economic relationship is a subject that is as complex as it is emotional. Any effective analysis must account for multiple layers of reality. This book represents the efforts of a relatively objective, longtime observer of U.S.–Japanese economic relations to comprehensively explain the sources of the incessant trade frictions and the failures of any policy responses to date to correct the core problem: *a systemic imbalance of competitive forces that significantly favors Japanese industry and is magnified by a communication gap.*

Shared perceptions between the two countries are as rare as unequivocal facts. A "two cultures" phenomenon exists twice over, once in the differing historical experience of Americans and Japanese and second in differing economic theories and business-political considerations. In the social sciences where precise laboratory experimentation is precluded, "truth" is inevitably mostly in the eye of beholder. Pursuant to the cognitive process model of decision making, that people tend to mentally process incoming data to fit preconceived beliefs, the greater the ambiguity of the data, the more likely that points compatible with expectations will be assimilated while incompatible points are downgraded or dismissed. (Hence, one measure of the success of this study will be its ability to change minds.)

I start with four objectives: (1) to provide a historical explanation of bilateral problems with Japan and offer a guide for future relations; (2) to explain the extreme differences between the United States and Japan in interpreting reality; (3) to determine the causes and measure the costs of Japanese export success and the relative failure of the United States to penetrate the Japanese market; and (4) to raise a sense of urgency and recommend policies to reverse both U.S. market access difficulties in Japan and Japan's widening competitive edge in industry vis-à-vis the United States. In pursuing these objectives, I see no need to adopt either a pro-Japanese or a pro-American point of view, nor to avoid ambiguities. Rather, I urge an eclectic approach based on the assumption that both countries share the blame for the past and the need for a better future.

If there is a "constituency" that I favor, it is not any one country, but rather a healthy, efficient, and stable international economic order beneficial to all countries. This kind of system would be difficult to impossible to achieve in the wake of unmanageable strains in U.S.–Japanese trade relations, a negative sum game in which everyone would lose.

Econometric efforts are of minimal value in defining what is an "appropriate" bilateral trade balance. Analysts of international economic relations have difficulty using vigorous scientific techniques to produce a single incontrovertible interpretation as to what is acceptable and what is unacceptable in international trade relationships. There inevitably will be multiple shades of truth as to the nature of U.S.-Japanese trade frictions. There also will be multiple shades of gray in a balanced diagnosis of this subject. Perhaps the only generalization endorsed in this book is that all *single* factor explanations of how U.S. and Japanese economic behavior interact are wrong.

Beliefs and perceptions are difficult to quantify. The dividing line between politics and economics is inevitably blurred, and the addition of cultural factors exacerbates methodological problems. Perfect techniques do not exist for distinguishing between cause and effect, source and symptom, the transitory and the permanent, unique events and long-standing trends, or the symbolic and the real. I make no claim to have reached any final answers; I will be content if I have raised the right questions. Throughout the book, I have attempted to strike a proper balance between what is similar and dissimilar, what is compatible and incompatible— between the cowboy and samurai schools of capitalism.

I begin in the next two chapters with an empirical consideration of the serious, prolonged bilateral frictions that began in 1969. The two subsequent chapters analyze the cultural and economic foundations of Japan and the United States. I move on to contrast the all but total differences in philosophy, objectives, and circumstances of what I call the cowboy and samurai approaches to international economic policy, most specifically trade, monetary, and investment issues.

Chapters 7 through 9 focus on details of the policy mismatch and value differences that have not been adequately recognized by either side. After examining the bilateral negotiating process as manifesting the cowboy-samurai dichotomy more than a search for solutions, the book looks more closely at the communication gap between the countries and attempts to provide a definitive argument of the Japanese case against the United States and then the American case against Japan. Having by then sifted the multiple layers of "truth," the book offers conclusions in Chapter 10 as to the relative merits of the opposing arguments as to what is really going on. Chapter 11 looks at the unfavorable prospects for U.S. competitiveness and forecasts the costs of continuing unresponsiveness to the warning signs. The final chapter proposes policy changes for both countries to attain better equilibrium and harmony in bilateral economic relations.

CHAPTER 2

A History of Contemporary Bilateral Trade Relations

Why is it every time we get someplace in the world, the big powers push us down?

      —Frequently asked Japanese question

The nail that sticks up gets hammered down.

      —Traditional Japanese proverb

Three subordinate trends dominate the past two decades of conflict. The first is the steady rise in the relative strength of Japan's export capability that destroyed, debilitated, or put off balance a growing number of American industries. The second trend is the equally uninterrupted demands by the U.S. government for greater access to the relatively inaccessible Japanese home market for American exports. Together, these two trends spawned a third: mounting frustrations and disillusionment as a steady series of efforts at conflict resolution failed to make any significant or lasting dent in resolving the issue at the heart of the bilateral economic problem: Japanese export success and American export failure. Disillusionment set in on the Japanese side as repeated export restraint efforts were unable to stem the continuing American demands for more restraints. Disillusionment set in on the American side as the uncountable number of liberalization measures regularly rolling out of Tokyo were unable to make exporting to the Japanese market comparable to exporting to other industrialized countries. Repeated efforts at ad hoc, piecemeal responses, often interpreted differently by the two governments, created a long lasting, intensifying series of economic clashes.

THE UNITED STATES BECOMES DEFENSIVE: THE TWILIGHT'S FIRST GLEAMING

U.S. anxiety about Japan's economic prowess is far from a recent phenomenon. In the opening years of this century Japan was described as affording us "the amazing spectacle of an Eastern society maintaining all the outward forms of Western civilization; using with unquestionable efficiency, the applied science of the Occident; accomplishing by prodigious effort, the work of centuries within the time of three decades."[1] One year later, in 1905, the Japanese worker was described as "ingenious, artistic, inventive, industrious and intelligent, wearing almost no clothes and living on less than would support a mechanic's dog in this country."[2]

In 1962, a U.S. economist identified the central dilemma that exists to this day in the West's response to Japan: "The problem is how to integrate Japan's export capability agreeably into the trade pattern of the Free World."[3]

Similarly, friction and disagreement are anything but new phenomena in U.S.–Japanese economic relations. Believers in omens can point to the unpleasant manner in which the U.S.–Japanese trading relationship began. Commodore Matthew Perry was only the first in a long line of U.S. officials to confront the Japanese with U.S. demands about the responsibilities inherent in international economic interdependence; Perry was also the first U.S. official to be frustrated in his efforts to open the Japanese market to U.S. goods. The Treaty of Kanagawa, signed in March 1854, was limited to protection of ships and crews in distress and the opening of two Japanese ports for purchasing fuel and food supplies. For several more years, the Japanese successfully rejected the opening of formal bilateral trade relations.

In the late 1850s the United States and the West European powers imposed the "unequal treaties" on the Japanese, stripping Japan's government of tariff-making authority until the end of the nineteenth century. Bilateral trade grew rapidly in the first two decades of the twentieth century despite widespread imposition of tariff barriers by both countries. But in the 1930s, trading was sharply disrupted worldwide. The United States implemented the Smoot-Hawley Tariff Act in 1930, raising average U.S. tariff rates to slightly above 50 percent—their highest level in history. When the worldwide Great Depression followed a couple of years later, there was widespread resort to import restrictions as many countries sought to preserve employment at home at the expense of their trading partners. In 1937, an informal agreement was reached that led to four years of Japanese restraints on their exports of cotton fabrics to the United States, a harbinger of things to come. Japanese–U.S. trade relations moved down yet another rocky path in 1940, when President Roosevelt imposed export controls on petroleum products and scrap metal to express dissatisfaction with Japanese military expansion in Asia.

After World War II, the bilateral economic relationship revolved around the Occupation and U.S. efforts to help Japan rebuild its political and economic vigor. This phase of relations terminated at the end of the 1950s, when the first signs of Japan's resurgence began to appear. Japan implemented "voluntary" export restraints—in response to U.S. pressures—on a number of labor-intensive, unsophisticated products, including cotton textiles, bicycles, bolts and nuts, flatware, baseball gloves, and ceramics.

A major reversal of trade patterns began in the latter part of the 1960s. Burdened by inflation and overvaluation of the dollar, the once large and stable U.S. multilateral trade surplus shriveled. Aided by productivity growth, governmental export incentives, and undervaluation of the yen, the wobbly Japanese trade balance shifted from red ink to stable surpluses.

Although far from clear at the time, the period of post–World War II U.S. international economic hegemony was ending and the period of Japanese industrial power was beginning. The only indication in the United States of this monumental transition was that the bilateral trade relationship moved up from a matter of virtually total indifference among senior Washington policymakers to an issue of at least secondary importance. By 1970, the U.S. government was becoming alarmed about its deteriorating trade position and aroused Japanese sensitivity to that country's steadily rising trade surpluses.

Until the mid-sixties, the closed door import policies of Japan and the open door import policies of the United States had made good economic sense. The policies made no political waves. But the tranquility of this period was the calm before the storm. By the end of decade, reluctantly, belatedly, and inadequately, both sides had begun adjustments in their trade policies to accommodate the steady reversal in their relative competitive positions. The policy actions taken were viewed as isolated, self-correcting measures that would restore harmony between the two countries; no one could have foreseen the approaching discord.

First came the successful effort by the Johnson administration in 1968 to coax the Japanese (and the Europeans) into signing a three-year voluntary steel export restraint agreement. This temporary arrangement was to allow the domestic U.S. steel industry to regroup from a surge, also presumed to be temporary, in imports.

The ensuing textile dispute (early 1969 to late 1971) marked the end of Japan's transition from a political-military dependent of the United States to its chief commercial nemesis. For three years an irresistible force faced an immovable object. President Richard Nixon's unflinching commitment to a campaign obligation was opposed by a stubborn and defiant Japanese textile industry. The great textile dispute was the first major resistance by postwar Japan to a U.S. trade initiative; neither the Japanese government nor the Japanese textile industry was intimidated by a firm U.S. economic demand. The period of unquestioned Japanese acceptance of U.S. economic leadership had ended.

By almost any measure, the nearly three years of acrimonious talks on synthetic textiles were extraordinary. Seldom has so much political capital been consumed in pursuit of the economically inconsequential. Despite the personal involvement of President Nixon and Prime Minister Sato, the trade policy decision-making processes in both countries seemed paralyzed in their efforts to produce a mutually acceptable compromise. Confronted by some of the worst aspects of the U.S. system of political economy, the Japanese government responded in kind.

Japan's hard-line, no-compromise stance reflected both the intransigence of the Japanese textile industry and its misreading of the U.S. position. Given the doubtful existence of import-induced dislocations in the U.S. textile industry, Japanese industry and government were convinced that in the face of strong resistance the United States would abandon its demand for reduced Japanese exports. The Japanese presumed, incorrectly, that the Nixon administration would consider its political obligation to the U.S. textile industry fulfilled by verbal demonstrations. The Japanese were slow to comprehend the determination of President Nixon personally to fulfill his campaign pledge to ease the textile industry's import competition.

The failure of the technical-level talks initiated in the summer of 1969 was quickly overshadowed by the political fallout of the first Sato-Nixon summit meeting, held in the White House in November of that year. For Prime Minister Sato, the reversion of the island of Okinawa to Japanese sovereignty was the paramount foreign policy issue. Textiles mattered only as they threatened agreement on reversion.

The meeting between the two heads of government was one of the great unintended fiascoes in the bilateral relationship. It has been unofficially reported that in response to Nixon's suggestion that Sato reciprocate for the reversion of Okinawa with textile export restraints, the Japanese prime minister said, in Japanese, *"zensho shimasu."* Apparently this phrase was translated as "I will take appropriate measures" or "I will take care of it." While literally correct, the translator failed to make clear that the phrase implies no results should be expected. The translation might better have been, "I'll look into it, but don't hold your breath."

While the exact wording of this crucial exchange may never be known, the outcome is now clear. First, no agreement ever emerged from the meeting. Second, President Nixon came away convinced that a scenario for settlement of the textile dispute was firmly in place. Third, the prime minister never was in a position to impose any agreement on the Japanese textile industry. Fourth, the extreme secrecy of the discussion in the Oval Office complicated subsequent negotiations by lower-ranking officials.

The final phase of the dispute did not begin until many months later, in the summer of 1971. A shake-up in the Sato cabinet was announced on 5 July. Kakuei Tanaka became the minister of International Trade and Industry, and Takeo Fukuda became foreign minister. Since both men were interested in succeeding Sato as prime minister, both were prepared to subordinate the usual Ministry of International Trade and Industry (MITI)–Foreign Ministry rivalry to curry favor with the incumbent prime minister. Helping settle the textile struggle was clearly a way of impressing Sato and gaining his support on the succession.

The conclusion of a negotiated settlement on the textile dispute was highly dramatic, fully befitting the many months of intrigue that had preceded it. The general terms of the deal were concluded in the early fall of 1971 by MITI Minister Tanaka and David Kennedy, formerly the secretary of Treasury, who had become an ambassador-at-large in the State Department. Tanaka publicly declared opposition to an agreement, but took the opposite tack in his confidential private talks with Kennedy. Tanaka suggested that the U.S. government officially confront Japan with credible threats of an imminent imposition of unilateral import quotas. This threat of overwhelming economic force would then be used by Tanaka to justify imposing a government textile agreement on the still-uncompromising, intransigent Japanese textile industry.[4]

The Nixon administration obliged Tanaka by announcing its intention of imposing harsh quotas on 15 October 1971 if no agreement had been reached. The law chosen as the legal basis of this potential action bore an unfortunate name: the Trading with the Enemy Act. Originally passed during World War I, the act delegated broad authority to the president to regulate foreign commerce in periods of declared national emergency. Such an emergency had been declared shortly after China entered the Korean War, and it had never been rescinded. Considerable legal doubt existed as to the applicability of the act to Japanese textile imports, but the Japanese government did not want to argue legal technicalities; it wanted a dramatic gesture that would allow government officials to blame extreme U.S. pressure for the need to settle the textile dispute.

The tenacious U.S. demands were grossly out of proportion to the situation. It is true that the percentage increases in the value of U.S. synthetic textile imports had grown considerably in the late 1960s. But in economics everything is relative. U.S. consumption and production also were increasing rapidly, in percentage and absolute terms. Imports averaged 5.1 percent of total U.S. consumption of synthetic textile products in 1969–70,[5] and Japan accounted for less than one-third of the import total. Three years of tumult and a near reversion in the United States to protectionist trade legislation were deemed acceptable in order to put a ceiling on imports from Japan that accounted for less than 2 percent of the total value of the U.S. market for manmade textiles![6]

In a modern-day version of the Japanese capitulation to the demands made by Admiral Perry from the black ships, the government of Japan acquiesced in mid-October to a textile export restraint formula acceptable to Washington. Bilateral restraint agreements with the other major Asian textile suppliers followed. When it was all over, the Nixon administration had achieved its goal and demonstrated the value of persistence, but a dubious economic victory came at a high cost in political goodwill lost in Japan. To this day, the Japanese harbor resentment. The only shared experience in the great textile dispute may have been the feeling on each side that the other was unreasonable.

While the textile dispute dragged on, other notable events were occurring. The first was the near passage of protectionist trade legislation in 1970 by a restless Congress unrestrained by an administration seemingly willing to restrict imports of Japanese textiles at all costs. Then, in August 1971, the realization that the United States had a structural balance of payments problem led to a dramatic reversal of U.S. economic policies. President Nixon shocked everyone by imposing shock therapy on the U.S. economy in his New Economic Policy. A ninety-day freeze on wages and prices dominated the domestic package. The new external economic policy featured a 10 percent surcharge on all existing U.S. tariffs and suspension of the obligation to convert dollars held by foreign central banks into gold at the rate of $35 per ounce. The president's program signaled the end of the postwar phase of U.S. foreign economic policy that unequivocally placed foreign policy objectives over domestic needs.

The Japanese, by this time, had already taken several steps in the opposite direction, adjusting their previously total commitment to internal priorities to external exigencies. Blanket "infant industry" protection was no longer needed. Japanese companies had become world-class competitors in steel, electronics, shipbuilding, cameras, and other industries. By the end of the 1960s, the Japanese were ready to begin dismantling the vast postwar export-promotion and import-retarding mechanisms that they had assembled to accelerate economic recovery. Initial targets of the new liberalization were export inducements and residual import quotas. Though the latter were technically illegal after Japan accepted the obligations of membership in the General Agreement on Tariffs and Trade (GATT), more than 150 import quotas remained.

The new liberalization resulted mainly from two external forces: the foreign exchange market had begun taking notice of Japan's strengthening trade balances, with increased yen purchases, and the U.S. intensified pressure for access to Japan's markets. The first installment of the promised reduction-by-half in import quotas was announced on 1 October 1969. Additional measures followed. Thirty-three residual quotas remained after an eighth installment in April 1972. The Automatic Import Quota system, which discouraged imports by requiring prior licenses, was also abolished in that year.

When quantitative restraints on computers and related accessories and components were removed in 1975, only twenty-seven quotas remained. Of this total, twenty-two were in the agricultural sector—an area given protection throughout the world—and marine products (fish and seaweed). The remainder applied to leather goods and footwear, an outgrowth of an historical Japanese social prejudice that still limits job opportunities in other sectors for descendants of leather workers. By 1983, quotas accounted for only a miniscule portion of the market access complaints lodged by the United States and Japan's other trading partners.

The elimination of most import quotas, together with the other measures implemented in the 1970s and early 1980s had the effect of putting

Japan's *formal* import barriers on an equal level with those of other industrial countries. The continued surpluses in trade with the United States meant that every remaining barrier to potential U.S. exports (citrus fruit, meat, and cigarettes, for example) was a source of discontent deeply felt in the United States, as were informal, but formidable barriers such as restrictive government procurement practices and testing standards. Similar attitudes were taken by European and Asian countries.

With the conclusion of the textile dispute, Japan's main international economic concern was that the demise of the 1949 exchange rate (360 yen to the dollar) would undermine Japan's newly acquired capacity regularly to balance its trade account, that is, export enough to pay for imports. As part of the Smithsonian Agreement of December 1971, in which the exchange rates of all the major currencies were realigned, the yen had appreciated by a total of 17 percent against the dollar—more than any other currency. Japanese concerns, epitomized by the finance minister's warning in August 1971 of a "glorious kind of suffering," proved unfounded. Japan's multilateral trade surplus continued to increase, as did its bilateral surplus with the United States.

Japanese economic policy now shifted to preventing a second revaluation of the yen. The seven-point program announced in May 1972 largely duplicated the weaknesses of its predecessor, the eight-point program, of June 1971. Both were long on rhetoric; both made but marginal changes in fundamental economic realities.[7] Further action soon became necessary to dampen speculation in the foreign exchange markets that the yen again would increase in value.

The Japanese government's third effort to stabilize pressures on the yen and to reduce Japan's overall trade surplus was formulated during September and October 1972. Like its predecessors, the new program promised to enlarge import quotas, phase out remaining export incentives, reduce nontariff barriers to imports, accelerate decontrol of international capital transactions, and increase foreign aid on an untied basis (meaning that recipient countries could spend the funds received anywhere they chose). In addition, an across-the-board tariff cut of 20 percent on manufactured goods and processed agricultural goods was promised for 1973. Finally, MITI announced its intention to begin more vigorous efforts to maintain orderly growth in exports with the authority granted to it by the Export Trade Control Order.

U.S. government officials greeted the new program with undisguised skepticism. An internal memorandum of the U.S.–Japan Trade Council reported that among executive branch economists "there is a complete consensus that the program is a waste of time because it will fail in its major objective: preventing revaluation of the yen. Instead of expending energy on implementing the . . . program, it is argued that Japanese energy should be expended on effective measures such as revaluation or an export tax."[8]

Nineteen seventy-three was a year for structural changes in the international economic order. In March, the international monetary system switched from the Bretton Woods system of fixed exchange rates to a floating rate system directed by market forces rather than government fiat. By July, the yen had risen to 263 per dollar, an appreciation of 27 percent over the 360 rate of July 1971.[9] International trade problems then shifted from the traditional concerns about import barriers to coping with the effects of governmental export controls. In June, the Nixon administration engineered another sudden switch in U.S. economic policy, imposing export controls on soybeans because of exaggerated fears of domestic shortages.

The soybean episode was soon upstaged by economic events outside the control of either the United States or Japan. The course of modern international economic relations was radically altered by the first of many increases in the price of petroleum ordered by the Organization of Petroleum Exporting Countries (OPEC). Between the summer of 1973 and January 1974, the posted price of OPEC petroleum jumped from about $3 per barrel to $11.65. A number of observers foresaw the imminent collapse of the international financial system under the burden of history's largest shift ever of international purchasing power. By 1975, OPEC's estimated total oil export revenues were $100 billion above 1973 earnings. The oil import bills for Japan increased from $6.7 billion in 1973 to $21 billion in the next year. The U.S. oil import bill of $26 billion in 1974 was more than three times as large as its previous year's total of $8 billion. Japan's overall trade surplus shrank from a surplus of $3.7 billion in 1973 to a mere $1.5 billion in 1974, the lowest since the mid-1960s. The descent of the international economy into what was at that time the worst postwar recession overshadowed all bilateral trade difficulties between Japan and the United States.

As Table 2.1 shows, the U.S. recession in the wake of skyrocketing oil prices, together with the lag effects of the December 1971 exchange rate realignment, temporarily halted the deterioration in the U.S. trade balance with Japan begun in the early seventies. Changes in exchange rates and business cycles—then and now—can reduce, but not eliminate, Japan's rising competitiveness vis-à-vis the United States.

In the longer term, Japan's economic system would display its recuperative powers and underlying strengths in adjusting well to the first oil price shock. On the other side of the Pacific, U.S. government officials were talking in 1974 about the imminent collapse of OPEC and an inevitable decline in oil prices. In a further display of wishful thinking, they began planning a futile program to achieve U.S. energy independence. U.S. citizens preferred to believe in a joint Arab–oil company price-boosting plot rather than accept a genuine energy crisis requiring painful adjustments, while Japan decided to work harder and use less petroleum. This divergence of response had profound implications for economic relations in the late 1970s and early 1980s.

Table 2.1 U.S.–Japanese Trade Relations, 1969–75

	U.S. Bilateral Deficit (Billions)	U.S. Imports from Japan (Billions)	Increase from Previous Year of U.S. Imports from Japan	U.S. Exports to Japan (Billions)	Increase from Previous Year of U.S. Exports to Japan
1969	−$1.4	$ 4.9	20 %	$ 3.5	17 %
1970	1.2	5.9	20	4.7	34
1971	3.2	7.3	24	4.1	−13
1972	4.2	9.1	25	4.9	19.5
1973	1.3	9.6	5.5	8.3	69
1974	1.6	12.3	28	10.7	28.5
1975	1.7	11.3	−9	9.6	−10.4

SOURCE: Unpublished U.S. Commerce Department data and author's calculations.

THE LATE 1970S: INTO THE PERILOUS FIGHT

By the latter half of the 1970s, Japan had become a force to be reckoned with in the international trading system. It was on the verge of becoming a bona fide economic superpower. Trade relations with the United States remained cordial. Mutual goodwill marked efforts in both countries to deal with the new U.S. demands for greater market access in Japan and Japanese restraint in exporting certain manufactured products to the U.S. market. Efforts at conflict management were ad hoc, focusing on one problem at a time, an arrangement reflecting the special political, military, and economic bonds between the two countries. They chose to ignore on most occasions the established multilateral procedures for the resolution of foreign trade disputes, including the safeguard mechanism (Article XIX) and basic principles (such as nondiscrimination) enshrined in the GATT.

If international power is defined as the ability to influence the actions of other countries, then the United States clearly was more powerful in this period. Export restraints and relaxed import restrictions were policy measures reluctantly undertaken by the Japanese only after the application of pressure by the U.S. government. Despite a general lack of sympathy for U.S. demands, Japan was forced to be responsive out of respect for the fact that the United States is its military protector, its chief overseas political ally, and its largest export market. Then as now, Japan's number one foreign policy priority was maintenance of political, military, and commercial ties with the United States.

U.S. pressures emanated mainly from perceptions of awesome commercial power in many segments of Japan's industrial sector. Japanese responses were based on the presumption that a few ad hoc concessions would assuage U.S. demands and prevent retaliatory actions by a temporarily angered United States. Ironically, both sides focused on their own weaknesses, virtually ignoring their respective strengths. In the late 1970s, each side viewed the other as more powerful.

The U.S. and Japanese economies had responded very differently to the first OPEC oil shock—a factor that significantly shaped the evolution of the bilateral trade relationship. Japan's feelings of weakness and vulnerability fostered an intense collective determination to overcome the country's latest economic misfortune. The Japanese have repeatedly demonstrated a powerful ability to transform economic adversity into advantage, and now rolled up their sleeves and worked harder to offset the financial effects of the mammoth increase in their oil import bill.

The U.S. response in 1974 resembled Japan's only to the extent that it too conformed with a historical pattern. Long-standing financial strength abroad and rich domestic energy resources have always given the United States a buffer against crisis. The relative lack of need for a dramatic internal economic response to the OPEC oil shock fed resistance to changes in economic policy. The United States was content to dream of energy independence and accept the economically unwise but politically attractive distortions of price controls on domestically produced oil and natural gas. As for paying its soaring oil import bill, the United States had the unique luxury of merely printing additional dollars.

Not even Japan could avoid a recession in the wake of the near quadrupling of oil prices between mid-1973 and January 1975. However, recession, large wage increases, inflation, and export stagnation did not last long. Japan's economic adjustment, relative to other countries, was superb.

Japanese management vigorously and successfully pursued greater production efficiency and lower break-even points. Nominal wage increases dropped dramatically as Japanese labor did its part to adjust to a weakened economic environment. By 1978, the rate of increase in manufacturing productivity was approximately the same (7 to 8 percent annually) as wage increases. In other words, unit labor cost increases for Japanese manufacturing firms were effectively zero in 1978 and for several years thereafter.[10]

The widening Japanese lead in industrial efficiency and export competitiveness showed in the growing Japanese bilateral trade surplus. U.S. misgivings about the equitableness of the relationship became fixated on these numbers. Japan's cumulative trade surplus with the United States in the six-year period of 1970–75 was about $13 billion (according to U.S. government statistics). In the six-year period beginning in 1976, the cumulative Japanese bilateral trade surplus spurted to about $60 billion.

Data for bilateral trade in the 1976–80 period (table 2.2) suggest that only the depreciation of the dollar against the yen in 1977–78 interrupted U.S. deterioration. It should be noted, however, that even the dollar's relatively large drop (about 33 percent) in those two years was insufficient to bring the bilateral balance even close to equilibrium. Insight into the relative *multilateral* trade performances—frustration versus muscle—from 1976 to 1982 can be gleaned from table 2.3. While the U.S. trade deficit remained constant, Japan's growing trade surplus once again was briefly thrown for a loop by the second upsurge in oil prices in 1979–80, and once again quickly recovered.

The expanding stream of imports associated with the continuing flow of red ink in the U.S. trade account triggered two responses. First, increasingly vulnerable U.S. corporations accelerated efforts to secure relief from foreign competition. Second, in 1975 the U.S. Congress cooperated by relaxing the statutory criteria for proving import-induced injury under the so-called escape clause. This is the provision in U.S. trade law by which domestic producers can receive temporary relief (higher tariffs and/or quotas) from intensifying, albeit fair foreign competition—if they can demonstrate "injury" as described in the statute. After a prolonged period of steadily rejecting private sector petitions for relief under the escape clause, the U.S. International Trade Commission changed course in January, 1976. A majority of commissioners found that imports of specialty steel

Table 2.2 U.S.–Japanese Trade Relations, 1976–80

	U.S. Bilateral Deficit (Billions)	U.S. Imports from Japan (Billions)	Increase from Previous Year of U.S. Imports from Japan	U.S. Exports to Japan (Billions)	Change from Previous Year of U.S. Exports	U.S. Exports to Japan as Percentage of U.S. Imports from Japan
1976	$ 5.3	$15.5	37%	$10.2	6%	66%
1977	8.0	18.6	20	10.5	3	56
1978	12.6	25.5	37	13.0	24	51
1979	8.7	26.2	3	17.6	35	67
1980	9.9	30.7	17	20.8	18	68

NOTE: Imports measured FAS.

SOURCE: Unpublished U.S. Commerce Department data and author's calculations.

Table 2.3   Multilateral Trade Balances, 1976–82
(billions of U.S. dollars)

	Japan	United States
1976	+10.0	−8.3
1977	+17.3	−29.2
1978	+24.6	−31.0
1979	+ 1.8	−27.6
1980	+ 2.0	−24.6
1981	+20.0	−27.3
1982	+18.2	−31.8

NOTE: Imports measured FAS.

SOURCE: U.S. Department of Commerce, *International Economic Indicators,* various issues.

were "a substantial cause of serious injury, or threat thereof, to the domestic industry." Accordingly, they recommended the president impose import quotas for five years.

Ensuing events became the prototype of trade settlements in the style that was soon dubbed the "new protectionism," referring to the practice of a negotiated reduction in the exports of specified goods when an importing country judges them to be politically or economically excessive. This course provides both sides with a middle ground between the political imperative of reducing intense foreign competition in a period of relatively slow economic growth and the proven economic stupidity of the unilateral "beggar your neighbor" policies practiced widely in the 1930s. In place of either unilateral import restrictions or the grievance procedures spelled out in the GATT, import pressures more and more have come to be relieved by means of an orderly marketing agreement (OMA) or a voluntary export restraint—practices specially sanctioned in the U.S. Trade Act of 1974.

The U.S. government, faced with a statutory time limit for responding to the ITC decision on specialty steels, convinced Japan to undertake a three-year voluntary restraint agreement. Other exporters of specialty steel refused such an arrangement, and in the quotas imposed for the three-year period beginning in June 1976, Japan received favorable treatment.

An OMA covering color televisions followed in May 1977. As with specialty steel, the ITC had found color TV imports increasing in sufficient numbers to warrant sanctions. Unlike the steel case, the upsurge in TV imports truly was dramatic and significant. Between 1971 and 1977, more than 60,000 jobs were lost in the U.S. color TV industry, and the number of manufacturers dwindled from twenty to five. In 1976 alone, Japanese color TV exports to the United States jumped by more than 150 percent. Their market share reached 40 percent in that year, a proportion more than double their share of approximately 15 percent in 1975.[11]

The OMA signed by Japan and the United States stipulated that for three years beginning in July 1977, Japanese color TV exports to the United States would not exceed 1.75 million sets annually. This figure represented a 41 percent decline from the 1976 figure of 3 million units, which most analysts believed had been inflated by accelerated shipments in anticipation of an escape clause decision. Like the specialty steel OMA, the television OMA was strictly a bilateral deal. In violation of the spirit of GATT principles, the United States specifically discriminated against Japanese goods—at least until 1979, when bilateral export restraint agreements were signed with South Korea and Taiwan. In addition, the U.S. government offered no compensation to Japan for the Japanese TV industry's reduced export opportunities.

An interesting dimension of the TV episode was the unusual intensity and persistence of the U.S. industry in trying to reduce competition from Japanese imports. Led by Zenith, several U.S. TV producers launched an attack on all fronts in the early 1970s that began with complaints under the escape clause and antidumping statutes. In addition, a case was filed (and later rejected by the ITC) under Section 337 of the Tariff Act of 1930; Japanese TV producers were accused of a variety of unfair and anticompetitive business practices. Also, a civil antitrust suit was filed in U.S. federal court alleging price fixing and restraint of trade. (This case was dismissed in April 1981.) Finally, Zenith filed a petition under the U.S. countervailing duty statute (a provision of U.S. trade law designed to neutralize the effects of foreign governments subsidizing their exporters) alleging that the nonpayment of domestic commodity taxes by Japanese companies on television sets they export constituted an illegal "bounty or grant" by the government of Japan. This complex case was eventually settled by a Supreme Court decision in 1978 that rejected Zenith's subsidy argument.

In retrospect, it seems that the Japanese industry's highly successful TV offensive of the early 1970s was deliberate, large-scale dumping and price collusion, met with indifference by U.S. officials charged with enforcing the dumping laws. Japanese consumers staged a temporary boycott when a U.S. study showed that Japanese-made TVs were selling in Japan at retail prices 50 percent higher than those exported to the United States.[12] Meanwhile, several major U.S. distributors, including Sears, were charged by the U.S. government with fraud for accepting illegal kickbacks by Japanese TV producers, a practice which, of course, made selling U.S.-made televisions less attractive to profit-conscious retailers. Some estimates of the cost to U.S. industry of Japanese TV dumping ran into the hundreds of millions of dollars.

Although the domestic TV industry was reeling, legal sanctions were not forthcoming to halt unfair trade practices by Japan. Only after protracted legal bickering did the U.S. government, in 1980, settle both the complex TV dumping case (originally filed in 1968) and the fraud case for a payment of $76 million by Japanese TV producers.[13] (The seeming indifference of the Treasury Department throughout the dumping investigation was a motivating factor in the later decision to transfer enforcement of the antidumping statute to the more industry-sensitive Department of Commerce.) Zenith's dissatisfaction with the penalties imposed on the Japanese led to legal appeals that dragged on, without success, until 1987.

The pattern of single-product disputes was broken in the late 1970s by a series of unique efforts at macroeconomic diplomacy. In 1977, U.S. international economic policy priorities turned toward trilateralism. One of the Carter administration's earliest foreign policy initiatives was the urging of expansionary macroeconomic policies in the other industrialized countries to induce faster growth, and in turn an increased demand for imports, in the relatively sluggish Japanese and European economies.

The Japanese prime minister, Takeo Fukuda, made two important promises at the economic summit meeting held in London in May 1977. He committed his administration to a specific, if unrealistic, goal of real GNP growth of 6.7 percent for the Japanese fiscal year (JFY) ending March 1978. Fukuda also suggested to his fellow heads of government that Japan's current account surplus would soon be replaced by a small deficit. When Japan's GNP failed to grow as rapidly as promised and its current account surplus subsequently widened, feelings of bitterness became apparent in both the United States and Europe.

The next major chapter in macroeconomic diplomacy consisted of a bilateral effort by the Carter administration to quell rising U.S. frustrations with Japan through a comprehensive agreement covering a range of economic issues. The Strauss-Ushiba agreement of mid-January 1978 was distinctive mainly for the breadth of issues associated with the "changing world conditions" referred to in the official communiqué. But in other respects, it followed the familiar pattern of a bilateral agreement negotiated in a near-crisis atmosphere, with an impact more symbolic than economic. Virtually all concessions and promised policy changes were made unilaterally by the Japanese. It served the useful political function of cooling tempers in the short run, but without satisfactorily addressing the underlying economic forces that caused the tensions.

On the macroeconomic level, the Strauss-Ushiba agreement, as reported in the official communiqué, called for action in four broad areas:

1. Increased Growth. "Both sides agreed to take major steps to achieve high levels of non-inflationary economic growth," and Japan reiterated its recently adopted real growth target of 7 percent for JFY 1978.

2. Balance of Payments Adjustment. Japan agreed to undertake steps "aimed at achieving a marked diminution of its current account surplus." The minister for external economic affairs

added that in Japan's 1979 fiscal year and "thereafter, under present international economic conditions, all reasonable efforts would be continued with a view to further reducing Japan's current account surplus, aiming at equilibrium, with deficit accepted if it should occur."

3. Increased foreign aid.

4. Japanese import liberalization. The inevitable list included:

- Advanced tariff reductions on the equivalent of $2 billion of imports;

- Removal of quota controls on twelve products (subcategories of existing products protected by quota);

- Increased quota ceilings for meat, oranges, and citrus juices;

- A sweeping review of Japan's foreign exchange controls; and

- Improved access for foreign-produced goods through such measures as eased government procurement procedures, simplified inspection requirements, and expanded import credits.[14]

U.S. trade negotiators were pleased with the agreement. U.S. Trade Representative Robert Strauss told reporters that the communiqué "represented a change of direction and a new philosophy for Japan." U.S. economic policy officials should have known better. As is not surprising, Japan's ambitious targets for growth rates and current account balances were not achieved (see tables 2.4 and 2.5). The growth target would have been difficult to achieve even in a communist, or command, economy; only the advent of the second oil price shock in 1979 caused a diminution of Japan's current account surplus, and then only temporarily.

THE EARLY 1980S: THE ROCKETS' RED GLARE

By the 1980s, a clear pattern of conflict in U.S.–Japanese relations had become apparent, with each side convinced it was the victim of the other's excesses. Most Japanese identified continuing U.S. demands for concessions as the acts of a political bully incapable of making needed economic self-improvements. Most Americans (at least among those who followed trade issues) felt themselves to be victims of a double standard by which the Japanese coordinated an export onslaught with an aversion to importing manufactured goods. On both sides emotion and oversimplification stood in for systematic analysis.

The market opening measures announced by the government of Japan

Table 2.4   Real Growth
in Japan's GNP, 1976–80
(percentage increase by
Japanese fiscal year)

1977	5.3
1978	5.1
1979	5.3
1980	3.7

SOURCE: Japan Economic
Planning Agency data, repro-
duced in "Twenty-five Ques-
tions and Answers on
Japan–U.S. Trade Relations"
(Consulate General of Japan:
New York, 1983).

Table 2.5   Japan's
Current Account Position
(millions of U.S. dollars)

1976	3,680
1977	10,918
1978	16,534
1979	− 8,754
1980	− 10,746
1981	4,770
1982	6,896

SOURCE: Economic and For-
eign Affairs Research Association [of Japan], *Statistical
Survey of Japan's Economy,*
various issues.

in 1980 were the first of a long series, without precedent in their volume, their tentativeness, and their failure to produce any significant change in Japanese import patterns. In almost every case, Japan's liberalization efforts were aimed at specific goods or services of special interest to U.S. business, reflecting the political and economic importance attached by Japan to good relations with the United States. The resulting extensive negotiating framework caused some trade analysts to worry that the relationship between the two countries threatened the multilateral principles of nondiscrimination embodied in the GATT. Additional problems resulted from the fact that only pressures from Washington, not an indigenous desire to increase the access of the Japanese people to cheap imports, inspired the removal of Japanese import and investment barriers. The

Japanese government did not want more imports; it only wanted to silence U.S. demands. This sentiment was (and still is) the prime cause of the general failure of U.S. manufactures exports to grow significantly despite the easing of overt import barriers.

The first liberalization program eased restrictions on international capital flows and foreign direct investment in Japan with amendments to the thirty-year-old Foreign Exchange and Foreign Trade Control Law. The revisions permitted foreign direct investment after prior notification—no longer requiring government consent—in all but a few specified industries. Capital transactions (except bank deposits) were to be treated similarly by the Ministry of Finance.

These initial measures exemplified the protracted process of negotiations and multistage actions needed to satisfy U.S. demands for results. A later package designed to give U.S. tobacco products greater market access in Japan included a reduction in cigarette tariffs from 90 to 35 percent as well as an easing of official restrictions on advertising, distribution, and test-marketing cigarettes, cigars, and pipe tobacco. The seemingly generous decline in the tariff rate must be discounted, however, since prior to announcing this concession, Japan never had revealed the exact tariff level, if in fact there even was one; U.S. exporters were simply told by the official Japanese tobacco monopoly what their final retail prices would be.[15] Furthermore—in a classic case of one step forward and two steps back—the tariff cut actually caused the price of U.S. cigarettes in Japan to go *up*. This result was brought about by a new excise tax based on the after-tariff price of the cigarettes. Not surprisingly, the market share (less than 3 percent) of U.S. cigarettes remained unchanged.

Despite a second round of tobacco liberalization in 1983, U.S. cigarette makers continued to complain about tariffs, the excise tax, discriminatory distribution practices, and limits on marketing operations and pricing discretion. Settlement came only in the fall of 1986, five full years after the inception of tobacco liberalization, and then only to head off retaliation by the Reagan administration under Section 301, a catchall provision of the Trade Act of 1974 authorizing retaliation in kind against foreign discrimination against U.S. exports.

An even longer-running dispute also had its origins in 1980, with the reluctant agreement by Nippon Telegraph and Telephone Public Corporation (NTT) to allow foreign firms to bid on its multibillion dollar telecommunications equipment contracts. In the Tokyo Round of Multilateral Trade Negotiations, Japan agreed to a new Government Procurement Code that opened NTT's "Buy Japan" bidding. When the U.S. threatened to forbid Japanese companies from bidding on all U.S. government contracts, the Japanese agreed to open a significant portion of NTT procurement contracts to international bidding and to provide special opportunities to U.S. companies to bid on about $1.5 billion equivalent annually in high-technology communications equipment.[16] Suspicions that the prejudice against outside suppliers continued after this change in the regulations were supported by the statement by NTT's chairman to the effect that the most likely goods to be purchased from abroad were mops and telephone poles.[17] Slowly, U.S. and Canadian suppliers received isolated orders for sophisticated gear. After a decade of intense U.S. pressure and the privatization of NTT, the dispute continues at this writing over the level of Japanese imports of U.S. telecommunications equipment and the sizeable bilateral deficit (in excess of $3 billion annually) in this sector.

Automobiles joined the growing list of items subject to "voluntary" export restraints as the result of a Japanese government decision made on 1 May 1981. The three-year restraint program that began in JFY 1981 started at 1.68 million cars and was to be adjusted upward in the following years according to growth in annual U.S. automobile sales. (In fact, this total remained unchanged because of a slump in U.S. sales.) Japanese car exports to the United States had increased rapidly with a relatively high-quality, price-competitive, and fuel-efficient product. Once again, Japanese commercial aggressiveness gained rapid increases in export volume and market penetration.* And once again, the combination of strong Japanese producers and a weakened domestic U.S. industry resulted in economic dislocations and a political backlash in Washington. The Japanese government was pressured to constrain its private sector's export push by the menace of protectionist-minded U.S. members of Congress.[18] (An automobile quota bill sponsored by Senator John Danforth of Missouri came to no result, but attracted considerable congressional support.)

Despite surface similarities with the pattern of previous voluntary export restraints, the 1981 automobile settlement possessed several unique characteristics. First, it cannot officially be described as a formal agreement: the three-year restraint commitment emanated from an informal series of bilateral "non-negotiations." This situation reflected the unprecedented reversal of roles between governments. The Japanese government, mainly through MITI, sent clear signals to Washington in 1980 that it was willing to establish quantitative export restraints on automobiles; the Reagan administration responded with a vagueness that seemed the essence of what Westerners refer to as Japanese inscrutability. The Japanese government, accustomed to U.S. specificity in trade demands, had to judge the U.S. mood by instinct, reading between the lines, and guessing how serious Congress was in demanding that, one way or another, reductions be made in shipments of Japanese cars to the U.S. market.

A second unique characteristic of the automobile restraints was the unprecedented refusal by the Reagan administration to drop its efforts to restrain Japanese automobiles even after the International Trade Commis-

---

*U.S. imports of Japanese cars rose from 792,000 in 1974 to just under two million in 1980; Japan's share of the U.S. market rose from 8.5 percent to 22.3 percent between these two years (U.S. Department of Commerce data).

sion had ruled that imports were not a substantial cause of injury to a domestic industry. In all previous cases, when an industry had lost its appeal for import relief under the escape clause, the administration gladly adopted a nonprotectionist posture. A third unique factor was the magnitude of the costs—billions of dollars annually—imposed on U.S. consumers by more expensive domestic and Japanese cars. As the number of Japanese cars fell short of demand and their prices rose, Detroit quickly followed with its own price increases. Estimates placed the cost per job saved in the U.S. automobile sector (relative to incremental prices) in excess of $100,000 annually.[19] A fourth unusual aspect of the automobile cutback was its duration: the initially three-year arrangement has now entered its second decade with no end in sight. In recent years, the U.S. government has said outright it no longer wants an extension, so Japan's decision to continue to limit automobile exports is now genuinely voluntary.

Bilateral economic tensions were partially overshadowed in the early eighties by extraordinary strains in the international economy. The aftermath of the second oil price shock produced not only the worst global recession since the 1930's but an international debt crisis as well. Both U.S. and European eyes noted new increases in Japanese trade surpluses following Japan's rapid adjustment to higher oil import prices. To stanch rising foreign criticism Japan liberalized imports. Given the persistence of Japan's low marginal propensity to import manufactured goods, the government had to crank out market-opening measures on a mass production basis. A late 1981 cabinet decision led to a January 1982 announcement of a sixty-seven point package. Most of the promised changes responded to foreign complaints about such Japanese nontariff trade barriers as customs procedures, product standards, and testing requirements. While applauding the scope and detail of the package, foreign reaction was skeptical of the results. The U.S. Commerce Department argued that only a small minority of the items represented changes that could quickly be implemented. About 80 percent of the measures were dismissed as having already been implemented in the past or as being "of no importance to U.S. trade interests."[20] Privately, U.S. officials complained that many of the measures were merely recycled versions of previously announced actions.

The January trade package also established the Office of Trade Ombudsman in the Japanese government. Supervised by the deputy chief cabinet secretary, the ombudsman was to expedite settlement of foreign trade grievances by receiving written complaints, directing them to senior officials in appropriate ministries, and ensuring that a response is given. In fact, the office served as little more than a ceremonial middleman and effectively disappeared from view by the end of the 1980s.

A more comprehensive import liberalization package was unveiled in Tokyo only four months later in May 1982. Tariff reductions or eliminations, effective 1 April 1983, were announced on more than 200 items, including photographic film, computers and components, medical equipment, and others of major interest to U.S. exporters. Further changes promised for the future were to ease product standard requirements and customs procedures, as well as streamline the distribution system.[21]

The U.S. response to this effort was more favorable than to the January package. The Reagan administration was favorably impressed with the appeal by Zenko Suzuki, then prime minister, to the Japanese people to "welcome foreign products" and to cease discriminating against imports. In an effort to defuse short-term bilateral political tensions, the decision was made in Washington to give the new package the benefit of the doubt. U.S. trade officials subsequently went public with their complaints that many of the promised liberalization measures had not been implemented. A series of visits paid to Tokyo in the second half of 1982 by U.S. officials demonstrated a suspicion of Japanese foot dragging and half-hearted efforts by Japanese officials charged with implementing the new liberalization measures. Overall, the 1982 measures had no success. Neither liberalization package addressed the major U.S. demands on market access for citrus fruits and meat or reduced the growing competitive threat of Japanese high-technology exports. Neither package would have any significant impact on the large bilateral deficit or on Japan's overall export success in the industrial sector. Neither package caused U.S. anger to abate.

On the other side of the communication gap, the Japanese, proud of what they viewed as politically painful responses to foreign pressures, suggested that no further comprehensive import liberalization packages were possible. They claimed that only scattered, politically sensitive restrictions remained. Nevertheless, one of Prime Minister Yatsuhiro Nakasone's earliest acts in office was to order his cabinet to draw up a new list of measures to further open Japanese markets to foreign goods. The new prime minister thus continued what has become an old tradition: the liberalization package. The tariff reductions on seventy-five products announced in January 1983 with promises of further simplifications in the country's product standards requirements, testing criteria, and customs procedures were remarkably similar to those made earlier. Goaded by continuing U.S. pressure and static imports of manufactured goods, the Japanese government announced additional market-opening packages on a more or less semiannual basis. Amendments to sixteen laws governing product standards and testing procedures were passed in May 1983. A more splashy economic package unveiled in October of that year contained domestic stimulative measures, such as public works spending, a proposed income tax cut, and a discount rate cut, along with another easing of import barriers. Tariff cuts agreed to in the Tokyo Round of Multilateral Trade Negotiations were to be accelerated on hundreds of items, with reductions in nontariff barriers and relaxation of restrictions on international capital flows.

The first of two 1984 packages, announced in April, featured numerous promises to do more in areas where action previously had been announced, with no specifics as to how key measures would be implemented. In addition to many reductions and a few eliminations of tariffs, the government promised to ease access to the market for such high-technology goods as communications satellites and telecommunications equipment, to improve access for foreign direct investment in Japan, to pursue more financial market liberalization, and to reduce restrictions on foreign lawyers practicing in Japan. Near year end, a package designed to help less developed countries was announced; its most important component was accelerated tariff cuts on more than 1,000 items.

By the time the parade of antiprotectionist packages peaked in 1985, Japan claimed to have the world's lowest overt tariff and nontariff trade measures. In a continuing effort to demonstrate the government's commitment to a more open market in Japan for imported goods and services, Prime Minister Nakasone went on national television in April 1985 to announce a three-year drive to free the Japanese market of import restraints, except in cases involving special circumstances and national security. Details of the "action program" to achieve this goal, unveiled over ensuing months, included major regulatory relaxations in product standards, customs approval, and testing procedures for imports. Tariff cuts of at least 20 percent were promised on approximately three-quarters of all the goods on Japan's tariff schedule. The seemingly inevitable year-end follow-up to the spring initiative consisted in 1985 of measures to stimulate faltering domestic demand, with an acceleration in the timetable for import market-opening measures.

U.S. pressures elicited a radically new round of Japanese concessions, beginning in 1984, with the advent of bilateral negotiations on financial liberalization. The efforts of the Ad Hoc Group on Yen/Dollar Exchange Rate, Financial and Capital Market Issues produced a series of regulatory changes aimed at two broad goals. The first was the increased internationalization of the yen. The U.S. Treasury Department believed that increased use of the yen by foreigners in international transactions would contribute to yen appreciation, thereby improving U.S. competitiveness. The Japanese agreed to technical innovations such as creation of a yen-denominated bankers' acceptance market and the facilitation of floating yen-denominated bonds outside of Japan (the so-called Euro-yen market). The second broad goal of enhanced market access in Japan for foreign financial institutions was to be met by such changes as permission for foreign banks to conduct trust business in Japan and foreign membership on the Tokyo Stock Exchange.

Few of the trade measures impressed U.S. negotiators. In the absence of any significant improvement in market performance by U.S. exports, U.S. demands became even more prolific than Japan's many market-opening packages. By the mid-1980s, U.S. pressure escalated to a level viewed as improper and dangerously aggressive, though many Americans viewed U.S. actions as belated, inadequate, and lacking follow-through.

The first of the new U.S. trade initiatives was the drafting (but not passage) of a "reciprocity" bill in the Senate. While the U.S. government also complained about trade barriers erected by the Europeans (especially on agricultural goods), the Canadians, and the less developed countries (LDCs) objections to perceived Japanese double standards were the principal inspiration of the proposed statute. According to congressional supporters, the reciprocity bill had nothing at all to do with restricting imports. Congressional sponsors said that the United States no longer could tolerate the refusal of other countries to open their markets to the same degree as the United States had done for foreign-made goods. They felt a new law was needed that would present Japan and other countries with the simple choice of either opening their markets to a degree deemed by U.S. officials as being comparable to levels of U.S. openness or facing retaliatory restrictions. It was supposed that the Japanese would choose the first option. Despite general support for this approach, the Senate yielded to the administration's request that the president be given considerable flexibility in imposing retaliations against foreign import barriers. Congressional failure to complete legislative action in 1982 did little to dispel Japanese feelings of having been unfairly singled out in the reciprocity debate. Japan's siege mentality was heightened by efforts in the House of Representatives to impose local-content requirements on most imports of Japanese-made cars in the United States. If the bill had become law, a stipulated minimum percentage of the components of imported cars would need to have been made in the United States.

A new dimension in U.S.–Japanese frictions opened in the spring of 1982 when a little-known company filed a complaint under an obscure tax law. Houdaille Industries, a machine tool maker, submitted the first-ever petition under Section 103 of the Revenue Act of 1971. Section 103 authorizes the president to suspend eligibility of foreign-made products for the investment tax credit in the United States upon a determination that a foreign government has unjustifiably restricted U.S. commerce by its "tolerance of international cartels." In this case, given the potential tax savings associated with eligibility for investment tax credits, the effective price of Japanese-made machine tools would have increased almost 15 percent.

The Reagan administration faced the unprecedented question of deciding if certain Japanese industrial policies (some of which were made public for the first time by research conducted in Japan by Houdaille's counsel) bestowed unfair competitive benefits under U.S. law on exporters to the United States. The traditional trade policy issue of domestic injury from imports was completely overshadowed by far more significant matters: Japanese internal policies were, in effect, on trial in Washington. Furthermore, a decision in favor of the machine tool company could open a flood of similar requests by other U.S. producers of capital goods, for most of the economic policies challenged by Houdaille applied to many industrial sectors besides machine tools.

The final decision in the Houdaille case is draped with sensationalism. It was widely believed in the Washington trade community that personal intervention by Prime Minister Nakasone with President Ronald Reagan led to a ruling in favor of Japan.[22] Having apparently gotten wind of deep divisions in the U.S. bureaucracy, the Japanese embassy seems to have convinced Nakasone to call on the personal relationship with his fellow conservative in the White House for a political favor in exchange for efforts at home to get Japan to meet U.S. demands for increased defense expenditures.

The dispute over metal baseball bats waged at this same time lacked the high-level intervention and potential ramifications of the Houdaille petition, but the symbolic value of this product generated a level of emotion in the United States far in excess of the economic effect. The long-drawn-out efforts to get the Japanese to relax their product standards and testing requirements, together with the subsequent inability of U.S. exporters to regain the market they had lost in the seventies when domestic Japanese production of metal bats began, make this disagreement something of an exemplar for U.S. trade frustration. Despite years of disproportionate exertion by the U.S. government to close one loophole after another in Japan's regulatory defense against bat imports, no significant export market ever developed. The reasons for this failure, as explained to the author at various times, elicit little sympathy from most Americans; the excuses range from a lack of after-sales follow-up by U.S. companies (for a very simple product with no replacement parts) to a dislike by many Japanese ball players of the pinging sound made by U.S. bats when they strike the ball.

Simultaneous with the ping controversy came the sting controversy. In June 1982, the FBI arrested employees of Hitachi Ltd. on suspicion of buying stolen IBM trade secrets. Alerted to the priority given by Hitachi and Mitsubishi Electric to keeping up with innovations in mainframe computers, IBM arranged with the FBI to secretly videotape illegal transactions between the Japanese buyers and FBI agents posing as consultants who had obtained the proprietary data. To avoid an embarrassing trial, Hitachi pled guilty to criminal charges, and in a later civil suit, agreed to pay millions of dollars in damages to IBM and to allow IBM for several years to inspect new Hitachi products to assure that no unauthorized IBM technology had been incorporated into them. As notable as IBM's legal one-upmanship was the matching of U.S. outrage at Japanese corporate piracy by Japanese outrage at the carefully executed sting operation. Sensationalist Japanese newspapers portrayed Hitachi as the victim of yet another crude U.S. exercise in Japan bashing; to the Japanese, IBM was a villain who deserved to lose sales to mistreated Hitachi.

Yet another problem arose in the related field of copyright protection for computer software. High-level U.S. government protests and threats of retaliation defeated a proposal within the Japanese government that would have diluted and shortened copyright protection for software, a product area where the United States retains competitive leadership.

More traditional negotiations in the mid-1980s involved steel, specifically, U.S. demands for Japanese "voluntary" export restraint. The beginning was a finding in an escape clause investigation by the ITC in 1983 that imports of specialty (stainless and alloy) steel products were a substantial cause of injury to the domestic producers of this high-value-added product. The European Community again accepted unilateral U.S. import restrictions, but the Japanese government insisted on working out a four-year orderly marketing agreement negotiating annual export ceilings product by product.

By the fall of the next year, U.S. trade negotiators were back in Tokyo, this time to explain the virtues of voluntary export restraints on traditional carbon steel products. In an impressive feat of election-year political dexterity, President Reagan had rejected the ITC's recommendation of relief from import injury under the escape clause, but immediately announced that he intended to use new legislative authority to negotiate comprehensive "voluntary" export restraints to prevent future import surges and offset the unfair effects of widespread foreign subsidies for steel. To cooperate with the administration's effort to limit imports to 20 percent of total U.S. Steel consumption, Japan agreed to limit its exports to a 5.8 percent market share in return for assurances that no further legal harassments on steel shipments would be forthcoming.

Although bilateral trade problems have been and still are handled within the relationship, the United States has submitted grievances against Japan to the GATT. Frustrated with Japanese intransigence, the Reagan administration requested the GATT to convene a council of mediators to determine the extent to which the Japanese had acted illegally in (1) maintaining import quotas on leather and (2) imposing stringent testing requirements on imports of metal U.S. baseball bats. In 1983, the U.S. government asked the GATT to investigate Japanese agricultural import quotas. With a GATT ruling against Japan, the United States would be legally entitled to retaliate if Japan refused to alter its restrictions.

In 1982, the European Community had joined the United States in invoking the GATT's negotiating procedures to gain further access to the Japanese Market. The Europeans filed a complaint under Article 23 of the GATT, alleging that barriers to imports were still sufficiently stringent to suggest that Japan was violating the spirit of the GATT. Arguing that its trading rights had been impaired, the Europeans successfully demanded the initiation of bilateral consultations. These forestalled a threat to go one step further: to request formation of a formal GATT panel to investigate allegations of Japanese discrimination against foreign-made manufactured goods.

None of these actions resulted in any substantial change in Japan's trade policy or import figures. In some cases, limited agreements reached "out of court" forestalled retaliation. It was not until 1988 that Japan finally agreed to phase out quotas on eleven relatively minor agricultural products; this action was taken in the wake of recommendations made by the GATT dispute panel convened to consider the U.S. complaint originally filed in 1983.

THE LATE 1980S: BOMBS BURSTING IN AIR

Japan dominated American trade policy thinking in the late 1980s more than ever before. No questioning of the status quo, no desire to avenge questionable foreign trade practices, and no sense of insecurity in trade policy or U.S. competitiveness failed to involve Japan in some manner. An uneasy Congress sought a solution to the "Japan problem" through a number of new legislative ideas and alterations to existing trade laws. The executive branch made demand upon demand for Japanese concessions, conducting bilateral negotiations on an unprecedented number of issues. Private sector analysts and some members of Congress wondered out loud whether retention of a liberal trade policy made any sense in view of Japan's successful application of an industrial policy that seemed to be hastening the continuing downward slide of the United States in industrial competitiveness. (See table 2.6 for a comparison of the divergent multilateral trade performances of the two countries.)

Fear of or frustration with Japan was the source of many new terms in the U.S. trade vocabulary. Trade and competitiveness debates revolved around such concepts as induced competitive advantage, adversarial trade,

Table 2.6 Multilateral U.S. and Japanese Trade Balances, 1983–89
(billions of U.S. dollars)

	Japan	United States
1983	+31.5	−57.6
1984	+44.3	−107.9
1985	+56.0	−117.7
1986	+92.8	−138.2
1987	+96.5	−152.1
1988	+95.0	−118.7
1989	+77.1	−108.6

NOTE: Imports measured FAS.

SOURCES: U.S. Department of Commerce, "U.S. Foreign Trade Flash Tables" for the United States; International Monetary Fund data (by telephone), for Japan.

strategic trade theory, results-oriented negotiations, and industrial targeting. The United States was waking up to the magnitude of the bilateral
economic problem, though it was not yet ready to move beyond rhetoric.

The mood in Japan was radically different, with a growing sense of
achievement, confidence, and power. Gratitude for postwar U.S. assistance
was turning into irritation and disdain at the strident tones of a declining
superpower that preferred complaining to self-improvement. Corporate
profits, prices of land and common stock, and an inflow of dollars from the
continuing current account surplus all reached heights that would have
been considered impossible as recently as the onset of the decade. Despite
an apparent embarrassment of riches with which the Japanese can buy
their way out of many international economic difficulties (such as by
foreign direct investment), the continuing importance of the U.S. market
and the political relationship with the United States combined to postpone
the day when the Japanese refuse to talk to or cooperate with U.S. trade
negotiators.

The most important development in the bilateral dialogue in 1985 was
the advent of the Market-Oriented Sector-Selective (MOSS) talks.* The
purpose of this new negotiating format was to avoid tedious case-by-case
dealings with U.S. trade complaints and threats of retaliation. The MOSS
talks were to address all identifiable trade barriers within a Japanese industry where (1) U.S. companies were competitive in the international marketplace, but (2) had poor results in exporting to Japan.

Varying results were achieved by year end in the four sectors where
efforts initially were concentrated. First, the Japanese government offered
a number of concessions to prevent any disadvantage to U.S. suppliers of
telecommunications equipment or services as the result of the privatization
of NTT and deregulation of the telecommunications sector that coinciden-
tally were in progress at this time. The Japanese agreed to accept the results
of certain equipment-testing procedures conducted in the would-be exporter's country and to make operating standards for telecommunications
equipment more closely comparable to those in the United States. Considerable red tape was eliminated in a second sector, medical equipment and
pharmaceuticals, as Japan eased requirements for testing and test data
(some foreign clinical test results would now be acceptable), for approval
of existing products, and for introduction of new products; the Japanese
regulators in this sector were ordered to be more available and responsive
to foreign companies. Modest tariff reductions were the only notable
concessions granted in the final two sectors, forest products and electronics.

In June 1985, yet another emergency import package, this one in the

---

*The depth of some U.S. trade negotiators' cynicism towards Japan is revealed in the
joke that circulated among trade specialists that MOSS really stood for "More of the
Same Shit."

$2 to $3 billion range, was announced by the Japanese government in an effort to reduce its trade surplus and foreign complaints.

Meanwhile Washington had become the center of activity for the U.S.–Japanese economic partnership. In 1985 Congress came so close to passing protectionist legislation that the Reagan administration finally retreated from its free-market approach toward the deteriorating trade balance and the appreciating dollar. Alarmed by the administration's inaction and apparent indifference, Congress attempted to force a policy shift by initiating its own. Approximately 300 bills to impede imports were introduced in the Ninty-ninth Congress. In addition, some members of Congress openly discussed an across-the-board surcharge on imports as a means of simultaneously enhancing U.S. competitiveness and raising revenue to reduce the federal budget deficit.

Three prominent Democrats (Senator Lloyd Bentsen, chairman of the Finance Committee; Representative Dan Rostenkowski, chairman of the Ways and Means Committee; and Representative Richard Gephardt, a trade hawk) introduced legislation in mid-July mandating import surcharges on all goods of "major trading countries that maintain an inequitable surplus in their trade with the U.S. or with the world as a whole" and refuse to take measures to reduce such surpluses. The aggressive provisions of this bill formed the core of the Gephardt amendment to the omnibus trade bill that was passed by the House in 1987, but subsequently diluted in the conference committee with the Senate. A textile quota bill mandating a sizeable import rollback was the only protectionist bill to reach the president, but he vetoed it.

Although the dollar overvaluation and the mounting budget deficit increased the U.S. trade deficit worldwide, Japan was the focus of congressional demands for policies more aggressively serving domestic U.S. interests. As shown in table 2.7, Japan became the single largest contributor to the deteriorating U.S. trade balance, and the bilateral deficit grew steadily throughout most of the decade. Overnight, momentum led to Senate approval of a nonbinding resolution introduced by Senator John Danforth (R., MO) in March 1985 that categorized Japan as an unfair trader, denying U.S. products fair access to Japanese markets despite its ready access to the U.S. market, and instructed the president to take "all appropriate and feasible action" to rectify the situation. After scathing rhetoric during floor debate, the resolution was passed by a vote of 92 to 0. A similarly worded resolution sailed through the House of Representatives a few days later.

Although none of the proposed protectionist measures, including the mandatory version of the aforementioned resolution, was enacted into law, the new Treasury secretary, James A. Baker III, decided not to call Congress's bluff. Soon after taking office in early 1985, he launched a major shift in U.S. international economic policy to halt both the U.S. trade deficit's upward spiral and the protectionist fury on Capitol Hill. Key to

Table 2.7   Trends in Bilateral U.S.–Japanese Trade Relations in the 1980s

	U.S. Bilateral Deficit (Billions)	U.S. Imports from Japan (Billions)	Increase from Previous Year of U.S. Imports from Japan	U.S. Exports to Japan (Billions)	Increase from Previous Year of U.S. Exports to Japan	U.S. Exports as a Percentage of U.S. Imports
1980	$ 9.9	$30.7	17 %	$20.8	18%	68%
1981	15.8	37.6	22.5	21.8	5	58
1982	16.7	37.7	—	21.0	-4	56
1983	19.3	41.2	9	21.9	4	53
1984	33.6	57.1	39	23.6	8	41
1985	46.2	68.8	20.5	22.6	-4	33
1986	55.0	81.8	19	26.9	19	33
1987	56.3	84.6	3	28.2	5	33
1988	52.1	89.8	6	37.7	34	42
1989	49.0	93.6	4	44.6	18	48

Cumulative U.S. Bilateral Trade Deficits, 1980–89 $353.9 billion
Increase of U.S. Imports from Japan, 1989/1980   205%
Increase of U.S. Exports to Japan, 1989/1980   114%

NOTE: Imports measured FAS.
SOURCE: U.S. Department of Commerce, unpublished data.

this strategy were the multilateral effort to push down the dollar's exchange rate (beginning with the Plaza Agreement in September 1985) and the enhanced assault on foreign trade barriers, centered on an interagency strike force to challenge foreign trade barriers, announced by President Reagan in September.[23]

A more traditional approach to bilateral problems returned in 1986. New products and services were discussed, but in a familiar pattern of U.S. efforts to secure new market-opening measures as well as "voluntary" Japanese export restraints. Only the U.S. rice industry failed in what was its initial attempt to secure government assistance in reducing Japan's near-total restrictions on imports of that product. On the services side, U.S. trade negotiators worked at improving access for U.S. construction and engineering companies to the gigantic public works projects getting under way in Japan, partly as the result of the fiscal stimulus programs. U.S. dissatisfaction centered on the multibillion-dollar Kansai International Airport outside Osaka. High-level talks produced nominal progress in opening the Japanese legal system to U.S. lawyers.

A principal focus for Japanese export restraint was machine tools. President Reagan responded to a request by that industry for import relief on national security grounds by negotiating export restraint agreements with the main foreign shippers of machine tools.

U.S. displeasure in the semiconductor sector produced the unique situation of a bilateral agreement simultaneously involving arrangements for improved market access and for altered Japanese export behavior. This important dispute, illustrating all major aspects of bilateral trade frictions, will be analyzed in depth in the next chapter.

A new pattern of bilateral cooperation was set outside trade policy in the so-called Baker-Miyazawa accord concluded in the fall of 1986. The two finance ministers essentially swapped a promise for fiscal stimulus in Japan for a joint effort to stabilize exchange rates at a time when a rising yen discomfitted Japan's export sector. Japan's economically rational decision to implement expansionary fiscal measures provided a political pay off as well: this initiative engendered a favorable, "let's avoid retaliation" attitude towards Japan in Treasury secretary Baker, at that time the most important voice in U.S. international economic policy-making.

Reagan administration officials were greatly encouraged as to prospects for structural reforms in the Japanese economy by a naively exaggerated reading of the so-called Maekawa Commission report. Too good to be true from a U.S. perspective, the recommendations to the Japanese prime minister included greater reliance on domestic growth, encouraging consumption in Japan through higher wages and fewer working hours, reducing Japan's current account surplus, and increasing market access for foreign goods. Regrettably, the report remains an ambitious, never realized blueprint.

Several unsettling events in 1987 overshadowed efforts to follow up on the continuing issues of automobile parts, Kansai Airport construction, supercomputers, telecommunications, legal services, financial restrictions, and bilateral macroeconomic cooperation. The first of two boat-rocking events was the first unilateral U.S. retaliation against Japanese trade practices in the postwar period, undertaken because of alleged violations of the bilateral semiconductor agreement (see chapter 3). A second retaliatory act followed in December, when Congress passed a one-year ban on Japanese companies bidding on most federally funded construction projects—a message of dissatisfaction at the continuing inability of U.S. construction firms to win major contracts for the Osaka airport and other Japanese public works projects.

Then came the surprise revelation that two companies, one Norwegian and one Japanese (the Toshiba Machine Company), had violated export control laws and sold advanced milling machines and control equipment to the Soviet Union, enabling the latter to improve the propellers on submarines so they operated more quietly. No one disputed that this technology leak was a serious breach of security for the United States and its allies, including Japan. The thought of quieter Soviet submarines prowling the world's oceans because of Japanese corporate sales hunger, on top of Japan's reputation for lax export control, provoked outrage in the U.S. Congress. Congress was not mollified by the quick response by the Japanese government, strengthening export control enforcement capabilities and punishing the Toshiba Machine Company. Congress wanted a five-year ban on the import into the United States of any product produced by Toshiba or the Norwegian company, a measure that could have cost Toshiba $3 billion annually. Strenuous opposition from the executive branch and lobbying by Toshiba's U.S. customers succeeded in watering down the retaliatory provisions in the 1988 Trade act. (Toshiba escaped the three-year import sanctions imposed on its machine tool subsidiary, but was restricted as to bidding on federal procurement contracts.)

U.S. pressure for greater access to the Japanese market continued in 1988. The major success stories were Japan's agreement to phase out quotas on beef and citrus fruits (tariffs would be substituted) and relax allegedly discriminatory technical standards imposed on foreign companies offering computerized data transmission facilities known as international value-added networks. Notable failures to change the market access status quo included a second rejection by the Reagan administration of the U.S. rice industry's petition for retaliation for continued Japanese import barriers. In the politically sensitive case of rice, the U.S. government recognized a sector where the cost of obtaining concessions was disproportionate to any benefit. A bilateral agreement in the spring of 1988 was to improve access for U.S. construction and engineering companies, but when few major contracts were won by U.S. firms, the United States initiated a formal investigation of Japanese barriers in these sectors.

Two important harbingers of future trends emerged in 1988. First, in

Washington, came the Omnibus Trade and Competitiveness Act. Three years in the making, the bill was the outcome of three broad congressional concerns: (1) lagging U.S. competitiveness; (2) unaggressive U.S. trade policy; and (3) presidential subordination of international trade issues to foreign policy considerations. With an eye on Japan, Congress passed the new "Super 301" provision requiring the president to seek reductions in "priority" foreign barriers. This amendment to the old section 301 added export targeting and government tolerance of cartels to the list of "unreasonable" trade practices and required reciprocity in the treatment of foreign securities firms acting as primary dealers in the trade of government debt instruments.

A second turning point was the controversy over the 1988 agreement for joint development and construction of the new jet fighter known as the FSX. This agreement represented a compromise by the Japanese, who had been reluctant to buy their new fighter from U.S. defense contractors. The backlash in Washington against the technology "giveaway" forced the Bush administration to tighten up understandings in the agreements on technology transfers in both directions and work-share guarantees for U.S. companies. The political significance of this backlash lies in the apparently irreversible inclusion of international economic policy concerns in U.S. national security policy formulation involving Japan. The Pentagon can no longer urge Japanese militarization without considering the impacts on U.S. industrial and technological competitiveness. The FSX is also significant in signaling Japan's intention to develop domestic aerospace technology.

As the turbulent 1980s drew to a close, new economic concerns broke into traditional patterns of bilateral relations. On a familiar note, the United States threatened retaliation against what appeared to be blatant discrimination in the Japanese telecommunications sector. Negotiations resolved the complaints of one U.S. company (Motorola) about restrictive Japanese government regulations imposed on its exports to Japan of technologically advanced mobile radios and cellular telephones.

Also on a familiar note, at the end of 1989, the Japanese government announced an "unparalleled" import promotion program—this one centering on tax incentives. Tax credits were to be offered to companies that increased imports of specified manufactured products by at least 10 percent annually. The package additionally promised to eliminate tariffs on 1,004 items.

Additional Japanese market-opening measures followed the 1988 U.S. trade bill. After being included on the list of countries whose trade barriers were to be targeted under "Super 301" treatment, the Japanese agreed to reduce import barriers on three priority products—supercomputers, satellites, and wood products. As so many times before, when the United States presented product-specific demands in one hand and waved a big club and a final deadline in the other, Japanese concessions were forthcoming—though the actual increases in U.S. sales remained uncertain.

Apparently to placate Japanese sensitivities, a number of other un-
resolved market-access complaints, such as rice, soda ash, and semiconductors, were omitted from the initial Super 301 negotiating list, and in a
classic bit of bureaucratic compromise, the most salient Japanese import-
retarding factors—domestic business practices and attitudes—were relegated to separate, informal negotiations without legal mandate or time
limit. Thus the Structural Impediments Initiative was born, and the 1990s
began with a genuine breakthrough in trade relations. The United States
moved beyond its concern with explicit trade regulations to demand modification of such indirect internal barriers to imports as Japanese pricing
mechanisms, business structure and practices, land policy, goods distribution, and working hours. The Japanese countered with demands that the
United States rectify internal problems such as the budget deficit and
inadequate investment.

Another new element in U.S.–Japanese trade relations that had
emerged in the late eighties was the thesis increasingly popular in the U.S.
private sector that the continuing ineffectiveness of Japanese concessions
called for radically changing the mode of negotiations. A so-called results-
oriented approach to bilateral problems was suggested as the better alternative. Since the United States was interested only in bottom-line
results—ends rather than means—specific, quantitative standards for U.S.
export expansion could be set, leaving the Japanese to decide among themselves how the demands would be implemented. Managed trade would
replace the unfulfilled promises of Japanese liberalization packages. Different targets, such as absolute and percentage reductions in the overall
bilateral trade deficit and minimum U.S. export levels to Japan in sectors
where the United States is otherwise internationally competitive, were
suggested by influential sources, including the presidential Advisory Committee for Trade Policy and Negotiations, the Emergency Committee for
American Trade (a coalition of large U.S. multinationals), and Henry
Kissinger and Cyrus Vance (in a 1988 *Foreign Affairs* article).

A third important development in bilateral relations involved a growing U.S. backlash against the large capital inflows from Japan that are the
natural consequence of its persistent trade surpluses. The financial facts of
life are that these inflows were the principal means by which the United
States financed its $100 billion-plus current account deficits in the mid and
late 1980s. The U.S. Treasury Department still turns ashen at the thought
of Japanese investors reducing or terminating purchases estimated to be as
much as 30 percent of new issues of U.S. government debt instruments.
Even the rumor of reduced Japanese buying at the next auction of Treasury
IOUs causes nervous investors to send U.S. interest rates spiraling upward.
Meanwhile, state and local governments compete shamelessly with one
another to attract Japanese capital inflows by offering lucrative financial
packages to lure new Japanese manufacturing plants.

Concern over the "selling of America" to foreigners dominated the
U.S. reaction to these vitally needed Japanese capital inflows. The popular

press sensationalized the purchase by Japanese companies of such cultural icons as Rockefeller Center and the Columbia motion picture studio. Congress began responding to warnings that more comprehensive statistics and national security limitations on foreign direct investments are necessary. But with the United States having amassed foreign debts approaching $700 billion by 1990, need continues for foreign capital inflows, by direct investment and otherwise.

Although Japan is not the largest foreign direct investor in the United States—Great Britain is—the large, persistent Japanese bilateral trade surpluses have resulted in Japan having the fastest growth rate of any country for U.S. capital inflows from abroad. Total Japanese assets held in the United States increased tenfold from an estimated $35 billion in 1980 to about $350 billion at the end of 1989. Japanese purchases of U.S. corporate bonds rose from $3 billion in 1984 to $30 billion in 1988, and investments in common stocks jumped from $1 billion to $16 billion during the same period.[24] The more politically sensitive direct investment from Japan expanded sevenfold during the 1980s, rising from an estimated $10 billion in 1982 to just under $70 billion in 1989 (see figure 2.1).[25]

CONCLUSION

Nineteen sixty-nine was a watershed year in U.S.–Japanese trade relations. Previously submerged economic trends began to surface; the first signs

Figure 2.1   **Japanese Direct Investment in the United States
(billions of U.S. dollars)**

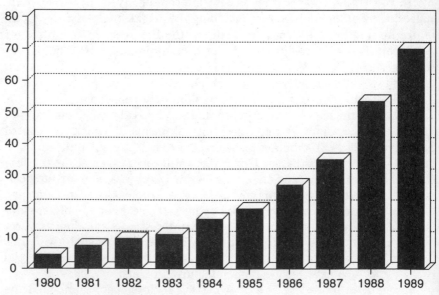

SOURCE: U.S. Department of Commerce.

appeared of frictions associated with Japan's export zeal and low marginal propensity to import manufactured goods.

In the two decades that followed, a consistent pattern of behavior developed. Nonstop efforts to resolve commercial differences through ad hoc agreements failed to alter either underlying economic conditions or the bilateral trade disequilibrium. The Japanese repeatedly liberalized their overt barriers to imports of manufactured goods and foreign direct investment. They repeatedly responded to U.S. demands for restraints on the volume of exports. Nevertheless, given the minimal effects of Japan's liberalization and the significant impact of that country's escalating export success, most Americans perceived Japan as an unfair trader.

Most Japanese attributed their economic success to hard work, and they viewed U.S. complaints as ill-informed demands by a country that preferred to blame someone else for its own economic shortcomings. At the same time, Americans attributed their bilateral shortcomings to the cynical refusal of the Japanese to accept the principle of equity in their import and export policies. While most American observers were perceiving a self-indulgent effort by Japan to maximize exports and minimize imports of manufactured goods, most Japanese observers of bilateral economic relations were perceiving a self-indulgent effort by the United States to restrain Japan's economic success. The failure to recognize the structural nature of the economic problem and the cultural differences that created and sustained a gap in communication prevented the two countries from resolving the twin problems of inadequate U.S. market success in Japan and booming Japanese export success in the U.S. market.

The result was a constant repetition and broadening of trade frictions, to the point of disrupting one of the most important bilateral relationships in the present world order. After two decades of conflict management, it seems clear that no enduring solutions will be forthcoming without a better understanding of why the contemporary relationship between the cowboy and the samurai economic and cultural systems developed as it did.

CHAPTER 3

The Semiconductor Dispute

The more technology advances, the more the U.S. and the Soviet Union will become dependent upon the initiative of the Japanese people . . . America's semiconductor industry . . . is losing its superiority minute by minute. . . . Very soon now, the defense of America will become dependent upon supply sources abroad.

—Shintaro Ishihara (1989)

The U.S.–Japanese semiconductor dispute in the mid-1980s is a classic case in contemporary bilateral economic relations. All of the basic questions, arguments, and dilemmas are present: a U.S. industry in apparent decline allegedly over-aggressive price discounting by the Japanese, incompatible industrial structures, limited access for U.S. exports to the Japanese market, U.S. domestic inability to meet a Japanese import threat, and so on. Also present were broad issues such as maintaining important high-technology industries and the perennial lack of definitive answers on the subjective question of what is good versus bad in economic policy.

Semiconductors are variously referred to as the DNA, the petroleum, or the rice of modern industry. They lie at the heart of the information-processing revolution that has altered every aspect of the economy; they represent the key to today's fastest-growing and best-paying consumer, capital, and military goods industries. Worldwide, the semiconductor industry is expected to grow from $40 billion to more than $100 billion by the next century. And semiconductor chips are the key to systems worth a large multiple of their value. They are increasingly critical, for example, in the electronics industry (estimated already to exceed $250 billion in the United States alone) that encompasses such technologies as computers, telecommunications, control and measuring instruments, consumer electronics, and robotics. Chips are also widely used by the capital goods, aerospace, and automobile industries. To economists, the semiconductor industry is a prime example of "externalities," where economic and knowledge benefits flow from one sector to others.

ORIGINS OF THE DISPUTE

Lack of plentiful, cheap, state-of-the-art semiconductor chips jeopardizes a modern country's international industrial competitiveness across a broad spectrum.

The establishment of a competitive domestic semiconductor industry by the Japanese was a calculated, pragmatic move designed to achieve global leadership in production of low-cost, high performance computers and other advanced electronics. (Even if this is an unprovable hypothesis, the leading Japanese semiconductor producers also manufacture computers.) The doubling over the past decade in Japan's world market share in computers is more than coincidental to the United States's flagging performance after long-standing global computer supremacy.

The U.S. semiconductor industry has had limited market success in Japan. Despite the termination in the early 1980s of formal legal or administrative barriers to the import of semiconductors in Japan, the U.S. market share percentages have remained remarkably unchanged. The net cause of this situation, as between Japanese market structure and protectionist instincts and American lack of efforts and short-term horizons, is in dispute. What is clear is the tremendous current and long-term costs to the U.S. industry of curtailed sales opportunities in what is both the world's largest market for semiconductors and the home of the world's most efficient volume producer of memory chips.

The U.S. Semiconductor Industry Association (SIA), based in northern California and led by a group of freewheeling, market-oriented entrepreneurs who were at first uncomfortable with the idea of government bail-outs, soon perfected lobbying techniques for galvanizing the U.S. trade policy–making apparatus into action. By 1981, the SIA was complaining of Japanese dumping of 64k—the "k" is shorthand for kilobit, the capability of a chip to store approximately 1,000 bits of information—dynamic random access memory (DRAM) chips and continuing poor sales by U.S. firms in Japan. The situation was exacerbated in 1985 and 1986 by a sudden, severe downturn in the semiconductor market. DRAM prices eroded steadily in the face of what might have been as much as a 30 percent decline in demand. By the end of 1985, prices for 64k and 256k DRAMS had dropped to one-fourth of the price at the beginning of the year. The U.S. International Trade Commission documented a price decline for some 256k DRAM products of more than 90 percent between September–October 1984 and November 1985.[1] In the wake of mounting United States industry losses—an estimated $2 billion in 1985 and 1986—six U.S. companies abandoned the manufacture of memory chips, the highest volume component of the market, leaving only three domestic companies in the field. Seemingly impervious to losses estimated at $4 billion during these two years, Japanese producers watched their share of the U.S. memory chip market rise to nearly 90 percent. The U.S. producers, on the other hand, watched their market share in Japan slide back down to its historically meager 10 percent as new customers from the 1983–84 upswing returned to Japanese suppliers. Within the SIA, confidence sank that the domestic industry could survive.

Mounting frustration in Washington about the deteriorating U.S. trade position created a favorable environment for the flurry of legal actions against Japanese imports initiated in mid-1985 by the U.S. semiconductor industry. Dumping petitions (accusations of sales at less than fair value) were filed against imports from Japan of 64k DRAMs and erasable programmable read only memory chips (EPROMs). In December 1985, the administration took the unprecedented step of ordering the Commerce Department to self-initiate a dumping investigation of 256k DRAM chips—and all ensuing generations of chips with expanded memory capacity, whether or not currently in production—rather than await an industry complaint. (The rationale was that a memory chip was the same basic product, no matter what its capacity, and that dumping penalties should not be circumvented by such devious means as bringing out, say, a 257k DRAM.) Micron Technology Corporation had already, in September 1985, filed an antitrust suit alleging a Japanese conspiracy to fix prices and monopolize the market in 64k DRAMs. In January 1986, Texas Instruments filed a suit for patent infringement against eight Japanese and one Korean semiconductor producers.

With at least tacit encouragement by senior U.S. trade officials, the SIA filed a Section 301 complaint; this provision can provide redress from foreigner's economic practices (usually internal) that are unjustifiable, unreasonable, or burdensome to U.S. commerce. The gist of the SIA's petition was that the Japanese domestic semiconductor market was protected by structural barriers that were an outgrowth of industrial targeting. The SIA claimed the barriers: (1) relegated U.S. suppliers to residual or marginal status, and (2) allowed the Japanese industry to overinvest and overproduce without regard to market conditions. In short, the oligopolistic structure of the Japanese semiconductor industry, which discouraged competition, and the policies that financed and shaped it allegedly distorted trade. Relief was requested through an end to Japanese dumping and the guarantee of a U.S. market share in Japan commensurate with that enjoyed by the U.S. semiconductor industry in other key markets such as Western Europe.

The U.S. accusations raised complex questions. Were the Japanese really guilty of dumping as a practical, economic matter (as opposed to the rarified legal standard)? What were the real reasons for the limited U.S. success in Japan? Were the statistics used by the U.S. companies biased? Was the counterlobby launched by Japan appropriate or equitable?

Final answers to these questions cannot yet be conclusively known; any evaluation of the semiconductor agreement and its effects on the U.S. economy and U.S.–Japanese relations is less an exercise in divining unassailable truths than an indirect exposition of a relatively arcane theory of political decision-making known as cognitive process. It holds that people tend to mentally process incoming data to fit with their preexisting beliefs and images in order to perceive what they expect to be there. The greater the ambiguity of the data, the more likely it is that points compatible with expectations will be assimilated and incompatible points will be down-graded or dismissed.

THE AGREEMENT

As it became increasingly apparent that the United States would take unilateral action against imports of Japanese semiconductors, both governments moved fitfully toward a negotiated settlement. As usual, the U.S. government hesitated to impose sanctions contrary to the liberal trade ethic, especially against its key ally in the Western Pacific, while the Japanese pursued their usual time-consuming search for exploitable divisiveness in the U.S. government.

In June 1986 the U.S. Department of Commerce imposed dumping duties in the range of 12 to 35 percent on imports of Japanese 64k DRAMs. Dumping margins of 60 to 188 percent (meaning that prices were pegged at about one-third of estimated fair value) loomed for imports of EPROMs from various Japanese companies. Preliminary findings of dumping margins of 20 to 109 percent had been announced by the Department of Commerce for 256k chips. Unlike a Section 301 investigation, dumping cases permit no flexibility for the president once sales at less than fair value and material injury to the petitioning domestic industry have been determined. Thus, the Japanese had to cut a deal if they were to avoid paying dumping duties and being branded an unfair trader.

A comprehensive semiconductor agreement was initialed late on the night of 30 July 1986, minutes before the legal deadline for notifying the petitioners that the dumping duties on EPROMs would be suspended. The Section 301 case was withdrawn, and the U.S. government indefinitely suspended action in the EPROM and 256k DRAM dumping cases. In return, the Japanese government agreed to two initiatives that were familiar in bilateral agreements.

First, the Japanese government would monitor the prices of semiconductors exported to the United States and third-country markets so as to prevent further sales at less than fair value. The United States insisted on the "third-country" provision to avoid becoming the high-price market for Japanese-made chips that allegedly would be dumped everywhere else. The major Japanese exporters separately agreed to abide by a confidential, custom-tailored fair market price list to be issued quarterly by the U.S. Commerce Department. Minimum prices, specified company by company, sometimes for hundreds of individual items, became the means by which the U.S. government would prevent Japanese dumping in the U.S. market. (Semiconductors incorporated into finished products were not covered by the agreement.)

Second, Japan agreed to assist in enlarging the Japanese market share for all foreign semiconductor producers over a five-year period, in part by encouraging domestic consumers to expand imports. In a secret, still-unacknowledged side letter, the Japanese government said that it *"recognizes* the U.S. semiconductor industry's expectation that semiconductor sales in Japan of foreign capital–affiliated companies will grow to at least slightly above 20 percent of the Japanese market in five years [and] considers that this can be realized and welcomes its realization [emphasis added]."[2]

The semiconductor agreement was an ad hoc solution rather than a part of any preexisting grand strategy to save the U.S. high-tech sector. No symbolic line was drawn in the dirt to divide the global market for semiconductors. The 1986 agreement might never have been concluded or the Section 301 case been pressed but for the SIA's adroit lobbying. The domestic industry marketed its case shrewdly in Washington, focusing on redress from unfair competition and avoiding the specter of protectionism. The SIA asked only that the market mechanism (as Americans define it) be allowed to operate—free from import barriers and free from a draining contest of which country's industry could lose money the longest: the formal request was only that the Japanese competition sell its products in the U.S. market above production costs and that U.S. companies get a fair shot at selling in the Japanese market.

CLAIMS, COUNTERCLAIMS, AND CONFUSION

Even before the semiconductor pact was signed, controversy had risen about its provisions. The specifics of the arguments reproduce in microcosm the complexities of what does and does not constitute legitimate market activity within the contentious U.S.–Japanese economic relationship.

The first round of claims, counterclaims, half-truths, and multiple layers of truth centered on the issues of market access and dumping. On the surface, the question of market access seems straightforward, something that can be measured by simple arithmetic. Private research firms regularly publish information about Japanese purchases of semiconductors from different producers. The United States argues that the volume of Japanese chip imports has been artificially limited. While imports recently have increased, they remain so low as to violate the promises made in the secret letter mentioned above. Some U.S. trade and industry officials view the small U.S. market share in Japan as symptomatic of larger patterns of that country's import behavior, including a preference for defusing tensions by restricting exports rather than increasing imports, retention of an import substitution mentality if not an unofficial import substitution policy, and informal as well as formal market-sharing arrangements not normally open to foreigners.

The SIA distributes what it calls "the worm chart" (see figure 3.1), in

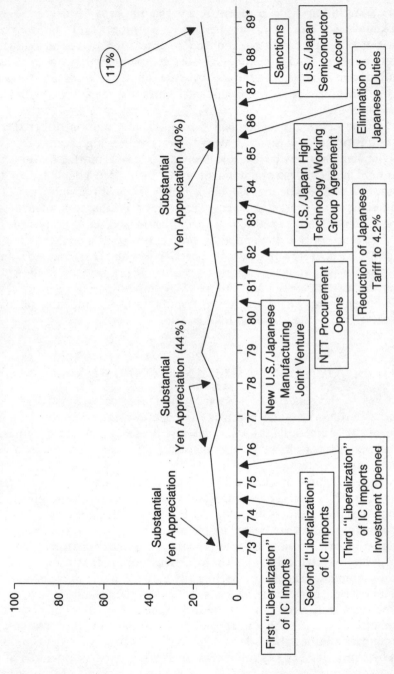

Figure 3.1 U.S. Share of Japanese Semiconductor Market

*Preliminary figures
SOURCE: Semiconductor Industry Association.

(IC = integrated circuit)

which U.S. market share in Japan is depicted in graph form as an almost horizontal line (helped along slightly by drawing the graph to large proportions) at 10 percent. U.S. market share held steady from 1973 into 1987, despite numerous measures ostensibly opening the market: liberalization of import and foreign direct investment controls, procurement reforms by Nippon Telegraph and Telephone, the High Technology Working Group, total elimination of tariffs on semiconductors, substantial yen appreciation, and the 1986 bilateral agreement, among others.

The Electronics Industry Association of Japan has stated publicly that the U.S. accusations of bad faith "are entirely groundless and ordinarily would not warrant a reply." A rebuttal was forthcoming, the association continued, only because of intensifying bilateral trade frictions and spreading misconceptions about Japanese economic and business practices.[3]

The Japanese also point to the rapid increase, measured in absolute dollar terms, of U.S. semiconductor exports to Japan, from $682 million in 1988 to $906 million in 1989. Because U.S. exports rose at a faster rate than overall Japanese consumption, market share in that country for U.S.-owned semiconductor firms exceeded 12 percent by the end of 1989.[4] This moderate progress notwithstanding, it is inconceivable that the U.S. market share will even approach the supposedly agreed-upon level of 20 percent by the end of 1991. The all-important question is why? Who and what are to blame?

Much of the ongoing market access debate revolves around the legitimacy of the 20 percent goal/commitment. The Japanese emphasize three points. The first is that even if Japan recognized the side letter, it constitutes no legal commitment to a specific market share (recall that the conveniently vague language stipulates only "recognition" of the goal of a 20 percent market share). The Japanese also point out that U.S. estimates for chip exports excluded those of two in-house or "captive" producers, IBM and AT&T, who release no data. A third argument supporting the Japanese position is that it would be unrealistic to expect a linear, or straight-line progression in the growth of U.S. market share; rather a "gradual and steady" increase over the five-year life of the bilateral agreement should be expected in a noncommand market economy.

The United States makes three points of its own with regard to the market share brouhaha. First, this number was not arbitrarily invented by the U.S. government. Trade negotiators for both countries surveyed data on the Japanese market, identifying some fifty-five submarkets for chips before agreeing on the figure of 20 percent, much below the 30 to 40 percent originally demanded by the Reagan administration.[5] (Further, the 20 percent figure includes production within Japan by U.S.-owned companies as well as third-country exports.)

Another point that seems to support U.S. claims is the discrepancy between the performance of U.S. chip companies in Japan and elsewhere. As seen in table 3.1, U.S. success in all other markets dramatically exceeds

Table 3.1 Estimated Global Market Shares in Semiconductors, 1988

World Companies	Regional Markets				
	North America	Japan	Europe	Rest of World	Total
North American	70%	9%	43%	31%	37%
Japanese	21	90	17	45	51
European	6	1	38	10	10
All others	3	0	2	13	3
Total	100%	100%	100%	100%	100%

NOTE: Geographical home of companies is on vertical axis, market share of each producing country or region in each major geographical area is on horizontal axis; thus, European companies have 6% of the North American market.

SOURCE: Dataquest Inc.

the level in Japan; in the case of Western Europe, higher relative U.S. semiconductor sales reflect in part more extensive operations (and presumably sales efforts) by U.S. subsidiaries than in more expensive, more forbidding Japan.

Even if allowance is made for the special historic and cultural difficulties in exporting to the Japanese market, it is difficult to reconcile widely published estimates that U.S. companies account for about 70 percent of the global market for semiconductor chips used in automobiles, while their Japanese market share for such devices is no more than 1 percent.[6]

Third, the United States reasonably challenges the Japanese contention that it is unrealistic to think that in the late 1980s, MITI retained the power and influence to force a change in corporate buying habits. It is a dubious proposition that MITI could not enforce a 20 percent commitment even if it wanted to, because of its diminished capacity in a liberalized economy dominated by large, cash-rich corporations. MITI presumably did not need formal power, but merely the ability to articulate common sense, to motivate the big six producer/consumers of semiconductors in Japan (Fujitsu, Hitachi, Matsushita, Mitsubishi, NEC, and Toshiba) to import more chips. They were made to recognize the threat of escalating U.S. anger to their multibillion-dollar export market in the United States. In point of fact, by 1989, the six were closest to reaching the 20 percent mark for their share of chips bought from American and other foreign-owned companies for use in their electronics products.

Conflicting views of "the truth" about Japanese dumping cloud any objective quantification of an important issue in the semiconductor agreement: the extraordinary application of U.S. antidumping law. Typically, dumping involves export sales at prices below those prevailing in the home market. In the semiconductor case, domestic Japanese prices were low, and so the claim depended on the "constructed value" to determine whether export prices were less than fair value. Dumping can be demonstrated to exist (no matter what the foreigner's domestic price is) if the landed costs of imports in the United States are not sufficiently high to offset direct and indirect production costs and provide a profit of at least 8 percent.

Determination of constructed value is difficult even in mature, relatively static industries like televisions or steel; the economics of the semiconductor industry presented unprecedented problems to Commerce Department analysts. Technology in the industry is evolving rapidly. The learning curve is so important that on average a doubling of production of any particular device has lowered costs by up to 30 percent. At the same time, unusually short product life cycles—past levels of memory storage have become obsolete after three to four years—necessitate a fairly quick payback of incremental development costs.

Another major complication arises in calculating overhead costs. Assumptions must be made on allocating ongoing and overlapping R&D and the costs of expensive manufacturing equipment specific to each model of semiconductor. Additionally, manufacturing costs vary considerably from company to company according to "yield," the percentage of usable chips produced from a wafer of silicon. The unusually fast-pace of semiconductor technology may have rendered obsolete the traditional statistical measurement of dumping.

The United States government defends the earnest, objective, and meticulous efforts of the Commerce Department to develop the most accurate and up-to-date cost estimates, even without adequate data from all Japanese producers. It was also argued that Commerce's margin of error could hardly be so large as to invent dumping margins of 188 percent; even if some findings were high, some dumping was almost certainly present. Another argument suggests that Japanese chips were being sold at home and abroad in the down markets of 1985–86 at prices too low to recoup the costs of developing and introducing the 64k and 256k generations of DRAMs within their short life cycles. Price declines for these devices was far steeper than allowed for by the traditional ratio between increased production and cost reductions. Imposition of dumping duties in 1986 was thus seen as absolutely necessary to staunch the flow of red ink in U.S. industry before IBM and the two surviving merchant producers of DRAMs abandoned production and left the Japanese to control the U.S. market.

The Japanese counter that in addition to being unable to keep up with production innovations, the dumping investigators ignored the importance of "forward pricing" in the semiconductor market. Given the learning-curve phenomenon and the resultant utility of increased demand, no chip producer expects to recoup development and production costs for a new product at the outset. Instead, prices are averaged over an extended period and initial losses are offset when economies of scale are achieved later in the manufacturing cycle.

The characterization of "extraordinary" also applies to the unprecedented extension of the semiconductor agreement to third-country markets. The United States justified this extraterritoriality on the grounds that cheap (read dumped) Japanese chips in Mexico, the Far East, or elsewhere would have driven U.S. computer makers and other assemblers of electronic equipment offshore, a painful economic setback to the U.S. economy. The move offshore also would have complicated the domestic political situation by widening the schism between the semiconductor industry and its customers in the electronics industry.

A second phase of claims, counterclaims, and confusion began in 1987 when alleged Japanese noncompliance with two of the three major provisions of the agreement—increased market access in Japan and third-country dumping—sparked retaliation by a surprisingly unified Reagan administration. Throughout late 1986 and early 1987, anger swelled in the executive branch as Japanese promises to increase U.S. market share and stop third-country dumping failed to materialize. Early on, MITI's failure to establish a promised semiconductor sales promotion organization was seen in U.S. trade policy agencies as a measure of MITI's insincerity on the market access issue.[7]

Meanwhile, the administration received a steady stream of reports via U.S. semiconductor companies, commercial counselors in U.S. embassies, and intelligence sources that Japanese chips were being offered in Asia for prices below what the U.S. government considered fair market value. A U.S. sting operation caught a Japanese chip producer in Hong Kong quoting low prices by telex to a female "customer" who later vanished.[8] Denying corporate duplicity, Japanese semiconductor companies point to the flourishing gray market in their chips, with middlemen allegedly filling suitcases with cheap chips in Japan and profitably selling them overseas at prices still below the official fair market levels.

Despite formal warnings to Japan of retaliation and specific deadlines, no improvement of the situation was evident to the Reagan administration when the cabinet-level Economic Policy Council met in late March 1987. No one—not even the theoretical economists or the enthusiasts for the budding Ron-Yasu relationship between the two countries' heads of government—argued that the violations could be ignored. A formal government-to-government agreement had been flouted; the consensus in the United States was that U.S. credibility would be undermined if Washington turned the other cheek. Furthermore, Congress was moving toward passage of legislation restricting the president's flexibility in retaliating against unfair foreign trade practices.

In yet another example of the extraordinary situation surrounding the semiconductor agreement, for the first time since the end of World War II, the U.S. government unilaterally imposed trade sanctions in retaliation against what was deemed to be unacceptable Japanese trade behavior. The surprisingly decisive U.S. action slapped prohibitive 100 percent duties on selected Japanese electronics products made by divisions of the big Japanese semiconductor manufacturers. Penalty duties on imported semiconductors were bypassed, lest the U.S. electronics industry be made to suffer. When third-country dumping ceased (for reasons discussed below), the administration removed the higher tariffs on nearly one-half of the targeted $300 million in Japanese imports. (The 100 percent tariffs on the rest remain in effect as of this writing, by way of imposing retaliatory costs equivalent to the estimated losses of the lagging U.S. market share for chips in Japan.)

UNINTENDED CONSEQUENCES

A major lesson of the semiconductor agreement has been that government interventions to reduce market distortions, internal or external, produce distortions of equal or, more likely, greater magnitude. The 1986 pact did serve to create a slightly more level playing field for the U.S. semiconductor industry. As expected, Japanese export prices increased and so did U.S. export sales. But from the perspective of the U.S. government (and possibly that of the Japanese as well), the agreement also triggered enough unintended, unexpected, and undesirable consequences that a cost-benefit analysis suggests, at best, a dubious outcome.

Immediately after the agreement was signed, the Commerce Department presented Japanese semiconductor producers with their minimum fair market value prices. Because the lists were based on data from 1985 (when the dumping investigations had been conducted), sizeable increases were immediately ordered by the Department of Commerce, and prices in the U.S. market for DRAMs and EPROMs increased 100 to 500 percent. A significant downward revision of the prices in October relaxed tensions—for the moment.

The market rapidly turned around in 1987. Within a matter of months, prices of memory chips doubled and tripled amidst growing shortages. Part of the cause was a cyclical upsurge in demand by computer and VCR producers. The press reported production cutbacks by some chip-starved U.S. computer companies and instances of Japanese exporters discriminating against U.S. companies in allocating scarce chips or making special demands, such as augmentation of memory chip orders by purchases of customized logic chips. The ensuing supply-demand disequilibrium was exacerbated by production delays associated with the initial transition in Japan from 256k to 1-megabit (capable of storing one million bits of information) DRAMs.

But the number one factor by far behind the growing shortages appears to have been the production cutback foisted by MITI on the Japanese semiconductor industry. The intensifying U.S. complaints over third-country dumping led the Japanese government to conclude it needed to go beyond the measures contained in the original agreement.

The United States now was hoisted on its own petard. Its demands that the Japanese chip producers make profits and refrain from dumping led to MITI actions that replaced free-wheeling price competition with a de facto Japanese semiconductor cartel. The cartel arrangement implemented production rollbacks that successfully destroyed the economic logic of dumping increasingly scarce semiconductors anywhere in the world. In the larger interest of enabling the Japanese government to keep its word in an international agreement, MITI effectively restrained domestic production. At the U.S. insistence, MITI had created an industry-specific version of the worst U.S. nightmare—Japan, Incorporated.

With the Japanese producers enjoying ballooning profits, MITI officially denied the existence of a formal cartel. Although MITI does, in fact, lack legal authority to order production cutbacks, there emerged a continuing, uncanny correlation between the supply/demand forecasts for semiconductors issued quarterly by MITI and actual production totals. At a minimum, the evidence points to a pattern familiar from previous MITI-led efforts to defuse U.S. trade complaints: voluntary corporate compliance with prorated production cutbacks implicit in so-called weather forecasts that foresaw lowered demand.[9] Here was a classic case of the Japanese market's controlled competition. The situation changed only after the Reagan administration once again actively sought a shift in Japanese policies; beginning in late 1987, production levels were allowed to rise in response to market demands, and prices leveled off in the following year.

No one in Washington intended the 1986 agreement to provide a financial windfall for Japan's semiconductor industry. Nevertheless, Japanese producers of 1- and 4- megabit DRAMs continue to enjoy what economists call rents, unusually high profit margins accruing from market domination by sellers. Another widely accepted, but empirically unverified estimate is that during the 1987–88 demand/supply disequilibrium, Japanese semiconductor exporters enjoyed economic rents of perhaps $2 billion dollars—the antithesis of their 1985–86 supply glut. Most of this windfall went not to increased common stock dividends, but rather into incremental R&D and capital investment. The future looks better than ever for the Japanese industry as it moves ahead in the preliminary designs and production for DRAMs of 16 and higher megabits as well as the sophisticated logic chips, such as microprocessors and application specific integrated circuits (ASICs) that are the last bastions of U.S. chip strength.

It certainly had not been intended that the semiconductor agreement would result in no more than a minimal effort by U.S. industry to reenter DRAM production. Another lesson here is that when debilitating import competition causes an industry to shut down plant and capacity, there is a reluctance to commit resources to reclaiming lost market share on the basis of protective import barriers that may or may not be permanent. This same reluctance can be seen with exchange rate depreciation that may or may not be reversed in a few months' time.

The creation of U.S. Memories, Inc., announced in mid-1989, represented an innovative effort to revive DRAM manufacturing (as opposed to manufacturing technology) in the United States through a new form of intersectoral corporate cooperation. The projected new consortium was premised on private funding from both the computer and semiconductor industries and the commitment of IBM to license the new company to produce its state-of-the-art 4-megabit (and beyond) DRAMs for sale to U.S. computer companies. It seems even mighty IBM was running scared. Longtime corporate presence in Japan had given IBM unusually clear insight into the tactics, strategy, and potential of the Japanese semiconductor and computer companies. By now indirectly providing its most advanced chips to other U.S. computer makers, IBM was gearing up to apply its leadership and material resources to revive memory chip capacity in the United States and contain further Japanese inroads in the U.S. electronics market.

Unfortunately for the idea, it ran afoul of the old maxim that timing is everything. The relatively abundant supply of memory devices in the United States in late 1989 and early 1990 softened prices and discouraged U.S. computer makers from committing sufficient capital to back even a scaled-down version of U.S. Memories. The project aborted amidst acrimonious talk about short-sighted U.S. business executives and Japanese duplicity. (One scholar suggested a more sinister explanation: the Japanese may have helped undermine U.S. Memories by deliberately reducing DRAM prices while the project was being considered and then announcing production cuts and price increases shortly after it was abandoned.)[10]

CONCLUSION

The semiconductor agreement signed in 1986 by the U.S. and Japanese governments epitomizes the notion that there is a difference between legitimacy and success. The agreement was completely consistent with international trade law in responding to indications of Japanese dumping, but it did little or nothing to resolve the structural factors that underlay the weakness of the U.S. industry. U.S. economic policies continue to suffer from the lack of a cost-effective alternative to a rely-on-market-mechanism-no-matter-what approach.

To deal with the exigencies of the moment, the agreement was and is necessary, if imperfect. It did induce market-opening measures in Japan that probably would not have occurred otherwise. It gave a strategic U.S. industry at least temporary breathing space from savage price competition in memory chips from Japan. The indefinite period of dumping avoidance by the Japanese semiconductor industry provided a "better than nothing" opportunity for the U.S. industry to gear up for what may be its final attempt to escape a permanently defensive, secondary status to its Japanese counterpart. The United States economically and politically cannot afford to be pushed out of the critically important semiconductor industry. Nor can it afford the desperation move of adopting protectionism to preserve a viable industry: this option would subsidize mediocrity and further punish end users of chips, especially the U.S. computer industry.

The direct costs to the U.S. economy by Japanese dominance in DRAMs in 1987–88 runs into the billions of dollars. This short-term price of forcing the Japanese to impose generous profit margins on 256k and 1-megabit chips sold in the U.S. market might be considered preferable to risking greater, long-term costs in the future from current inaction. Permanent Japanese domination in memory chips could lead to even higher markups and larger shortages in another upswing in demand. Such dominance might also lead to eventual Japanese leadership in the production of logic chips. It is difficult to dismiss the behind-the-scenes alarm expressed by the knowledgeable IBM Corporation about the dangers inherent in the potential demise of a meaningful domestic semiconductor capability in the United States. It is difficult to understand, therefore, how U.S. national interests would have been served if the Reagan administration had subverted the U.S. antidumping statute and sat on its hands.

There was no good reason in July 1986 to think that Japanese semiconductor companies had exhausted their ability to sustain losses. Sales at less than production costs could have continued to the further detriment of the surviving U.S. DRAM producers. Without the agreement, the Reagan administration would have had no choice but to enforce the law and apply dumping duties on Japanese semiconductor imports to offset the less than fair sales prices. But unilateral action on dumping would not have addressed the third-country dumping issue or improved access to the Japanese market for U.S. chip exports. Many of the ensuing market distortions were inevitable.

All the same, the agreement that grew out of the U.S.–Japanese semiconductor dispute must be deemed a failure in its net accomplishments. Now after four years, the shortcomings can be seen to be numerous and serious:

- The U.S. semiconductor industry has not regained sustained competitive strength, nor can the pact provide the industry with the technological, manufacturing, and financial revitalization it needs. Meanwhile, the Japanese give every indication of accelerating already formidable production and financial strengths and innovative skills.

- The actions taken by Japanese producers of memory chips to avoid charges of dumping and maximize profits have harmed U.S. interests:

    A strategy to maximize profit rather than market share provides new financial resources to Japanese producers for expanded R&D in product design and process technology;

Windfall profits by Japanese semiconductor companies were made at the expense of U.S. electronics systems manufacturers, mainly the computer industry, whose Japanese competitors have access to lower-priced chips.

- The pact will fail to achieve the desired 20 percent U. S. market share in Japan by the end of 1991.

- There has been no significant reentry by U.S. semiconductor companies into DRAM production; both the existence and the success of future ventures remain uncertain.

While U.S. trade officials may have been slow in assisting the domestic industry fend off unfair practices by the Japanese chip industry, the main cause of failure lies outside trade policy, in the failure of senior Reagan administration officials to separately insist on commitments by both the government and U.S. industry to remedy internal causes of the competitive problem.

One of the main lessons of the semiconductor agreement is how easy it is to produce third best economic policy when inappropriate remedies are applied to a Japanese industrial tour de force. The U.S. government is seriously out of synch with contemporary global market realities and thus unable to integrate trade policies with domestic industrial policies. The government was intellectually, institutionally, ideologically, and instinctively incapable of determining what really was needed to enable the U.S. semiconductor industry to hold its own with, let alone surpass its Japanese competition.

To this day, the United States remains without a comprehensive offensive strategy in microelectronics competition (to some, this is a perfectly appropriate state of affairs). There are only piecemeal defensive tactics. The executive branch retains its long-standing contention that an unwavering, hands-off free-market response is the only way to deal with the at times devastating inroads of superior and/or unfair Japanese industrial performance. The result is the pattern seen—not for the first time—in the case of semiconductors: Washington's anti-import efforts to compensate for Japanese trade strengths leading to even greater economic distortions.

The transcendent lesson of the semiconductor incident is the inherent limitation of using trade policy to solve the broader industrial competitiveness problems that have been brought into the limelight by the successes of our most potent foreign competitor. U.S. trade laws and trade theory were conceived in a much simpler time, when technological change was slower and less expensive and before industrial structure began reflecting *successful* industrial policies among some U.S. trading partners, notably Japan. Any correlation between trade agreements with Japan (even on market access and antidumping) and long-term creation (or restoration) of U.S. competitiveness in any industry is purely coincidental. Unfair trade practice laws are designed to neutralize unfair trade practices, that is, to equalize prices; they cannot be expected to create an internationally aggressive, competitive domestic industry out of whole cloth. Both the problem and the cure begin at home. The 1986 semiconductor agreement might be thought a moderately successful surgical operation, but the patient—the U.S. semiconductor industry—has a cloudy prognosis.

CHAPTER 4

The Domestic Foundations of Japan's Foreign Trade Performance

"The strength in Japanese industry is in finding many ways to turn basic technology into products and using basic technology. . . . Turning technology into products is where Japan is number one in the world."

—Akio Morita (1989)

To understand Japan's phenomenal foreign trade success since the late 1960s, it is first necessary to understand the sources of its phenomenal domestic success since the late 1950s. The contemporary economic success of Japan was neither accidental nor conspiratorial. Rather it was the logical outgrowth of a critical confluence of factors. Japan's post World War II economic metamorphosis was rooted in an unusually strong national consensus about the need for economic recovery and catching up with the industrially advanced countries, mainly the United States. The foreign trade sector, like all others, became subordinated to the grand design of industrial expansion. Much has been written about the Japanese economic "miracle." I will take a different approach to identifying the reasons for Japan's uniquely successful industrial sector—the base from which its export-generating capabilities were launched. Above all, I will avoid the central fallacy of most English-language analyses of Japanese economic success: the search for a single explanation.

The true cause seems to lie in the mix of cultural values, historical circumstances, management strategies, production know-how, and official policies reinforcing one another in a uniquely positive environment for industrial growth. The extraordinary interplay of these factors might be equated with synergy, the natural science phenomenon in which a number of substances or organisms combine to achieve an effect that none is capable of producing on an individual basis. If any of the principal ingredients of Japan's industrial strength described in this chapter had been absent, Japan's economic recovery would have been radically altered.

That Japan's economy recovered after World War II and kept growing was far from preordained. Indeed, Japan's success has been improbable, overcoming obstacles far more frequently than exploiting natural advantages. Japan was and remains a small, densely populated island possessing a minimum of natural resources. Among the other characteristics that militate against the market-driven recipe for industrial success are labor immobility and a rigid seniority system, concentrated industries (domination by a relatively few companies), lax antitrust enforcement, and active government involvement in economic planning.

A holistic approach is the most appropriate methodology for explaining Japan's economic ascendancy. The Japanese economic process violates a rule of geometry: it is larger than the sum of its parts. Regrettably, there exists no methodology for assigning the basic factors a precise degree of importance or for quantifying the ways each affects the other. Another critical point in assessing the relative importance of the factors contributing to Japanese economic success is that their importance varies according to the period being examined. The respective impact of each of the sources of strength to be discussed in this chapter has varied over the past forty years and can be expected to change again in the future.

Nevertheless, my central hypothesis, that all single-factor explanations of Japan's domestic economic success are inadequate, holds up well under critical scrutiny. Japan's bureaucratic planners had great long-term strategic vision and a knack for choosing the appropriate implementing tactics. However, it was the business sector that actually produced low-cost, high-quality goods and implemented successful overseas marketing strategies. And it was a skilled, productive, and compliant labor force that literally forged the tools of economic strength. Moreover, by the 1980s, many Japanese industrial companies had become so large, successful, and cash rich that they had outgrown their dependency on governmental financial support and hence the constraint to comply automatically with governmental desires.

Those who point to cultural factors as the source of Japan's post-war resurgence tend to forget that these values are many centuries older than Japan's emergence as an international economic superpower. For those who argue on behalf of the central role of government policies, I would ask this: Why haven't other countries replicated the Japanese economic miracle by simply copying the directives, incentives, aids, guarantees, and forecasting techniques adopted by the Japanese government? The correct response is that Japan's economic policies cannot be neatly transplanted elsewhere. Otherwise, government planning and control would have demonstrated universal success in achieving economic prosperity. Similarly, the argument that management excellence and hard work alone produced economic success is dubious. Japan's industrial managers were and are very good. But they benefited from indigenous factors beyond their production lines and marketing skills in the support they received from social values and government assistance.

CULTURE AND HISTORY

Unique cultural and historical factors have combined to produce a unique strain of capitalism in Japan. The American sociologist Daniel Bell has argued that what ultimately provides direction for an economy is not the price system for goods but the value system of the culture in which the economy is located. This assertion seems especially relevant to Japan, where more than elsewhere economic success cannot be explained strictly in economic terms. Japan's uniquely distinctive culture is the source of important social values, attitudes, and priorities that helped overcome the major obstacles to economic resurgence: war damage, lack of capital, and lack of natural resources.[1]

A number of basic Japanese values are invaluable for economic success: the work ethic, honesty, frugality, and an orientation towards collective goals. The shape and spirit of Japanese capitalism also have been molded by a second level of values that include emphasis on the group over the individual, stress on social harmony, mutual trust, simultaneous competition and cooperation, acceptance of a deep sense of obligation, respect for hierarchy, and belief in long-term, binding business commitments.[2] What might be termed the third and most abstract level of cultural values includes a complex set of deeply emotional attitudes towards foreigners and their inroads into what the Japanese perceive as the private preserve of their social order.

Many of the major cultural characteristics of modern Japan became ingrained during the two and one-half centuries of the Tokugawa period. From 1600 until 1868, the human environment in Japan was tightly controlled. The overriding political objective of the ruling shoguns during this period was the preservation of their absolute rule. To this end, the Tokugawa shogunate emphasized regimentation and established a centralized feudal structure controlled by regional lords (daimyō). The social order, stressing the concept of hierarchy, was based on a rigid class system with the samurai at the top. The samurai, or warrior class, epitomized the moral virtues of loyalty, righteousness, and propriety. (Although the term *samurai* literally stands for the type of feudalistic hierarchy practiced in medieval Japan, the more common designation will be used here.) Only samurai carried weapons, and they could use them on common people virtually at will. In return, the samurai were expected to pursue self-fulfillment though total devotion to the interests of their lord's—including having no second thought about laying down their lives to protect them from any challenge from rival samurai. This all-encompassing subjugation of self put financial gain very low on the samurai's list of priorities. (When the samurai were transformed into government and business leaders after the Meiji Restoration, they became proselytizers as well as practitioners of these values, calling upon farmers, tradesmen, and artisans to vigorously adhere to the notion of group loyalty and the other Confucian ethics that had guided the samurai tradition.)

The government imposed near-total isolation of Japan from the rest of the world, lest potential dissidents obtain foreign ideas or weapons. Many of the roots of contemporary Japanese attitudes toward self, employer, and government can be traced to the formalized social order that developed during this era of Japan's history.

A gradual but inevitable consequence of the emphasis on hierarchy and obedience to ritual was the suppression of individualism. Individual identity and self-esteem became a function of social class. In Tokugawa Japan, this meant that status and value as a citizen reflected the proximity to or distance from performing service to one's superior, the regional lord. Personal characteristics and achievements were relatively less important. One's own happiness or unhappiness became a secondary consideration.

The prevailing feudal value system emphasized unselfishness and derivation of self-identity by relating oneself to a group or organization. Within Japan's regimented society, no one could be self-made. "Thus the competitive, adventurous Japanese of the sixteenth century became, by the nineteenth century, a docile people depending mainly on their rulers for leadership and following all orders from above with few questions."[3] A major ingredient of Japanese culture for generations has been the widespread signals in everyday life that actively promote the notion that submerging individual personalities into larger social entities is normal, desirable, and ultimately self-fulfilling.

Japanese school children are indoctrinated from a young age to be part of a team: the very special Japanese race. As they go through life, Japanese are bombarded with explicit and implicit messages about fitting in with the group. They repeatedly hear they must accept as inevitable that their intellectual and psychological growth is restrained not so much by personal abilities as by the will of the collectivity. To sugarcoat the pill, this supposedly collective will is presented by parents and bosses as benevolent, devoid of power, and wholly determined by a unique culture.[4]

Be it as school children or workers, the Japanese people have complied stoically with demands that would be branded as unjustifiable burdens or outright exploitation by the U.S. value system. Personal sacrifice, persevering in the face of adversity, patience, and endurance are viewed in Japan as virtues that signify dignity, strength of character, and maturity. Making a fuss over being cheated over one's just desserts suggests immaturity and selfishness, characteristics inimical to the collective good.

As Edwin Reischauer has written, "Each person, each thing, fits into an accepted order of prestige and power. Position on this scale must be clear so that one can distinguish the superior from the inferior and know where the authority lies."[5] The gradations of politeness and deference in the Japanese vocabulary reinforce the concept of hierarchy. Students of linguistics know that there is a reason for the many forms of personal pronouns in the Japanese language as opposed to the simple "I" and "you" in the English language. Japanese have a far keener sensitivity to their relative social status and their attitudes toward their environment at the time they speak. The language allows them to express these feelings, as well as the concept of being inside *(uchi)* or outside *(soto)* a certain group.

Consensus, capitalism, and the special circumstances of Japan's economic history collectively produced a system in which the samurai of the Tokugawa era seem to have been transformed into the new breed of managers and bureaucrats who guide modern Japanese corporations and government agencies. Large corporations can be seen as contemporary versions of the regional lords to whom so much loyalty was extended. White-collar workers are modern-day samurai in that they are fiercely loyal, hard working, and group oriented. They are at the top of the social and professional pyramids. They willingly compromise when dealing with associates but demonstrate aggressiveness and relentless determination toward rivals inside and outside of Japan. The "private sector samurai" also have a tradition of cooperating with government officials on issues of economic policy.

Is the accumulation of personal wealth the primary driving force behind the "new samurai"? Not likely. Once again, historical continuity seems to prevail. The contempt of the spartan-living samurai for the relatively wealthy merchants of feudal times continues. Amassing and displaying personal wealth is not emphasized in modern Japan. The "good life" is appreciated, just as it is in the West; the Japanese are not masochists who have taken vows of poverty. Status is merely experienced in a different manner, such as through the use of expense accounts for various forms of evening entertainment.[6] The salaries of Japanese business leaders and professionals are very small in comparison with those of their U.S. counterparts.

The Japanese value system simply does not fit the Western notion of economic activity as collective decisions of economically rational people going through life making selfishly sophisticated cost-benefit decisions. Nor does the Japanese value system fit the notion self-evident to Americans that efficient domestic production and a liberal foreign trade policy should serve the unequivocal ends of maximizing consumption, lowering prices, and increasing the variety of goods available to consumers. Japanese culture places self-discipline and self-denial above self-gratification.

Japan has never conformed to the free-market, consumption-oriented model that Americans like to think prevails in all capitalist countries. Japan, argues James Fallows, has long subordinated consumer welfare to a different priority:

> preserving every person's place in the productive system. The primary reward of working hard in Japan is to continue to be able to work. Japan has consistently protected its producers—farmers,

unions, small shops, big corporations—at the expense of Japanese consumers, who must pay exorbitant prices for everything they buy. Japan . . . has continually expanded its market share, but only at the price of living more austerely than its customers do. . . . "The Japanese have never really caught up with Adam Smith," wrote the sociologist Ronald Dore. "They don't *believe* in the invisible hand. They believe—like all good Confucianists—that you cannot get a decent, moral society, not even an efficient society, simply out of the mechanisms of the market powered by the motivational fuel of self-interest. . . . The morality has got to come from the hearts, the wills and motives of the individuals in it."[7]

The large corporations that account for the bulk of Japan's exports demand a lot from their employees. Simply put, they expect total commitment and dedication. They want employees to believe that their personal interests are served mainly by the growth and prosperity of the company. Work is depicted as a fulfilling human experience, only secondarily providing wages—the work ethic is not just an economic concept but a philosophy of life. In the words of longtime Japan observer Karel van Wolferen:

The salaryman's intensive involvement in his company makes necessary a reassuring symbolism, confirming that his time, energy and personal interests are being sacrificed for a worthy cause; the company must appear to be something more than an organization established for the purpose of making a profit or providing its employees with a livelihood. It is generally presented as having intrinsic value. . . . The passionate clinging to the symbols of the firm, the founder and the corporate ideology; the singing of the company song; the joint calisthenics: all are symbolic acts designed to reassure the employee of his membership in the company and of its nurturing powers.[8]

To be sure, the offer of lifetime employment by big corporations (usually to male workers only) justifies more loyalty than workers in other countries feel to employers that might lay them off at the onset of the next recession. Employees in Japan are looked on as important assets to be cultivated. Workers are encouraged to believe that they and the company are bound together in a common destiny where short-term sacrifices will produce long-term payouts. Big companies require long work hours and mandatory after-hours production meetings, but they also provide such fringe benefits as subsidized housing, vacation resorts, and company stores. In turn, employees find a company success a source of pride and self-satisfaction. Hard work that contributes to this end is its own reward. Thus, rigid adherence to the seniority system has done little to stifle economic success in Japan, though it would if applied in the U.S. business sector. A feeling of personal importance and accomplishment is primarily based on the degree to which workers contribute to the better performance of their work area, factory, company, and country.

Individuals in every society are subject to peer group pressures. The average person wants to fit in with friends and coworkers. In some societies this means limiting one's work efforts to rigid work practices established by powerful unions, and joining in frequent work stoppages. In Japan it means after-hours work in quality circles, refusal to take all of one's allowable vacation time, and attendance at company-sponsored social events.

Western workers who pursue their own interests, maximize their leisure time, and use the monopoly power of unions to secure the highest possible wages would find themselves outcasts in the Japanese system. Any Japanese embracing such Western tendencies would be severely chastised as a selfish person unconcerned with the harmonious and successful functioning of the corporate group.

Social pressure is a more likely cause than some genetic predilection for self-denial for the Japanese worker's unusual sublimation to the corporation's needs. Management is the major perpetuator of the credo putting employers' interests before family. Why? Because this credo lowers production costs and contributes to output. It is a profitable and convenient credo for business and the nation, but the number of bars in Japan and the social license to criticize one's bosses (to their faces) when under the influence of alcohol suggest what lies behind the facade of the happy Japanese worker content to be endlessly, feverishly serving the company without thought of recreation or family life.

Japanese values are not "better" than those of Western societies in any absolute sense, but they are integral to the success of the Japanese that Westerners envy. The sense of loyalty and duty to family, company, and society has economic implications, as does the notion that the self is not to be pampered. In a country recovering from the devastation of World War II and dedicated to catching up economically to its overseas competitors, a tremendous force of human energy was unleashed from a base of existing cultural and social patterns. Japan is one of the few countries in which economic modernization has not destroyed historic national values.

Throughout history the outside world has been a source of both fear and inspiration to Japan. The country's economic policies have been affected by the social goal of limiting foreign influence. One of the most insular of nations, Japan possesses ambivalent attitudes toward other countries. The Japanese demonstrate a classic case of love-hate attitudes: feelings of arrogance and vulnerability, and attitudes of superiority and inferiority toward the outside world. To this day, Japan retains a strong sense of distinctiveness and a seemingly innate capability for preserving a national sense of self-identity despite "modernization." Japanese resistance to Western hegemony began in earnest in the late nineteenth century with a remarkably fruitful effort to preserve the nation's sovereignty and economic viability. Ironically, this long-standing accomplishment has partially been based on study and widespread utilization of foreign activities and accomplishments.

As China had done in the sixth and seventh centuries, Europe and the United States provided a source of inspiration and guidance for Japan in the nineteenth and twentieth centuries. "Japanese spirit, Western techniques" *(wakon yosai)* became the road to economic maturity—but not at the cost of surrendering either basic cultural values or the inner feeling of being a distinctive, important nation with a special destiny. Japan's rulers long ago developed an uncanny instinct for selectively importing those foreign practices that could successfully be grafted onto the basic Japanese value system without causing radical change in existing social patterns.

From the time of the Meiji Restoration in 1868, the building of a modern state capable of maintaining political independence and social identity against all outside threats has been a driving ambition in Japan. Until 1945, this priority included military power as well as economic strength. Although military disparities are no longer relevant, the Japanese continue to practice a conscientious effort to maximize commercial and technological strength in their effort to achieve a high ranking in the international hierarchy of economic accomplishment. To overtake the United States and Europe has been an extremely strong motivating force in Japan. The typical worker's desire to contribute to Japan's economic progress is based at least as much on collective national pride as on an individual's desire for personal enrichment. Now an equal to the United States in overall economic and technological prowess, Japan faces new, more difficult challenges. Chasing a front-runner was easy compared to determining national goals and roles as an economic superpower. MITI and other government agencies can no longer concentrate single-mindedly on industrial development and export expansion. Japan's internal needs and external responsibilities have changed radically.

Hesitancy and ambiguity may continue to characterize Japan's reactions to its economic success for some time. However, one should not anticipate the general acceptance of the virtues of relaxation and diminished effort. Industrial strength will not exempt Japan from a continuing reliance on the rest of the world, both for raw materials and export markets. Consequently, there will come no right time for the Japanese to abandon their overriding historical goal of controlling foreign influence through industrial superiority. A willingness by the Japanese elite to accept the place of second best in any critical commercial technology is just not in the cards. The national consensus that economic strength is the key to preserving the Japanese system and maintaining prosperity will not likely be subordinated in the foreseeable future to clearly *secondary* goals of placating U.S. demands for improved market access and providing more domestic consumer goods and leisure to Japanese citizens.

CORPORATE STRATEGIES, MANAGEMENT PRACTICES, AND PRODUCTION EXCELLENCE

An appealing explanation for Japan's industrial success is that Japanese corporations produce better products at lower prices than do other countries. On the one hand, there is no doubt that it is through having more imagination, more innovation, more determination, better production techniques, and working harder that a large number of Japan's industrial companies have become world leaders in pleasing users of both consumer and capital goods. On the other hand, corporate brilliance does not arise in a vacuum. Japanese industrialists function in an extraordinary legal and social context that features a distinctive set of growth-encouraging institutions and economic and regulatory policies—financial, antitrust, labor, trade, and more.

Japanese business managers differ from their U.S. and European counterparts in priorities, rewards, and cultural values. (As one Honda official is said to have put it, U.S. and Japanese management are 95 percent alike but differ in all important respects.) The typical Japanese manager looks at his company (there are an infinitesimal number of female Japanese business managers) in a broad, long-term context. He will stay with that firm until retirement; he looks to his company to grow and contribute to Japanese society.

The primary indication of successful corporate performance in postwar Japan has been market share. The fight for increased market share over the long term has been the main battlefield of Japanese corporate competition, primarily because the Japanese recognize that the company with the highest growth rate for production of a given product was most likely to become the lowest-cost producer. A sharp, absolute increase in sales in a rapidly expanding market is not enough to assure long-term corporate survival, let alone high profits. Sales increases tend to be less important than lowering marginal production costs below one's competitors, an objective tied to maximizing volume and market share. Emphasis on sales growth in Japan led to a unique and effective corporate strategy that effectively produced a self-fulfilling prophecy:

> Managements with a bias toward growth have distinct mind-sets which include the expectation of continued growth, decisions and plans formulated to produce growth, and the unfaltering pursuit of growth unless the very life of the organization is threatened. Companies with a bias toward growth add physical and human capacity ahead of demand. Prices are set not at the level that the market will bear, but as low as necessary to expand the market to fit the available capacity. Costs are programmed to come down to support the pricing policies and investments are made in anticipation of increased demand.[9]

Executives also place a high priority on increasing the prestige and reputation of their company within the home market as well as in foreign markets. Possessed of a very competitive, very rank-conscious society insistent on buying goods associated with quality and status, Japan is not a market in which product mediocrity can flourish. Profits are important but not ends in themselves. It is assumed that if quality and sales growth are maintained, adequate profits will follow naturally.

A simple, practical reason for Japanese industry's freedom to look beyond short-term profits is the relatively limited role stockholders play in the operations of a Japanese corporation. At least through the early 1980s, commercial bank borrowing was a far more important source of investment capital to the typical Japanese company than sale of equity—common stock—than is the case in the United States. Japanese banks especially if members of the same industrial group (known in Japanese as *keiretsu* and best exemplified by such names as Mitsui and Mitsubishi) as the borrower, placed greater emphasis on the longer-term outlook for corporate growth and national need than on immediate profitability as means of measuring creditworthiness. In earlier years, the Ministry of Finance signaled commercial banks which industrial sectors were of special interest to the government. Lending to favored industries was implicitly a low-risk proposition; capital was made available to the banks for such lending and loan losses presumably would be covered by the central bank.

Two other factors further diminish the role of shareholders. Companies in the same *keiretsu* hold considerable amounts of stock in each other and form a kind of interlocking directorate. In addition, ordinary shareholders are as satisfied with appreciation of share prices through steady corporate growth as with dividends, because individuals pay only nominal long-term capital gains taxes on profits made from the sale of stocks. The bottom line is that for Japanese companies, customers come first and shareholders second, the reverse of priorities for U.S. companies.

Heavy reliance on bank debt resulted in interest payments becoming a major fixed cost to most Japanese corporations, and rapid sales growth is one of the best methods to reduce the burden of fixed costs. Bank borrowing is now becoming less of a force in the strategy of the larger Japanese manufacturers, however. By the mid-eighties, many of the larger companies had weaned themselves from bank borrowing: sales were strong, cash flows were often augmented by real estate and stock market speculation, and capital could be borrowed at nominal costs in the Euro-bond market.

One of the single most important ingredients of Japanese industrial success appears to be the relentless, unstinting use of applied technology by that country's manufacturers to develop and refine many of the most efficient, lowest cost production techniques in the world. Common sense, intelligence, and a sense of urgency were the primary factors in determining Japan's world class achievements in process technology—the total planning and execution of the manufacturing process from product design through final assembly.

Cultural factors are involved to the extent that Japanese pay extraordinary attention to details, that their emphasis on teamwork maximizes communication between engineers and knowledgeable assembly line workers, and that most Japanese managers are sufficiently motivated that no given plateau of improved production technique is accepted for long. Since the time of the Occupation, Japanese corporations have assiduously studied U.S. production techniques, frequently adapting and improving upon them. Dedicated students often become teachers: by the early 1980s, Japanese management had become the leading innovators worldwide and U.S. managers slowly became the students and copiers. The Japanese government helped shape the country's overall industrial structure and influenced some aspects of corporate behavior. However, the continuing revolution that has occurred on the factory floor in Japan was born of the competitive drive, determination, pride, and, to a lesser extent, insecurity of Japan's private sector in its zeal to beat domestic and foreign competitors.

An illustration of the unquenchable Japanese thirst for continuous incremental improvement in production processes was provided on a visit made to a Hitachi plant near Tokyo by a Motorola executive. Asking about the "P200" message emblazoned on a flag flying outside the factory, he learned it stood for the lofty 200 percent productivity improvement the plant hoped to achieve that year; the plant manager expressed disappointment that they had so far reached a productivity increase of "only" 160 percent. The American executive quickly sent a warning to corporate headquarters that if Motorola did not dramatically raise its own productivity goals for pocket pagers—it then considered a 20 percent annual increase to be pretty impressive—it risked being pushed out of the business.[10]

Above all, Japanese industrialists have applied nonstop brain power and physical effort to making products in the most efficient manner possible. The result was an evolutionary process in which Japan displaced the United States as the leading innovator in assembly line methods. Japan also moved to world leadership in investment and robotics. Japanese industry eventually dwarfed the rate at which its U.S. counterpart expands and upgrades capital stock.

The initial rise to international eminence of postwar Japanese industry reflected the simple use of sustained increases in production runs for such standard goods as steel and television sets. Maintaining market share in the rapidly growing domestic market (double-digit real-growth rates were the norm in Japan during the 1960s) and penetrating foreign markets produced sufficient increases in volume to make Japan a master at economies of scale. The constantly expanding production base allowed many Japanese companies to move quickly down the learning curve of production costs as they mastered all of the tricks of streamlining the costs and time involved in the production process. Sustained increases in production volume also reduced production costs by allowing Japanese companies to amortize fixed cost (such as labor, interest payments, R&D) and by encouraging them to inves in the latest available capital equipment when capacity needed to be ex panded.

By the 1970s, many Japanese corporations had shifted into what U.S business scholars dubbed "focused" manufacturing. This strategy wa necessitated by the fact that most Japanese manufacturing companies re mained smaller than their major competitors in the United States anc Europe. To compete most effectively in foreign markets, Japanese compa nies focused production on a limited number of models or product varia tions. By maximizing production in a narrow product line where marke demand was strongest, total production costs could be brought below thos of the more overextended, full-line producers. With sales increases in Japa and in foreign markets came continuous reductions in overhead and mate rials costs. This was the strategy that by the early 1970s enabled Toyot to sell a forklift truck in Western Europe at prices just slightly above th costs of materials to a larger Western manufacturer of this equipment.[1]

The most recent—and thus far most important—step in Japanese pro cess technology is generally referred to as flexible manufacturing. Goin beyond the economies of scale associated with mass volume, flexible manu facturing permits complex production schedules, the assembly of man different models of a product on the same production line, and the intro duction of new models and styles in the most rapid and lowest-cost manne possible. That the Japanese have become the overall world leaders i intricate production techniques that don't require mass production shoulc give pause to those who scoff at the notion of the Japanese dominatin industries such as aerospace.

Another aspect of flexible manufacturing is known as just-in-tim delivery (kanban). The seemingly innocuous practice of scheduling deliv eries of parts and components from subcontractors on the day they are t be assembled into the final product in fact dramatically increases efficienc in many parts of the production process. Significant cuts in fixed cost follow from reductions in the number of factory workers, the cost o maintaining inventory, the size of factory floor space needed, and the tim required to move materials on the production line and manufacture th final product. Flexible manufacturing also reduces the time that machiner sits idle.[12]

Continuous improvements on the production line have placed Japa nese factories in a class by themselves in managing complex assembl operations. On average, the Japanese have the fastest turnaround times, b it in shifting a machine from one task to another or in getting a nev product off the drawing board and onto the assembly line. Many of thes techniques involve nothing more exotic than redesigning the configuratio of capital equipment or the position of machines on the assembly line floo so that a single worker can operate more than one machine. A dramati example of the results was Toyota's reduction of the changeover time required for altering the output of a bolt-making machine from eight hours to just one minute![13]

In a study comparing Japanese and U.S. applications of flexible manufacturing systems (computer-controlled integration of work stations for manufacturing complex parts produced in low volumes and switching back and forth between product models), Professor Ramchandran Jaikumar concluded that the Japanese were refining this technique more quickly and using it far more effectively: "The battle is on, and the United States is losing badly. . . . No magic here—just an intelligent process of thinking through what new technology means for how work should be organized."[14] The Japanese are also using flexible manufacturing systems more extensively. In studying metal-cutting operations among machine tool producers, Jaikumar found that a typical Japanese factory required 100 workers to make a certain number of machine parts, but only 43 workers after the introduction of flexible automation. The "before" number of workers for a comparable U.S. plant was 194, and there was no "after" number because the author could not find a U.S. machine tool plant with such a process on line[15] (a situation that may explain the recent U.S. request for voluntary export restraints by Japanese machine tool makers).

The narrowing gap between Japanese and Western wage rates (in real terms) means that the much-praised Japanese management runs out of miracles when the manufacturing process is relatively simple, such as in paper and chemicals. The simpler the manufacturing process, the less likely it is that Japanese industry will be able to exhibit superior international competitiveness through higher productivity. The greater the number of steps and the more demanding the engineering involved in the manufacturing process, the greater is the probability that higher Japanese productivity can be combined with a long-term marketing strategy (that is, a willingness to look beyond short-run profits) to produce a mighty competitive force. Of course, most important new technologies require a high degree of manufacturing precision and complexity.

There are many examples of Japanese industry mastering the details of process technology. Most Japanese manufacturers exert far greater efforts than their foreign counterparts to integrate research and development with product design and production. Scientists and engineers are not physically or spiritually distant from the production line personnel. Key suppliers often are brought into the planning and design stages, thereby reducing later production glitches and helping to assure that subcontractors meet stringent quality control standards.

The emphasis on teamwork allows almost simultaneous development of products, machinery, and assembly line layout. A speedier transition from new ideas to actual output and a simpler, less error-prone assembly operation result. In most Japanese companies, products and manufacturing processes undergo continuous experimentation and review, as researchers, engineers, technicians, and machinery operators collectively seek new ideas and improvements. The nonstop effort extends to developing advanced models of, and new commercial applications for, existing products.

Japan's industrial success in general and its process technology accomplishments in particular are related to its being in the vanguard of global leadership in quality control. Japanese practices can be traced back to W. Edwards Deming, an American whose ideas of how simultaneously to increase productivity and quality were largely ignored in his own country. Present-day Japanese techniques reflect Deming's principles:

- Refuse to allow commonly accepted levels of delay for mistakes, defective material, and defective workmanship;

- Eliminate the need for mass inspection;

- Reduce the number of suppliers and buy on statistical evidence of dependability, not price;

- Search continually for problems in the system and seek ways to improve it;

- Break down barriers between departments; encourage problem solving through teamwork;

- Institute modern methods of training, using statistics;

- Use statistical methods for continuing improvement of quality and productivity.[16]

Quality control in the typical Japanese factory is implemented by well-educated, well-trained, dedicated employees who take pride in their workmanship; they set production standards and continually review existing production procedures. The goal of zero defects is not imposed on production line workers from above by whip-cracking managers, but instead pursued by "quality circles" of peers. With management support, worker groups concentrate on identifying problems within their individual sections, using complex statistical approaches to propose better, more dependable assembly procedures.

Manufacturing high quality goods that work properly from the start has proven a classic case of getting the best of two worlds. First, high grades from consumers for dependability and longevity increase sales and in some cases (such as automobiles) permit higher prices. Secondly, the Japanese have discovered that production line efforts to prevent defects in the first place and avoid repairing a finished product after it has been assembled or even sold to a customer reduce costs in the long term. In effect, quality control can be costless.

Any analysis of the superb competitive performance of the typical large Japanese industrial company would be incomplete and misleading without looking beyond state-of-the-art factories and lifetime employment.

The high overseas visibility of these large companies obscures the fact that barely 30 percent of the Japanese labor force works for companies employing more than 100 workers. Many of the smaller companies are so dependent on selling to a single manufacturing giant that they are helpless to resist harsh demands for different production schedules or lower prices.

> Almost half Japan's manufacturing workforce is engaged in factories with fewer than fifty workers. These are often no more than sweatshops in which husband and wife may work ten or more hours a day. As subcontractors, these small companies—which make parts, or assemble finished products for distribution by the famous firms—provide cheap labour, and in times of economic downturn absorb much of the shock. When the yen doubled in value against the U.S. dollar between 1985 and 1987 these small companies were asked to bear a large share of the loss in profits of companies eager to hang on to foreign market shares.[17]

Exploited small suppliers are not the only shadow to the bright image of productive excellence and dedicated hard work. By U.S. standards, most Japanese workers are exploited through limited salaries, long working hours, high consumer prices, and a relatively underdeveloped social infrastructure, that is, inadequate housing, parks, roads, and the like. Although the average Japanese today lives better in material terms (such as household appliances, clothing, travel) than he or she did twenty years ago, the overall amenities of daily living seem to have advanced little in this time period. Relative to other developed nations, the average city-dwelling Japanese clearly has lower real spending power and lesser comforts, suggesting a lower quality of life than most Westerners take for granted. Nevertheless, demands by the work force for increased wages or improved government services are seldom heard in this land in which "looking out for number one" means looking out for the group.

Despite these apparent causes for complaint by workers, wanting a more enjoyable life style, labor-management relations in Japan reflect to this day a harmony unknown in the West. Surely this harmony—or acceptance of exploitation—is an outgrowth of a culture that discourages individualism and an industrial sector that is never satisfied with the competitive status quo. Integral to harmony are the discouraging of internal strife and the encouraging of self-fulfillment through group participation. In general, Japanese workers, especially women, have had less freedom of expression and lower paychecks than their U.S. counterparts. Such deprivations are accepted because most Japanese workers have a greater respect for authority and more loyalty than Americans in promoting their company's well-being. The net economic result is an extraordinarily productive, relatively inexpensive work force in Japan's industrial sector.

Japanese industry combines a skilled work force, amenable to technological innovation, with by far the highest rate of corporate investment as a percentage of GNP among the industrial countries. This combination provides a potent source of competitive advantage. Hard work per se is insufficient to achieve efficiency without capital investment, as can be seen from the high costs in the primary (agriculture and mining) and tertiary (services) sectors in Japan. Relative to the secondary (manufacturing) sector, those sectors are inefficient and overstaffed. This arrangement yields political and social benefits, however, protecting farmers and encouraging full employment through use of underemployed workers in the service sector. The perennially poor performance of the Japanese consumer price index relative to the wholesale price index confirms industry as the crown jewel of the Japanese economy.[18] But this provides little solace to foreigners bemoaning the onslaught of Japanese exports of manufactures.

As seen from abroad, there seems to be an informal social contract in Japan. Industrial workers are the builders of Japan's international position and the earners of vitally needed foreign exchange, and Japan's international economic strength depends on these workers exercising restraint in wage demands. Industrial workers in Japan do not practice their U.S. counterparts' effort to grab all wage and benefits increases oligopoly (or monopoly) union negotiating practices allow. Productivity increases in the United States do not necessarily establish a ceiling on wage increases. Conversely, the failure of Japanese industrial workers, since the 1970s, to obtain wage increases equivalent to productivity increases suggests that in this country as well, productivity increases do not closely correlate with wage increases. The key difference is that productivity growth in Japan establishes no floor, or minimum, on wage increases. The competitive and financial positions of individual companies—as determined by management—and the health of the Japanese economy seem to be the main determining factors of annual wage increases in the industrial sector.

Internationally, this social conscience gives Japanese producers a large competitive advantage in prices. Domestically, the failure of Japanese industrial workers to secure wage gains commensurate with productivity gains amounts to a de facto subsidy to the inefficient but labor-absorbing service sector, especially in distribution and retailing. The pursuit of full employment is related to pursuit of a stable social order and group harmony at the national level.

Japanese industrial companies are blessed with workers who are tops among major industrial countries in increasing their productivity (output per worker hour) and well below average for increases in unit labor costs (wage costs divided by output). As shown in table 4.1, the Japanese increase in manufacturing productivity, 55 percent between 1980 and 1988, considerably exceeds the U.S. figure of 34 percent. In the same time period, unit labor costs declined by just over 8 percent in Japan while U.S. costs rose 9 percent (see table 4.2). Part of this discrepancy can be accounted for by hourly compensation costs, which in national currency terms for

Table 4.1   Output per Hour in Manufacturing (1977=100)

	Japan	United States	Germany	France	United Kingdom
1960	23.2	62.2	40.3	37.4	55.9
1970	64.8	80.8	71.2	71.4	80.3
1980	122.7	101.4	108.6	110.6	101.9
1985	161.1	123.6	123.4	132.7	133.9
1988	184.7	136.0	125.7	145.9	155.6
1989	195.4	138.7	131.3	152.7	163.6

SOURCES: U.S. Department of Labor, *Monthly Labor Review,* September 1989; and unpublished data from the Bureau of Labor Statistics, U.S. Department of Labor.

**Table 4.2   Unit Labor Costs in Manufacturing
(in national currencies; 1977=100 for all countries)**

	Japan	United States	Germany	France	United Kingdom
1960	38.4	58.7	46.6	40.2	27.2
1970	52.3	71.0	67.4	50.8	39.1
1980	98.4	130.6	115.7	134.3	165.5
1985	94.0	142.7	128.3	200.0	193.9
1988	89.9	144.1	142.4	207.9	203.0
1989	90.8	147.3	142.4	207.8	212.7

SOURCES: U.S. Department of Labor, *Monthly Labor Review,* September 1989; and unpublished data from the Bureau of Labor Statistics, U.S. Department of Labor.

manufacturing workers during this period increased in Japan only 29 percent, or about one-half of productivity gains, but increased 41 percent in the United States, well above productivity gains.[19]

In sum, an important determinant of Japanese industrial competitiveness relative to the United States is the discrepancy in the need for (or willingness of) management in the two countries to reward labor for gains in productivity. In dollars, Japanese wages are more comparable: hourly compensation costs in manufacturing were roughly 91 percent of U.S. costs in 1988, but the figure for 1984, the year before yen appreciation began, was only 51 percent.[20] While dollar depreciation partially offsets relatively greater Japanese productivity gains and lesser wage increases, it cannot hide the fact that the pay side of labor-management relations is conducted very differently in the two countries. It would be a serious error, however, to believe that *cheap* labor explains Japan's economic and foreign trade success since the end of the 1970s. Labor is now expensive in Japan, even if still underrewarded.

It should be noted in conclusion that investment, the raw material of increased labor productivity, is in turn dependent on a country's savings rate: the more savings, the greater is the supply of capital and the greater is the probability of low borrowing costs, that is, interest rates. Once again, the Japanese performance is superb; data for the mid-1980s indicate that the Japanese saved at a rate three times as great as Americans did. The historic Japanese pattern of thrift has been further encouraged by tax incentives, large lump-sum year-end bonus payments, minimal retirement programs, and expensive housing. Japan and the United States have long had among the highest and lowest savings rates, respectively, of the major industrial countries. In 1987, for example, Japan's net household savings as a percentage of disposable household income was 16.8 percent, five times the U.S. rate of 3.3 percent.[21] Differences in calculating the savings rate can explain some, but not all of this gap, even in those years when the gap is smaller.

THE ROLE OF GOVERNMENT ECONOMIC POLICIES

People who believe in the unequivocal power of the marketplace will not welcome the suggestion that Japan's miraculous domestic economic recovery and foreign trade success are partly due to government intervention. Despite the previously discussed excellence of the industrial sector, there is an abundance of evidence that since the 1950s, the Japanese government has guided the invisible hand of the market in directions and with speed that probably would not have occurred without active official involvement. Examples of controlled competition, collaboration, and collusion (all of which come together in such tactics as directing some companies to develop technology aimed at one specialized segment of a product market while other companies concentrate on perfecting other specific segments) emerge repeatedly, as in semiconductors. Professors Laura Tyson and John Zysman argue:

> Whether it is joint planning of expansion in capital-intensive industries to avoid excess capacity and to assure the introduction of plants of sufficient size to capture scale economies, or joint research on generic technologies, or reallocation of domestic market share in the aluminum industry to firms that move production offshore, or efforts to allocate domestic market to foreign firms—the evidence is overwhelming that competition is bounded and orchestrated. The deals may or may not be stable; that is, the market divisions may or may not be fixed. However, market outcomes are certainly different because such mechanisms for collaboration, collusion, and bargains exist.[22]

Mistakes were inevitable, but relatively few. Failures were also inevitable, but also relatively few. On balance, the role of the government has been positive, constantly changing in accordance with the evolution of Japan's economy.

Nothing was left to chance in the promotion of Japan's post–World War II economic recovery and expansion. The bureaucracy neither trusted the market mechanism to produce on its own the desired economic expansion nor frustrated or displaced a capitalist system. Government policies helped the market system along, nudging it into directions determined beforehand to be desirable and appropriate.

Although a precise quantitative assessment of government's impact is impossible, three broad themes seem clear. First, the ability of the Japanese government to influence the economy is partially a function of cultural and historical factors peculiar to Japan, such as a relatively passive, cohesive citizenry willing to follow the strong bureaucracy's grand design for catching up with the more advanced Western societies. Second, the cumulative effect of government policies on the operation of the Japanese economy since the 1950s is probably the most successful effort of its kind in recent history. Third, the fact that one can point to examples of companies and entire industries prospering without official assistance does not negate the fact that most industries flourished in the sunshine of official policies.

Ambiguity surrounding the exact impact of the economic planners is also an outgrowth of the fact that their power, priorities, and practices have changed over time. Reconstruction and development of heavy industry were closely controlled in the initial postwar period. Decontrol of both internal restrictions and imports dominated the 1960s. The encouragement of knowledge-intensive industries in the 1970s and the promotion of advanced high-technology industries in the 1980s were accomplished mainly, but not exclusively, by indirect inducements such as collaborative research consortia.

The recent emergence in Japan of large, cash-rich corporations again alters the role of government in its continuing pursuit of the transcendent national goal of industrial self-reliance and strength. The private sector seems with increasing frequency to view the major economic ministries as meddlers, and the economic planners no longer can rely on legal authority as the primary means to impose their will. But there is no reason to believe that Japan's powerful business organizations seek a no-holds-barred free-market battleground. MITI continues to alter corporate behavior by using the power of reason to offer an informed concern or warning about current or planned business activity. There was nothing surprising in the Japanese press reports in late 1989 of MITI's strong (and ultimately successful) pressures on Mazda to pare down the scale of a proposed automobile assembly plant. It was just another example of official concern to avoid industrial overcapacity.

It is common wisdom in the Japanese business community that the ministries have a long institutional memory and are likely to take revenge against a once-insolent industry later seeking favors. The author has been told that it is still common for the bureaucracy to apply muscle (such as threats of exclusion from bidding on government contracts or of tax audit) to smaller companies who act too independently of what officialdom deems to be the collective economic good.

Government's ability to keep on top of present-day Japan's bigger, more complex economy is surely strained by limited personnel resources. Further, the legal clout of the economic ministries is slipping in a liberalized economy. On the other hand, they continue to achieve priority goals, even against private sector opposition. It is far too early to count out senior civil servants as key players in the economy. The tradition in Japan of respecting government institutions seems to be changing at no more than a snail's pace, and MITI and the Finance Ministry have no trouble attracting elite graduates from the country's best universities. Most Japanese businesspeople, consciously or unconsciously, continue to respect the ability of the bureaucracy as protector of the collective interest. Other reasons for the continued clout of the Japanese bureaucracy include the facts that even the biggest companies remain reluctant to flout the Finance Ministry or MITI, and retiring senior civil servants still find lucrative positions awaiting them in industry.

Government officials in democratic capitalist countries do not produce or market goods for internal or foreign consumption. They produce policies, programs, and regulations. The government sets a climate: by the actions it takes or does not take, government establishes a context in which the business sector functions. The highly positive atmosphere created by the Japanese government since the 1950s has included guidance, tax incentives, financial guarantees, direct subsidies, and protection from foreign competition to an extent completely unknown in the United States. Professor Chalmers Johnson calls modern Japan a capitalist developmental state, the dominant feature of which is the setting of economic and social goals. Industrial policy, defined as concern with the current and future structure and international competitiveness of domestic industry, represents the goal-oriented approach to setting economic policy. The United States exemplifies a regulatory, or market-rational, state, where the government concerns itself with the forms and procedures of competition rather than economic strategy; rules and legalisms are stressed more than goals.[23]

History and necessity are the keys to understanding the extraordinary impact of the government on the modern Japanese economy. Laissez faire economic principles have never flourished; bureaucratic involvement has been an established fact of life in Japan at least since the Meiji Restoration. The very purpose of the Restoration was to preserve Japanese society through the development of an economy sufficiently strong and modern to resist intrusion by the colonial powers of the West. Without the shogun, day-to-day management of the economy was taken over by an elite group of powerful bureaucrats, often former samurai, who ruled in the emperor's name without specific statutory authority. Rapid industrialization was directed by the government, which built or financed factories. In the early 1880s, the government switched from direct control to indirect protection of industry by virtually giving away what it had developed. An economic oligarchy evolved, consisting of politically privileged financial houses that were beholden to the ruling elite. "The *jinmyaku* networks—built on kinship, marriage, bribes or friendships dating from school—that played such a striking role in the course of Japan's modern economic development" were functioning by the beginning of the twentieth century.[24]

Official guidance of the economy continued in the twentieth century, accelerating in the 1930s in response to the Great Depression and the country's military operations in Asia. Ironically, bureaucratic control seems to have reached its zenith during the effort by the Occupation forces to initiate the rebuilding of the war-shattered economy. The later decision to adopt economic policies on the basis of maximizing economic growth was not a matter of casual choice in postwar Japan, but a necessity in the wake of wartime devastation in a proud, ambitious country desirous of a strong industrial base.

By the 1950s, the government had assumed the duty of articulating the rationale and techniques for restoring economic vigor to Japan. It was aided in its efforts by the previous history of government guidance to the economy and the historical tendency of the Japanese to accept with minimal dissent the policy goals of government officials. These two factors combined with the harsh realities of the immediate postwar period to shape the nearly unanimous Japanese consensus to emphasize rapid economic growth. The civil servants in the main economic ministries became an elite corps of well-educated, powerful managers of public policy, commanding respect and influence.

The promotion by the government of heavy and basic industries and the subsequent nurturing of knowledge-intensive high-tech industries beginning in the 1970s bore little resemblance to Adam Smith's concept of the "invisible hand." Japan's modern economic development has been heavily influenced by the semivisible hands of MITI, the Ministry of Finance, and the Economic Planning Agency. Sometimes these hands pointed in a specific direction; sometimes they dispersed financial inducements to industrialists; sometimes they were in the shape of a clenched fist. The guiding strategy remained unchanged: the industrial sector was the key to Japan's economic restoration and its ability to pay for imports.

In an unusually candid speech in 1970, Yoshihisa Ojimi, then vice-minister of MITI, said that if Japan had obeyed basic market forces in the 1950s, it would have relied on the labor-intensive industries that had "manufactured and exported masses of junk before the war." The results of continued specialization, he argued, would have been to relegate Japan to the Asian pattern of stagnation and poverty. The government and the bureaucrats decided it was necessary to alter the "natural" course of Japan's economic history. In Ojimi's words, the following chain of events unfolded:

The Ministry of International Trade and Industry decided to establish in Japan industries which require intensive employment of capital and technology, industries that in consideration of comparative cost of production should be the most inappropriate for Japan, industries such as steel, oil refining, petro-chemicals, automobiles, aircraft, all sorts of industrial machinery, and electronics, including electronic computers. From a short-run, static viewpoint, encouragement of such industries would seem to conflict with economic rationalism. But, from a long-range viewpoint, these are precisely the industries of which income elasticity of demand is high, technological progress is rapid, and labor productivity rises fast. [It] was clear that without these industries it would be difficult to employ a population of 100 million and raise their standard of living to that of Europe and America with light industries alone. . . . In a fast-growing economy, banks find it essential to select growth industries . . . to finance if they want to maintain and expand their share of business. In judging what makes a growth industry, banks relied on the judgment of the MITI as one of their chief criteria.[25]

The brilliance of the economic policies pursued by Japan after World War II lies mainly in the way that incipient market forces were encouraged. The economic planners had learned from their prewar mistakes. They did not try to unilaterally invent nonexistent market trends or thwart existing market forces. An extensive two-way dialogue between industry and bureaucracy was based on mutual stimulus and response. The official sector cajoled and enticed; it seldom dictated. The Industrial Structure Council and other advisory bodies involved the private sector in shaping economic priorities and policy strategy. The bureaucrats wisely decided to remain behind the scenes and, like movie directors, guided others in the starring roles. After the U.S. Occupation ended in 1952, the government did more than pave the roads for industrial development: its articulation of goals and establishment of supporting policies provided a safety net for the private sector. When capitalists helped the government realize economic goals by developing certain industries, their risks were minimized and rewards maximized. This situation was as clear to the banking community as it was to the industrialists.

Two broad categories of policies promoted Japan's sensational industrial achievements. The first category includes the two components of macroeconomic policy, monetary and fiscal policy, controlled by the Finance Ministry. In brief, the banking system has operated in such a manner that adequate capital is made available on attractive terms to favored growth industries. The ministry closely regulates interest rates, and in return for protecting banks against insolvency, indirectly ensures that the direction and volume of bank lending activities support industrial policies. With liberalization, the process has grown more indirect and subtle. Banks are naturally inclined to lend to officially targeted industries. They are glad to supplement loans from official institutions to these "glamour" industries. In the past, the Ministry of Finance exercised such extensive controls over commercial banks and was such an important source of liquidity that a de facto credit-rationing system existed. To this day, the private credit allocation process is supplemented by the lending activities of the government-owned Japan Development Bank and quasi-official long-term credit institutions. Clearly, the Japanese government has been looked upon as lender and loan guarantor of last resort.

The corporate tax system is designed to encourage growth and capital formation. Tax rates have been low relative to most other countries. Generous tax deductions have been granted for a wide range of business expenses: accelerated depreciation, large write-offs for R&D, deductions for the start-up costs for overseas market development, and so forth. The relatively low rate of taxation is not without social costs. Welfare programs and infrastructure lag behind their counterparts in the other large industrial countries.

Industrial policy is the second part of the Japanese government's economic presence. The broad effort by the commercial ministry, MITI, to influence, at the micro level, the development of Japan's industrial structure is perhaps best described by dividing it into four basic, interrelated components, the mix of which in any particular case depends upon the characteristics and competitive position of individual industries.

The first component of industrial policy consists of international trade policies. A wide variety of measures have been utilized over the past thirty years to protect the home market and encourage and subsidize exports. (These policies will be discussed in greater detail in chapter 6.)

A second important component of industrial policy is indicative planning and goal setting. The periodic publication of MITI "visions" epitomizes the government's effort to indicate on a general but comprehensive level the desirable directions for the Japanese economy to take. These statements, like the work of the Industrial Structure Council, grow out of consultations between the manufacturing sector, the financial community, and the government as well as with selected politicians, labor officials, scholars, and members of the business press. The impact of the "visions" document has been succinctly described by a MITI official:

> Since the vision is . . . the reflection of the actual state and trends of the economy, it is widely accepted by many, including the industrial and financial sectors. It also serves to assist in the formation of a consensus at all levels and minimize any uncertainties. Thus the vision encourages private industry to proceed with voluntary and positive adjustment, and occasionally with the help of indirect policy measures, it greatly contributes to the modernization of the industrial structure in Japan.[26]

MITI's version of economic planning is not an exercise in simple extrapolation of trends. It is not a precise forecast, and it is not based on wishful thinking. Rather, Japanese indicative planning articulates a consensus view of the desirable and attainable economic directions and achievement and has been a kind of self-fulfilling prophesy.

Japanese economic planners have been remarkably successful in looking ahead to determine growth industries of the future, to encourage faster expansion of product lines complementary with Japanese production capabilities, and to ensure that adequate capital was made available to those industries designated winners. MITI successes were related to a rejection of a static theory of comparative advantage in favor of a dynamic concept of competitive advantage, based on the conviction that competitiveness in certain industries could and should be induced under supportive, long-term government policies. Official planning efforts shrewdly selected industries for official cultivation that met the following criteria:

1. An industry should be able to produce increasing "returns to scale"; that is, after a large initial investment in plant and equipment, the average cost of production is significantly lowered as the volume of output increases.

2. A relatively high income elasticity of demand for the product produced could be expected in the home and foreign markets.

3. The industry could be expected to sell successfully in foreign markets, thereby earning needed foreign exchange while helping domestic production achieve economies of scale.

4. An industry should promote economic expansion in general as well as contribute to technological progress in related industries.[27]

The government's goals have been compatible with those of corporate Japan. Pursuit of these goals offers growth, financial well-being, and international prestige to the industrial sector. No one is forced to invest or produce in a targeted sector. Companies are encouraged to do so by three things. The first is an optimal mix of government-enhanced market forces. The second is a desire to see a prosperous, strong, and internationally respected Japan. The third is the twin prospects of sales growth and profits.

The third component of industrial policy is activated when the government sets out to induce the desired corporate actions by creating the market for products and the conditions for high returns. As seen from the viewpoint of management, the Japanese government's policies

> helped provide cash for investment, tax breaks to assure cash flow that maintained liquidity, research and development support for technology, and aid to promote exports. These public policies changed the options of companies. Without the protected markets, the initial investment could not in many cases have been justified

by private companies. Without external debt finance, the funds to make the investments would not have been available to the firms.[28]

The primary beneficiaries today of government financial assistance are the so-called targeted industries. Since the 1970s, the Japanese government has wisely determined that the future was to be found in nonpolluting, knowledge- and capital-intensive industries such as computers, semiconductors, electronics, robotics, aerospace, biotechnology, and telecommunications. These industries thus become eligible for a number of special privileges and benefits. A major government goal is to assist high-tech firms achieve the maximum levels of basic scientific research and know-how in the commercial application of newly developed technology. To promote the developments at reasonable costs to corporations, the Japanese government provides targeted industries with grants, loans, special tax subsidies, exemptions from antitrust prosecution, and favorable government procurement practices. Government-sponsored research develops technology that is made available to all interested companies. The machinery industry, for example, received revenue to support research efforts from such sources as the pool of funds generated from government-controlled betting on bicycle and motorcycle races.

The prestige and status afforded by designation as a targeted industry extend to preferential treatment in the private sector. Bankers, suppliers, and the general public show special respect for those industries deemed important to Japan's industrial future. Domestic customers think long and hard before rejecting the products of targeted industries in favor of price-competitive imports from abroad.

The fourth and final component of industrial policy is the mixture of administrative guidance and industry "rationalization" that influences corporate behavior and sectoral structure. Administrative guidance comes in the form of informal government pressure—requests, suggestions, warnings, and urgings—when there is an absence of formal statutory authority to demand compliance.

An important manifestation of MITI's administrative guidance is organizing an industry in a manner deemed "rational" by MITI, that is, with an optimal amount of corporate competition. Cartels are openly encouraged for such purposes as preventing "excessive competition," reducing production costs, shrinking production capacities, and encouraging price stabilization. In some industries (such as machine tools), MITI has suggested that in the name of efficiency, a producer drop a particular product or model if the company's market share for that product drops below an arbitrarily selected minimum.

Japanese civil servants have set an international standard for understanding business trends and fulfilling planning objectives. This success is inextricably linked with a government-business-labor communication process, corporate strategies, and social factors that are present only in Japan.

The fact of the matter is that Japan's industrial policies operate within a larger context that is uniquely Japanese.

CONCLUSION

There was no conspiracy behind Japan's industrial resurgence. Nor was it a matter of luck. Japan's strong domestic economic base was the outgrowth of a uniquely favorable configuration of a supportive cultural environment, supportive economic policies, and aggressive, shrewd business strategies; the absence of any one of these three factors would have changed economic history. The Japanese recognized their economic weaknesses, embraced a desire for economic prosperity, and calculated the most efficient methods of accomplishing their objectives. The combination of foresight, cooperative spirit, teamwork, intelligence, and an accommodating international trading order worked miracles. The absence of any serious, irremediable economic or business mistakes also helped considerably.

However, even this favorable synergy probably would have produced slower and less dramatic results if it had not operated in the context of the historical national consensus that economic inferiority to the West was unacceptable. Rapid economic recovery after World War II was seen by almost all Japanese as an absolute necessity and an absolute priority. In the words of Karel van Wolferen, longtime resident in Japan, "To a degree virtually inconceivable to Westerners, many Japanese—with no religion beyond mere socio-political demands—found the ultimate meaning of life, their existential lodestar, in the survival and welfare of the nation."[29]

Japan's modern economic system heavily favors large manufacturing corporations over individuals, an arrangement that has provided the Japanese a better and quicker opportunity than the invisible hand of the free market to foster a strong home base and international competitiveness in a wide range of industries. Those benefits come at costs acceptable to the Japanese public, but a majority of Americans surely would denounce them as unacceptably limiting the quest for self-gratification, encouraging anti-competitive price behavior, and allocating resources inappropriately to the overall public welfare.

For whatever reason, economic, historical, or cultural, the Japanese have been tolerant of a capitalist system that largely consists of an oligopolistic market structure. Collusive business conduct and aggressive export drives are not viewed with the degree of concern they meet with in the United States. Instead, the existing market structure is seen as necessary for desired economies of scale, and instances of collusion are shrugged off as an inevitable side effect of achieving rapid economic growth:

> Because of this view, held with little variation for over a century
> of Japanese industrialization, the various forms of government

involvement in aiding the efforts of the large firms to increase their productive efficiency are widely accepted as socially necessary and not regarded as an undesirable intrusion in market activities.[30]

Successful exporting grew out of successful domestic industrial production; the insecurity accompanying a large import bill for food, fuel, and other primary products; and the drive to attain international status and independence through commercial achievements. The large, continuing trade surplus that has long rankled Japan's trading partners is, in turn, the natural outgrowth of a society that does not view increased consumption as the prime purpose of increased output. Japan's trade surplus could not have endured without its peculiar propensity to consume far less than the national output.

The synergy which spawned the Japanese economic miracle remains vigorous. Countless forecasts of its demise have proven incorrect, partly because the forcefulness of purpose and intelligence of the Japanese people lie at the base of this synergy. The economic challenges of the twenty-first century would not seem too daunting to the demonstrated strengths of Japanese culture, management strategies, production know-how, and industrial policy, all consciously or unconsciously aimed at the goal of keeping the industrial sector in the forefront of important emerging technologies.

CHAPTER 5

The Domestic Foundations of the U.S. Trade Performance

I've always believed that this blessed land was set apart in a special way—
that some divine plan placed this great continent here between the oceans
to be found by people from every corner of the earth who had a special love
for freedom.

—Ronald Reagan (1982)

New Yorkers can have their pooches transported to groomers, vets or even
the airport in Lincoln Town Cars or limousines by Princess Car Service. Pet
transport, which costs $30 an hour plus 20% tip, is now 25% of Princess'
business.

—*Wall Street Journal* (1990)

During the same time that the Japanese industrial sector experienced peak
synergistic growth, the U.S. industrial sector overall suffered from a negative synergy. I argue here that the competitive performance of American
industry as a whole was sadly lacking over the past two decades.

Few agree in their assessments of U.S. economic performance over
recent decades. While one economic analyst says "America's industrial
decline is undisputed,"[1] another claims "The U.S. has a trade deficit because the Reagan tax-rate reductions made the U.S. a good place to invest
money. . . . [T]oday a trade deficit can be a sign of investors' confidence
and serve as a leading success indicator.[2]

The rise of Japan's industrial might coincided with a period in which
government policies, corporate management practices, and cultural norms
in the United States made the latter vulnerable to those few foreign competitors that gave priority to manufacturing success over national security
or domestic consumption *and* did the right things to achieve this success.
U.S. laws and policies, at least through the 1980s, have not been designed
primarily to directly contribute to international commercial success in the
industrial sector. Intents and priorities have long rested elsewhere: social

justice at home, democracy on a global scale, and individual consumption. These are certainly rational goals, and many observers cheer victories in these categories as outweighing the trade deficit that has developed with the world as a whole and Japan in particular. Others look beyond present industrial problems, preferring instead to embrace an optimistic scenario of an advanced postindustrial economy based on services.

These domestic concerns are not without relevance for Japan's international trade performance. As is the case with the Japanese surplus, the roots of the U.S. trade deficit are domestic, and the underlying assumption of this analysis is that over the long run, the often painful dislocations in the manufacturing sector inflicted by the external sector are costly, dangerous, far from inevitable, and on balance undesirable. The continuing strengths of the primary (agriculture and raw materials) and tertiary (services) sectors in the U.S. economy remain insufficient to offset the deteriorating international competitiveness in the secondary (manufacturing) sector, as measured quantitatively by the composition and amount of trade flows and qualitatively by leadership in key technologies.

Despite real problems in the U.S. economy, undiluted pessimism appears unjustified. The United States suffers from neither uncorrectable weakness nor permanent disability, but rather from a lack of understanding of or will to respond to the new, intensified level of international competition embodied by Japan. As yet, it seems, the price has not yet become high enough to motivate the government, corporations, investors, and workers of the United States to modify their behavior to effectively counter twenty years of increasingly successful Japanese competition.

CULTURE AND HISTORY

The United States, like Japan, is unique in many respects. It is the youngest of the major industrial countries. It is one of the few countries born out of a genuine revolution. It is the only country in the world to be formed by people from every other country in the world; one of a handful of nations whose citizenship statutes are tolerant and embracing. It is a country without feudal or class patterns, having been founded by immigrants who came overwhelmingly from the lower classes.

The United States was founded by and for people escaping the wretched excess of government authority in other countries. Independence was declared from Great Britain only after extended soul-searching and debate. The new country united a group of individual states that insisted on a Constitution that minimized the concentration of power in the hands of the national government, lest the British king reappear in a different, localized form. Here is a sharp contrast to the Meiji Restoration, the closest modern Japan has come to a genuine revolution. The Meiji Restoration's raison d'être was to give the government extensive authority swiftly to modernize the economy, not to maximize civil liberties.

The priority given political, economic, and religious self-expression and the universal nature of U.S. immigration indelibly etched two characteristics into the American value system: individualism and pluralism. Along with democracy, capitalism and entrepreneurialism became dominant philosophies.

The efforts by Americans to exalt rugged individualism, maximize self-gratification, pursue endless frontiers, and scorn government interference have given rise to the metaphor of a cowboy culture. While these traits do not portray a completely accurate historical portrait of cowboys, a widespread *perception* persists that the cowboy lifestyle embodies the preferred U.S. lifestyle. The lingering reverence for cowboy virtues has been cleverly exploited to produce one of the most successful, long-lasting advertising images of all time: the Marlboro man.

Economic resources have been viewed as being best allocated by the market, with government ownership kept to a minimum. Indeed, the U.S. government is unique in never having owned a commercial airline, a radio or television network, or telecommunications facilities. The government is supposed to keep a low profile in the economy; entrepreneurs are supposed to be free of government restrictions. These notions are seen as consistent with vigorous official enforcement of antitrust laws—as a means of guaranteeing competition.

Government and manufacturing never wanted much to do with one another. Big business is supposed to sink or swim on its own. An organizational manifestation of this philosophy is the U.S. Commerce Department's being the weakest commercial ministry, in terms of policy impact, in any major industrial country. The United States offers little honor or monetary reward to its civil service. The private sector expects, and usually gets, assistance from the federal government only after a bad situation has gotten out of hand, that is, a bail-out from impending bankruptcy or a respite from intensifying import competition. Yet, these attitudes are not universal.

The agricultural sector, for example, for reasons not completely clear, historically has maintained a much closer, more cooperative relationship with the Agriculture Department. The latter provides financial support as well as technical and export expansion assistance to a community happy to have official friends in Washington. Defense and aerospace contractors work so closely with government agencies that it is sometimes difficult to tell them apart.

The laissez faire model does not explain the totality of the "culture" of U.S. economic policy. Despite the formal separation of church and state, the United States practices a "let the seller beware" philosophy of Judeo-Christian origins, manifesting itself as consumer, environmental, and worker protection laws. Corporations can expect to be punished by the government if they are not good corporate citizens, but they should not expect special treatment like significant amounts of nondefense R&D funding, tax subsidies, or subsidized export financing.

Although tolerance of and even demand for governmental intervention in the economy has varied over time, the burden of proof is almost always on those who advocate government activism—a stance consistent with the fundamental desire to let everyone live up to his or her potential in as free an economic and social order as is feasible. Americans see no need for rules or institutions by which government, business, and labor could collaborate formally in preparing for the future. Instead, Americans continue to rely on a pluralistic process of competition among organized interests and single-issue groups.

Americans believe that government should not drain the wealth of individuals, even of those making millions of dollars annually. The United States is arguably the easiest country in which to become a millionaire and is certainly the easiest industrialized country in which to retain such wealth. It is, however, not the most comfortable country for the poor, especially the "underclass" of undereducated and unskilled persons. Transfer payments are provided grudgingly and parsimoniously to any except retirees. Americans dislike welfare, be it for the jobless, unwed mothers, or companies unable to compete with import competition.

Richard Darman, the first director of the Office of Management and Budget in the Bush administration, characterizes American economic culture as "Now-now-ism." The American obsession with the here and now makes Americans consume as if there were no tomorrow: "Our current impatience is that of the consumer not the builder, the self-indulgent not the pioneer. It borders dangerously on imprudence."[3]

A cowboy culture exalting the individual and encouraging adversarial dealings with others also manifests itself in the relationship between labor and management. Historically, maximizing union members' wages, fringe benefits, and working conditions took priority for organized labor over both the economic health of employers and the larger interests of society as a whole. Many industrial unions became large enough to take on the attributes of an oligopoly. During most of the twentieth century, union negotiating power was a larger factor in setting wages than economic contribution by the work force. Existing labor benefits usually were non-negotiable, and efforts by management to increase competitiveness by introducing new machinery, part-time nonunion labor, new work rules, or anything else that threatened to change the workers' status quo were resisted by unions. Failure to increase benefits in renegotiating labor contracts almost always meant a strike. Well-financed union strike funds, greater access to welfare benefits by striking workers, and public support have made strikes part of economic life in the United States: they are acceptable manifestations of interest group warfare.

Management is hardly blameless for U.S. workers' negative attitudes. Working conditions prior to the union movement were often harsh and dangerous. Once established, unions were viewed as meddling adversaries. Workers in many companies are treated not as partners in production but as fungible assets to be laid off at will. Plants are closed with little or no notice, sometimes to move production overseas.

In prosperous times, management prefers to accept excessive labor demands rather than absorb a long, debilitating strike. There was no real problem with this arrangement as long as costs could be passed on to the consumer. With industry-wide unions, management could assume that competitors' labor costs would increase comparably; this assumption has been undermined by the globalization of manufacturing competition and the rapid industrial productivity increases of Japan in particular. Basic economics, not coincidence, quickly revealed Japan's competitive edge in steel and automobiles: at the onset of the 1980s, U.S. workers in those sectors enjoyed wage rates more than 50 percent above the average for the manufacturing sector.

Two events of the early 1980s changed the adversarial tradition in U.S. labor-management relations: the severe recession of 1981–82 that left workers unusually insecure and the increasingly intense foreign competition, especially from Japan, that was further intensified by the overvaluation of the dollar. Unprecedented "givebacks" of previously negotiated wage increases and benefits were conceded by production line workers, with a few plants being shut down in the wake of workers refusing such concessions. Management became sufficiently alarmed at their precarious competitive situation to adopt some basic principles of the Japanese management system, such as autonomy for production line workers, reductions in middle management, job security, and limiting the number of suppliers.

GOVERNMENT ECONOMIC POLICIES

The U.S. government in the period under review lacked the authority, will, and expertise to duplicate the success of Japan's ministries of Finance and International Trade and Industry (MITI). The majesty and national security power of the presidency tend to overshadow the limitations of that office in economic matters. The separation of powers written into the U.S. Constitution has evolved into a government decision-making process that now operates at an advanced stage of fragmentation. The central bank, the Federal Reserve System, independently formulates monetary policy, while Congress must enact taxes and approve all executive branch spending. Congressional decision-making also has become more fragmented and time consuming in recent years with the decline in the authority of the leadership of the two political parties over rank-and-file members and the decentralizing proliferation of subcommittees. The judicial branch in general and the Supreme Court in particular have also become major factors in determining national economic policies.

The substance of American economic policy in the latter part of the twentieth century was radically different from that of Japanese economic policies—a reflection of different ideologies, priorities, and values. Although no conclusive proof exists that domestic American economic policies were inferior to those of Japan, it probably was not coincidence that the external performances of the two countries also were very different. In contradistinction to the Japanese government's developmental approach, the United States remains an example of what Chalmers Johnson calls the regulatory, or market-rational, state. The U.S. government concerns itself with rules of economic competition and the size and behavior of firms, rather than determining which industries ought to be nurtured and which phased out.[4]

Overall, the U.S. government's policy sometimes seems to be to have no policy. The market mechanism is supposed to determine matters like civilian technology, productivity levels, the structure of industry (such as mergers or joint research), output, the cost of capital, and international competitiveness. The economic and social programs that emerge from Washington have had little deliberate consistency or cohesion in the industrial sector. There was no grand design, just a collection of mostly ad hoc measures, not one of which had any great positive impact. Some, such as import barriers, were the antithesis of the market mechanism. Others, such as forcing the Japanese into "voluntary" automobile export restraints, were flat out negative in their effect on the overall economy. For example, after the imposition of Japanese quotas, the prices of all new cars sold in the United States rose so much that the estimated annual cost of each domestic job saved was far in excess of the salaries of the jobs saved, with the net result of fattening the profit margins of U.S. and Japanese car makers.

"Industrial policy" is a term whose ability to foment controversy in the United States is exceeded only by the elusiveness of its precise definition. For present purposes, a minimalist definition will suffice: government programs to encourage and expedite economic trends that would not occur on their own and on a comparable basis in a completely free market and free trade environment. While a case against the ability of industrial policy to succeed in the United States can be argued, it is difficult to deny that the United States already has a series of sectoral industrial policies that have been quite successful, such as defense industries, space technology, agriculture, and highway construction, with housing being a moderately successful targeted industry.

Thus, in fact, the United States has an industrial policy, albeit disjointed, semivisible, and missing what in the long-term is arguably the most important sector of all: commercial high technology. By a curious blockage of the intellect Americans reject the notion that the proven ability of the U.S. government to strengthen other targeted sectors could be applied to civilian technology. An organizational manifestation of this attitude is the fact that the closest Washington counterpart of Japan's MITI is not the Commerce Department, but the Defense Advanced Research Projects Agency (DARPA), the Pentagon's outlet for financing new weapons technology and dual-use technology such as semiconductors, computers, and, to a lesser extent, high-definition television. (In a sense, Japan's defense ministry is MITI, industrial strength being deemed more important to long-term security in Japan than meeting the military threat from Russians or anyone else.)

The Reagan and Bush administrations have held to the philosophy that DARPA—and all government agencies—should stay out of commercial technology; that commercial ventures can and should be financed by private capital; and that the ability to raise capital in the private sector is the best test of a project's feasibility. Efforts in 1989–90 to increase DARPA's funding of R&D in the high-technology sector, as well as a congressional proposal to create a separate civilian counterpart to DARPA, were vigorously opposed by the Bush administration.

The tentative support in Washington for the nondefense high-tech sector applies also in tax policy, where, for example, Congress has been unwilling to extend even limited tax credits for R&D on a permanent basis. Existing tax credits for only a small portion of incremental R&D spending continue to be approved for limited time periods, with no guarantee of renewal.

Yet another example of the government's lack of interest in the civilian, as opposed to the defense, sector appears from an examination of the very impressive aggregate statistics for total U.S. R&D expenditures and total government funding of R&D. Of the approximately $125 billion in total expenditures in 1987, the federal government provided about $60 billion, a sum just slightly less than total R&D outlays in Japan, the country with the second biggest R&D effort. However, all but $18 billion of the U.S. expenditures were defense related.[5]

Although there are "spillovers" from the defense to the commercial sectors, their infrequency and uncertain timing underscore the inefficiency of the disjointed, industrial-policy-by-proxy approach. The different levels of involvement by the Japanese and U.S. governments shows in the product composition of the two countries: Japan is strong in a range of high-tech consumer and capital goods, while the United States is strongest in industries tied to the defense effort, such as aerospace. In an excellent summation of the haphazard approach of the U.S. government to industrial policy, Ira Magaziner and Robert Reich argue:

> while U.S. defense procurement and defense-related research and development programs have spawned some highly competitive industries, these programs have been undertaken without regard to their effects on the commercial development of civilian markets. . . . For reasons of ideology or politics, or both, the U.S. has failed to acknowledge the practical choices confronting it. Instead, it has clung tenaciously to the notion that government can and should be "neutral" with regard to market adjustments. The vast array of

U.S. tariffs, quotas, "voluntary" export agreements, and bail-outs for declining businesses are viewed as isolated exceptions to the rule of neutrality; its defense-related expenditures, tax breaks, and assorted subsidies for other industries are seen as being somehow unrelated to industrial development or to market dynamics. Consequently, the U.S. has neither neutrality nor rationality. Meanwhile, its trading partners are becoming ever more efficient in designing and administering policies to aid their industries in adapting to market changes.[6]

Federal actions in the 1969–89 period were aimed at regulating the alleged excesses of business and enhancing the quality of society rather than promoting the civilian industrial sector and international competitiveness. One study of forty-five regulatory statutes passed between 1962 and 1982 calculated that the direct federal expenditures for regulation increased from $800 million in 1970 to $5.9 billion in 1980, with most of the increases in environmental protection, worker antidiscrimination and protection, and consumer safety.[7] It is likely that the indirect costs of private sector compliance—higher prices and reduced international competitiveness—exceeded the direct budgetary costs. No one has yet developed an effective formula for quantifying the economic costs of regulations and weighing them against social benefits.

Prior to the intensification of foreign competition, these attitudes were not a cause for great economic concern. The United States entered the 1970s with an unparalleled standard of living, an abundance of natural resources, and an apparently safe cushion from foreign industrial competition (exclusive of labor-intensive goods such as textiles and shoes). U.S. policymakers should have turned around and looked behind them. More than one thing was gaining on them: the Japanese economic miracle and the energy crisis. The inexorable forces of international economic interdependence were making the U.S. economy highly vulnerable to external forces for the first time in the twentieth century.

Some observers have concluded that the failure of the U.S. government to come up with better, more proactive economic policies over the past twenty years accounts in part for shortcomings in economic performance. A congressional Technology Policy Task Force concluded in December 1988 that

America's economic problems began in the 1960s when increases in productivity began to level off and U.S. industrial managers failed to make investments in new machinery. These shortcomings were compounded in the 1970s by the increase of new laws and regulations in response to heightened concerns about the environment, energy, and public health and safety.[8]

Other criteria show the economy performing satisfactorily in the 1980s with government actions as they were: the record peacetime expansion in real GNP beginning in late 1982, continued moderate inflation despite this record expansionary cycle, and the creation of more than 18 million new jobs in the domestic economy. I find that U.S. government economic policies must be criticized for lacking the long-term commitment to industrial competitiveness found in Japan, for encouraging the financing of domestic growth by external borrowing in amounts that are not sustainable, and for failing to adequately address the critical dilemma of lagging productivity increases.

Many of the external economic problems that emerged in the United States in the 1980s can be traced to this domestic economic policy malaise. Nowhere is this unfortunate linkage more apparent than in the seemingly intractable budget deficit predicament. It all began with the absurd claim that massive tax reductions could be made in the federal tax base amidst the largest U.S. peacetime military buildup without incurring record budget deficits or gutting the domestic income-support system. While some economists profess unconcern about the deficit even now—although the public debt tripled in the 1980s with an absolute increase of $2 trillion—it is hard to dismiss the possibility of worrisome future consequences. In the words of one academic writer, "America has thrown itself a party and billed the tab to the future. The costs, which are only beginning to come due, will include a lower standard of living for individual Americans and reduced American influence and importance in world affairs."[9]

Fallout from the triple-digit budget deficits that have prevailed since fiscal year 1982 includes escalating doubt about the integrity or backbone of the federal government. Skepticism mounted in the wake of the increasingly obvious use of "smoke and mirrors" in congressional compliance with the deficit ceilings imposed by the loophole-ridden and amended-when-necessary Gramm-Rudman-Hollings statute. Congress openly resorted to such blatant accounting deceptions as rescheduling expenditures from the next fiscal year to the current fiscal year (targets only apply to the upcoming fiscal year); passing supplemental budgets after the initial target was met; moving large expenditures like some of the savings and loan bail-out off budget; counting Social Security receipts as current income; and making overly optimistic assumptions on revenue growth, borrowing costs, and receipts from the sales of government assets—all in lieu of conforming with its self-imposed budget limit.

Another consequence of the large budget deficits and the poor prospect for their genuine reduction has been a deterioration in the U.S. trade balance. The combination of expansionary fiscal policy and heavy governmental demands on the available supply of capital have produced undesirable trends in the monetary policy side of the macroeconomic policy equation. Budget deficits have tended to keep interest rates relatively high, a major factor in maintaining a high (strong) exchange rate of the dollar that in turn works against reducing the triple-digit trade deficits that developed in the immediate wake of the advent of Reaganomics.

High interest rates relative to those in Japan harmed U.S. international competitiveness by raising the cost of capital acquisition to U.S. corporations. The high cost of borrowed capital, in the words of U.S. Treasury Secretary Nicholas Brady,

> makes long-term investments too expensive and forces capital into short-term projects. High capital costs mean projects have to pay off more quickly, and a short-term focus may mean pressure to earn short-term profits. But let me tell you what it doesn't mean. It doesn't mean innovation. It doesn't mean long-term risk-taking. And it doesn't mean competitive prices.[10]

The continuing budget deficits in combination with an inadequate rate of saving create an economic condition that perpetuates the U.S. trade deficit, even after the depreciation of the dollar from its 1985 peak. In mathematical terms, a country's current account (goods and services) in its balance of payments is equal to the sum of saving minus net government expenditures (revenues minus outlays) and minus investment. That this is no idle theory can be seen in the continuing close relationship between these balances in table 5.1.

Unless offset by a massive increase in private sector saving, large trade

---

Table 5.1   U.S. Saving and Investment 1985–89
(billions of dollars)

	Private Savings	Government Savings	Private Investment	Saving-Investment Imbalance	Actual Current Account Balance
1985	$665.3	$−131.8	$643.1	$−109.6	$−115.2
1986	669.5	−144.1	659.4	−134.0	−138.8
1987	663.8	−110.1	699.9	−146.2	−154.0
1988	738.6	−96.2	750.3	−107.9	−126.5
1989	806.2*	−104.6	773.5	−71.9	−105.9

*Preliminary figure.

NOTE: The widening statistical discrepancy beginning in 1988 between the saving-investment imbalance and the current account deficit may be due to a combination of the increasing use of "off-budget" federal expenditures, such as those involved in the savings and loan bail-out, and an overstatement of the preliminary estimate for private savings in 1989. It is also possible that the real size of the current account deficit is becoming increasingly exaggerated by inadequate data.

SOURCE: U.S. Department of Commerce.

deficits will continue to accompany large domestic budget deficits. The U.S. preference for consumption over savings is a costly, self-inflicted drain on U.S. industrial competitiveness. The U.S. savings performance, as shown in figure 5.1, is poor in comparison with all other industrial countries, not just Japan. Given the present tax discrimination against saving— no exemption for earned interest and dividends—no sharp increase in savings can be expected.

While seldom considered a matter of economic policy, education has become an increasingly important factor inhibiting growth in U.S. industrial productivity. U.S. corporations spend billions of dollars annually to teach rudimentary reading and mathematics skills to blue-collar workers. Simultaneously, the need grows for production line workers to handle complex, computer-controlled machinery and perform multiple jobs with less supervision as well as to comprehend the overall production process sufficiently to be able to make suggestions for enhancing efficiency. This demand for increasingly skilled labor is running up against an educational system producing students who consistently finish in the bottom half on standardized tests (especially in science and mathematics) administered to international groups. The North Carolina subsidiary of a Japanese semiconductor company was reportedly forced to hire university graduate

Figure 5.1   Net Disposable Savings as a Percent of Disposable Income (1980–88 average)

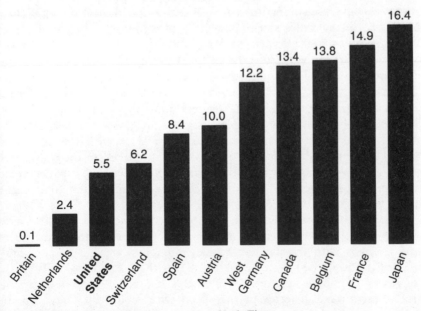

SOURCE: OECD data published in the *New York Times.*

students in mathematics to perform statistical calculations for quality control procedures that in Japan are handled by production workers with high school educations.

A lower percentage of U.S. college graduates receive degrees in engineering than in almost any other industrial country; and Japan reportedly graduates a higher number of engineers than the United States. In 1983, the National Commission on Excellence in Education reported that "the educational foundations of our society are presently being eroded by a rising tide of mediocrity that threatens our very future as a Nation." The commission admonished that with knowledge, training, and skilled intelligence being the "new raw materials of international commerce," the United States needed to reform its educational system "if only to keep and improve on the slim competitive edge we still retain in world markets."[11] Hopes for quick improvements in the U.S. educational system were dashed by the early 1990 Department of Education report that national test results showed schoolchildren's reading and writing skills had improved only very slightly in the late 1980s, the introduction of numerous educational reforms at the state and local levels notwithstanding.

SHORTCOMINGS OF U.S. BUSINESS STRATEGIES AND MANAGEMENT PRACTICES

Through the 1970s, few U.S. manufacturing companies recognized the severity of Japanese competition or took any steps to meet the challenge. The record of the 1980s shows but slight improvement. U.S. companies have simply not been performing satisfactorily, even if we discount the disadvantages they faced from the cultural emphasis on quick self-gratification and the absence of supportive governmental policies. The manufacturing sector as a whole has underperformed in critical areas such as productivity growth, technological leadership, and production line know-how. The implication is inescapable: a significant, if not precisely measurable, portion of the U.S. economic problem rests with the corporate sector's flagging abilities to develop, make, and market, at the right price and quality, the kinds of products that compete successfully in the world marketplace. Management's performance has been inadequate to meet the rapidly changing market conditions.

U.S. industrial managers as a group have not done as good a job as their Japanese counterparts did in preparing for the future. They never came to grips with the inevitable unsustainability of the extraordinary advantages the United States experienced in the immediate post–World War II era. Pursuing short-term profits, U.S. companies developed a comparative advantage in terms of the speed with which they gave up the competitive fight and dropped product lines that came under heavy import competition. Executives paid more attention to legal and financial issues than manufacturing, productivity, and labor costs. In the 1970s, the time horizons in corporate boardrooms were further shortened with the mania for mergers, acquisitions, and buy-outs.

The lack of managerial foresight prevalent among senior U.S. business leaders was summed up eloquently by an entrepreneur in Silicon Valley:

> They didn't invest in the future. The steel industry, the auto industry, the centerline of American industries, their mentality was not to change. They would define the marketplace. It didn't matter what anybody else thought. That's the mentality they operated under. . . .
>
> They weren't prepared to make the changes. They thought in terms that were dictatorial and they got caught.
>
> It's all a matter of orientation. The only thing that stays the same is that things change. The ways that worked last week are thrown away entirely. . . .
>
> The unions are a problem not because they help the workers but because they make costs higher and they don't get the productivity we need. But if there were no unions, we still would have lost to the Japanese because we weren't building the right products.[12]

The shortcomings of U.S. management relative to the Japanese competition are largely attributable to rational responses to an increasingly obsolete reward system. Executive performance and, by implication, managerial excellence are usually measured by the size and regularity of current profits and returns on current investment. An important ingredient in this system is the relative importance of equity financing (as opposed to debt financing) to most U.S. corporations. Intense pressures to please stockholders—the company's owners—result. Performance evaluation within the average industrial company, as well as externally in stock market prices, is geared to current profits, the so-called bottom line. All too frequently, senior management and Wall Street analysts ignore the potential future payoff of investments for increased plant productivity and new products. Since pay and bonuses for corporate executives often are tied to current stock prices, sales, and profits, managers are tempted to ignore their company's long-term growth and productivity in favor of making today's accounting numbers look good. These managers are neither irresponsible nor dishonest; they are only adhering to the reward systems of their milieu. It takes tremendous courage for a senior executive who is getting close to retirement to jeopardize current earnings by investing in costly new projects, the uncertain payoffs of which are, at best, several years in the future.

Many aspects of modern corporate culture direct the priorities of U.S. business executives away from long-term market share and better production techniques. Few senior executives are innovators or masters of the production process. The fastest route to the top in major U.S. companies, which now offer total pay, bonus, and stock option packages averaging in excess of $1 million annually, is through marketing and finance, not production. Too many companies became burdened with middle management. Instead of exuding frontier spirit, too many executives become risk-averse functionaries who do little to expedite communication between the R&D side of the company and the production line. The net result, to use the term coined by Richard Darman in 1986 when he was deputy secretary of Treasury, was the emergence of an overly cautious, unimaginative "corpocracy."

The mind-set and priorities of untold numbers of senior U.S. business executives is surely tied in with the potentially unhealthy U.S. mania with casino capitalism: mergers, acquisitions (friendly and otherwise), and leveraged buy-outs. Business problem solving has become increasingly financial and legal in nature and less concerned with engineering and science than is the case in Japan. Generalizations are suspect because every corporate restructuring is financially unique, but it is difficult to see how potential benefits of rewarding shareholders, investment bankers, and lawyers, and of occasionally pushing aside inept or unsuccessful management will outweigh the long-term dangers to the economy of increased debt loads and ever more highly leveraged companies. That the ability to service that debt is subject to occasional loss of confidence in the investment community was demonstrated by the sudden, unexpected weakness in the junk bond market in late 1989. A recession and/or higher interest rates may prove disastrous, especially to those rearranged companies whose debt service is close to or above current income flows. The wisdom of the marketplace is further placed in question by the likelihood that at least some of these deals would not have been made in the first place were it not for tax incentives. (A company is able to reduce its income tax liability by writing off interest payments, a factor that normally makes debt instruments more attractive than sales of equity, that is, stock.)

It is even more difficult to see how rearranging the slices, without enlarging the size, of the U.S. economic pie by manipulating balance sheets can benefit long-term international competitiveness. While the Japanese industrial sector pushes new products, investment, and exports, many U.S. companies have become phobic about short-term performance and current stock prices as part of their efforts to encourage or repel corporate raiders or to redeem company stock from so-called greenmailers.

Companies wanting to be "acquirees" as well as the acquirers saddled with high debt burdens can be expected to cut back on longer-term priorities such as capital investment, market development, employee training, and R&D. The slowdown in the rate of increase in corporate R&D detected in 1988 by the National Science Foundation[13] appears to be an early result of merger mania encouraging short-term corporate thinking and nonproductive corporate activity. "We can't be competitive on a world-class basis unless we invest substantially in new technology, and we can't do that with a balance sheet heavily burdened with debt," the vice chairman of the Eaton Corporation has said.[14] Nor can a company expect to become or remain internationally competitive if top management is keeping at least one eye on acquisitions possibilities (often to his or her financial benefit) or defense against a hostile takeover. Either situation leaves less time, energy, and money for what the Japanese do best: designing and assembling goods in accordance with superior process and production technology, all part of putting priority on what happens on the factory floor. Another adverse effect of merger mania is that the big bucks for financial middlemen have been luring the best and brightest of U.S. youth into becoming asset-shuffling lawyers and bankers ("paper entrepreneurialism") instead of production and managerial functions.

A harsh but appropriate critique of U.S. industry was made by Akio Morita, cofounder and chairman of the Sony Corporation in his Japanese-language book, *The Japan That Can Say No*: "Real business entails adding value to things by adding knowledge to them, but America is steadily forgetting this. That terrifies me. America no longer makes things, it only takes pleasure in making profits from moving money around." In criticizing the short time horizon of U.S. executives, Morita comes close to denigrating an important insight through an exaggerated extrapolation. When a U.S. money trader says he plans ahead by only ten minutes, Morita concludes "If Americans think only in terms of ten minute action, while we Japanese think in ten year terms, America assuredly faces gradual decline" because it will not be able to compete with Japan.[15] Finally, Morita laments the declining innovation of U.S. industry: "America is by no means lacking in technology. But it does lack the creativity to apply new technologies commercially. This, I believe, is America's biggest problem. On the other hand, it is Japan's strongest point."[16]

A more thorough, scholarly study of the U.S. industrial performance conducted by an interdisciplinary team, the Commission on Industrial Productivity, assembled in late 1986 by the Massachusetts Institute of Technology (MIT), came to these no kinder or more optimistic conclusions:

> The verdict is that American industry indeed shows worrisome signs of weakness. In many important sectors of the economy, U.S. firms are losing ground to their competitors abroad.
>
> Determining the causes of these trends and gauging their significance also calls for human judgment. From our industry studies we have concluded that the setbacks many firms suffered are not merely random events or part of the normal process by which firms constantly come and go; they are symptoms of more systematic and pervasive ills. We believe the situation will not be remedied simply by trying harder to do the same things that have failed to work in

the past. The international business environment has changed ir-
revocably, and the United States must adapt its practices to this
new world.

. . . the weaknesses we discovered concern the way people
cooperate, manage, and organize themselves, as well as the ways
they use technology, learn a new job, and interact with government. These weaknesses are not at all unique to manufacturing.[17]

While the commission assigned blame to governmental economic and
regulatory policies, five of the six broad areas of weakness were internal
to U.S. companies:

- Outdated production strategies, with too much emphasis on
  mass production and too little on flexible manufacturing;

- Excessively short time horizons;

- Technological weaknesses in development and production
  techniques, including poor coordination between the design
  and assembly function, lack of interest in the manufacturing
  process per se, and inadequate efforts to improve either products or production techniques;

- Neglect of human resources, with inadequate education and
  training of workers;

- Lack of cooperation within the company, between labor and
  management, between firms and suppliers, and between firms
  and customers.

The commission noted examples of well-designed and effective management strategies that drew on the strengths of the U.S. system, but its
two major conclusions were not kind to U.S. management capabilities and
business strategies:

First, relative to other nations and relative to its own history,
America does indeed have a serious productivity problem. This
problem in productive performance, as we call it, is . . . manifested
by sluggish productivity growth and by shortcomings in the quality
and innovativeness of the nation's products. Left unattended, the
problem will impoverish America relative to other nations that
have adapted more quickly and effectively to pervasive changes in
technology and markets.

Second, the causes of this problem go well beyond macroeconomic explanations of high capital costs and inadequate savings to
the attitudinal and organizational weaknesses that pervade America's production system. These weaknesses are deeply rooted. They
affect the way people and organizations interact with one another

and with new technology; they affect the way businesses deal with long-term technological and market risks; and they affect the way business, government, and educational institutions go about the task of developing the nation's most precious asset, its human resources. They introduce rigidities into the nation's production system at a time of extraordinarily rapid change in the international economic environment.[18]

The MIT commission's findings are consistent with a growing body of literature identifying the failure of U.S. industry to continuously apply the latest technology to the manufacturing process as one of the most important reasons that it has lost ground to its Japanese competition. Two senior members of the Berkeley Roundtable on the International Economy have argued that U.S. industry's basic shortcoming

is not our technology or our workers, but how our corporations organize production and use people in the manufacturing process, how they set automation strategies and goals for product innovation. U.S. industry has contributed massively to its own undoing [and] must assume much of the responsibility for turning things around.[19]

The level of excellence in process technology reached by many Japanese companies is less a question of investing large sums in new equipment and automation than how effectively new equipment is used. As noted in the previous chapter, the Japanese appear to be well out in front in understanding how to use and improve upon flexible manufacturing techniques. The U.S. lag here appears to be a major factor in the gap in performance between the two countries' industrial sectors.

The biggest example—literally—of the ineffectiveness of money and size to offset corporate shortcomings in mastering the manufacturing process is the lack of return on General Motors's estimated $45 billion outlay (an amount larger than the GNP of many countries) during the 1980s. Despite this investment, designed to boost the productivity of its U.S. assembly plants, GM had the dubious distinction at the end of the decade of being the highest-cost producer (mainly because of the need for a higher labor content) of the Big Three U.S. auto producers and the operator of fifteen of the sixteen least efficient automobile assembly plants in the United States.[20] Inappropriate application of production and design technology, along with a stubborn corporate culture, limited GM to a nominal increase in productivity in the eighties. How well technology is applied to the production process, not how much money is invested, seems to be the key factor in lowering costs. (The U.S. Postal Service provides another example of large investments in automation achieving little increased efficiency.)

Not all U.S. companies are slow to grasp the importance of the production line and of constant improvements in process technology and product innovation. Many U.S. high-tech firms never lost their competitiveness. Others companies have used the pressures associated with potentially fatal Japanese competition to turn themselves around, principally by adapting many of the demonstrably successful management techniques perfected in Japan (though sometimes conceived in the United States).

The Xerox Corporation, the developer of photocopying machines, decided to strike back in the early 1980s when it saw its world market share plummet alarmingly. Comparison with its best Japanese competition showed the latter were superior in every important category. Japanese companies were producing copying machines at one-half Xerox's production costs and with ten to thirty times fewer defective parts. Furthermore, new products were being introduced in one-half the time, with one-half as many people on the development team.[21] Xerox then placed new emphasis on quality, design, production techniques (increasing worker involvement on the production line), and after-sales service. The company reduced the layers of middle management, slashed the number of its suppliers (by more than 90 percent), and turned to the best competing product or service as its standard for each phase of corporate performance ("benchmarking"). Xerox has since enjoyed a significant increase in both its market share and reputation for reliability. In 1989, Xerox's Business Products and Systems Division was one of the two corporate winners of the U.S. government's Malcolm Baldrige National Quality Award which annually recognizes "preeminent quality leadership" in U.S. business.

Motorola's experience suggests a strong link between corporate zeal in manufacturing and U.S. success at competing head-to-head with Japanese companies, even in their home market. Motorola's global success in such products as pocket pagers and cellular telephones reflects a corporate strategy to "out-Japan" Japan, in which Motorola has stressed market share, quality control, product innovation, simplified assembly operations, customer satisfaction, worker training, R&D, and a long-term planning horizon (the company also appealed to the U.S. government for help against dirty tricks by Japanese government agencies and corporations). Motorola's new smaller cellular phone has just 400 parts, about 12 percent as many as its first cellular phone, and as of 1989, it can be assembled in two hours rather than the forty hours required just four years previously.[22] Motorola has joined Xerox and other concerned corporations in imposing new quality control standards on their suppliers, in some cases insisting that the latter be good enough to seriously apply for the Baldrige award.

CONCLUSION

In the absence of intensified global industrial competition, U.S. economic performance would be worthy of high praise for growth, increased employment, the quality of basic research, and more. The failure to anticipate the advanced international economic interdependence meant a lack of preparedness in the U.S. government, in the business community, and in organized labor. Only in the 1980s, after an increasing number of companies and whole industries were threatened with extinction from import competition—often from Japan—have the costs and implications of the failures of business practices, government policies, and cultural forces become clear.

The U.S. idea of economic efficiency—a collection of individuals pursuing the dream that only personal limitations should limit success, a government minimally interfering in the economy, business managers operating under the strict discipline of maximizing current profits—together with the sheer size of the economy was good, but not quite as good as the Japanese synergy in inspiring industrial competitiveness. The unabashed pursuit of personal enrichment, the adversarial system, and short time horizons resulted in a lack of focus, harmony, or concern for international competitive position.

The United States unquestionably has a very good economic system. As the world's largest and richest national economy, the United States retains a comfortable (albeit shrinking) margin of error in its economic performance. But increasing weaknesses and inadequacies in both economic policy and management practices have been exposed by comparison with the totally committed, highly motivated, and brilliantly conceived drive by Japan to become an international industrial superpower. Perhaps the best that can be said for U.S. domestic industrial performance is that some companies and unions responded brilliantly to the danger of being wiped out by their Japanese competition. Given the serious degeneration of U.S. competitiveness, these improvements are insufficient to correct the bilateral imbalance and may not even be enough to prevent a widening of the bilateral competitive gap. An eloquent elegy on the inadequacies of the U.S. economic order was provided in 1989 by Colby H. Chandler, then chairman of the Eastman Kodak Company:

> America, like Britain before, has been dissipating world economic leadership through complacent self-indulgence, blind to ever more forceful world competition. If we do not save and invest substantially more, American living standards will decline and stagflation will be the rule. We will become a low-wage nation in the industrial world, quarreling over an undersized pie. . . .
>
> We cannot continue to save far less than our competitors, underinvest in our future and yet hope to stay on top or even close.
>
> The signs of mounting trouble are everywhere. A striking illustration comes from my home town. Fully 5 percent of the workforce in Rochester is illiterate; another 10 to 15 percent is well below high school equivalency. Yet less than 2 percent of the jobs that need to be filled can be described as unskilled. How can we

hope to compete in a high technology world with an undereducated workforce?

The rest of the world is not waiting for America to catch up. Today's developing country will be tomorrow's manufacturing powerhouse. We are like a wounded elephant, very large and still powerful but increasingly weakened. Can we heal our wounds? Do we have the national resolve and political leadership to correct our mistakes and meet the challenges ahead? It is hard to know since we do not even have a blueprint, let alone the commitment.[23]

CHAPTER 6

A Comparison of Japanese and U.S. International Economic Policies

The Japanese don't understand why the U.S. doesn't play by their trade rules; the reason is that the U.S. does not realize that it is in a [competitive] race.

—Senior U.S. Commerce Department official (1982)

Thus far, Japan has viewed its economic, technological, and trade policies, including its negotiations with the United States, as a continuation of competition and predation by other means.

—Charles H. Ferguson (1989)

The loss of U.S. industrial competitiveness to Japan was too rapid and pervasive to be explainable solely in terms of *domestic* economic policies, management practices, and cultural differences. Radically different international economic philosophies and priorities contributed to the systemic imbalance in the competitive performances of the two countries in the 1969–89 period.

These dissimilar international economic policies were themselves outgrowths of different domestic economic situations, ideologies, and priorities. The United States has not shared the Japanese belief that an interventionist foreign trade policy could effectively promote domestic manufacturing. The United States views foreign trade more as a means to achieving foreign policy objectives and maximizing consumption. The Japanese government considers import barriers on manufactured goods as integral to a long-term industrial policy while U.S. officials see such barriers as occasional detours necessitated by domestic political considerations but irrelevant to long-term interests.

Foreign trade policies are also inextricably linked with international monetary and international investment considerations. U.S. companies have the unique luxury of selling in the world's largest national market. Most large U.S. companies utilizing a global marketing strategy opted to serve overseas customers through foreign direct investment or licensing, not by the traditional route of exporting. Japanese companies, at least through the early eighties, kept production at home, while aggressively pursuing exports as means to obtain critically important economies of scale and maximize market share.

While the Japanese stubbornly clung to an "export or die" mentality (exporting was seen as the prerequisite for paying for vitally needed raw materials and energy imports), Americans as a whole clung just as stubbornly to a lackadaisical attitude toward exporting. The national mood unconsciously reflected the unique advantage of possessing the world's international reserve and transactions currency: the United States could pay for all of its imports with its own currency. It did not have to *earn* foreign exchange; it could *print* it. The door was open for the United States to have trade priorities different from those of Japan.

Import policy priorities also differ between the two countries, one nation linking them to consumer satisfaction and the other to promoting industrial development.

JAPANESE FOREIGN TRADE IDEOLOGY AND PRACTICES

Japan's relatively self-centered, narrowly focused view of the international trading system is typical of trade policy practiced by most countries. Japan differs primarily in the intensity of its feelings toward trade. This attitude is rooted in the self-perception of a relatively weak and vulnerable country—a feeling associated with dependence on foreigners for most of its raw materials. From the time that it literally was forced to become part of the Western-dominated trading system, Japan has struggled to overcome the perceived weakness of being an industrial latecomer. Moving up the hierarchy of international economic power has long been a priority shaping internal and external economic policies.

Catching up with its trading partners, as measured by the ability to substitute domestic production for an ever-expanding array of sophisticated manufactured goods, has been the informal national past-time in Japan for more than a century. The sacrifices required to close external competitive gaps seemingly are offset by the psychic income that comes with reduced dependence on and awe of foreigners/outsiders. The growth and preservation of commercially competitive industries and firms are viewed as the essence of Japan's national security. The government as a whole views these industries and firms as the determinants of Japan's domestic prosperity; thus, they are much too important to be left to fight on their own, living and dying by the abstraction of free market competition.

Japan's post–World War II success in achieving rapid economic growth and international competitiveness has yet to erase the country's long-standing feelings of at once superiority and vulnerability. Nor do the Japanese feel they can relax and live on their laurels. Remaining an isolated island country subject to natural disasters, lacking in raw materials, possessor of an extraordinary inner drive to preserve its cherished cultural heritage—a country with only one close overseas political alliance—Japan remains susceptible to intense feelings of defensiveness and nationalism toward international trade to an extent unknown in the United States. In the words of Masataka Kosaka:

> Ultranationalism was discredited by the Second World War, but the views and experiences of the 1920s and 1930s have remained in Japanese consciousness: as Japan has no natural resources, its first priority must be their acquisition; extraordinary efforts to increase exports are necessary in order to pay for raw materials; Japan is in a weak position because it is less industrialized than the Western countries; and Japan is in a disadvantageous position politically because it is the only nonwhite industrial country. These feelings make up the underpinnings for Japan's defensive and nationalistic international economic policy.[1]

Most Japanese in the immediate post–World War II period viewed the international trading system as a means of national survival. With a shattered economy, the Japanese had neither the power nor the conceptual orientation to adopt a global perspective comparable to that taken by the United States. Japan, like most other countries, reacted to, rather than initiated, international trade developments. The primary question was how the international trading system could assist internal objectives, namely, the rebuilding of the economy, economic growth, and international commercial competitiveness. Trade policy was subordinated to the priority goals articulated in industrial policy—a very different approach from that taken by a hegemonic United States.

Consistency between domestic industrial policy and international trade policy was infinitely more important to the Japanese than dismantling barriers to imports. Japanese import policy has been no philosophical pursuit of free trade, but pragmatic response to specific situations. The Japanese view of the world usually produces a preference for calculated responses to international events that are designed to secure maximum national benefits. Modern Japan has seldom tried to create or change the distant, often confusing, international environment that appears to be fully controlled by foreigners. Few Japanese are intellectually committed to the concept of a liberalized world trading order as an end in itself. But most Japanese are committed emotionally to the enhancement of their country's economic strength.

In contrast with the postwar U.S. ambitions to reshape the international order in its own image and resurrect the economies of nonCommunist countries, until the 1970s, the Japanese felt little obligation to contribute to the liberalization of the international trade order. As one Japanese observer has written,

There does not exist in Japan a real feeling that Japan and the
Japanese, with their individuality, are related with other nations
. . . [or] that the Japanese contribute to the civilization of others,
and others to the civilization of Japan. . . . The world has been a
"given" surrounding Japan, which makes a real impact on Japan,
but which cannot be modified by the efforts of the Japanese. The
world is nothing but the "framework" or the setting which can
change only mysteriously.[2]

Japan's trade policy has not been dominated by abstract trade theory.
Rather, it has been guided by the effort to maximize domestic economic
output. From the 1950s through the 1980s, Japan's trade strategy was
straightforward: build a strong, export-oriented industrial sector and limit
imports of any manufactured goods that could be produced "reasonably"
efficiently in Japan. Comparative advantage need not flow directly from a
given endowment of land, labor, and capital. Global competitiveness could
be induced by government influence on private sector allocations of financial and human capital. In an enhanced "infant industry" trade strategy,
targeted industries designated by government-business sector consensus as
being appropriate for special nourishment were and usually still are given
a nearly impenetrable shield from import competition.

Restrictive import policies were part of the larger industrial strategy,
first of recovery and later of fostering the growth industries of the future.
This policy encouraged the domestic flow of financial, entrepreneurial, and
labor resources into the industries that would become the backbone of
Japan's industrial strength. In addition to a comprehensive system of
arithmetic quotas, Japan's domestic market was protected by an intricate
tariff system, with low duties on primary products and many capital goods
and high rates on most finished goods and consumer goods. Imports of
manufactured goods that directly competed with key industries were
viewed as nothing less than enemies of the state by many policymakers.
The Japanese are far from sharing the U.S. view of import barriers as
unfortunate but unavoidable responses to short-term political pressures.

The unprecedented speed and magnitude of Japan's industrial resurgence behind a protectionist import policy suggest there are flaws in the
market-oriented liberal trade philosophy embraced by most Americans.
Japan has enjoyed continuing prosperity since the 1960s without benefit of
the discipline of vigorous import competition; differences in Japan's economic system apparently exempt it from the need for an open import
policy. The rate of rising industrial competitiveness was not slowed by
introducing liberalization measures only after the achievement of international strength.

Japan's postwar experience, with an import policy that first formally
restricted, and later informally retarded, imports of manufactured goods,
has been exactly the opposite of the U.S. trade experience. A large number
of Japanese companies became world-class competitors without meaning-

ful import competition. During the same time, many U.S. companies in the basic industries suffered a collapse in their competitiveness—despite the pressure of the world's most liberal import policies. Still it is *inconceivable* that the U.S. basic industrial sector—steel, automobiles, textiles, consumer electronics, footwear, and so forth—would have voluntarily expanded investment outlays and revamped production techniques to become more competitive, more quality conscious, and more export oriented if it had received the import protection provided its Japanese counterpart. The world has seen very few examples, outside Japan, where companies given infant industry treatment so frequently became world-class competitors. Japanese industry has shown an extraordinary ability to outgrow the need for import barriers.

Foreigners tend to dismiss the merits of Japan's comprehensive effort throughout the 1969–89 period to eliminate and reduce formal barriers to imports. It must be puzzling to that country that its liberalization program has received so little recognition from the United States and other trading partners. There are at least three reasons for the failure of other countries to express gratitude. First, while imports in a few sectors (textiles, petrochemicals, aluminum, luxury automobiles, and so forth) have increased significantly, imports of manufactured goods as a percentage of GNP or of total imports remain exceptionally small by the standards of any other industrialized country. Second, the United States and other countries still perceive, rightly or wrongly, that due to formal, informal, and cultural barriers, exporters have extreme difficulty succeeding in Japan.

Third, foreign perceptions of the Japanese liberalization effort suggest that this effort was taken only reluctantly in the wake of mounting foreign pressures. There are few, if any, indications to foreign observers that Japan was liberalizing because it wanted to or because the economic theory of liberal trade suggested it was a positive step for Japanese consumers. The impression remains that Japan liberalized under duress to prevent other countries, particularly the United States, from discarding their liberal import policies.

Most puzzling about Japanese imports today is not the disdain for importing high-value-added goods, but the success of informal barriers to discourage, if not prevent, their entry. By the mid-1980s, indirect and attitudinal barriers (discussed in detail in chapter 9) had displaced formal barriers as the scourge of would-be foreign exporters. The oft-repeated assertion that the total elimination of formal import barriers in Japan would increase U.S. exports by only a very few billion dollars is probably true, but it is also irrelevant to an understanding of the contemporary dynamics of the Japanese import sector. While informal barriers cannot impose any absolute barriers (unless the government is the sole purchaser), they can and do act as de facto tariff barriers forcing foreign-made goods to demonstrate unusually wide differentials in price and/or advanced technology if they are to be successfully exported to Japan.

From the Japanese perspective, it is logical and appropriate that their foreign trade consist overwhelmingly of importing raw materials, adding value to them, and then exporting manufactured goods. They apparently see nothing inevitable, or even desirable, in importing manufactured goods, except in three situations—labor- or energy-intensive goods that the Japanese cannot even come close to making competitively; items like large aircraft and advanced microprocessors where the technology or licensing arrangements are unavailable domestically; and luxury consumer goods. The inability to produce all important state of the art technologies seems to trigger that extraordinarily intense, long engrained Japanese determination to catch up with the foreigners. The success of the Japanese trade strategy built on adding value instead of importing it is vividly illustrated by their 1987 figures for imports of an estimated 617 million tons of goods and exports of an estimated 71 million tons of goods[3] with a trade surplus for the year exceeding $95 billion.

The fact of the matter is that to this day Japan has little need for a genuinely open door import policy to ensure industrial efficiency. Japan, however, does need a liberal international trade order. A breakdown in liberal trade would put at risk the Japanese ability to earn the foreign exchange necessary to pay rising raw materials import bills. With a large economy but few indigenous natural resources, Japan is the second-largest consumer (after the United States) of raw materials in the noncommunist world. Japan's percentage dependence on imports of raw materials is the world's largest.

Japanese dislike of manufactured imports displacing domestic producers and workers—or preventing Japanese entry into a new sector—is exceeded only by a passion for exporting. In blunt terms, Japan is a master practitioner of mercantilism, the old theory that the measure of a country's foreign trade success is the size of its trade surplus. Western economists relegated this still politically popular idea to the status of old wives' tale after the publication in 1776 of Adam Smith's book, *The Wealth of Nations,* arguing ever since that *importing* goods that can be made more efficiently abroad is the true source of acquiring benefits from trade.

For a country largely devoid of natural resources, and one that cares less about increasing consumption than preserving its cultural identity, importing your way to wealth is still an alien concept. Given Japanese internal priorities, no thought has been given to imitating the uniquely U.S. practice of using export controls to pursue foreign policy and humanitarian goals. As late as 1970, before Japanese exports grew so large that they could pay twice over for necessary imports of food, energy, and industrial raw materials, Japan's fixation with export expansion could be completely explained in traditional economic terms. Today, however, the export imperative seems to have become a strategy for enhancing the domestic production of high-tech goods. If a country is to reach the cutting edge of industrial production—and stay there—it needs to be the low-cost producer, generally by achieving economies of scale, increasing global market share, and keeping foreign competition on the defensive. Export strength is the first line of defense in perpetuating the long-term pursuit of sufficient industrial power to keep dependency on foreigners at a minimum and strength relative to other countries at the maximum.

In the early postwar years the Japanese government did not miss a trick in providing maximum assistance to the export promotion effort. It devised a broad range of export incentives: export price subsidies, some of which allowed companies to sell products abroad below production costs; formation of the Japan External Trade Organization; generous export-financing facilities; and encouragement of industry export associations. Tax incentives included special deductions for export income, an overseas market development reserve, and accelerated depreciation for capital equipment that produced exports. As Japanese export strength became a source of contention in the late 1970s, virtually all special incentives were terminated. However, the phaseout of export support measures did no more to switch off the Japanese export machine than the phaseout of import barriers did to create a boom in imports. As was the case in the United States, commercial factors did not change much, only the official rhetoric changed. Special delegations went abroad on buying missions or to educate foreign producers about the correct means of marketing in Japan. On average, official import restrictions fell to levels below those of the United States and the European Community, and the Japanese became the leading practitioners of voluntary export restraints.

That exports were also vitally important to Japan's private sector is suggested by the aggressive international marketing strategies pursued by a large number of industrial corporations. A virtual army of smart, zeal-ous, hard-working business executives went overseas to master foreign tastes, laws, customs, and languages. Although the domestic market usu-ally takes precedence, foreign markets have become integral to corporate growth strategies. Short-term profits in overseas markets were subor-dinated to the longer-term goal of increased export shipments and market shares. A corporation began with a well-defined product with high-volume sales potential, typically at the cheaper, less glamorous end of a product line. Since such products typically have low profit margins, they seldom were a focus of marketing efforts by U.S. producers. Once a beachhead was secured, the exporting company sought to increase market share for its product, looking to move up to the middle and upper ranges of the product line, while maintaining consumer satisfaction through low prices and high quality.

The emphasis on low pricing led to a growing U.S. perception of a Japanese propensity to export goods at less than fair value prices—an unfair trade practice known as dumping. This perception was encouraged by Japan's being by far the most frequently named country in petitions filed in U.S. antidumping proceedings. The onerous cost of distributing goods within the Japanese market often had the effect of making home market prices legitimately higher than export prices, but undoubtedly, some Japanese companies also engaged in dumping on a calculated basis in order to build a sales base for the future. In other cases, dumping was unintentional, occurring either because an export manager failed to check on domestic prices or because honest mistakes were made as to exactly where the arbitrary dividing line would be drawn under U.S. antidumping law between a fair and unfair price. In still other cases, there was deliberate harassment by U.S. producers hoping to scare Japanese competitors into major price increases. Although no one knows the exact frequency, magnitude, or deliberateness of Japan's dumping actions, many Americans assume it remains a common Japanese export tactic.

That many Japanese companies employ a two-tier price structure, one for home and the other for exports, used to be a source of the once mildly amusing joke that Japanese trade delegations visiting the United States loaded up on Japanese goods to take home because they were so much cheaper in U.S. stores. The reality of thousands of Japanese overseas tourists on buying sprees, reenforcing the realization that prices for most consumer goods are unusually high in Japan, has caused this joke to become very stale. Whatever humor may have remained disappeared with the stories (see chapter 9) of entrepreneurs and individuals importing back into Japan goods that had been made there, exported, and put on sale abroad at a fraction of the price they were selling for in Japan. Such a situation could not exist in the open, entrepreneurial, consumer oriented economy of the United States. As soon as major price discrepancies were discovered between U.S.–made goods in the home market and their prices abroad, people would re-import in such quantities that differentials would be closed. That this arbitrage mechanism is seldom if ever evident in Japan is yet another example of the differences in market dynamics between the two countries.

Japan's general trading companies, or *sogo shosha,* provide an additional resource in the country's export drive. These companies are specialists in importing and exporting, thereby freeing Japanese manufacturers to concentrate on planning and producing products. The general trading companies have developed an unparalleled international commercial intelligence network and miss few outlets for Japanese exports or sources of cheap raw materials to ship back to Japan. Working on small sales commissions and large volume, the larger trading companies operate in more than one hundred countries, individually generating export sales valued at tens of billions of dollars annually. The perfecting of the trading company model illustrates yet again the Japanese practice of turning weakness into strength. Two Japanese professors explain:

> It is important to remember that when Japan was opened to international trade in the mid-19th century, it quickly recognised that its lack of preparation was a source of commercial inequality and therefore set out to foster its own trading companies to replace

foreign traders in intermediating Japan's exports and imports.
. . . The net result has been the emergence of unique mercantile
institutions whose performance and efficiency in both intermediating trade and organising overseas ventures are unrivalled in the
world. Japan has thus turned its original disadvantage into one of
its trump cards for trade and investment.[4]

Aside from the problems to foreigners inherent in the rapid annual
increases in Japan's exports and its mammoth trade surplus in manufactured goods is the fact that these exports are concentrated in a relatively
few industries, all thriving overseas prior to the onslaught of Japanese
competition and many in the highly visible consumer (as opposed to capital
goods) sector. Japanese success in exporting such goods as automobiles,
consumer electronics, motorcycles, cameras, watches, office machines,
semiconductor chips, machine tools, and steel has triggered a high degree
of foreign sensitivity to Japan's export surge. In contrast, foreign reaction
to U.S. exports has been docile. The best explanation for this difference
may be the relative lack of displacement caused by U.S. exports of agricultural products in short supply elsewhere (such as soybeans) and high-tech
goods not being produced elsewhere (for example, jumbo jets).

Officially Japan has shifted from a trade policy emphasizing export
expansion to one emphasizing import enhancement. Programs to expand
imports have been instituted, and most export enhancement programs
were long ago phased out by the government. But there has been little
change in the product composition of Japan's trade flows and little reason
to expect change in the future. Japanese thinking about the purpose and
goals of trade has not changed. There is no easing up in the pursuit of
industrial strength, no dropping existing business relationships when a
foreign supplier comes along with a slightly better deal, no endangering
targeted industries through buying of competing imports. Nor is there any
commitment to the major reorganization of the Japanese distribution system necessary to make it more favorable to imported goods. One needs to
look beyond what the Japanese say about their changing trade priorities
and more closely at what they do.

U.S. FOREIGN TRADE IDEOLOGY AND PRACTICES

When U.S. and Japanese policymakers looked at the international trading
system at the conclusion of World War II, they saw different things. The
two countries had little in common when it came to memories, needs,
traditions, ambitions, and motivations. Only the general desire to make the
process of importing and exporting serve the "national interest" was a
shared experience.

In the late 1940s the United States abandoned the isolationist foreign
policy that dated back to the founding of the country. Its relatively sudden

emergence as an international superpower quickly imbued it with a genuinely global perspective on political, military, and economic affairs. The United States perceived a unique opportunity to shape the international economic order in accordance with its own economic values. Liberal international trading and monetary systems—unfettered by government controls—were viewed as the best guarantees that the Great Depression would not be repeated and that postwar economic reconstruction would be accelerated. The advent of the cold war between democratic and communist-bloc countries accentuated the U.S. feeling of global mission.

Most Americans then believed (and still believe) that the principle of comparative advantage emerges naturally from market forces. There was (and is) widespread belief that global economic production will be maximized under an international specialization of labor in which all countries produce goods for which they possess a natural efficiency. Import restrictions undesirably frustrate the marketplace's invisible hand. It was later recognized, however, that political needs can force deviation from this economic ideology. Relatively inefficient or declining industries with political clout would be given protection to minimize factory closures and job losses, not to conform with long-term official planning. Whenever politically feasible, companies and industries would be forced to live and die by competition in the free market.

Ensuring political stability in Western Europe and Japan became the top overseas priority of the U.S. government. International economic growth, in turn, was viewed as indispensable to political stability. The United States used its influence and financial resources to establish such multilateral programs and institutions as the General Agreement on Tariffs and Trade (GATT), the International Monetary Fund (IMF), and the World Bank to encourage an expanding international economic order by means of maximization of the market mechanism and minimization of government interference in the flow of international commerce and capital. The anticipated increase in economic output was seen as the most efficient path to a durable peace, democracy, and international economic prosperity. Until U.S. hegemony began to be questioned by the Europeans in the 1960s, good U.S. international economic policy was deemed to be exactly equivalent to good national security policy. There were in fact no serious conflicts between the goals of the two policies. Americans generally saw their political and economic interests being advanced by the recovery of the European and Japanese economies. The United States was so strong in material terms that it literally sought to spread its wealth overseas in pursuit of national security objectives.

Import competition was of minimal concern to U.S. industry in the early postwar era. Exports were of no significant concern to the U.S. government, and foreign sales were left almost completely in the hands of the private sector. Given the chronic trade surplus, government export promotion programs were almost completely nonexistent. Export opportunities through the 1950s were limited mainly by shortages of dollar holdings in foreign countries. Indeed, the United States openly accepted the discriminatory treatment imposed on U.S. goods by Japan as well as the European Payments Union, a regional economic organization that operated in the 1950s. The best long-term stimulus to U.S. exports, it was generally agreed, was the rejuvenation of the European and Japanese economies. Once their economies recovered, U.S. policy planners assumed, these countries would liberalize trade policies.

U.S. international economic policies and aid programs were major factors inducing the boom in international trade and capital flows during the fifties and sixties, the so-called golden age of the world economy. In retrospect, U.S. international economic policies may have been too generous. The abilities of the Japanese and West European economies to recover had been severely underestimated. One of the most serious weaknesses in the postwar international economic order was the failure to foresee, recognize, and adjust to the unexpectedly rapid increase in Japanese and European industrial competitiveness relative to the United States.

The Vietnamese experience fanned fires of disillusionment with the burden of responsibilities associated with global leadership. Resulting feelings of fatigue and the reassessment of U.S. priorities centered in part on the international economic order: patterns of trading relations began to look unfair to more and more Americans. The emphasis placed on foreign policy considerations by U.S. trade policy began to look excessively costly. As the United States struggled with a stubborn inflation, a deteriorating position in foreign trade, high defense costs, and mounting unemployment, its chronic balance of payments deficit suddenly ballooned and was perceived to be the major source of international monetary instability. Western Europe and Japan, on the contrary, were characterized by price stability, full employment, continuing balance of payments surpluses, strong foreign trade positions, and comparatively low defense costs. To most Americans, the time had come for a fundamental reorientation in international economic policy.

The axis of U.S. foreign trade policy began to shift at the end of the sixties. An early sign of this reappraisal was President Nixon's New Economic Policy of August 1971. Subsequent efforts to reduce the accessibility to the U.S. market for certain Japanese goods were the later manifestations of the shifting emphasis of U.S. trade policy. Despite the trauma associated with the erosion in U.S. international competitive strength and a persistent trade deficit, protectionism is still viewed by most U.S. citizens and all its economists as a second-best economic solution. Import restrictions have been considered by most U.S. policymakers to be incompatible with the long-term wisdom of the marketplace. Companies coming before government agencies to plead for import relief usually suffer a loss of face; hence U.S. industry does not like to beg for government charity. Nor is the Washington bureaucracy disposed to dispense import protection to inefficient industries.

When protection from fair foreign competition is granted, the executive branch frequently treats the case as exceptional and not to be viewed as setting a precedent. Since most Americans believe in liberal trade, most restrictions imposed on imports are viewed as government bail-outs, semi-legitimate at best. Most efforts to restrict foreign shipments into the U.S. market are criticized (for good reason) by economic analysts as not being cost-effective, in that the higher prices imposed on society as a whole far outweigh the advantages of preserving a few domestic jobs. The most important consideration in U.S. import policy remains maximizing competition and minimizing the prices of consumer and capital goods. Promoting a predesigned industrial structure is not even on the official policy agenda.

All recent presidents have taken the implicit position that the need for import restraints would decline in direct proportion to relaxation by other countries of barriers to U.S. exports. Having no official industrial strategy with which to be concerned, U.S. trade policymakers sincerely view increased foreign market access—not protectionism—as the optimal adjustment to domestic disruptions from increased imports. Increased access to foreign markets has come to mean an opening of foreign markets to the same extent that most Americans perceive the U.S. market to be open to imports. A significant number of U.S. economists, however, remain unconcerned about foreign trade barriers in an era of floating exchange rates. They believe that in the long term, trade disequilibria self-correct as exchange rates will eventually change by sufficient magnitudes to induce balance in trade accounts.

While the U.S. government has been accused of ignoring the peril of rising import competition, it has been even more widely criticized as being worse than useless in the promotion of exports. Indeed, U.S. government policies have been more efficient in restricting exports than in promoting them, a situation that begins with the subordination of international industrial competitiveness to national security. While it is difficult to put a dollar figure on reductions in overseas shipments, U.S. exporters clearly are burdened by a series of official practices that would be unthinkable in Japan or any other country. The following laws are but a sample of an export policy long on morality and short on commercial considerations:

- The Foreign Corrupt Practices Act prohibits the use of illegal and illicit payments by U.S. companies to secure overseas contracts. The vague wording of the law has been a major source of discomfort to U.S. exporters.

- The Export Administration Act allows the president to restrict exports in connection with (1) national security, (2) foreign policy, or (3) domestic shortages. This statute is still the legal source of U.S. export controls affecting East-West trade. Despite recent changes in the bill, the U.S. export control list is still much larger than those maintained by the Europeans and Japan.

- Antitrust legislation restricts cooperative efforts by U.S. companies to jointly bid on large foreign contracts.[5]

The increased sophistication of competition in international markets has not yet moved the United States to adopt the export-at-all-costs policies prevalent in Japan and most other countries. The United States may or may not be foolish and naïve in trying to emphasize the export of U.S. morality ahead of the export of U.S. goods; this is more an ethical than an economics question. The important point is one illustrated by the willingness of President Reagan in 1982 to restrict the export of U.S.–made equipment for use in constructing the Soviet natural gas pipeline to Western Europe: the international competitive position of U.S. industries did not receive as high a priority as national security objectives in the value system of U.S. public policy.

Japan and the United States continue to use very different cost-benefit equations in establishing operational trade policies. Although Japan's strong international competitive position and the very large U.S. trade deficits have contributed to some convergence in their previously diametrically different postures toward promoting exports and retarding imports, major differences in ideology and programs remain. The United States remains extremely cautious about any government measures designed specifically to assist exporters. Programs designed to discriminate in favor of exporters are largely viewed as inequitable and inefficient. Severe cutbacks in the Export-Import Bank's export financing operations were made in the midst of massive U.S. trade deficits.

In the meantime, export-oriented constituencies, mainly multinational corporations and the agricultural community, continue to lobby vigorously and effectively for a liberal trade policy. Presidents continue to see a link between a U.S. move to protectionism and a potential collapse of the world trading order. U.S. government bureaucrats who argue either the need to reverse the sagging international competitiveness of U.S. industry or the advantage of retaliating against foreigners' discriminatory economic actions still remain in the minority.

The depth of the U.S. philosophical commitment to liberal trade and opposition to government import controls was demonstrated repeatedly throughout the 1980s. Early in the decade, the Reagan administration turned a blind eye to deteriorating U.S. global competitiveness brought on by the overvaluation of the dollar. The dollar's appreciation was viewed by the administration as a symbol of U.S. revived economic vigor; concerns about overvaluation were turned aside on the notion that the foreign exchange markets were in a much better position to know the proper dollar exchange rate than a handful of government officials (or private sector economists). Given the subsequent rise in the U.S. trade deficit, it is hardly hyperbole to suggest that no parliamentary government in Western Europe or Japan could have survived with comparable indifference to legitimate business concerns.

The growing congressional threat of protectionist trade legislation finally convinced the administration to modify its international economic stance in 1985.[6] Measures to reduce foreign trade barriers and dollar depreciation, not import restrictions, were initiated to placate most members of Congress. Despite several consecutive years of trade deficits in excess of $100 billion and with no relief in sight, the omnibus trade bill passed by Congress in 1988 avoided any suggestion that imposing unilateral import barriers would be an effective or efficient policy response. The only such provisions included in the bill were to punish the two foreign companies that had violated their own countries' export control laws in exporting technology to the Russians for reducing submarine propeller noise. The major change brought about by the bill was to escalate pressure on the executive branch (mainly through the new "Super 301" provision) to negotiate the reduction or elimination of foreign trade barriers.

The U.S. policymaking process reflects the underlying value system that influences trade policy substance. The United States is the only major industrialized country with no one ministry having overall jurisdiction in trade policy. (The extraordinary trade policy power of the legislative branch is another unique aspect.) The Commerce Department has always been a minor player in U.S. economic policy formulation; neither the industrial sector nor Washington has ever wanted a powerful commercial ministry. Americans are quite comfortable viewing foreign trade policy as completely distinguishable from domestic economic policy; the major exception is that in both policies, the short-term interests of consumers must be respected.

THE IMPACT OF INTERNATIONAL MONETARY RELATIONS ON BILATERAL TRADE

International monetary factors affect the U.S.–Japanese bilateral trade relationship in two principal ways. The first has to do with the impacts on U.S. trade priorities of the extraordinary international role of the dollar, the second with the extraordinarily limited degree to which the floating exchange rates have adjusted the bilateral trade disequilibrium. Although the international monetary system can be a major cause of this imbalance, it offers only faint hope of a correction.

The United States has fewer concerns than any other country about earning foreign exchange: no other country can use its own currency to pay for *all* of its imports of raw materials, manufactured goods, and services. The discipline imposed by balance of payments constraints are thus largely absent.

The unique role of the U.S. dollar as the primary international reserve and transactions currency has caused the U.S. balance of payments position to be unique. There are two kinds of national balance of payments structures, one applying to the United States, the other to all other countries. During the 1950s and 1960s, when fixed exchange rates prevailed, a strong trade performance and a chronic current account surplus were offset by a larger deficit in the capital account; this was caused by the outflow of private capital seeking to maximize profits (foreign direct investment and overseas bank loans) as well as official expenditures for foreign aid and an overseas military presence. Also unique was the means by which the United States financed the longest and largest continuing balance of payments deficit in modern economic history. The United States remains alone among deficit countries in not having to worry about exhausting its foreign exchange reserves. Except for a relatively small outflow of gold reserves in the mid-1960s, the United States continues to finance its deficits by the willingness of foreign central banks and businesses to hold dollars as part of their reserves. (Under the floating exchange rate system, the United States often has been in the unique position of experiencing a sufficiently strong foreign demand for its currency in the midst of a deteriorating foreign trade position that no exchange rate depreciation ensues.)

To demonstrate just how extraordinary is the U.S. balance of payments position, one needs only point to the fact that for much of the 1980s the United States was able to finance record-breaking annual current account (trade plus services) deficits with equally record-breaking net capital inflows. Furthermore, in spite of cumulative current account deficits well above $600 billion in the last half of the 1980s, the dollar's exchange rate finished out the decade *higher* than most analysts thought appropriate for the level of U.S. trade competitiveness.

This seemingly cost-free (at least in the short term) trade deficit raises the question who is conning whom. In terms of economic theory, the United States is coming out ahead by exchanging paper money for real economic resources—goods and services that enhance the U.S. standard of living. Countries like Japan with large trade surpluses are assisting the United States to consume beyond its ability to produce or save; a large portion of the dollars generated from the trade surpluses is then invested in or lent to the United States in the form of capital inflows. Whenever the dollar depreciates against the yen, Japanese dollar assets, measured in yen, will drop immediately, raising further questions about the value to Japan of chronic trade surpluses, beyond the psychic income of industrial self-sufficiency and dominance.

On a social welfare basis, the United States does much better than Japan. Instead of using their capital to improve the underdeveloped infrastructure, such as housing, roads, and parks, the Japanese, by returning a significant amount of capital to the United States, subsidize the U.S. standard of living. To an economic theorist, it is not clear who is sillier: Americans who complain about their multilateral and bilateral trade deficits, or Japanese who work long hours in part to obtain the dubious output of the U.S. government's currency printing presses.

From the business and long-term economic points of view, the U.S. trade deficits are, respectively, undesirable and unsustainable. The United States should neither welcome a secular deterioration in its industrial competitiveness nor expect an unlimited inflow of foreign capital to finance its current account deficits. Nevertheless, in the short-term, the United States retains an extraordinary nonchalance about the potential long-term costs of inadequate increases in exports relative to import growth. The situation for Japan is very different. Japan is typical of other countries in having to earn dollars the old-fashioned way—through exporting. Japan is untypical only in its success, as discussed earlier, and the degree to which its unusually heavy dependence on imports of foodstuffs, raw materials, and energy and its feelings of uniqueness, geographic isolation, and helplessness to prevent external shocks combine to create an extraordinary sense of vulnerability.

A second critically important impact of international monetary factors on the bilateral trade relationship involves the frequent undervaluation of the yen relative to the dollar since the 1960s that favored Japanese exports and inhibited U.S. exports. Even after exchange rates started floating in the early 1970s, the relative value of these two currencies has seldom seemed to mesh with the relative commercial competitiveness of the two countries. The net effect has been extended periods of time in which the competitiveness of Japanese goods in the U.S. market has been enhanced and extended periods of time in which of the competitiveness of U.S. goods (when denominated in yen) in the Japanese market has been reduced.

A major weakness of the Bretton Woods international monetary system, in force from 1945 to its formal collapse in 1973, was the rigidity of exchange rates. Even after the dollar became overvalued relative to most industrialized countries' currencies beginning in the late 1960s, countries with balance of payments surpluses remained extremely reluctant to adjust their exchange rates upwards (revaluing their currencies) in order to preserve the price competitiveness of their exports. It was this failure of declining U.S. commercial competitiveness to be reflected in exchange rate realignments that led to the demise of the fixed exchange rate regime.

The yen-dollar exchange rate established in 1949 remained in force until the dramatic actions of President Nixon's New Economic Policy of August 1971 forced a temporary float and an eventual currency realignment in December of that year. From the U.S. viewpoint, this yen revaluation was long overdue but would not have occurred without drastic unilateral U.S. action. What was deemed prudent policy in Japan had come to be viewed in the United States as an intolerable mercantilistic effort to maximize exports and minimize imports by adhering to an undervalued exchange rate for the yen. Japanese fears in 1971 that immediate yen revaluation would be premature generated no sympathy in the United

States, for this was the beginning of the clear manifestation of a shift in bilateral trade competitiveness.

The floating exchange rate system that replaced the fixed rate system in the spring of 1973 was supposed to reflect changing relative rates of international competitiveness and induce balance of payments equilibrium. The subsequent two decades have demonstrated that floating exchange rates do not necessarily produce logical or appropriate exchange rate movements. It has also become clear that a floating rate system cannot ensure a dollar-yen exchange rate consistent with relative international competitiveness; the system is thus capable of perpetuating a trade balance disequilibrium. Exchange rates, even if floating "cleanly," reflect a variety of factors beyond bilateral commercial competitiveness and even beyond the multilateral trade balance.

Two important aspects of exchange rate adjustments were demonstrated in the 1971–89 period. First, yen revaluation can reduce, but not erase, a large Japanese trade surplus with the United States. The extremely large—30 percent—dollar depreciation in 1977–78 vis-à-vis the yen reduced the bilateral trade imbalance only modestly. An even more dramatic yen appreciation between February 1985 and the end of 1988, when the yen rose from 243 per dollar to 125 per dollar, also yielded disappointing results in either shrinking the Japanese bilateral surplus or altering the composition of U.S. exports. The salutary effects of rapid Japanese economic growth were fully offset by the U.S. macroeconomic position (the previously mentioned savings-investment imbalance), U.S. industrial shortcomings, and informal Japanese import barriers.

Numerous other factors limit the effect of exchange rate movements, particularly yen appreciation, in equalizing bilateral competitiveness:

1. Japanese exporters frequently reduce export prices, preferring a lower profit margin to reduced market share.

2. U.S. manufacturers and Japanese importers frequently raise their prices in the wake of lower yen costs for U.S.–made goods as a means of widening profit margins.

3. There is a relatively price inelastic demand in the United States for many Japanese products, especially those with reputations of high quality, such as automobiles, that brushes off price increases for these goods.

4. There is no U.S.–based competitor for certain Japanese exports, such as 35 mm cameras, fax machines, and video cassette recorders. Hence, price increases for imports lead to no resurgence of domestic production.

5. There is a relatively price inelastic demand in Japan for many U.S.–made products that brushes off price decreases for these goods; this tendency is compounded by the importance in

Japan of long-standing business relationships and the restrictive distribution system that is unfriendly to new entrants.

6. Japanese industries using imported raw materials receive a price windfall from yen appreciation that reduces production costs and partially offsets yen revaluation; the steel industry is the major example of this phenomenon.

7. The challenge to exports imposed by yen appreciation tends to induce a greater work effort by Japanese management and labor. This is a reflection of Japan's cultural ability to convert weakness into strength.

8. Exchange rate changes have to be adjusted for inflation differentials. Japanese inflation rates, as measured by the wholesale price index, were lower than those of the United States during the 1969–89 period.

All things considered, the Japanese business cycle in the 1970s was a far more important determinant of import volume than either yen appreciation or liberalization of import barriers.

The experience of the overly strong dollar, beginning in 1981 and extending through early 1985, suggests that foreign exchange markets can favor a country's currency despite an exchange rate far in excess of international commercial competitiveness. The upsurge in the dollar's exchange rate had a devastating impact on U.S. exporters and import-sensitive industries vis-à-vis all other industrial countries and Japan in particular. While nobody fully understands the persistent strength of the dollar during this period, the fall of the fixed exchange rate system demonstrated that central bankers can no longer impose their perceptions of "appropriate" exchange rates on the marketplace. Governments now lack the financial resources to outmaneuver the individuals and companies that buy and sell the equivalent of hundreds of billions of dollars worth of currency every working day in the world's foreign exchange markets.

Central bank intervention could "bend against the wind," but throughout most of the 1980s, it could not offset the many nontrade factors that attracted businesspeople, multinational corporations, investors, and speculators to dollar assets—factors such as relatively high U.S. interest rates, political malaise in Western Europe, a declining rate of U.S. inflation, a recovery in the U.S. stock market, and positive expectations about the future performance and pro-business attitudes of the U.S. economy. Beginning in 1982, the dollar-yen exchange rate moved exactly opposite the trend of trade competitiveness as measured by either the bilateral or a multilateral trade balance. There is no reason to suggest that it cannot happen again.

Nor is there reason to argue that if the yen does significantly appreciate in the future against the dollar, any significant reduction in the bilateral trade imbalance will follow. The financial press has quoted Japanese business leaders asserting that they can profitably compete with their U.S. counterparts at exchange rates of 100 yen per dollar or even higher. There is growing anecdotal evidence that Japan's major industrial firms have break-even points for production costs far below those associated with the exchange rates of the late eighties. *The Economist* concluded: "With so many options now available to them, big Japanese companies have become, to all intents and purposes, independent of the value of the yen against the dollar."[7] It appears that anything short of free-fall for the dollar in the early 1990s will barely trim very fat Japanese export profit margins.

To the extent that future exchange rate changes reduce multilateral trade imbalances, the urgency for remedying bilateral imbalances will drop. But if a large bilateral deficit with Japan continues amid overall U.S. trade balance correction, floating exchange rates probably will fail to reduce political disequilibrium. If future dollar depreciation fails to generate a sizeable increase in U.S. exports of high-tech manufactures to Japan, floating exchange rates can only marginally reduce frictions arising from the disparity in exports. In economic terms, smaller numbers for the bilateral trade disequilibrium are a necessary, but not sufficient, factor to guarantee a trade relationship with Japan accurately reflecting the true competitive advantage of U.S. industry.

THE IMPACT OF FOREIGN DIRECT INVESTMENT ON BILATERAL TRADE RELATIONS

There is an important similarity as well as a major difference in the current foreign direct investment activities of Japanese and U.S. manufacturers. One of the few parallels in their international activities is serving foreign markets through overseas production rather than simple exporting. Since the 1980s, major Japanese exporters have replicated the U.S. corporate strategy begun two decades earlier to protect mature export markets by establishing foreign subsidiaries in key countries. Foreign direct investment not only puts physical production and business decisions closer to distant consumers, it can circumvent trade barriers and minimize distortions from exchange rate fluctuations.

Foreign direct investment (generally defined as at least 10 percent of the voting stock of a local corporation being controlled by a foreign company) by U.S. companies is now of sufficient longevity for the effects to show in the domestic U.S. economy as well as on the U.S. trade sector. When a company decides to build a new plant abroad instead of at home, there is an opportunity cost to the domestic economy of corporate investment in plant, equipment, and jobs. During the decade beginning in 1957, one-third of all U.S. transportation equipment plants were located abroad. For chemicals, the ratio was 25 percent; for machinery, 20 percent. By the end of the 1970s, overseas profits accounted for a third or more of the overall profits for each of the 100 largest multinational producers and banks in the United States. In some corporations, the share was much higher. In 1979, for example, 94 percent of the profits of the Ford Motor Company came from overseas operations; for Coca Cola it was 63 percent. In 1977, Citicorp derived 83 percent of its banking profits from its overseas operations.[8]

The Japanese initially viewed foreign direct investment by domestic companies as an intolerable dissipation of the national industrial base. Threats of new trade barriers to their exports eroded this position, but an unusually intense emphasis remained on importing Japanese-made components or bringing along Japanese suppliers so as to minimize local content used in Japanese-owned factories abroad. The U.S. strategy of placing local employees in top management positions in foreign subsidiaries remains a very new concept in Japan, adopted by only a few companies. Many Japanese worry that foreign direct investment will lead to the "hollowing out" of corporations that has become a concern in the United States.

It may never be possible to measure the net costs and benefits of foreign direct investment on the domestic economy of the country whose companies head abroad. Some analysts consider a direct correlation between lost exports and overseas production to be self-evident. Others argue that overall exports are actually increased as the result of overseas direct investment operations, with overseas subsidiaries often captive customers for parts, components, product models, and machinery made for overseas purchase by the parent company. This argument is supported by anecdotal evidence from individual companies (such as the Compaq Computer Corporation being the fastest-growing major U.S. exporter in 1988 tracked by *Fortune* magazine, despite its reliance on a subsidiary in Scotland to serve the European computer market)[9]—and by aggregate data from the U.S. Commerce Department. In 1985, for example, an estimated 32 percent of all U.S. exports (minus petroleum and mining products) was shipped to foreign affiliates of U.S. companies; figures ranged from 48.4 percent for Canada and 30 percent for Western Europe to 10.6 percent for Japan.[10]

The correlation between export success and the foreign direct investment in a given market is confirmed by the U.S. experience in Europe. Extensive investment appears to be a factor in the perennial (interrupted only when the dollar was enormously overvalued in the mid-1980s) U.S. trade surplus with the European Community. The trade-investment correlation also appears, albeit in the negative, in patterns of U.S. trade and investment with Japan, that is, in the relationship between the relative paucity of U.S. exports of manufactured goods to Japan and the relative lack of U.S. majority-owned foreign investments in that country. The latest Commerce Department "Benchmark" survey of U.S. overseas investment activities shows that manufactured goods exports shipped by U.S. parent companies to their majority-owned subsidiaries in Japan were low compared to figures for Canada and the European Community; in 1987, shipments to Japan were more closely comparable to those to subsidiaries in the relatively tiny Dutch economy (see table 6.1).

A white paper on U.S. foreign direct investment published in 1980 by the American Chamber of Commerce in Japan concluded that:

> The evidence suggests a clear connection between the small extent of U.S. manufacturing operations in Japan and the continuing U.S. deficit in trade with Japan. . . . The results [of a previous study by the chamber] show that the Japanese market is a particularly relevant example of the positive link between investment and trade.[11]

The major dissimilarity in direct investment activities by the United States and Japan is the lack of opportunity for foreign direct investment in Japan. The historical reasons for the existence of formal restrictions were similar to those on postwar imports: the Japanese economy was to be rebuilt according to Japanese rules and traditions. Outsiders, who could not be expected to understand and comply with the written and unwritten rules of the Japanese system, would be more trouble than they were worth, merely second-best contributors to Japan's goal of industrial leadership and independence of foreigners. To this day, despite removal of almost all formal barriers, special circumstances discourage U.S. foreign direct investment in Japan. (The parallel with the experience in trade suggests the existence of systemic differences in the operation of the two markets.) Although almost all formal Japanese controls on foreign direct investment were long ago abolished, most U.S. companies setting up a manufacturing venture in Japan still find a Japanese business partner to be a lesser evil than setting up a wholly-owned subsidiary. (Acquiring an existing Japanese company is virtually out of the question.) Continuing inhibitions to establishing a new foreign direct investment in Japan include the costs of establishing a factory in Japan, the difficulty in recruiting good Japanese

Table 6.1 U.S. Exports of Manufactured Goods Shipped by U.S. Parent Companies in 1987 to Overseas Affiliates
(billions of dollars)

Japan	$ 1.9
Canada	29.7
European Community (total)	11.7
U.K.	3.1
Germany	2.3
Netherlands	1.4
Belgium	1.0
Malaysia	1.1

SOURCE: U.S. Department of Commerce, *U.S. Foreign Direct Investment Abroad . . . Preliminary 1987 Estimates,* table 16.

personnel, delays in the granting of zoning approvals, and difficulties in establishing new sales networks and weaning companies away from long-standing relationships with suppliers. The extraordinary complexities of doing business in Japan led a U.S. Treasury Department assessment of foreign direct investment obstacles in various countries to conclude that cultural and institutional impediments, not official barriers, create Japan's "relative impermeability to foreign investment."[12]

Japan accounted for only 5 percent of the total book value of U.S. foreign direct investment at the end of 1988 (5.9 percent of investment in the manufacturing sector). By the end of 1988, total Japanese foreign direct investment in the United States ($53.4 billion) was more than triple the book value of the U.S. investment in Japan; at $7.9 billion, U.S. investment in the Japanese manufacturing sector in that year was just a little over 10 percent of the U.S. total for the European Community. Given the extensive bilateral trade relationship and the size and growth of the Japanese economy, the dearth of U.S. foreign direct investment cannot be explained by U.S. corporate indifference to this market. Once again, the explanation lies in the unique Japanese economic and cultural system, which has never welcomed, and often banned, foreign investment. At least as far back as the Meiji Restoration in the late nineteenth century, the Japanese government has been concerned that an influx of foreign manufacturing investment might lead to dominance by foreigners of major sectors of Japanese industry.[13] This prospect could hardly be viewed enthusiastically by a country so bent on preserving its traditions and institutions.

The relative absence of direct investment in Japan by U.S. manufacturing companies over the past forty years has squelched the next-best alternative to exports as a means of selling in the Japanese market. U.S. companies, perceiving themselves shut out of the Japanese market by the unfavorable combination of import restrictions and foreign direct investment controls, early on contented themselves with licensing their technology and patents. In the short run, this practice was attractive: most of the fees and royalties received were pure profit; they increased cash flow and allowed growing companies to finance additional investment and R&D. In the long run, the fast and easy money received from licensing will mostly be phantom profits, reflecting recurring weaknesses in U.S. industry: absence of a long-term strategic planning, a tendency to underestimate the Japanese competition, and an apparently congenital weakness in maximizing the commercial application of newly developed technology.

The Japanese were quick to see the value of absorbing the latest state-of-the-art technology from abroad. They assiduously identified, evaluated, and leased a sizable percentage of major new scientific learning. Between 1950 and 1980, Japanese companies signed an estimated 30,000 licensing and technical agreements with U.S. and European companies. With this strategy Japan made a quantum jump over the obstacle of domestic technological shortcomings. The estimated cost to Japan in these years for licensing and fees was less then $10 billion; in return, Japanese companies acquired U.S. technology that had cost between $500 billion and $1 trillion to develop.[14]

Japanese industrialists have been smart in two ways. They understood their need for acquiring foreign technology and knew how to exploit it once they got it. More important than their ability to enhance U.S.–developed scientific advances has been their ability to apply new technology to commercial uses. Most Japanese firms have organized a much more efficient flow between research laboratory and production line than their U.S. competition. In an age of international interdependence, the ability to be the first to effectively *use* technology is more important than being the first to *discover* it. That the Japanese frequently are the first to convert U.S. technology into a marketable product is more than a source of embarrassment to U.S. industry. It also is a source of weakness. "The United States is an underdeveloped country when it comes to getting useful, proven technologies transferred to business and industry," in the opinion of an official in Congress's Office of Technology Assessment.[15]

Those persons doubting the long-term costs to U.S. industry of aiding the Japanese competition should ask, for example, the RCA Corporation whether, if they could do it over again, they would have licensed their color TV technology so quickly to Japanese TV manufacturers. Had other U.S. companies had the leverage and determination of IBM to successfully demand approval for a wholly-owned Japanese subsidiary, the ability of U.S. industry to penetrate the Japanese market might have been enhanced.

If less U.S. technology had been made available to Japanese companies, Japan's export boom would have been delayed. Instead, three familiar patterns have been repeated in technology acquisition. First, the Japanese cleverly turned their weaknesses into strength. Second, U.S. companies, frequently oblivious to the commercial potential of their new technology, were willing to profit in the short-term from the licensing of technology to the closed Japanese market. Third, U.S. companies seemed unable to recognize or correct actions debilitating their international competitiveness. Relatively recent U.S. technological breakthroughs were still flowing to Japan in 1990. The U.S. system is either incapable of or uninterested in retaining full control of even the most commercially significant technology. What is the relevance of comparative advantage when U.S. high-tech companies in semiconductors and aircraft deem it desirable (or necessary) to license state-of-the-art technology to Japanese companies who clearly want to become world-class competitors with their own version of cutting-edge technology?

Remaining a laggard relative to Japan in exporting and investing abroad, and having apparently learned nothing from the past, U.S. companies continue to turn over corporate assets to Japanese competitors through licensing. The firestorm of criticism in the United States in the wake of the joint agreement in 1989 to produce the FSX jet fighter showed that U.S. attitudes had changed enough to modify but not kill an arrangement providing a major infusion of assembly know-how to the budding Japanese aircraft industry.

If the Japanese had disguised their competitive ambitions in such high-technology sectors as military and civilian aircraft, the seemingly excessive generosity of U.S. industry might make sense. Instead, U.S. comparative advantage vis-à-vis Japan in the manufacturing sector continues to lie more in the export of blueprints than in the export of goods.

CONCLUSION

Japan and the United States have little in common when it comes to defining how foreign trade in particular and foreign economic policy in general should serve their national interests. Attitudes in the two countries toward exports are almost diametrically opposed. As for import policy, Clyde Prestowitz has argued that

> The Japanese cannot "open" in the American sense. They think of
> openness as removal of restrictions case by case, as the bureaucratic
> giving of permission, and have not the generic Western concept of
> an absence of the need for permission. With their strong perception
> of themselves as unique, to be Japanese is by definition to be
> different and to belong to an exclusive group of like people. Thus,
> to ask the Japanese to "open" is to ask them to become less exclu-
> sive and thus less Japanese.[16]

Some large Japanese manufacturers have recently followed the U.S. example of adding production overseas to protect lucrative foreign markets initially developed through exporting, but the two countries have shared few other common experiences over the past half-century of their participation in the global economy. The guiding philosophies of the two countries in the external sector are as different as the needs and goals to be met, a situation similar to the case in the domestic economic sector. The spacious gap in their relative competitive performance, therefore, should not be surprising. It is the failure to recognize the nature, breadth, and depth of these differences that occasions the potentially dangerous situation, to be discussed in the next chapter, of extended bilateral efforts to reduce economic tensions and disequilibria remaining largely ineffective. Ironically, the discrepancies in economic priorities that caused the problem in the first place have proved so profound as to induce both countries to live with the continuing failure to negotiate an end to the bilateral economic tensions that both agree are destabilizing.

CHAPTER 7

The Political Economy of the Bilateral Negotiating Process

We can improve the well-being of our people and we can enhance the forces for democracy, freedom, peace, and human fulfillment around the world, if we stand up for principles of trade expansion through freer markets . . . among nations. The United States took the lead after World War II in creating an international trading system . . . that limited government's ability to disrupt trade . . . because history had taught us the freer the flow of trade across borders, the greater the world economic progress and the greater the impetus for world peace.

—President Ronald Reagan, 1983

Japanese policy should . . . be that of keeping Americans and Europeans as much as possible at arm's length. . . . The Japanese should take every precaution to give as little foothold as possible to foreigners.

—Herbert Spencer, 1892

A permanent dialogue between Japan and the United States developed in the late 1960s over a new generation of bilateral trade problems. The negotiating agenda included Japan's manufactured goods export boom, allegations of Japanese protectionism, and negative U.S. reaction to the $1.4 billion bilateral trade deficit that emerged in 1969. Two exhausting decades later, the two sides were discussing Japan's export boom, allegations of Japanese protectionism, and hostile U.S. reactions to an annual bilateral trade deficit stuck at $50 billion.

Only systemic differences between the samurai and cowboy approaches to economic policy in general and trade policy in particular can explain why so many persons talking so earnestly and so extensively about so many issues accomplished so little. In negotiations, process meets substance: if this book's central thesis about the existence of a systemic problem is correct, we should find fundamental differences in the approach to bilateral bargaining.

In fact, for more than twenty years, the intense bilateral dialogue has

141

afforded a picture-perfect reflection of the differences between one party naively concerned with short-term gratification, consumption, and free-market dynamics and the other party shrewdly concerned with competitiveness, production, and exports.

NEGOTIATING SYMBOLS, NOT SUBSTANCE

Japan and the United States tend to talk *at* more than *to* each other and therefore do not communicate effectively. The divergences in both economic situation and cultural orientation has fostered a stopgap form of economic diplomacy in which the same problems continually resurface. Remedies, arguments, and counterarguments are regularly recycled. The limitations and contradictions of the negotiating process became a part of the substantive problem. The negotiations bought time, but they did not, and could not, remedy the core problem: the structural strength and goal orientation of the Japanese economic system overwhelming the feeble effort of the United States to mount an effective competitive response.

An assessment of the negotiating dynamics requires distinguishing between two levels of accomplishment. On the lower, or micro, level, dozens of specific agreements were implemented, and the process of providing a concession here, a reduced trade barrier there, sufficed to prevent a serious rupture. Japan had no real demands to make on the United States, but needed to demonstrate good-faith movement in the direction of U.S. visions of how trade should be carried on. The higher, or macro, level involving structural problems must be judged a failure. No bilateral negotiations to date have reconciled the basic differences in values and priorities. Pursuant to a tacit agreement to deal with more manageable symbols of commercial disagreement and economic divergence, both sides avoided even placing the larger, conceptual causes of the steadily rising trade imbalance on the negotiating table.

Criticism of the futile effort to contain trade frictions should be qualified in two respects. First, the causal factors of trade problems were deeply rooted in domestic trends. The internal seeds of the Japanese economic miracle and the relative decline in U.S. industrial competitiveness, as suggested in earlier chapters, are so complex that only now, after a long passage of time, do they emerge clearly. It would be foolish to argue that trade negotiators should have possessed sufficient wisdom and foresight in the 1970s to appreciate the sudden, large structural changes that combined with cyclical factors to induce a radical realignment of economic power. Even in the 1980s—as exemplified by the semiconductor agreement—it was asking too much of trade negotiations to deal satisfactorily with larger, structural industrial problems.

Nevertheless, at some point, at least some trade negotiators must have realized the negotiating process was too narrowly focused. Why didn't they speak up? Probably because of the downright scary notion that virtually the entire Japanese and U.S. economic systems lay at the heart of the problem. The burden of negotiating on such a scale would be awesome. The U.S. government would be forced to admit weakness in U.S. capabilities and intrude deeply into Japanese domestic affairs, where meaningful changes would have been forthcoming only if Japan were a fully subordinated client state of the United States.

Self-interest also militated against U.S. trade negotiations involving structural causes of the bilateral imbalance: results were more easily achievable with regard to narrow, tangible items of U.S. dissatisfaction, and negotiators, after all, are charged with achieving results. Although the Structural Impediments Initiative of 1989 (see page 49) was intended to finally get down to the nitty-gritty in the Japanese economic-cultural system, the talks could never have been expected to accomplish much, since they lacked a formal legal basis and a deadline for completion.

The second reason for the failure of bilateral negotiations to contain the basic forces causing trade frictions begins with the notion that the process was a political exercise in which each country sought to maximize very different values and minimize the costs of achieving them. Ironically, both countries found their interests served by limiting efforts to an ad hoc exercise in pursuing symbolic actions instead of reforming underlying causes of the competitive imbalance.

Reduced to its basics, the world market was viewed by Japan as a vehicle for enhancing economic growth at home and, most important, as a means of ensuring economic security for Japan. Because competitive imports and foreign direct investments diluted control over industrial policy objectives, they were opposed. A protected home market, and the ensured volume of demand that it provided, was a major element in an industrial policy that does not welcome the disturbing forces of foreign competition in high-value-added industries within Japan.

Purchases of foreign-made goods have been generally viewed as a challenge to the growth and strength of Japan's domestic corporations. Genuine import liberalization normally has been delayed until after Japanese producers are powerful enough to flourish without the aid of import restrictions. Foreign direct investment was not encouraged because foreigners could not be trusted to play by the informal obligations of the Japanese system. The bilateral negotiating process therefore was looked upon by Japan as a means for allowing the country to pursue an essentially mercantilist, self-centered trade strategy at minimal costs. None of Japan's "concessions" to world public opinion either slowed the relative growth of its industrial strength or significantly altered the product composition of its foreign trade flows.

The United States felt little pressure to force changes in Japan's trade strategies. Downplaying the importance of both exports and retaliation against import barriers, the United States emphasized such "noble" ideas as an open international trading system, comparative advantage, competition, and consumer sovereignty. U.S. companies and unions seeking import protection from fair competition are usually viewed in Washington as losers, victims of their own relative inefficiency. Import restrictions usually are viewed as politically necessitated deviations from the free market. Local governments, unlike their Japanese counterparts, actively seek out foreign direct investment, equating it with job creation and income enhancement.

Implicitly, U.S. trade policymakers, from the president down, recognize the importance of foreign competition in imparting discipline to management and labor. U.S. policymakers understand that almost any action taken to punish the Japanese for lack of reciprocity would hurt the U.S. economy more than that of Japan. U.S. policymakers also recognize that export promotion policies do not need the same "make or break" priority that dominates the thinking in Japan and many other countries. In sum, both sides accepted the twin failures to (1) significantly increase U.S. exports to Japan and (2) increase U.S. efficiency so as to reduce the manifestation of Japanese industrial strength in the U.S. market.

The United States has never developed any comprehensive or long-term vision of exactly what it wants from Japan or, hence, a strategy to obtain it. The resultant lack of a carefully designed, detailed strategy nurtured the mutually confusing approach that occasionally put out fires only to have both sides surprised when new sparks flew. The lack of continuity in U.S. policy minimized the costs to Japan of merely going through the motions of making its markets more accessible to imports. While the Japanese publicly congratulated themselves on dozens of politically painful regulatory alterations, in fact they had defused U.S. anger with a minimum of real change in trade flows.

This spectacle of the deaf outwitting the blind began to cause more serious problems by the early 1980s. With product-specific trade disputes erupting faster than the two bureaucracies could effectively respond, the continuing failure to address underlying causes increased the risk of a trade war. Not fully aware of the potential threat to its industrial base, the U.S. government still wore the ideological blinders that precluded any serious attempt to respond more forcefully to aggressive foreign industrial and export policies. U.S. negotiators preferred to focus on the market access issue, deluding themselves that balanced trade could be achieved by reducing overt barriers in Japan to U.S. exports. Even more discouraging, trade negotiators lacked expertise and authority to end the trend of one Japanese industry after another beating the United States in its own home market

By the late 1980s, U.S. government fear and frustration had escalated to the point of taking unilateral retaliatory measures against Japan's semiconductor manufacturers and the Toshiba Machine Company and restricting Japanese bidding for federal construction contracts. Although breaking a longtime precedent, these measures reflected special situations rather than any fundamental shift in U.S. ideology or trade strategy. Complaints continued of evidence of closed Japanese markets, import-inhospitable Japanese industrial structure and policy, and unfair Japanese business practices, adding volume and numbers to the chorus calling for blood. Nevertheless, as of this writing at the onset of the 1990s, there appears little likelihood of the United States clobbering the Japanese with major protectionist measures or changing the basics of its own domestic economy. Urgency is not sufficient to shift values and priorities or force the move from negotiating symbols to taking substantive actions.

NEGOTIATING IN CIRCLES

The bilateral negotiating process has failed to correct either trade asymmetries or trade frictions, although the United States dragged Japan kicking and screaming to the pursuit of import liberalization efforts. As Japan's bilateral trade position was geometrically more out of balance in 1989 than in 1969, the official negotiating process after 1969 can be criticized for failing even to preserve the status quo. Tensions escalated along with the trade imbalance and competitive disequilibria. A steady stream of bilateral agreements was no substitute for the missing long-term strategy to address structural economic problems and political needs. No definitive settlement could be possible in the context of ad hoc agreements focused on symptoms instead of causes.

Many specialized negotiating groups were created to deal with specific disagreements in a proliferation of forums. This reflects the basic beliefs of the two countries that theirs is the world's most important economic relationship (and possibly most contentious) and that dissimilarities in the government structures of Japan and the United States are too vast to permit any effective, permanent conduit for resolving the multiple disagreements.

The most specialized negotiating forums bring together narrowly focused delegations under a limited mandate to arrange some specific export restraint agreement (steel, color televisions, automobiles) or market access agreement (beef, citrus, supercomputers, construction). This product-specific format was only much later expanded to encompass broader issues in the MOSS and Structural Impediments Initiative talks. A second category of forum consists of more general, permanent meetings, working groups, and consultative bodies convened by both the official and business sectors—one example is the series of regular meetings between the U.S. president and Japanese prime minister. The U.S.–Japan Subcabinet Meeting brings senior officials together semiannually. The more specialized Trade Committee meets at least once a year at the assistant secretary level to discuss a narrower agenda. The annual series of meetings for senior business leaders convened by the U.S.–Japan Business Conference frequently produces jointly written reports on what both sides see as the tasks ahead.

All of these forums share the unfortunate characteristic of negotiating in circles. The sense of repetition pervades any assessment of the major results of the bilateral negotiating process:

- Innumerable voluntary export restraints by Japan when the domestic U.S. industry mounted a credible political fight against rising market penetration by imports. In virtually every case, however, the breather provided to U.S. industry did not result in the promised upsurge in ability to compete against imports.

- Innumerable "packages" of import liberalization, domestic economic policy shifts, studies of further remedies, and so forth. Japan typically announces a package when U.S. anger approaches the boiling point, promising great changes and suggesting this is the final package that ever will be assembled.

- A barrage of Japanese public relations activities and embarrassing, inconsequential trade promotion efforts, perhaps best epitomized by the sailing in 1979 of *Boatique America,* a Japanese ship that was converted into a floating market of U.S. consumer goods and visited various Japanese ports (the sponsors may have believed that Japanese consumers are more amenable to buying foreign goods once they step off of their home soil).

- Gaps between Japanese promises and implementation. This phenomenon partly reflects the cumbersome Japanese decision-making process and partly their expertise in sweet-talking Americans. Japan has long made commitments on trade policy changes that take many years to materialize in practice—for example, Nippon Telegraph and Telephone's procurement of sophisticated electronic equipment from foreign suppliers.

The most consistent element in the negotiations may be U.S. anger—as opposed to action. Rising fear and sinking credibility about Japanese intentions have resulted in a torrent of criticism and threats directed against this country that is perceived to live by one standard—unlimited expansion—for its own exports and another standard—a closed door—for foreign access to its market. On innumerable occasions, U.S. trade officials have declared that frustrations with Japan had reached a "critical stage" and the imbalance was "simply unacceptable," with warnings that passage of protectionist legislation in Congress was imminent. Typically, a pro forma Japanese response would then calm U.S. tempers. Failure by the Japanese to offer *major* results-generating concessions may yet lead to unilateral protectionist actions in the United States. U.S. patience with Japan has its limits. None of the Japanese concessions made between 1969 and 1989 significantly increased U.S. market share in Japan for a major manufactured good or allowed U.S. industries to emerge from the shadow of superior Japanese competition. Japanese liberalization packages have been political crisis management tools rather than levers of economic change.

Japan long ago mastered the U.S. negotiating style, perfecting an ability to recognize U.S. bluff and bluster. The vast majority of U.S. threats never come close to realization, and some have been repeated so frequently they have lost all credibility. Despite its protectionist posturing, Congress passed no binding, unilateral import-restricting laws between 1969 and the time of this writing (1990) affecting access of Japanese goods to the U.S. market, with the one exception of punishing Toshiba Machine Company for its illegal technology sales to the Soviet Union (see chapter 2).

The Japanese position that their market had become open by the late 1970s led them to adopt a negotiating posture built around the request that the United States give them specific examples of protectionism. With the Americans content to respond on this level, the negotiating process typically was relegated to the micro, or product-specific, level. Again, this was mutually agreeable. Discussions of radical structural shifts in the pro-export, anti-import bias of the Japanese "system" were avoided. U.S. negotiators could realistically hope to achieve measurable results in response to the specific trade complaints of specific industries or companies. As political appointees with a short time horizon, senior U.S. trade policy-makers preferred to deal with effects, not basic causes. Hence, negotiations dealt with the more tangible secondary issues such as quotas, dumping, Japanese import inspection standards, and so forth.

In terms of economic theory, the situation is very different from the one measured in commercial terms. The United States has unconsciously exploited Japan's mercantilist attitude by exchanging its home-grown paper money (dollars) for ever-increasing amounts of real economic resources. In political-commercial terms, Japan consciously exploited the process by learning how to go through the motions. Structural changes in the relative size and composition of its imports were the exception rather than the rule.

The quixotic nature of the search for an acceptable equilibrium in the relationship was quite rational. The marginal amount of value-added produced by the negotiating process served both countries' needs. Both sides got essentially what they were seeking. The United States got free-market purity, served the interests of its consumers, and politically defused the anger of most import-impacted industrial sectors; Japan got trade purity

(exports maximized relative to imports), served the interests of its producers, and politically defused the anger of its most important trading partner. Bilateral bargaining straddled the divergent inner feelings of both sides
with regard to how foreign trade should be used to serve national interests.
The process repeatedly defused dangerous situations while preserving the
basic friendship of the two countries. Neither side suffered costs that it
truly found intolerable.

The built-in limitations on achieving meaningful results produced a
clearly second-best approach to problem solving. The resulting exercise in
frustration introduces bizarre elements of repetition and time standing still.
Most U.S. criticisms of Japanese trade policy made in the early 1970s are
still being made twenty years later with no alterations. President Nixon's
Foreign Policy Report to Congress of March 1971 said "Japan's position
as a major beneficiary of a liberal international economic system is not
consistent with her slowness in removing the restrictions which limit the
access of others to her own vibrant economy. . . . [T]he future will require
adjustments in the U.S.–Japanese relationship." The then assistant secretary of state for economic affairs, Philip Trezise, argued in 1970 "in the
eyes of the United States, key Japanese foreign economic policies are out
of step with the requirements of the international economic system, incompatible with Japan's economic status, and contrary to the interests of the
United States and other of Japan's trading partners."[1]

A personal experience by the author provides another example of how
the negotiating process was long on ceremony but short on real substance.
In my research for this book, I came upon a long-forgotten memorandum
I wrote in the spring of 1970 in my capacity as chief economist for the
U.S.–Japan Trade Council. Entitled "Executive Branch Attitudes Toward
Trade," it contains two paragraphs that word for word portray with un-
canny accuracy the tone of American attitudes in the early 1990s:

> There is widespread belief that Japan's trade policies are consistent
> neither with its current economic strength nor with the ground
> rules of reciprocity which the U.S. feels its own liberal trade poli-
> cies warrant. The list of Japan's liberalization measures notwith-
> standing, there is a common assertion that the cards are stacked
> against American industrial exporters (administrative guidance is
> a favorite example) and that Japan's idea of liberal trade is limited
> to assuring open markets for its exports. Regardless of the merits
> of this line of thinking, it is very real, widely held, and deeply
> believed. Generally, all that differs among the U.S. officials is the
> degree of impatience with Japan. State and STR (Office of the
> Special Trade Representative) people still emphasize the use of
> negotiations to correct the current situation. The Commerce De-
> partment, in general, has lost faith in further talk and feels that
> the U.S. must now turn to action to spur . . . Japan to take the

measures which have long and unsuccessfully been sought by this country. . . .

Despite the large number of exchanges between Japan and the U.S., a real communications gap still seems to exist. Most government officials to whom I've spoken accept the fact that the Japanese are not deliberately trying to live by a special set of trade rules applicable only to Japan. They do feel that the Japanese government sincerely believes that the current pace of liberalization fully demonstrates its good faith. However, they argue that U.S. grievances against Japan are sufficiently numerous and justifiable (as evidenced by the current U.S.–Japan trade balance) to make it very difficult to forestall indefinitely hard line trade policies.

Repetitive patterns also appear in one tactic used to pressure a reluctant Japan into line with Western standards. An apparent absence of institutional memory led to repetitiveness in the proposal for a special, discriminatory tariff on Japanese goods. The first public mention of this idea was a *New York Times* article 24 May 1971. The unnamed source (later revealed to be the deputy undersecretary of the Treasury)[2] told a reporter such a duty might be necessary unless the yen were to be revalued to correct its extreme (up to 20 percent) undervaluation against the dollar. A variant of this idea was proposed in mid-1978 when the then chairman of the House Ways and Means Subcommittee on Trade urged President Carter to invoke the obscure balance of payments authority of the Trade Act of 1974 to impose temporary import surcharges of up to 15 percent to correct the destabilizing bilateral trade imbalance.[3] Senator Lloyd Bentsen of Texas got into the act in 1979, while chairman of the Joint Economic Committee of Congress; he suggested "a surcharge or other barriers" against Japanese imports.[4] In March 1985, Senator John Heinz (R., PA) introduced a bill (S. 770) that would have imposed a 20 percent tariff surcharge on all imports from Japan. Most of the advocates of "results-oriented" trade negotiations (see page 49) have suggested similar penalties in the absence of desired results.

Countless bills have been introduced into Congress, not necessarily with expectations of their being enacted into law. Most, like a 1982 proposal to limit U.S. purchases of Japanese goods to the level of U.S. exports to Japan of manufactured and processed agricultural goods, are intended to send a message to Japan. Congress is not as blatantly protectionist as it is often accused of being. As an institution, it has developed a decipherable set of signals to express its judgment that another country's trade practices have gotten too extreme and are in need of moderating, preferably by voluntary action, not necessarily by unilateral U.S. legislation.

Another repetitive pattern in bilateral negotiations is the solemn warning to the Japanese by yet another well-meaning U.S. official or business leader that bilateral relations are on the brink of a trade war and immediate

Japanese concessions are essential. A classic was the alarm sounded during an August 1985 visit to Tokyo by Congressman Sam Gibbons (D., FL), the liberal-trade–oriented chairman of the House Ways and Means Subcommittee on Trade: "The time is very, very late and the situation is very, very critical." Newspaper readers have come to recognize "Administration Gives Japan Stern Warning on Trade" as a perennial, all-purpose headline comparable to "Fighting Between Rival Factions Erupts in Lebanon." One can almost hear the Japanese saying to one another, "It's the silly season again, but let's put a look of concern on our faces and pretend to take the cliches seriously." After twenty years of listening to the same lectures and threats, the Japanese can be forgiven for becoming a bit blasé.

The pattern of repetition is so strong—and so likely to continue—it may be helpful at this point to offer two all-purpose scripts for future U.S.–Japanese confrontations. The first presents the sequence of U.S. anxieties mounting about increased competition from a particular Japanese industry; the second outlines the dialogue for the seemingly endless U.S. effort to strip away Japan's apparently inexhaustible supply of barriers to imports.

U.S. Protectionism Version

1. Japanese exporters initiate a blitzkrieg export strategy, catch U.S. competition napping, and capture a sizeable (more than 15 percent) share of the U.S. market.

2. U.S. producers launch an initiative in Washington to secure import relief. Political superstars like textile and automobile manufacturers go directly to the White House or Congress, while others like producers of color TVs, specialty steels, semiconductors, machine tools, and motorcycles apply to lower-level officials for erection of trade barriers under the various existing U.S. import relief laws.

3. The Japanese emphasize their efficiency and claim they have the U.S. consumer's best interest in mind. U.S. protectionism, they say, will hurt the U.S. economy most of all.

4. In an optional but very dramatic scene, members of Congress friendly to the petitioning industry introduce legislation that would impose severe, mandatory import controls. Word gets out that this action is a means of scaring both sides into negotiating a compromise, namely a "voluntary" export restraint agreement. For best legislative performances in this role, I cite Congressman Wilbur Mills's actions in 1969–70 on behalf of textiles and Senator John Danforth in 1981 on behalf of automobiles.

5. The U.S. government swears allegiance to the liberal trade ethic but forlornly tells the Japanese that reality calls for pragmatic behavior. Translation: a voluntary restraint agreement will allow the executive branch to beat back the forces of protectionism on Capitol Hill and elsewhere.

6. U.S.–Japanese negotiators haggle over export ceiling numbers. After reaching compromise, each side expresses hope for long-lasting tranquility in trade relations.

7. U.S. producers complain that protection given to them is too little, too late, and too brief. Adjustment to Japanese competition, they warn, won't come quickly or easily.

8. The Japanese criticize U.S. hypocrisy, congratulate themselves on willingness to cooperate in solving U.S. industrial problems, and begin to search for ways to exploit loopholes in the voluntary export restraint agreement.

9. U.S. economists argue that import restrictions will not provide positive contributions to domestic productivity and efficiency.

10. Both sides express dismay when yet another U.S. industry is put on the defensive by aggressive Japanese exporters. Return to scene 1.

Improved Market Access Version

1. The U.S. private sector complains bitterly of the lack of reciprocity in Japan's trade practices. Overt barriers, cultural practices, industrial structure, and dirty tricks are cited as restricting market access.

2. The U.S. government warns that grave consequences are in store for Japan if it does nothing to correct its trade disequilibrium by allowing other countries to sell more to it.

3. The Japanese envision the reappearance of black ships in Tokyo Bay and accuse the U.S. government of shamelessly and misguidedly meddling in their domestic affairs. Americans are advised that they need to work harder, get better organized, and invest more energy in understanding the Japanese market.

4. Japanese "internationalists" quietly thank Americans for vivid threats, saying that they are useful levers in internal debates. They point out to Japanese protectionists that export growth is at risk if foreign antagonists are not quieted, perhaps

by Japan's constructing a package of pleasant gestures and symbolic actions; substance is optional.

5. The government of Japan throws together another package of miscellaneous liberalization measures advertised as the cure for U.S. export problems and the source of Japanese political complications. The Japanese definition of implementation bears little resemblance to the U.S. definition. Subsequent increases in market share of U.S. manufactures exports require a microscope to measure.

6. The U.S. government expresses dismay that the Japanese don't realize it is in their own interests to go further in opening their market. It is said to be Japan's responsibility to act in a manner that protects the liberal trading order from its protectionist foes.

7. Japanese lobbyists and American intellectuals warn that U.S. bully tactics are a wasteful expenditure of political capital that eventually will undermine Japan's pro–United States foreign policy.

8. After a brief interlude, both sides express dismay at the continued enormity of the bilateral trade surplus. Return to scene 1.

BUREAUCRATIC MISMATCH

Because the course of bilateral economic relations is so much more important to Japan than to the United States, the Japanese apply relatively greater allocations of time, effort, organization, manpower, planning, money, and, last but not least, common sense to the negotiating process. The result is a subtle and occasionally not so subtle tilting of the negotiating table in favor of Japanese interests. Clyde Prestowitz, Jr. presents a sobering summary in his insider's look at the negotiating process: "the United States is outclassed. Its negotiators nearly always face a better-staffed, better-trained, and better-organized opponent. That they will not be successful is almost inevitable."[5]

The very size and power of the United States obviate the need for aggressive government efforts on behalf of the private sector, but a price must be paid for Washington's refusal to give priority to bilateral economic relations: the Japanese are more likely to get more of what they want. Japan's manipulating the percentages to its favor is, at the margin, a factor in enhancing the strength of the samurai system relative to the cowboy system.

The lack of a long-term Japan strategy, authority to carry it out, or backing by a unified public lies at the root of the bureaucratic mismatch that frequently puts the U.S. government at a significant disadvantage in negotiations. There is yet no effective vehicle for formulating and implementing U.S. economic strategy vis-à-vis Japan. Scattered and transitory authority means that coherence and consistency are rare in U.S. policy. Detailed knowledge of industry by senior officials is also rare. Behind the bluster and deals lie two disquieting realities that conjure visions of a powerful, but naked emperor. First, throughout the 1980s, the White House steadfastly argued that the source of U.S. internal economic shortcomings was excessive government interference, not the absence of effective government initiatives. The U.S. government was said to be the source of the problem, not the solution. Yet, admitted shortcomings, like the budget deficit and short-term corporate planning horizons, are perpetuated—the very antithesis of Japan's approach to economic policy.

Secondly, U.S. trade policy towards Japan remains devoid of direction, substance, and backbone. The only strategy employed with even minimal effectiveness in Tokyo is for the U.S. executive and legislative branches to repeatedly play the roles of, respectively, good cop and bad cop. Long since reduced to a cliche, the action starts with a ritual warning by the liberal trade–loving administrative branch that the protectionists on Capitol Hill are on the brink of passing severely protectionist legislation. The predictable result is a ritual, halfhearted Japanese concession for either more market access or less export pressure. To quote Prestowitz again, when U.S. trade negotiators try to frighten the Japanese with the vision of Congress out of control,

> Implicitly we were linking ourselves in common cause with the Japanese and creating a false sense that free-traders on both sides were fighting against the black hats in Congress. The negotiation thus changed direction: originally a matter of U.S. government requests, it became one of mutually calibrating just how much action would be necessary to keep Congress leashed. Instead of a negotiator, the U.S. trade team became an adviser to the government of Japan on how to handle the U.S. Congress.[6]

As suggested before, the Congress's bark on Japanese trade matters tends to be worse than its bite. The not-really-so-bad cop fears a repetition of the political dynamics that brought about the highly protectionist, highly damaging Smoot-Hawley legislation of 1930. It has become axiomatic that Congress will back off from final passage of anti-Japanese legislation as long as negotiations are under way or even seriously planned for the near future. Indeed, an almost audible sigh of relief usually emanates from Capitol Hill when the initiation of negotiations gives Congress a reason not to act, and the astute Japanese respond with an emphasis on polite process rather than substance.

The U.S. executive branch's shallow, piecemeal, and often leaderless trade policy toward Japan offers the latter a bureaucratic adversary usually so pre-divided that conquest seldom requires much effort. The pickings can be easy: a 1989 report by the U.S. Advisory Committee for Trade Policy and Negotiations noted that "By pitting one U.S. agency against another, the Japanese are able to delay the negotiations and prevent a consensus U.S. position from evolving."[7] U.S. departments and agencies are all too willing to cut separate deals with the Japanese, a trait reflecting the presence in Washington of many individual interests, public and private, with no single national interest accepted by all. The Japanese long ago mastered the art of playing the friendly bureaucratic ends against the hostile middle. Of course there are rivalries, turf battles, and policy disagreements among Japanese ministries and between the Japanese government and private sector, but the U.S. government and private sector remain amateurish in exploiting these relatively more subtle differences.

A clearly delineated three-way cleavage in the U.S. bureaucracy emerges regularly. The State Department and the National Security Council view the bilateral relationship as part of a larger political-military alliance that needs to be protected from the less important commercial squabbles; parts of the Defense Department join this camp while other parts look with growing anxiety at the growing dependence of U.S. weapons contractors on Japanese-made components and speak of a need for reviving U.S. industries. A second group, far less disposed toward a soft trade line, consists mainly of the Office of the U.S. Trade Representative and the Commerce Department; as officials charged with protecting U.S. trading interests, most have metaphorical scars from having hit their heads so often against the hard brick wall of Japanese negotiating tactics. Trade hawks remain in the minority and may do so indefinitely, even if the trade and competitive disequilibria persist. Although the hawks tend to speak loudly—because they carry such small negotiating sticks—they are frequently derided as protectionists and short-sighted Japan bashers. Their urge for a hard line going right to the jugular of Japanese trade practices is simply not the most widely accepted or popular agenda among the executive branch agencies with jurisdiction in bilateral relations.

The third school of thought includes pure neoclassical economists from the Treasury Department, the President's Council of Economic Advisers, and the Office of Management and Budget, who see their duty as protecting the workings of the free market. While the Treasury has forcefully and successfully urged the liberalization of Japan's financial markets, it is increasingly queasy at even the thought of retaliatory trade actions, fearing Japanese counterretaliation by slowing capital inflows into the United States or, worse, pulling out existing investment. Japan, in the view of the very powerful Treasury Department, is not so much a miscreant on trade as a cash cow providing a critical offset to the shortage in U.S. savings relative to the federal budget deficit.

Many stories have been told about the unflinching pro-Japanese bias of the U.S. embassy in Tokyo in the 1980s while Mike Mansfield was ambassador. Visiting members of Congress and businesspeople reportedly frequently avoided the embassy entirely, not wanting the soft-sell runaround. More disquieting were rumors that outgoing cables to Washington critical of Japanese economic policies were stifled and discouraged in the internecine warfare in which the soft-liners dominated the hard-liners.[8]

It is the exception rather than the rule for the U.S. trade bureaucracy to get its act together, retain unanimity, and maximize its leverage on Japan. Before and during many trade negotiations, the U.S. bureaucracy expends enormous amounts of time and energy on internal arguments over substance and over jurisdictional authority, i.e. turf. The result is the running inability to impose the concerted will of the U.S. government on its Japanese counterparts.

Japan's long tradition of an elite bureaucracy and close attention to detail gives its government at least five additional advantages above and beyond the big three of having a very specific agenda, being at the forefront of a national consensus on trade priorities, and presenting a relatively unified front to other governments. First, there are relatively more Japanese officials involved in bilateral trade matters, and they invariably speak and read English fluently and are knowledgeable about the subjects of U.S. trade policy and economic trends. Junior bureaucrats may not actively participate in negotiations, but they develop data to bolster Japanese positions while gaining valuable experience. By contrast, recent budget constraints have forced a reduction in the number of U.S. foreign commercial service officers stationed in Japan.

Two other Japanese advantages are interrelated: continuity and institutional memory among senior trade officials. Unlike the parliamentary system that relies on career officials up to the deputy minister level, the U.S. system contains a deep layer of political appointees at the top. Especially in trade, senior U.S. officials hold short tenure—on average, perhaps two years. This leads to the third Japanese advantage: a far better institutional memory.

Senior U.S. trade negotiators have inadequate time to learn historical detail and nuances or to cultivate close working relationships with either career U.S. civil servants or their Japanese counterparts. With their return to the private sector always looming, there is a natural tendency for most senior officials to opt for a quick, splashy agreement in lieu of ongoing technical negotiations to iron out details beforehand in the interests of a more effective, longer-lived agreement in the long run. Japanese trade officials have no such problems. The more talented bureaucrats slowly make their way up the ranks and stay there, with no revolving door for top officials in and out of the ministries. Details of Japanese negotiating arguments and objectives are meticulously passed on to carefully picked successors.

The Japanese must be amused to see the ever changing cast of U.S.

negotiators to whom they can sell "the same horse many times over. They know that if an issue is drawn out long enough the U.S. players will change, allowing the Japanese to offer the old proposals once more."[9] In complex, continuing disputes such as purchases of U.S. telecommunications equipment by Nippon Telegraph and Telephone (NTT), the lack of high-level U.S. continuity can preclude a solution satisfactory to U.S. producers. A former State Department official, now employed by a U.S. high-tech firm, laments that

> When you have average turnover . . . in the two-year range for the high level people, your ability to sustain that sort of negotiation is virtually nil. So the N.T.T. problem, almost by institutional definition, becomes insoluble.[10]

During the public works construction negotiations discussed in chapter 2, for example, the head of the U.S. delegation changed four times (the only constant was lack of experience in the construction industry). At one important point in the bargaining, the United States had to suspend the talks because its head of delegation had resigned and there was no one to replace him.[11]

Another advantage accruing to Japanese trade negotiators is their ability to use their language skills in the relatively open U.S. system to actively participate in influencing government attitudes and popular opinion. Media appearances, discussions with state and local officials, talks with U.S. businesspeople, college lectures, and the like give Japanese representatives both insight into and influence on U.S. perceptions and desires. By contrast, U.S. diplomats in Japan are isolated by attitudes and language barriers that discourage foreign involvement in or understanding of day-to-day events and public opinion.

A final and increasingly significant element in the bureaucratic mismatch is the vastly greater access of Japanese officials to lobbyists for amassing information and guidance in Washington and as contacts with the media and senior U.S. officials.

THE JAPAN LOBBY IN THE UNITED STATES

The Japanese system does not like external surprises. Japan's economic geography and its trade practices have made it unusually vulnerable to foreign imposition of import restrictions. Japan feels itself to be the most misunderstood of all U.S. trading partners. The Japanese system is methodical, it pays attention to detail, and it leaves little to chance. Furthermore, Japan has a lot to protect: the United States is worth $100 billion a year as an export market and the location of well over $300 billion in Japanese-owned assets, from Treasury bills to direct foreign investment. As might be expected, the Japanese have assembled in the United States the largest, most expensive, and most effective lobbying and foreign commercial intelligence operation in the world. Japan's trade interests and strategy are well served by a skilled network that is on top of all developments and trends in any way affecting U.S.–Japanese trade relations. The network gathers information, disseminates opinions and counterarguments, opens doors, and openly seeks to influence legislation and policy. It does all of this so well and so extensively that a backlash in the United States is developing.

Whereas the Chinese see a rising sun when they look toward Japan, Americans see opportunities for lucrative self-aggrandizement. Washington, D.C. is the mecca for Japan's hired guns in the United States, where a small army of lawyers, public relations specialists, advisor/lobbyists, economic consultants, local representatives of Japanese firms, and miscellaneous door openers, information gatherers, and influence peddlers promote the presumption of a commonality of economic interests between the two countries.

The lobbyists' raison d'être can be divided into five categories. Perhaps most important is influencing policy development in the executive branch. This is accomplished by such means as highlighting the costs to the United States of restrictive trade actions against Japan and explaining the Japanese side of the story, such as what they are doing to defuse tensions and why they cannot do more just now. A second category is the gathering of a seemingly endless stream of available—and some not so available—facts, rumors, figures, and forecasts about trends in U.S. international economic policies, the U.S. domestic economy, U.S. foreign policy, the personalities of U.S. economic policymakers, bureaucratic rivalries, and so forth. These data can be likened to inputs for the slow, painstaking Japanese decision-making process. Japan, like everyone else, was stung badly by the surprise announcement of the New Economic Policy in August 1971, and subsequently took steps to establish a comprehensive network of information and gossip collection. When important trade legislation is being drafted, the Japanese government can count on daily content analysis and forecasts of votes. When negotiations are in progress, a similar stream of analysis will examine the thinking inside relevant U.S. agencies. The third function of the lobbying effort is to present Japan's side of trade disputes to the U.S. public in the best possible light and mobilize the vested interests that benefit from bilateral trade (such as encouraging wheat farmers to oppose protectionist policies for the United States, lest foreign countries adopt protectionist policies as retaliation), and providing favorable data and film clips to the media. The fourth function is to represent Japanese industries in official proceedings where they are accused of injuring U.S. companies and workers. The job of the lawyers who represent Japanese interests in administrative import tribunals is to convince the U.S. government investigators that the domestic complaint has not met statutory criteria for triggering import restraints. A final, more limited function has been the direct effort to influence voting on pending legislation in Congress—for example, arguing against passage of the automobile local-content bill.

The Japanese thirst for information can reach absurd excesses, such as the 1981 decision by Toyota to retain at least ten different Washington organizations to monitor the auto import quota issue. Not knowing that they had all been given the same general assignment, the lobbyists descended on Capitol Hill seeking answers to identical questions. Exasperated congressional staff members finally told Toyota they would be happy to pass along information directly but refused to deal further with the company's squadron of lobbyists.[12] Washington insiders still express a mixture of amazement and jealousy about the reported $300,000 paid in 1977 to an economic consultant by Japanese TV manufacturers for a mere three months of part-time effort to contain the protectionist campaign of the U.S. TV industry.

The intelligence network in Washington is critical to Japan's need and ability to distinguish between U.S. bluff and genuine preparations for unilateral retaliation. The Japanese have developed a high degree of accuracy in predicting Washington's trade intentions by catching an early drift of bureaucratic thinking and evolving political pressures. Japan, viewing itself as an innocent victim of U.S. persecution, learned how to stay one step ahead of the sheriff. Most Japanese trade officials were probably surprised by their export success, but U.S. tolerance of a surging trade deficit was no surprise. The Japanese have an excellent idea of when to act and what minimum concessions will prevent a reversal in the liberal U.S. import policy.

There is no evidence of illegality or impropriety by the Japanese lobby; at worst, it exploits the openness of the U.S. system and the cowboy's penchant for putting self-interest ahead of societal interests. Nevertheless, the situation has disquieting aspects. Increasingly active and sophisticated Japanese lobbying has resulted in an enormous, potentially dangerous imbalance in the abilities of the two countries to affect the internal process of the other. The sheer magnitude of the monetary outlay by the Japanese forces one to take note. The sums reported annually to the U.S. Justice Department under the Foreign Agents Registration Act no longer indicate total lobbying outlays because of the rapid expansion of activities not covered by the law. But even the listings for Japanese lobbyists tend to be double those for the next-placed country, Canada. There has been no denial of the estimate by *Business Week* in the summer of 1988 that total Japanese spending on image making and influence molding in the United States, exclusive of advertising, would exceed $300 million that year.[13] The magazine's estimate of $50 million for direct lobbying in Washington may be conservative: estimates from other published sources are as high as $100 million annually.[14] The larger totals may apply in election years, for Japanese companies have become increasingly generous to both national parties. While federal law forbids direct contributions to political candidates by foreign interests, loopholes permit contributions from foreign-retained U.S. lobbyists and political action committees formed by U.S. employees of foreign subsidiaries. If Japanese lobbying expenditures are as high as estimated, they exceed the combined budgets of the five most influential U.S. national business coalitions, including the Chamber of Commerce and the National Association of Manufacturers. Some 250 Japanese government agencies, companies, and industry associations dispense funds to 200 or more firms and individuals in the U.S. capital, as well as $140 million in corporate philanthropy, $45 million in corporate public relations, and $17 million in university research contracts and gifts. As much as 80 percent of Japanese studies in U.S. universities may be funded from Japan; by 1989 the Japanese had funded sixteen chairs (at more than $1 million each) at MIT alone, with more on the way.

A worrisome aspect of the growing Japan lobby is a growing perception that big money is corrupting policy-making and may taint the thinking of persons in government, academia, research institutes, the law, and media, all of which are targets for Japanese largesse. There is no hard evidence of persons altering their views on Japan in return for money, but the growing numbers of organizations and individuals receiving Japanese funding means growing numbers with a vested interest in not offending or attacking Japan. The ranks of Washington's most influential and expensive lobbyists, those with the greatest access to high officials, would be much thinner and less affluent without the Japanese employers who tend not to quibble about price.

Some observers have begun wondering out loud about the objectivity of senior U.S. trade officials *while still in office* when so many of them go on to become attorneys or consultants for Japanese interests. Without much overstating the case, one writer worried that the Office of the U.S. Trade Representative (USTR) and the Commerce Department had become "virtual training camps" for the Japanese, "whose roster of lawyers, lobbyists, and consultants reads like an all-star team of former U.S. trade specialists."[15] The General Accounting Office identified seventy-six high level executive and legislative branch officials who left government between 1980 and 1985 to work for foreign interests.[16] In 1986 alone, fifteen members of the USTR reportedly became agents of foreign governments, mainly Japan.[17] A third estimate claimed that one-third of the forty-five top officials and all of the general counsels who left USTR during the Reagan administration became advisers to foreign interests, again mostly Japanese.

Uneasiness about the lure of big money in a society that respects wealth far more than public service is fueled by a growing number of cases demonstrating not even a pretense of separation between government service and cashing in on contacts and experience. Perhaps the best known recent example is Robert Watkins: while overseeing U.S. trade strategy in automobiles and auto parts as a deputy assistant secretary of Commerce in September 1987, he solicited work from Japanese automotive companies in a letter requesting that the companies consider hiring him to form a trade association to represent their interests in the United States. The letter read, in part, "I believe I am uniquely qualified to establish and lead an automotive association committed to market principles. . . . I am prepared to limit or end my responsibilities at the Department, when necessary . . ."[18] While still a commissioner on the U.S. International Trade Commission, Daniel Minchew actively solicited business in Tokyo.[19] Richard Allen, President Reagan's first assistant for national security affairs, who earlier had been forced to resign as a campaign adviser after his extensive business relations with Japanese companies became public, was forced from office after admitting that he accepted $1,000 for helping a Japanese magazine arrange an interview with Mrs. Reagan; he immediately resumed representing Japanese interests.[20] Recent examples of blurring the line between official propriety and Japanese money include James Lake, who retained his lucrative lobbying contracts with the Japanese while serving as a senior adviser to George Bush's 1988 presidential campaign. While negotiating with the Japanese government as a Defense Department official in 1988, James Auer solicited money from Japanese companies to fund a center for Japanese studies he planned to establish at Vanderbilt University.[21] It is difficult to dismiss as completely paranoid an unsubstantiated story that made the Washington trade gossip circuit in 1988, according to which the promotion of J. Michael Farren to undersecretary of Commerce had been blocked by representations from Japanese lobbyists unhappy with his tough stance on Japanese trade matters.

The diversification of intensive, effective Japanese lobbying outside Washington officially began with Toshiba Corporation's efforts in 1987–88 to defeat the import ban proposed by Congress in retaliation for the illegal technology sales discussed in chapter 2. Paid at least $9 million, the who's who list of lobbyists retained by Toshiba shrewdly expanded the argument that the parent company should not be punished for deeds it allegedly knew nothing about. Hundreds of American companies were galvanized to bombard Washington with the message that, as users of Toshiba parts and components, they and their workers would be hurt if imports of all Toshiba products were banned. The several thousand American workers of Toshiba's U.S. subsidiaries were urged to express to their senators and congressmen strong opposition to the proposed trade sanctions on the grounds that their jobs were at stake. Clever lobbying changed the image of Toshiba from a dispensable seller of consumer electronics in the United States to that of an irreplaceable vendor of inputs to U.S. manufacturers. The resulting Congressional retreat from its desire to impose strong sanctions on the company provides a vivid illustration of declining U.S. leverage in retaliating against Japanese imports at an acceptable cost.

The accusation that some Japanese foreign direct investment is made in politically strategic congressional districts may or may not be true. But U.S. employees—whose numbers are now counted in the hundreds of thousands—of Japanese manufacturing and service subsidiaries do write their congressional representatives to rebuke them for anti-Japanese legislation. And it is getting difficult to find governors, often the chief pitchmen for luring new foreign investments to their states, who are openly critical of Japanese trade practices. This spread of Japanese lobbying and influence buying caused a seemingly pro-Japanese State Department think tank to conclude "the United States has been penetrated—not only by Japanese autos and VCRs, but by Japanese influence peddling at every level."[22]

Can the prospect of six-digit retainers affect attitudes toward Japan by appointees taking a stint in the upper strata of U.S. trade policy-making? The correct answer probably is yes, for some people at some time to some degree. At best, persons with intimate knowledge of U.S. trade policy-making and access to influential officials help to enhance the economic position of their country's single greatest foreign competitor. At worst, a climate of suspicion is unfolding in which questions of impropriety arise ever more easily and more often, as in the decision by former president Ronald Reagan to accept a reported $2 million from a Japanese media company for a short speaking tour in 1989. Reports that Reagan defended Sony Corporation's purchase of Columbia Pictures at the same time his representatives were discussing a contribution from that company to the Reagan library[23] raise the implication that the sweet allure of Japanese megabucks might someday find its way into the Oval Office.

Another example of the growing climate of suspicion unfolded in January 1990, in the wake of the resignation of a Foreign Service officer to join the Washington office of the Fujitsu Corporation. His experience with formulating U.S. high-tech trade policy toward Japan generated major press stories for a job shift that just a few years ago would have gone completely unnoticed. While there were no suggestions of unethical behavior, fear was expressed that his insights would help his new employer outmaneuver the U.S. government—part of a larger perceived repercussion of the lobbying imbalance. Representatives of U.S. companies increasingly worry about disclosing proprietary business information when seeking official assistance: "We are reluctant to give the U.S. government basic data because it will go right to the Japanese," said one lawyer.[24]

A final disquieting factor is the failure of the U.S. government and U.S. industry to develop any significant lobby in Japan. Although Japanese-speaking U.S. business representatives and lawyers based in Tokyo are less rare than formerly, U.S. business interests face a much more closed society, where the very thought of trade officials leaving government to push U.S. imports is out of the question. In response to his inquiry what would happen if his company hired a high MITI official to represent it, a U.S. businessman was told by a friend in MITI "It would not happen, but if it did we would pay him not the slightest heed. We would treat him courteously, but he would become a social leper."[25] Under the Japanese system of *amakudari* (literally "descent from heaven"), retiring civil servants are

regularly placed in lucrative management positions with *Japanese* companies, often those that the bureaucrat had regulated.

Part of the responsibility for the lack of reciprocal lobbying rests with
U.S. business. Because so few U.S. manufacturers have built up a lucrative
export market in Japan, only a small handful of U.S. companies feel the
need to communicate directly with Japanese government officials and opinion makers or to pay out the large sums necessary to house U.S. lobbying
and public relations specialists in Tokyo.

The overall failure of more than two decades of U.S.–Japanese negotiations is only the surface manifestation of systemic factors promoting
Japan's trade and industrial ascendancy. The United States engaged in a
fantasy pursuit of export expansion and competitive parity with Japan's
industry. The long, detailed negotiating process produced numerous but
only marginal responses. Genuine progress was elusive because trade officials and political leaders in both countries found it comfortable to concentrate only on immediate, specific symptoms of the underlying economic
disequilibrium.

CHAPTER 8

Arguing Japan's Case Against the United States

The United States has continuously refused to admit its declining competitive power as the true cause of the existing trade friction and has continued to maintain that it has been a victim of cheap labor, dumping, and other unfair export practices by Japan.

—Naohiro Amaya, former MITI vice-minister, 1980

The inevitability of ambiguity and the preponderance of perception over reality have been recurring themes in this book. The Japanese version continues to differ radically from that of the United States, owing to the deeply divergent values and needs that each country brings to the area of foreign trade. The resultant communication gap is inherent in the systemic bilateral problem.

In this and the next chapter, we will take an unorthodox approach to the disparities with which each side views the causes and nature of trade frictions. The first effort at role-playing assumes the voice of a well-informed Japanese or pro-Japanese observer to give the Japanese position in the manner of a lawyer presenting the most complete, compelling argumentation possible in support of a client (not always limited to what the author thinks is accurate, fair, or consistent). This chapter should be read as a unit with the comparable effort to articulate the very dissimilar U.S. position in the chapter that follows.

AMBIGUOUS SELF-PERCEPTIONS: THE FRAGILE OUTSIDER

Japan's successful pursuit of international industrial power has failed to quench the country's long-standing, intense feelings of vulnerability and isolation. The growing self-perception of "Japan as Number One" continues to be tempered by a sense that the fates remain unkind to Japan. The Japanese see their culture, political system, and economy as fragile. The country lacks critical natural resources. It is subject to a variety of natural disasters. It is not part of any regional grouping of countries. Militarily, its small, crowded islands are especially vulnerable in the missile age. It continues to face a struggle already many centuries old to preserve its vastly different social order from encroachment by foreign cultures.

Few foreigners appreciate Japanese accomplishments or sympathize with their economically precarious position. Worse yet, it is widely believed that the physically and spiritually distant foreigners heavily influence the economic destiny of the country. Actions taken, or not taken, by most of the world have been and will continue to be major variables in the prosperity of the economy. The resulting sense of dependency on other countries has made the Japanese hypersensitive to foreign actions that are deemed injurious to their interests.

If a typical Japanese were asked to provide a brief history of the country's international economic relations since 1969, that person undoubtedly would focus on external shocks, not Japan's industrial export boom. The early 1970s included a U.S. triad of shocks in 1971—declaration of a New Economic Policy, a presidential visit to China, and threatened implementation of the Trading with the Enemy Act to end the textile dispute—and the soybean embargo of 1973. But the economic effects were mild compared with the two OPEC oil price increases of 1973–74 and 1979–80. Spiraling oil prices posed the greatest danger yet to the postwar economic prosperity and were incontrovertible proof to most Japanese that their economic fortunes ultimately depended on the actions of others. Suddenly, Japan was confronted with economic problems unknown since the 1940s: recession, sharp inflation, and shortages. The country saw all of this as a brutally clear signal that its luck had run out: the economic miracle had been derailed. The virtual 100 percent import dependence on oil only encouraged this notion.

Japan's growing trade surplus in the 1980s reflected its ability to organize itself better than other societies in the universal pursuit of economic prosperity. Japan should have been viewed abroad as a role model. Instead, jealousy and the inherent inability of foreigners to understand the Japanese culture caused Japan to be wrongly viewed as a predator and a threat to the economic stability of other countries. The continuation of the Japanese economic miracle in the eighties was all the more remarkable in view of the incessant pressures imposed by growing foreign protectionism, rapid yen appreciation, and nonstop foreign demands to reduce trade barriers and restructure business practices. Even the quick ability of the Japanese economy to recover from both of the OPEC price shocks has failed to instill a sense of serenity and security in the Japanese psyche. The overconfidence that prevailed in the United States through the 1970s was inappropriate for people who have suffered throughout their history from earthquakes, tidal waves, and typhoons and who in 1945 suffered atomic bombings.

The Japanese are not prone to gloating about their achievements, but it is galling to have their trading partners insist that Japan's gains were achieved outside of the realms of the natural and well deserved. Instead of learning from the Japanese, the other industrial countries keep Japan on the defensive, demanding greater access to its market and reduced exports. Japan's economic accomplishments generated little in the way of affection or respect by other countries. Discomfort and dismay were the common reactions in the United States and elsewhere.

Japan has become an elite minority. No matter how hard it worked, it could not envision itself achieving the social status and peace of mind possessed by the Anglo-Saxon establishment. At the back of its collective mind, Japan continued to worry about the Europeans and North Americans becoming actively hostile and turning on it. Economic success was inevitably precarious. Underdog status despite global economic superpower continues the historical pattern of Japan's being spiritually distant from other industrial countries. They have never welcomed Japan as a full partner in the community of nations. Twentieth-century Japan "has stood forlornly out in the cold, selling her wares to passers-by, and peering in longingly through the tightly closed windows of the world councils. Even when the door has been opened to Japanese participation, the Japanese have felt that they have not been treated as genuine equals."[1]

In a word, the common cultural bonds that link Western Europe and North America are not applicable to Japan; the Atlantic Alliance and the Atlantic Community have no Pacific counterparts. Sensitivities have also been magnified by the racial factor: It is not unusual when European imports are more tolerated in the United States and U.S.–European trade disputes are settled in a friendlier, more familylike manner.

A treaty concluded in 1922 at the Washington Naval Conference established a 5:5:3 ratio in heavy warships and aircraft carriers for the United States, the United Kingdom, and Japan, respectively. A conceptual similarity could be drawn between this hierarchy and the "voluntary" export quota agreements beginning with cotton textiles, negotiated since the early 1960s.

Japanese economic accomplishments are seldom appreciated or praised by other countries, and Japanese frustrations hardly can be put to rest by the typical U.S. and European responses to Japan's export successes. Japan's trade practices have been widely damned as being unfair. Respect for Japan's miraculous economic performance has been almost drowned in a stream of fatuous accusations of exploited labor, government subsidies, dumping, a rigged exchange rate, trade barriers, cultural prejudice against foreign-made products, industrial targeting, collusive business practices, and even of continuing World War II through economic aggression. In short, Western arrogance has sought solace in the belief that somehow the Japanese economy behaves *differently from, not better than* other capitalist economies. Whatever feelings of superiority that the Japanese might have relative to other countries are discounted in the global double standard that judges Japanese trade successes more harshly than all other countries. Hardly anyone notices or cares that West Germany's current account surplus is growing so rapidly that it is projected by the OECD to outpace Japan's in 1990 and 1991.[2] Nor is anyone bothered by the fact that the West German current account surplus, as a percentage of GNP, was well above Japan's from 1987 through 1989.[3] Despite the decline in Japan's current account surpluses and the rise in West Germany's, international criticism is virtually all directed towards the former.

"SCAPEGOATABILITY" AND RACISM

There is a widespread feeling among Japanese that they are made scapegoats for U.S. frustrations. The economic criticisms, demands, and hostility that have come to dominate the U.S. attitude toward Japan are viewed as poor substitutes for acceptance by the United States of its decline in industrial competitiveness. Instead of blaming reduced production, lost jobs, declining market shares, and a growing trade deficit on internal weaknesses and mistakes, it is more convenient to blame these problems on foreign duplicity. It is all too simple to say the source of these problems is the inequitable, unfair, and sometimes illegal trade practices used by a conspiratorial "Japan, Inc." to undermine U.S. industrial vigor.

By failing even remotely to reciprocate the scale of Japanese study of U.S. political and economic trends, the United States limits itself to a superficial understanding, leading to unfair criticism. Foreign ignorance of current Japanese economic realities is somewhat excused because of the mysteries of the Japanese language. Foreigners can be forgiven for being forced to rely on a handful of Western correspondents in Japan and occasional translations of books, articles, and speeches. Foreigners do not seem to be forgiven for not recognizing Japanese sincerity as presented in numerous goodwill missions in North America and Western Europe. The Japanese probably cannot understand why their message is not getting through. They feel that the problem goes beyond distorted images and obsolete impressions of their country. It is easy to read racist connotations in the internal European Community paper, leaked to the press in 1979, that branded the Japanese as economic animals who live in "what Westerners would regard as little more than rabbit hutches." Cultural factors are frivolously cited as allowing unfair economic advantages: exploitation of workers, chronic workaholic tendencies, vigorous government planning, acceptance of business cartels, and so forth. Japan's sense of equity is constantly being challenged in allegations that it applies different standards to the desirable flow of its exports and imports.

While admitting a tardiness in liberalizing tariff and nontariff barriers to imports, most Japanese are at a loss to understand why Americans and others refuse to accept the repeated contention that their market is now as open to foreign goods as that of any other country. Perhaps it is simpler for foreigners to complain than to engage in the hard work required to succeed in the Japanese market. Why, the Japanese wonder, don't more foreigners understand that success in their highly competitive market is difficult even for Japanese companies and that bankruptcies are common. U.S. credibility is further undermined in the eyes of the Japanese by the manner in which their numerous import liberalization packages have been greeted in the United States, invariably being dismissed as inconsequential, repetitious, or even devious. It might even be argued that more U.S. effort is put into finding loopholes and qualifications in new liberalization packages than in planning appropriate export promotion.

Until the Japanese perceive that U.S. companies are investing the same resources in penetrating their market as Japanese companies invest developing export markets, there will be little sympathy for foreign complaints about a closed market. "Effort gap" is often alluded to in official statements. The 1981 MITI White Paper on International Trade featured a large table comparing overseas representation. It showed that Japanese business had 21,644 employees stationed at 931 offices located in the United States and that U.S. business had 1,628 employees at 167 offices in Japan. If data were available on ability to speak fluently the native language, these statistical contrasts would have been far more dramatic.

There is little or no acceptance in Japan of the notion that its export success is a function of industrial policy, predatory dumping, a closed home market, a "free ride" in the international arena, or any other insidious or unfair practice. Instead, success is attributed to Japanese virtues and to shortcomings in the United States, Europe, and elsewhere. The Japanese would agree with Shakespeare's Julius Caesar that, "The fault, dear Brutus, is not in our stars, but in ourselves." They resolutely reject the popular U.S. conception that local industry is the hopeless victim of conspiracy by an export-crazed Japan, Inc.

There is agreement on both sides that someone is not doing the right thing. The Japanese believe that the United States and others are the transgressors because they work too little at staying competitive and spend too much time complaining. It is inexcusable to many Japanese that the United States (and Europe) would watch helplessly as Japan took over such a large market share for so many manufactured goods without taking drastic remedial efforts to beat the foreign competition. When Japan's mask of politeness is removed, as is now being done with increasing frequency, the result has been lectures to Westerners on their lack of will, misplaced priorities, loss of work ethic, and excessive emphasis on self-gratification. The Japanese have adopted the typical attitude of a country with a chronic trade or balance of payments surplus: the principal source of problems is the shortcomings of the deficit country; it is the latter that should take the blame and the bitter medicine to adjust. (This was precisely the European attitude toward the chronic U.S. balance of payments deficits in the 1960s.)

The Japanese, as scapegoats, feel no need to apologize. They refuse to serve as the excuse for others' weaknesses. In the words of Honda's former chairman, Hideo Sugiura, "What started with complaints about textiles and other manufactured goods turned into antidumping laws, escape clauses and attacks on Japanese culture. It seems the Americans feel they can no longer win in the marketplace—so they have to attack in other ways."[4]

Japanese distaste for their role as number one international trade scapegoat is summed up in a single question: Why must we be penalized for working hard and well? Neither the Americans nor any other foreign critic have been able to provide an adequate answer. In the breach, perhaps inevitably, the view has risen that the question has less to do with economics than with race. The emerging spokesman for this position is the controversial Shintaro Ishihara, a right-wing member of the Diet, former Transport Minister, and coauthor (with Akio Morita) of the best seller, *The Japan That Can Say No.* In a *New York Times* essay, he argues "At the root of Japanese-American tensions over defense, trade, and investment is the American establishment's smug assumption of racial superiority. . . . The United States must shed the pernicious delusion that modernization equals Westernization."[5] "Right now," he added, "the modern civilization built by whites is coming close to a period of practical end, and I feel that is adding to the irritation of Americans as the postwar representative of whites."[6] Failure of white societies to recognize the need to learn from the advances of Japan and other nonwhite societies, he believes, blinds the former to the need to adjust to a new technological era, causing them to fall further behind in the economic race. The 1988 U.S. omnibus trade bill appeared to direct so many provisions at Japan that Trade Minister Tamura was similarly moved to assert the legislation was protectionist and motivated by "anti-Japanese feeling and racial discrimination."[7]

UNCLE SAM: A LAZY BULLY?

The government and business leaders of postwar Japan have, until recently, all belonged to the generation that surrendered to the United States, lived under one of history's most benevolent military occupations, and continued to look to the United States as a source of both economic inspiration and political stability. Neither country was prepared for the speed and breadth of Japan's challenge to U.S. industry beginning in the late 1960s. Most Japanese viewed their growing trading power with bewilderment and supposed the situation could reverse itself at any minute. Nor were they prepared for what later became a habitual U.S. recourse to pressure tactics. Expectations that one more concession would put trade frictions to rest turned to despair in the 1980s, as it seemed the United

States would remain mired in a state of self-pity rather than get its own economic house in order.

Many Japanese believe that during the 1969–89 period, the United States acted in a manner unbecoming a political and economic superpower. A lot of mistakes were made, and attempts by Americans to correct them were too few and too late. Priorities drifted away from traditional U.S. values. Japan was resented for practicing some of them, such as hard work and risk taking. And perhaps worst of all, the United States was suddenly given to extreme, erratic actions—as exemplified by the Nixon shocks of 1971. Most Japanese, like most Americans, assumed that the problems facing U.S. productivity and competitiveness were reversible. Hence, there was little sympathy in Japan for the propensity of the United States to demand economic policy changes more from the Japanese than from themselves.

As the Americans stopped acting like Americans, they seemingly began to urge the Japanese not to act like Japanese. Former Commerce Secretary Malcolm Baldrige declared in December 1981 that because Japanese "cultural traditions" were a major cause of their bilateral trade surplus, they "simply have to be changed because . . . Japan now has the second largest economy in the free world."[8] The U.S. government was also perceived as preferring to change the rules of the international trading order rather than improve U.S. economic performance. One Japanese scholar argued:

> In some ways current U.S.–Japanese relations . . . resemble a card game where one player wins continuously. The loser, unwilling to accept the full blame for a poor showing, asserts that the rules of the game are unfair, while the winner is intent on explaining why the old rules are reasonable. Obviously, if it is mutually beneficial to continue the game, the rules will have to be changed with mutual agreement. U.S.–Japanese relations are now at the point where new rules must be sought and it is probable that both sides will be forced to make sacrifices.[9]

The Japanese have viewed continuing foreign demands for greater access to their market as punitive, rather than positive calls for a better international division of labor. The missionary zeal that sometimes characterizes U.S. negotiating objectives bewilders the Japanese. The general U.S. perception of Japan as a closed market often is dismissed as sheer ignorance of changing commercial conditions. Foreign complaints about Japan being an antiforeign, conspiratorial society, because of a unique mentality, a difficult language, and a tightly knit government-business relationship, are widely interpreted as insulting and outrageous distortions.

Japan's once-unequivocal image of superior U.S. economic strength, together with its dependence on the United States for military security, created a special sensitivity to U.S. demands. Until the 1980s, it seemed difficult for most Japanese to perceive that a vigorous bilateral dialogue could take place between economic, or at least industrial, equals. Demands for trade concessions were viewed as an inscrutable form of confrontation that threatened Japan's sovereignty. Sensationalized newspaper headlines spread the idea that the Japanese were becoming cornered. U.S. pressure tactics were deeply resented as intruding into Japanese domestic policy-making. Japanese sensitivities were eloquently summed up in the statement, "Many in the United States insist on attacking Japan's identity—its society, its economic structure, its political system, and its language. Yet the U.S. refuses to recognize the internal roots of its own failure."[10]

Some Japanese acknowledge that positive contributions can come from external U.S. pressures to force their government to initiate economically desirable but politically difficult trade liberalization measures. But the economic ends don't justify the harsh political means. An illogical U.S. negotiating cycle begins with a single U.S. industry's complaint and escalates to an issue of national importance. This symbol of commercial injustice is then relayed to the Japanese as a matter of urgency that requires response if unpleasant consequences, presumably retaliation, are to be avoided. Hajime Ohta, a Japanese economist writing for a U.S. audience, outlines what happens next:

> In response to these demands, Japan's reaction usually takes the form of a pledge to "try our best." After domestic negotiations and inter-ministerial adjustment, when Japan comes up with what it thinks is an adequate step toward improvement, these measures are evaluated by American negotiators as but a first step toward the ultimate goal. One after another, demands have been introduced in a similar pattern, dressed in political garb, on beef, citrus, leather, tobacco and government procurement. While there may have been some slight improvement in the bilateral trade figures as a result of American pressure on these items, many of them are of peripheral importance. Yet the political manner in which they were raised and the attention they received from the media gave the impression to the U.S. public that Japan is a closed market, and that the Japanese are the prime cause of the deficit in the American balance of payments figures. Neither Japanese nor American officials should view these problems as fundamental economic issues between the two countries.[11]

By the early 1980s, U.S. "aggressiveness" began to concentrate on the high-tech sector. The Japanese interpretation of the so-called IBM industrial espionage case well illustrates their reaction to this latest phase of the U.S. response to the Japanese challenge. The Japanese press probably gave at least ten times the coverage of the U.S. press to the 1982 arrest in

California of Hitachi and Mitsubishi Electric employees. In Japan, the wrongdoing of those companies in illegally purchasing secret, proprietary business information about IBM computers became a secondary issue to the perception of yet another form of "Japan bashing." Most Japanese believed that their country was being singled out and persecuted because of the rapid progress made by their computer industry and large bilateral trade surplus. The fact that the accused were caught in an undercover FBI operation—a tactic virtually unknown in Japan—added to the perception of unfairness. The mistaken belief that the IBM Corporation had masterminded the sting led to outright anger and calls for boycott against IBM Japan. The arrested Japanese businessmen retained public sympathy in their country even after transcripts of some of their conversations with undercover FBI agents were released, leaving no doubt about their guilt.

Each passing year brings new complaints and new forms of intimidation. What began as a series of disputes on specific products blossomed into comprehensive U.S. contempt for the Japanese economic system. This contempt, in turn, is seen as one part jealousy and two parts ignorance. Americans need to understand that Japan's comparative advantage is based on its blessing of skilled, dedicated managers and workers and the curse of minimal natural resources. The result is a distinctive, logical foreign trade structure: importing raw materials, adding value to them, and exporting finished goods. A few U.S. economists, such as Gary Saxonhouse, have concluded that "foreign access to the Japanese market would have to be considered excellent [and] foreign penetration of the Japanese market is equivalent to the experiences of other major industrial countries."[12] Quantitative studies have been unable to show that Japan's import behavior is different from other countries when allowances are made for differences in Japan's economic circumstances (resource endowment, geographic distance from trading partners, and so forth). Japan's export sector, 12 to 15 percent of overall GNP, is small in comparison with European countries. In sum, the Japanese believe that foreigners should understand that the pattern of their trade in fact reflects international market forces rather than government policies or cultural practices.

The government of Japan publicly rejects the notion that the imbalance in bilateral trade is an outgrowth of the closed nature of the Japanese market, asserting that Japanese import barriers—tariff and nontariff—compare favorably with those of any country, including the United States. The Report of the Japan–United States Economic Relations Group (the so-called Wisemen) in 1981 noted that "in terms of average tariff levels and quotas on manufactured products, Japan's market . . . will be no more closed than that of the United States. Indeed, given informal U.S. 'quotas' in the form of orderly marketing arrangements, Japan's market may well be less closed." While not denying that a number of informal practices and a bureaucratic legacy of administrative controls still inhibited imports, the report concluded "Japan appears to be generally meeting its international obligations to provide equal national treatment in those areas where there are treaties or international trade codes, and in this sense, Japan is playing according to the rules."[13]

Official sensitivity to charges that imports of manufactured goods are artificially low is seen in a government rebuttal to the statistic that Japan's annual imports of manufactured goods were approximately equivalent in value to those of Switzerland, a country with one-tenth the GNP.

> Such a comparison is misleading and illogical. Small countries in general are required to specialize in a narrow range of industries. (Switzerland, for instance, specializes in services.) Since they rely upon foreign countries for most of their manufactured goods, they have much higher ratios of manufactured goods to GNP than do larger nations. . . .
>
> If one uses this sort of twisted logic, then it would seem that the United States does not import enough manufactured goods, when compared with Belgium, for instance. America's GNP is 22 times larger than Belgium's, yet U.S. manufactured imports ($137 billion in 1980) are only about twice the value of Belgium's manufactured imports ($60 billion). Does this imply that the United States has a restrictive policy toward manufactured imports?[14]

U.S. businesspersons appear to be behind the times in realizing that economic trends are changing dramatically in Japan. In the wake of the the Group of Seven's macroeconomic policy changes with the September 1985 Plaza Agreement, Japan's economy has shifted from being export-driven to one based on domestic expansion. The number of foreign firms successfully selling in the Japanese market also has proliferated. Some things have not changed, however, such as the need for hard work, long-term commitment, and export hunger as the prerequisites for succeeding in Japan. Other Asian countries have begun to echo the long-standing Japanese complaint that all too many U.S. manufacturers, especially small and medium-sized ones, still fail to learn the details of exporting and refuse to adapt their production to the often specialized and demanding needs of foreign consumers. There is nothing in foreign trade theory that says Japanese officials need to beg U.S. companies to export or are obliged to establish export advisory facilities in the United States to offset the lack of overseas U.S. business representation.

Japanese trade statistics show that Japan's total imports of *manufactured* goods almost doubled from 1986 through 1988, rising from $44 to $85.6 billion in just two years. Japanese imports (of all goods) from the United States jumped by two-thirds from 1986 to 1989 ($29 billion to $48 billion).[15] The three main reasons for this upsurge—increasingly open markets, yen appreciation, and strong domestic growth—evidence a new phase in Japanese foreign trade relations. To the extent that imports of U.S.

products into the expanding Japanese market do not grow as fast on average as those from other major countries, the problem is in the U.S. export sector, not Japan's import sector.

In Japanese eyes the United States is a lazy bully that needs to clean up its act. To an increasing number of Japanese, the U.S. system is breaking down. Its arteries are hardening. Americans have it wrong about bilateral relations, and the Japanese are incorrectly being indicted as the source of the problem. Yielding to an endless series of unreasonable, unjustified American demands is neither a politically acceptable approach to the problem by a grown up Japan nor an economically rational path to a solution.

Some Japanese officials and economists continue to urge an acceleration in Japanese purchases of U.S. goods regardless of the legitimacy of U.S. demands: the United States may be a whining bully, but it is still the biggest player in the trade game. Increased imports by Japan could offset complaints of individual companies and workers adversely impacted by Japanese competition. Americans would call this a case of discretion being the better part of valor; the French might call it noblesse oblige. To the Japanese, it is a necessary sacrifice: appeasing unfair critics to avoid protectionist retaliation even after the need is ended to reduce import barriers, since they now exist only in the minds of lazy foreigners.

SHORTCOMINGS OF U.S. ECONOMIC POLICIES AND BUSINESS PRACTICES

The United States is seen by many Japanese as a country in permanent decline; sympathetic Japanese see some U.S. slippage in industrial competition as inevitable given the artificially high starting base after World War II. For the cynics, the explosion of the space shuttle Challenger in January 1986 was the benchmark for many Japanese for the snowballing downhill drift of U.S. technological leadership. Debilitated by violent crime, drugs, deteriorating inner cities, illiteracy, racial strife, the penchant for immediate self-gratification, as well as the mindless pursuit of mergers and acquisitions as if corporations were tradeable commodities, the United States is not even doing a good job in reversing the home-grown sources of its deterioration, let alone keeping pace with the drive and organization of Japan's industrial sector.

The Japanese see little *economic* significance in their bilateral trade surplus with the United States—a feeling exactly duplicated in U.S. thinking about the once-chronic U.S. trade surplus with European countries. Bilateral trade balances don't matter; it is the multilateral trade balance that is economically significant. The current account balance, which measures services as well as merchandise trade, is more important than the trade balance. The large U.S. services surpluses, mainly due to repatriated earnings from overseas investments, were sufficient in the late 1970s and early 1980s to either offset or exceed the U.S. multilateral merchandise trade deficit. With either minimal deficits or small surpluses in the overall current account, the U.S. trade deficit with Japan arguably should not have been viewed as a major drag on the overall U.S. balance of payments position.[16]

Economically sophisticated Japanese argue that the ballooning of the U.S. trade deficit in the mid-1980s was independent of economic events or conditions in Japan; the culprit was macroeconomic imbalance in the United States. The universal deterioration of the U.S. multilateral trade deficit—Japan's role being only proportional—is proof that the overvalued dollar and oversized federal budget deficit relative to savings caused the record trade deficits suffered by the United States since the advent of Reaganomics. Although the dollar's exchange rate has retreated from its peaks, there remains general agreement, even among U.S. economists, the trade deficit will persist as long as domestic savings fail to finance the government deficit and private investment (see page 106).

The advent of the structural impediments talks in 1989 (see page 49) gave the Japanese a long-awaited opportunity to vent their dismay and displeasure at a wide array of U.S. trade policies. Having made the discussion of U.S. structural impediments a quid pro quo for discussing Japanese structural impediments to balanced trade, the Japanese wasted no time in cataloguing instances of U.S. mismanagement. Besides reducing the federal deficit and increasing savings, the Japanese argue that the United States must relax its antitrust laws (the Justice Department case against IBM that spanned the 1970s was seen by many Japanese as extreme madness), lengthen the time horizon of U.S. business leaders, reduce the cost of capital to industry, accelerate corporate investment in plant and equipment, increase government incentives for corporate R&D, and ease export restrictions.[17] In addition, the Japanese pointed to the need for the United States to upgrade education, especially in the areas of science, mathematics, and foreign languages, as well as industrial programs for training and retraining workers.

Since the bilateral disequilibrium cannot be solved solely by changes within Japan, the Japanese argue that major changes in their remaining structural impediments to trade would be largely useless lacking U.S. reforms. The bottom line, therefore, is that the United States must remedy its own self-inflicted structural shortcomings in order to reverse its competitive inadequacies. This argument is developed further by Takashi Eguchi: Japanese internal measures cannot offset the external phenomenon of a rising U.S. demand for Japanese products. "Therefore, unless the U.S. begins to produce more goods that can compete against Japanese products, no matter how much effort is made by Japan to promote a restructuring and reduce the imbalance, such efforts will not be sufficient."[18]

If trade is viewed as a competitive game between corporations, U.S.

industrial companies are the primary culprits causing U.S. competitive inadequacies. They are more anxious to import Japanese capital and intermediate and consumer goods (the latter often with U.S. brand names affixed) into the United States than to export goods to Japan. U.S. companies indirectly encourage trade disequilibrium by failing to satisfy the demands of U.S. consumers. Japan is not selling too much; the United States is buying too much. The recognition of corporate shortcomings has become so ingrained that no one is particularly shocked when U.S. customer satisfaction surveys for automobiles find Japanese cars occupying six of the top ten slots (with German cars accounting for another two).[19] As one automobile specialist (an American) colorfully put it, "While Detroit flogged away at the bankrupt notion that Americans could be bamboozled into buying oversize, outdated, cheaply built cars covered with a layer of vinyl and chrome glitz, the Japanese recognized that technology was the key to future sales."[20]

Many Japanese business specialists believe that in some critical sectors, mainly electronics, U.S. industry has the wrong dimensions. Too many companies are too small to absorb short-term losses or afford sufficient capital commitments for investment and R&D. U.S. companies repeatedly make the mistake of failing to invest in timely additions to plant capacity and are later unable to satisfy intensified domestic demand. Japanese shipments of machine tools in the late 1970s and of semiconductors in the early 1980s boomed because of inadequate U.S. production relative to rising demand. It is all but impossible to find a Japanese analyst who thinks that small, inventive U.S. semiconductor companies can match the financial benefits of massive vertical integration accorded their Japanese competitors (see chapter 3).

Japanese criticism is increasingly targeted at the inherent limitations of the short time horizons of U.S. managers. Sony's Morita, in the controversial *The Japan That Can Say No,* may have immortalized the notion of the ten-minute U.S. time horizon and argued that with their ten-year time horizon, Japanese industrialists would always outcompete the United States. He spoke for many Japanese, who see industrial production as the foundation of a strong national economy, in adding a note of concern about the costs of a (still unprovable) evolution of the United States to a post-industrial economy:

> when people forget how to produce goods, and that appears to be the case in America, they will not be able to supply themselves even with their most basic needs. . . . Business, in my mind, is nothing but "value added;" we must add value and wisdom to things and this [omission] is the most deplorable aspect of America today.[21]

Japanese critics join some Americans in condemning the emphasis in U.S. industry on making money by juggling financial assets instead of generating profits by making high quality goods and selling them in volume. U.S. business culture has become jaded, according to Hajime Ohta, the economist quoted earlier:

> Ideally, corporate profits should be the direct result of risk taking, efficient management of production and administration, technological innovation and investment in research and development. One gets the impression, however, that these characteristics of American business are on the decline, and instead ingredients for an American success story today—particularly over the short term—are effective lobbyists, lawyers, public relations and advertising agencies. Another relevant factor is that the U.S. government has never had a strong institutionalized concern for the national economy. Its responses to industry and union pressures, and crises in different areas and sectors, are at best ad hoc.[22]

There is also a "dark side" of the Japanese case against the United States, consisting of a minority view of reverse racism and blatant mercantilism. Among those Japanese who view their race as purer than and superior to others, there have been numerous claims for special forgiveness for Japanese reluctance to import. In 1988, a Japanese politician attributed low meat imports to Japanese people having longer intestines than others and therefore having more difficulty in digesting beef.[23] Japan argued for extraordinary safety specifications for skis in the mid-1980s on the grounds that Japanese snow was different. While still prime minister, Yasuhiro Nakasone angered many in the United States by quietly saying that blacks and Hispanics lowered the U.S. literacy level.[24] A mid-level official of Nippon Telegraph and Telephone claimed in 1983 that Japan "can manufacture a product of uniformity and superior quality because the Japanese are a race of completely pure blood, not a mongrelized race as in the United States."[25]

A few Japanese believe Japanese industry is so big and so good that it can—or should—produce virtually every manufactured good needed by Japanese consumers. In the spring of 1983, the head of a bilateral trade committee smugly announced that Japan was "importing lots of things we need: Parker pens, Cross pencils, and French neckties."[26] In August 1985, a few months before he became MITI minister, Michio Watanabe publicly announced that he saw nothing in the United States that anyone in Japan would want to buy.[27]

RHETORIC VS. REALITY IN U.S. TRADE POLICIES

The oft-repeated U.S. claim of having the world's most open market is greeted with skepticism in Japan. Viewed from the other side of the Pacific, Americans look like hypocrites, for liberal import policies seldom are practiced beyond the point where foreign competition causes disruption.

The market mechanism is allowed to function only as long as it is politically convenient; and a significant percentage of Japanese exports to the United States (cars, steel, semiconductors, machine tools, textiles, and others) have been limited by some form of export restraint or import duty.

The average Japanese knows far more than the average American about the various statutory measures the U.S. government uses to provide import relief to domestic producers. There is a widespread impression in Japan that their goods have been the primary target of official efforts to impede imports into the United States. A people uncomfortable with the imprecision and uncertainties of legal technicalities, the Japanese view the U.S. escape clause provision (applied to fair import competition), as well as the antidumping and countervailing duty statutes (applied to the unfair trade practices of sales at less than fair value and government subsidies to exporters, respectively) as major impediments to their ability to sell in the U.S. market.

Japanese industrial corporations have fostered and enriched an entire generation of foreign trade lawyers in Washington. As the number one exporter of goods that compete directly with U.S.–made products, the Japanese industrial sector sees itself on the defensive in Washington's various trade tribunals under both the "standard" import relief laws (that is, the escape clause and antidumping statutes) and innovative applications of other measures, such as antitrust legislation and Houdaille Industries' use of the Revenue Act of 1971 (see page 39). The fact that the U.S. executive branch only once unilaterally imposed import barriers in the 1969–89 period is no cause for rejoicing in Japan, since legal proceedings and other pressures frequently end with "voluntary" export restraints. As seen from Japan, the U.S. offensive against foreign import barriers arises from emotion rather than established trade rules and procedures. The so-called Super 301 provision of the 1988 trade bill (see pages 48–49) is seen to dangerously and illogically emphasize unilateralism. A MITI-sponsored study argues that here the United States "has assumed the roles of both prosecutor and judge" in a "wrong prescription . . . not likely to bear any fruitful results."[28]

The uncertainties and imprecision of U.S. trade and regulatory law are viewed in Japan as de facto trade barriers. Americans and Japanese alike can be intimidated merely by the threat of legal action: the U.S. legal process in general is sufficiently long and costly that only the rich, brave, or foolish ignore a threat of litigation. Even unsuccessful domestic efforts to obtain official import relief can impose burdensome costs on foreign competitors in the forms of legal fees and administrative costs, such as data preparation, document translations, and travel by corporate executives to the United States. According to one trade lawyer, whose clients are mainly importers,

> The uncertainty of the trade laws, and in particular of the dumping standard, is itself a significant trade barrier. The fact

that importers generally cannot know what prices or practices will be condemned as unfair naturally tends to inhibit price competition and thereby to serve a protectionist interest. In addition the multiplicity and overlap of the trade laws, combined with various substantive and procedural features of the law, tend to create incentives for domestic firms to use strategies of legal harassment to impose costs, delays or penalties on their foreign competitors. As a result, the perception is spreading in Japan and elsewhere that the United States market, though basically "open," has become a hazardous and hostile environment in which to do business.[29]

The mere initiation of antidumping proceedings temporarily can impose a chilling effect on imports, even if the U.S. government eventually rejects the domestic company's accusation of sales at less than fair value. Upon a preliminary determination of dumping, importers must post bonds or cash deposits to cover potential dumping margins that might in the future be retroactively assessed as import duties. The final dumping margin cannot be known in advance, introducing new uncertainties into the exporting effort. The dumping duty could exceed the importer's profit margin.

The capriciousness of the U.S. antidumping legislation is beyond description outside a law school textbook. The statute is very imprecise, with little reliance on standard accounting practices. The multiple variables and details make it virtually impossible to predict the results of a dumping investigation. Even U.S. lawyers have difficulty making sense of the law, and foreign corporations are hard pressed to assemble the incredibly obscure data demanded by government investigators. Why, then, should the Japanese exporters accused of dumping not believe they are the victims of a bizarre judicial mugging? Lawrence Walders, a Washington-based lawyer who represents Japanese clients in antidumping cases, says, "The hardest thing for me as a lawyer is to explain to my client why the U.S. government is doing this to them."[30]

The Japanese grievance list continues. A number of extraordinary actions have been taken that collectively cause the Japanese to believe that despite an absence of tariff and nontariff barriers, the U.S. system is poised to counterattack foreigners successfully developing an export market. For example:

- The four-pronged U.S. color TV offensive, including charges of illegal export subsidies, antitrust violations, unfair trade practices, and injury under the escape clause.

- The 1982 petition by Houdaille Industries alleging that an illegal cartel had been constructed as an integral part of Japanese industrial policy. Not only did the Japanese deny the existence of a cartel conspiracy, but they objected to what was perceived as an unwarranted intrusion into domestic economic policies.

- In a late 1981 encounter with "America, Inc.," the Japanese computer manufacturer Fujitsu saw congressional pressure persuade the American Telephone and Telegraph Corporation to reject the Japanese company's low bid on a major optical fiber telephone cable link between the major cities of the northeastern United States. The contract subsequently was awarded to the lowest *domestic* bidder, for reasons of national security. In fact, lobbying by domestic suppliers had triggered a backlash against Japanese dominance in the U.S. market in fiber optics, a prestigious high-tech sector.

- In 1987, the then Commerce Secretary Malcolm Baldrige and the Defense Department raised sufficient fuss about national security that the Fujitsu company voluntarily withdrew its offer to buy the troubled Fairchild Semiconductor Company— then owned by a French company.

- In 1987 MIT broke off negotiations to acquire a Japanese-made supercomputer when informed by a senior Commerce Department official that purchasers of such equipment might be liable for dumping duties if a subsequent investigation found sales at less than fair value and ensuing domestic injury.

Sometimes the Japanese get caught between demands from U.S. trade officials for organized export restraint and Justice Department enforcement of antitrust legislation. This happened with steel after the initial export restraint agreement in 1969 and later with semiconductors. In early 1982, U.S. semiconductor manufacturers of random access memory devices (RAMs) accused the Japanese of aggressive pricing actions to obtain worldwide market dominance in 64k RAMs. Simultaneously, U.S. defense officials voiced concern about the national security implications of dependence on Japanese producers for an important computer memory device. Japanese exports of these RAMs slowed thereafter and prices rose. Then, to the surprise of almost everyone, the Justice Department announced in the summer of 1982, it was formally investigating the marketing practices of six major Japanese semiconductor producers to determine whether the Japanese had conspired to fix prices or impose supply restrictions on 64k RAMs exported to the United States. Coincident with rising U.S. worries about predatory pricing, the Japanese 64k RAM producers apparently were confronted with genuine shortages that led to higher prices and fewer exports. U.S. trade officials and industry experts at first assumed the Japanese semiconductor producers deliberately restrained their 64k chip exports to the United States to mute complaints about unfair and excessive competition. The Japanese vendors blamed the shortfall on their lack of capacity to meet a sudden spurt of demand from U.S. computer manufacturers—itself partly due to earlier Japanese price cutting—on top of an equally unexpected surge in demand from Japanese makers of data-processing equipment. This explanation of why the 64k RAM market shifted almost overnight from a buyer's market to a seller's market apparently did not ring true to antitrust lawyers in the Justice Department, even though it was supported by market conditions.[31] The department closed the investigation in 1984, finding insufficient evidence to warrant prosecution.

U.S. demands for export restraints and the dangers posed by U.S. protectionist legislation have had the ironic effect of resurrecting old non-market economic policies. To minimize dumping accusations and disruptions of U.S. markets, MITI has increased its influence on export-pricing decisions. A cartel-like arrangement becomes necessary when Japanese exporters must artificially apportion market share among themselves for products covered by export restraints. Some of the attributes of the Japanese economic system most disliked in the United States are in fact encouraged by U.S. trade policies.

JAPAN'S RAPIDLY CHANGING TRADE POSITION

Japanese trade data for any year prior to 1988 fail to foretell the rapid changes that emerged at the end of the decade. The decline in Japan's multilateral trade surpluses and the upsurge in imports of manufactured goods are very recent—the lagging results of market-opening measures and exchange rate realignment that make arguments about unusual Japanese trade behavior based on mid-1980s trade data obsolete.

The recent statistics demonstrate "normalization" of the Japanese import sector. In 1989, Japan's overall trade surplus declined for the fourth consecutive year; measured in yen, imports increased by 21 percent over 1988. Preliminary data show that imports of manufactured goods more than doubled between 1986 and 1989, raising the share of manufactured goods in total imports. Shipments to Japan are growing quite rapidly: U.S. exports to that country in 1988 were up 35 percent over the previous year, and for the third quarter of 1989, up 20 percent over the comparable quarter in 1988. U.S. exports to the European Community for these two time periods were up only 25.5 percent and 9 percent, respectively.[32] Japanese imports of manufactured goods from the newly industrialized countries of Asia rose on average almost 50 percent annually between 1986 and 1988.[33] Import penetration ratios at the end of the 1980s were much greater than at the start of the decade for many technologically mature goods, such as black-and-white televisions, cameras, calculators, radio cassettes, and electric fans.[34]

Further changes can be anticipated and should further hush critics of Japan. Imports of manufactured goods will be stimulated by special tax incentives for Japanese companies announced in early 1990, added efforts by trading companies, as well as the growing popularity among Japanese consumers of catalogue shopping and franchised retail outlets, operations that as a whole are more favorably disposed to imported goods. Conversely, future increases in the export of manufactured goods should be moderated by the growing reliance by Japan's industrial giants on foreign direct investment to serve foreign markets. Rising sales in Japan by U.S.–controlled companies will soon contribute a major offset to the bilateral trade imbalance.

CONCLUSION

Japanese attitudes toward their trading success vis-à-vis the United States are characterized by three diverse feelings: pride, prejudice, and persecution. The Japanese feel they worked harder and acted more intelligently on an overall basis than their U.S. competition and received in return only criticism and threats. Paternalistic U.S. attitudes had ended by 1969. Like a selfish parent talking to a grown child, Uncle Sam kept asking Japan, "What have you done for me lately?" The Japanese response fell on deaf ears: "We have repeatedly restricted our exports to a self-proclaimed open market and bowed to your pressures to change our import practices and reduce our controls on incoming foreign investments."

Instead of gaining respect and emulation, Japan's successes as democratic capitalists were held up to scorn. Japanese trade policies were criticized and threatened with retaliatory actions. The Japanese people were put in a false, distorted light by foreign critics not above using racist slurs. They were still the elite minority and economic scapegoats. The Japanese have found relatively little security and foreign acceptance in their industrial miracle, the continuation of which rests partly in the hands of jealous non-Japanese.

By the end of the eighties, the Japanese became increasingly unable to hide their growing contempt for what they widely viewed as serious shortcomings in U.S. economic policies and business strategies. Shedding the role of quiet, deferential junior partner in the bilateral relationship, the Japanese echoed many voices within the U.S. economics community that remedies were urgently needed for such home-grown deficiencies as an overvalued dollar (at least until 1985), an excessively large federal deficit and inadequate savings, excessively short time horizons for U.S. managers, and lagging rates of productivity increases. The once-great superpower and mentor to a recovering Japan, having become enfeebled by its own doing, now clutched desperately to its fading power and prestige in a futile effort to contain a resurgent Japanese economy via political pressures rather than economic self-healing. The long-standing feeling of obligation in Japan to respond to U.S. demands began to be displaced by scorn.

CHAPTER 9

Arguing the U.S. Case Against Japan

How courteous is the Japanese;
He always says, "Excuse it, please."
He climbs into his neighbor's garden,
And smiles, and says, "I beg your pardon";
He bows and grins a friendly grin,
And calls his hungry family in;
He grins, and bows a friendly bow;
"So sorry, this my garden now."

—Ogden Nash, 1938

Yes, things are changing in Japan. And yes, the United States is far from perfect. But a very, very different story can also be told. The recent signs of moderation in Japan's reluctance to import and in its export aggressiveness can be dismissed as too little and too late, insignificant ripples in a two-thousand-year campaign to keep all things foreign at arm's length. In the minds of most Americans, overwhelming evidence justifies a hostile reaction to Japan's trade attitudes and performance since the end of the 1960s. Very few Americans yet believe that their goods can enter Japan's market as freely as Japanese goods enter the U.S. market; the search for reciprocity and an end to disequilibrium is seen to call for continued strong U.S. pursuit of equity—a level playing field.

This chapter mirrors the preceding chapter, giving the definitive U.S. indictment of Japan's trade actions; again, the arguments do not necessarily represent the author's views as to what is accurate and fair. By once again seeking critical exposition in lieu of scholarly objectivity, this chapter produces an interpretation of the causes of trade friction that is virtually 180 degrees different from the just-concluded brief for the Japanese viewpoint.

A UNIQUELY SELF-CENTERED AND INSULAR VALUE SYSTEM

If there is one thing worse than a bad loser, it is an ungracious winner who does not know when to ease up. Americans are not alone in suspecting that

183

other countries are viewed from Japan as existing primarily to provide that country with export markets. The Japanese seem to be arch-mercantilists running amok in fanatical pursuit of global market shares and trade surpluses. The Japanese export compulsion, in the eyes of critics, is matched in intensity only by the subtlety of the web of devices and attitudes that enmesh foreigners seeking entry into Japanese markets.

Some see the Japanese mentality as so distant from the Western values that dominate the international trading system that Japan cannot help being the most conspicuous outsider of the global economic order. Advocates of this approach would agree that the opening lines of Ruth Benedict's now classic 1946 study of Japanese culture, *The Chrysanthemum and the Sword,* remain applicable to Japan's deviant international economic behavior in the 1990s:

> The Japanese were the most alien enemy the United States had ever fought in an all-out struggle. In no other war with a major foe had it been necessary to take into account such exceedingly different habits of acting and thinking.[1]

Henry Kissinger made a similar argument in his diplomatic memoirs:

> Two peoples could hardly be more different than the pragmatic, matter-of-fact, legally oriented, literal Americans, and the complex, subtle Japanese, operating by allusion and conveying their meaning through an indirect, almost aesthetic sensitivity rather than words. . . . Japan's achievements—and occasionally its setbacks—have grown out of a society whose structure, habits, and forms of decision-making are so unique as to insulate Japan from all other cultures.[2]

Japan's differences could be viewed abroad as quaint and charming only until the 1970s when it emerged as the world's most successful, aggressive exporter of manufactured goods. Japan's intense insular mentality might have remained of little note in other countries had its export ascendancy come more gradually or its imports of manufactured goods been greater. An annual trade surplus in manufactured goods that soars above $100 billion draws attention, and Japan's political leaders, senior bureaucrats, and business leaders were slow to respond to warnings from foreign friends about its increasingly disruptive impact on the international trading system. The Japanese establishment failed to anticipate or understand the intensity of the rest of the world's growing uneasiness with Japan's chronic trade surpluses and apparently closed market. Instead, it foolishly believed outsiders would respect the hard work that underlay the surpluses and patiently accept both Japan's sincerity and its unilateral timetable for only very gradually assuming greater international economic responsibilities.

Critics of Japan point to its failure to exercise responsible, visionary, benevolent international leadership commensurate with its expanding economic power. Japan's reluctance to spread its philosophy or promote its interests throughout the international order is very different from the attitude displayed by the United States in its "call to leadership" in the late 1940s, when virtually overnight it abandoned its isolationist foreign policy in favor of global responsibility. The United States assumed unprecedented burdens in the creation of a new international order: it defined its self-interest in the broadest possible terms, including the needs of new as well as old friends. Winston Churchill once said "the price of greatness is responsibility." During the 1970s and much of the 1980s, the Japanese felt no obligation to pay the price the United States deemed appropriate for them; they saw their responsibility limited to their own economy.

The Japanese are survivors rather than visionaries. Their insular, parochial society opens them to the criticism of remaining indifferent to the rest of the world. If a given country is not buying cars from Japan or selling it petroleum, "that society does not interest us at all," said a Japanese intellectual. "The rest of the world is interesting only as it affects Japan."[3] The typical Japanese citizen is unmoved by the economic plight of foreigners, and limited in the ability or desire to see situations from others' points of view. The suspicion endures that Japan's fondest wish is for self-sufficiency; autarky would free the Japanese of dependence on foreigners for raw materials and export markets. With an increasing sense of external economic responsibility throughout the 1980s, Japan has become a source of cash for needy countries, but not yet a source of ideas or an open market. It still lowers import barriers only under duress, not from any belief that economic liberalization to promote the free market is a virtue in itself. The Japanese economic system seems incapable of selflessness. In the harsh words of Senator John Danforth (R., MO): "What sets Japan apart is this: No other nation contributes so little to the open trading system of the world, in proportion to what it gains."[4]

Critics of Japanese trade actions and attitudes tire of listening to seemingly endless justifications and excuses. In explaining individual trees, Japan and its apologists have lost sight of the forest: all specific issues have now been swamped by the negative foreign perception generated by the totality of Japanese behavior. Even if particular Japanese rebuttals are reasonable,

> it is also reasonable to regard each of these arguments as simply self-serving, as a rationale advanced by a nation that defines its self-interest narrowly and takes selfish advantage whenever and wherever it can. All of Japan's interactions with the rest of the world in trade, investment, aid, and defense can be interpreted as those of a country acting purely in self-interest, with regard only to consequences for itself. Japan seems to change its international

policies only in response to threats, and thus appears to the rest of the world to act in a defensive and ungenerous manner. It is this perception of Japan, and the reactions and interactions that flow from this perception, that may well prove to be Japan's ultimate vulnerability.[5]

Individual anecdotes about extraordinary problems encountered by foreigners exporting to Japan long ago became too numerous to be accepted as aberrations that can be dismissed. These incidents cumulatively portray in a "meaningful way the operative Japanese policy towards foreigners in Japan. The anecdotes *are* Japanese policy; Japan is restrictive; it is a difficult place for foreigners to do business . . ."[6]

Japan's swift transitions between pleas for leniency for the "fatal fragility" of the Japanese economy—a term used by the MITI minister in 1982—and arrogance about Japan's economic superiority appear to illustrate a devious view of the world. In 1984, a Japanese businessman whose tongue had been loosened by alcohol explained the future shape of international comparative advantage: "Australia will be our mine and America will be our grain bowl . . . [and] Europe will be our boutique."[7]

Such a flippant remark may have been a careless personal indiscretion but it illustrates the animosity with which the Japanese historically have viewed foreigners—butter-smelling barbarians. In the seventeenth century, Japanese fishermen shipwrecked and rescued by a foreign boat were forbidden to return to Japan; they were tainted by the foreign contact. The Dutch residents on the islands off Nagasaki during the Tokugawa period could not be buried on Japanese soil when they died.[8] Japanese children who study abroad face problems of reassimilation and hazing unmatched anywhere else. Such justifications as different snow and unusually long intestines, mentioned in the previous chapter, can be viewed as ethnocentric absurdities, not legitimate argumentation. When other explanations are heard, such as the suggestion that foreign contracting firms would not be appropriate for building the new Osaka airport because Japanese soil is unique, suspicion is aroused that an entirely unique reasoning process is at work.

Japan's basic problem in dealing with the irresistible pull of international economic interdependence may come from its tenacious clinging to the exclusiveness that originated in the Tokugawa period of enforced isolation. Fear of outside influence, the domination of special interests, and the impermeable, interlocking social networks developed from political and historical factors rather than genetic predisposition; but these factors are not fading from the scene. "Totally rejecting and repelling outsiders— whether from another country or another 'fief'—is an old trait inherited from the . . . enclosed village society, where it was the main means of self-defense. Even today, if you enter a farming village, you will feel the full force of this utter exclusivity in operation."[9] Internationalization may be a fashionable concept in Japan today, but one long on hype and short on substance. The ancient tradition of taking from, but not giving to, the rest of the world is alive and well. The Japanese have thought themselves well advised

> to conclude friendly alliances, to send ships to foreign countries everywhere and conduct trade, to copy the foreigners where they are at their best and so repair our own shortcomings, to foster our national strength and complete our armaments, and so gradually subject the foreigners to our influence until in the end all the countries of the world know the blessings of perfect tranquility and our hegemony is acknowledged throughout the globe.[10]

These comments have a contemporary sound, but they date to 1857.

The outside world probably will always be regarded by the Japanese as threatening and unpleasant. It cannot be organized and regulated by the uniquely intricate discipline of intensely personal loyalties that keeps Japan running smoothly and consistently. When Sony, perhaps the prototype of the internationalized Japanese firm, made its official press announcement in October, 1989 that it had bought Columbia Pictures, the largest Japanese corporate overseas acquisition to date, it did so in a news conference closed to non-Japanese journalists.[11]

Frustration is the word to describe U.S.–Japanese economic relations, according to Senator John Heinz (R., PA), because the U.S. "experience is so different from Japan's that we cannot understand its closed society any more than they can understand our open one."[12] Japanese culture has spawned an economic ideology so fundamentally different from that of the United States that the world's two greatest capitalist powers do not really speak the same language. Karel van Wolferen observed in this regard:

> Freedom of the market is not considered a desirable goal in itself, but only one of several instruments for achieving predetermined effects that are totally subordinated to the ultimate goal of industrial expansion.[13]

> The USA stresses that Japan itself stands to gain from free trade and open markets, but what it means by this—greater choices for the Japanese consumers—is not at all what the Japanese administrators understand by gain. A truly open market would undermine the domestic order, so how, in their eyes, could this ever be considered a gain for Japan?[14]

George Soros, a U.S. investment manager with considerable international experience, flatly asserted "The Japanese treat markets as a means to an end and manipulate them accordingly."[15] Under pressure, the Japanese restrict exports to the United States or Western Europe, preferring a cartelized export sector to uncertainty and political tension. When British brokerage firms demanded that seats on the Tokyo Stock Exchange be open to foreign firms, the Japanese authorities refused to discuss abstract criteria for membership; the Finance Ministry only wanted to know what number of seats would mollify the British.[16]

A critic might also observe that Japan's self-centered insularity has made it the country from which U.S. congressional delegations are most likely to return home in a more hostile mood than when they departed. Consider the worrisome example of international misunderstanding in a 1983 meeting in Tokyo between a congressional group and the minister of MITI:

> As the meeting ended, [MITI Minister] Yamanaka disappeared behind a side door for a moment and emerged carrying a Kodak Instamatic camera. He bent down in what the congressmen took to be an exaggerated picture-taking position and snapped away at his guests, making sure that they knew he was photographing them with an American-made camera.
>
> He soon returned to his seat and reached for a cigarette, an American-made Pall Mall, silently but effectively reinforcing the point that U.S. products are sold in Japan. Then he pulled out an expensive gold lighter, opened it and struck the flint. "So sorry," said Yamanaka, looking first at the lighter and then at his guests, "French."
>
> "It was not a performance that sent any of us away from there with a feeling that they were about to give us a damn thing," said Democrat Al Swift of Washington. "In fact, it was a bravura performance of them telling us we could go [expletive deleted] ourselves."[17]

THE PERVERTED PRICE MECHANISM: AN INDIRECT IMPORT BARRIER

Japan's adoption of a market economy does not mean that the price mechanism works the same way there as it does in the United States. Similar corporate needs for profits and consumer desires for low prices notwithstanding, differences in the Japanese value system impose a hindrance—but not an absolute barrier—to imports unlike anything in the United States. The idiosyncratic Japanese price mechanism, along with the suspicious-to-hostile attitudes toward manufactured goods described earlier, and overt barriers to be discussed in the next section, add up to an extraordinarily difficult—but not impossible—task facing foreign manufacturers exporting to Japan.

A major cause of the relatively low import penetration of manufactured goods into Japan has been the limited ability of foreign goods to compete on the basis of price. Ironically, this limitation exists *despite* the fact that Japanese prices for most basic consumer necessities are the highest among the industrial countries, a situation which has precipitated no organized consumer revolt, only a buying frenzy by individual Japanese tourists traveling abroad. Survey after survey confirms what anyone knows who has shopped in the two countries: prices for goods are typically 50 percent to 500 percent (protected food products dominate the upper end) more expensive in Japan than they are in the United States. A package of six California oranges costs nearly $5 in Japan; rice can cost six times the world price. It has been estimated that Japanese workers must work five times longer than their U.S. counterparts to buy the same amount of fish or rice, three times longer to buy gasoline, and nine times longer to buy beef.[18] Airline tickets for travel to and from Japan are considerably more expensive if purchased there. The Japanese Economic Planning Agency's 1988 international price comparison, summarized in table 9.1, illustrates further price discrepancies, but may still understate the U.S.–Japanese differential in food prices; compare figures from the U.S. Department of Agriculture presented in table 9.2.

In a bizarre manifestation of Japan's price structure, above and beyond its acceptance by a Japanese public that stoically accepts an economic system heavily biased in favor of producers and against consumers, the OECD in its 1989 annual economic review of Japan, saw fit to urge this fabulously successful country—the export superstar and emerging banker to the world—to expend a greater effort to raise the country's living stan-

---

Table 9.1   Prices in New York and Hamburg, West Germany, Relative to Japan, November 1988

(Tokyo = 100)

	New York	Hamburg
Average	72	68
Food	69	64
Durable goods	76	88
Clothing and footwear	67	71
Other products	79	89
Utilities and water	44	70
Transportation	70	93
Health care	106	24
Education	108	52
Rental housing	54	51
Other services	118	78

SOURCE: Japanese Economic Planning Agency, *Price Report 1989.*

Table 9.2 Comparison of Food Prices in Tokyo and Washington, D.C., May 1989 (U.S. dollars)

Item*	Tokyo	Wash. D.C.
Steak, sirloin, boneless	25.88	4.86
Pork, roast, boneless	6.21	3.67
Broilers, whole	2.90	0.85
Cheese, Cheddar/Emmenthaler	4.19	3.52
Milk, whole (liter)	1.44	0.62
Oil, cooking (liter)	2.01	2.56
Potatoes	1.21	0.35
Apples	1.00	1.28
Oranges	1.32	0.53
Flour	0.69	0.29
Coffee	11.70	3.38

*Per pound, unless noted.

SOURCE: U.S. Department of Agriculture, Foreign Agricultural Service, Trade and Economics Information Division.

dards. "There is still a substantial discrepancy between the country's economic strength and the relatively poor quality of life," the report concluded, noting that the country ranks fifth among industrial countries in per capita income, but tenth in purchasing power.[19]

Japan's price structure exhibits the extraordinary oddity that even Japanese-made goods tend to cost less in the United States and other foreign markets than at home. Considerable publicity and some red faces were generated by the revelation in 1988 that a small trading company was re-importing cordless telephones made in Japan by Panasonic and exported to the United States. This Japanese entrepreneur briefly did a flourishing business, buying the phones for approximately $60 apiece in the United States and pricing them to sell at retail in Japan for the yen equivalent of $152; sales were both brisk and profitable because all other Japanese-made cordless phones were selling for four times that amount, i.e., above $600. This exercise in unleashing the invisible hand abruptly ended when Panasonic hurriedly bought up the re-imported phones, huffing that they were not built to meet higher Japanese telecommunications standards.[20] In 1986, the author purchased a Japanese-made camera in Washington, D.C. for about one-half the price quoted in Tokyo a few months earlier.

There are a few ways to get around the many impediments to the so-called gray market. Foreign residents of Japan often find it cheaper to ask overseas friends to send them Japanese-made goods rather than buy them locally. One person reported that he obtained Japanese floppy disks for one-fourth the price charged in Japanese stores, even with air parcel post charges.[21] In 1988, Business Week reported that re-imported Suntory whiskey could be purchased at a 45 percent discount in Tokyo, and that an increasing number of camera shops had bins of bargain-priced Japanese-made film originally intended for the Korean or Chinese markets.[22] But these examples are exceptions rather than the rule. There exists no systematic gray market in Japan seeking to exploit the opportunities presented by large price differentials for the same product. The Japanese dual-pricing system could never occur in the United States. Entrepreneurs would spring up by the hundreds to re-import any U.S.–made goods sold more cheaply abroad. Discount chains would welcome the merchandise, and antitrust laws would limit interference from distraught manufacturers.

The thin ranks of potential Japanese price entrepreneurs probably shrank further in the wake of what might be called the Lions Oil scandal. It began with the seemingly admirable effort of Lions president Taiji Sato to import a small amount of relatively inexpensive gasoline from Singapore so that a small number of gasoline stations could sell it at a modest discount below prices imposed by the major petroleum refiners. This initiative was just like the protruding nail in the Japanese proverb: it got pounded down by the unified force of the Japanese establishment. MITI lacked direct legal authority to prohibit the proposed gasoline imports but seems to have responded with a classic example of the unofficial power of administrative guidance; the bank financing the gasoline imports suddenly cancelled the loan and the discount gasoline proposal folded. The degree of government intimidation of the bank probably will never be known; it might have been no more than a dire warning of a (somewhat improbable) chain of events that might be set into motion: a potential price war that could harm national security (imports of discounted gasoline, it was argued, could lead to reductions in crude oil imports, and in turn, cause shortages in other petroleum products).[23]

The absence of any arbitrage mechanism in Japan evidences the different functioning of the market mechanism in that country. It also supports and prolongs the paradoxical willingness of Japanese manufacturers to subsidize U.S.—and other foreign—consumers by exploiting their fellow Japanese through higher domestic prices. Wider profit margins in the high-cost Japanese market allow Japanese manufacturers to offset lower export prices, potentially low enough to devastate U.S. competition or to protect Japanese market shares in the United States from goods exported by the newly industrialized countries of Asia.

In a truly bizarre example of "establishment capitalism," a major Japanese consumer organization expressed regret over a bilateral agreement in 1988 to relax Japanese trade barriers on citrus fruit and beef. The group was less interested in the possibility of lower food prices than in the probability that consumers would be worse off. How could this be? Because it felt distributors would pocket most of the potential savings from more plentiful imports and domestic cattle herds would be slaughtered, driving up milk prices.[24]

Each of the three possible justifications for this position would be rejected by any legitimate U.S. consumer group. First, the Japanese consumer group may have been willing to forego personal benefits to avoid possible losses in income for fellow Japanese, specifically, relatively inefficient farmers. Second, they may have felt suspicious of U.S. agricultural imports after seeing a scandalous film released by the politically potent Central Union of Agricultural Cooperatives (Zenchu), which maliciously, falsely, and graphically argued that chemicals applied to U.S. crops made them very dangerous to eat. Consider the film's contents: "Citrus is shown rotting on the docks at Yokohama, disfigured human fetuses float in laboratory jars, monkeys supposedly deformed by tainted food grovel in their pens, hospitalized children display mysterious skin diseases, airplanes spray clouds of chemicals on farm fields."[25] The third possible explanation is the most Japanese: many consumer groups are not independent entities, but themselves part of the establishment. The Consumer's Union of Japan, for example, was headed in the late 1980s by a former senior official of the Agriculture Ministry, a fact which possibly explains why that group, too, opposes removal of agricultural trade barriers as well as adjustment of product standards that would facilitate imports of consumer goods.[26]

The Japanese economy shows both consistency with its larger ideological setting and a pronounced double standard when it comes to the herculean efforts to offset the adverse competitive effects of yen appreciation on Japanese-made goods, as opposed to the feeble efforts made to pass along to consumers the benefits of cheaper import prices when the yen strengthens. When the yen appreciates, price changes are minimized for both imports and exports. The Japanese government did not contest U.S. complaints in the late 1980s that there was very little evidence of prices of U.S. goods in Japan being reduced in yen terms equivalent to the dollar depreciation vis-à-vis the yen. Comparing Japanese input prices, wholesale prices, and export prices, a 1988 study by the congressional Joint Economic Committee concluded

> Japanese manufacturers have not been passing on import cost savings fully to Japanese customers. At the same time, export prices have risen much less than either unit labor costs or wholesale prices. The gap between the unit labor cost index and export price index appears too wide to explain by cheaper imported inputs alone. The profits made from keeping the gains from cheaper imports and not passing them on to domestic customers may be subsidizing lower prices on exports.[27]

A study by the Federal Reserve Bank of Chicago concluded that "Japan passes on far less of its currency-induced cost increases than any of the other" major industrial countries.[28] The efforts of Japanese companies to further discriminate against Japanese consumers in order to minimize losses in overseas sales is tempered somewhat by the Japanese govern-

ment's efforts to minimize dislocations to domestic companies and producers from *endaka*—the strong yen. Subsidized loan programs offered official funding for corporate attempts to frustrate precisely what yen
appreciation is supposed to do: encourage Japanese imports and dampen
exports. The main obligation exhibited by the Japanese government toward
consumers is preventing "confusion," roughly a reference to brutal competition that would include price wars, corporate bankruptcies, and radical
change in business practices.

In the Japanese market, the price edge and/or technical superiority of
an import must be substantial, not merely interesting. A Japanese company's most likely response to a foreign proposal to supply goods at a lower
price is to challenge its current supplier to meet the *gaijin*'s bid or risk
losing both contract and face. Japanese vendors and subcontractors are
likely to rise to the occasion, mainly because they are used to being sub-
jected to—and meeting—punishing demands on price, quality, and delivery times. The bigger the buying company, the more likely the
responsiveness of the suppliers to the price mechanism—a benefit almost
unknown to Japanese consumers. Imagine the pressures on one branch of
a *keiretsu* to respond satisfactorily to the threat of another branch to
switch its supplier to a U.S. exporter if the product in question was not
made better and/or cheaper.

Naïve foreigners might do well to consider the response of a British
industrialist to the assertion by the eminent Harvard economics professor
Martin Feldstein that additional yen appreciation would alter Japan's
pattern of trade:

> I do not believe that selling in Japan is a matter of price, do not
> believe it ever has been a matter of price, and I personally don't
> believe it ever will be a matter of price.
>
> If you sell into Japan, by and large Japanese will only buy from
> you if there is no Japanese alternative. If there is a Japanese alterna-
> tive, they will match you on price, no matter what. It's a matter
> of national pride. I'm all in favor of trying to press them to import
> more, and I believe in the very long haul, Japan has got to open
> up more.[29]

PECULIAR TRADE PATTERNS

It is all too easy for defenders of Japan to massage statistics in order to
exaggerate the country's undisputable increases in manufactured goods
imports. Imports of all goods increased healthily at the end of the eighties,
at least in part because of the strong, above-average real-growth rates in
Japan's GNP (a rising tide raises all ships). Price declines in petroleum and
other major imported commodities artificially enhanced the percentage of

total imports represented by manufactured goods, however, and none of the available data suggest major absolute increases in manufactures imports other than labor-intensive and luxury consumer goods (mainly clothing and automobiles). Given the U.S. comparative advantage in high-tech capital goods, continuation of the buy-Japan syndrome in targeted industries must remain a matter of concern in bilateral trade relations.

Numerous statistical indices demonstrate that, for whatever underlying reasons, Japanese trade exhibits patterns very different from other major countries to a degree that the labels "protectionist" and "adversarial trader" are based on something more than mindless racism or a gross inability to understand Japan. In most cases, Japanese trends start at an idiosyncratic point and close gaps with other countries only slightly, or even move further away from the norm. As shown in table 9.3, Japan's ratio of imports to gross domestic product (GDP)* has, alone among major industrial countries, declined since 1956.

The recent absolute growth in Japan's imports of manufactured goods is overshadowed by two other factors above and beyond the basic observation that they were starting from a low statistical base. First, exports of such goods have been rising at a fast enough rate that Japan's surplus in manufactured goods continued to rise steadily throughout the 1980s, reaching a world-record $172 billion in 1988. Secondly, there has been no increase in imports of manufactured goods when expressed as a percentage of either total Japanese GDP or the domestic manufacturing sector. Between 1980 and 1988, imports of manufactured goods as a percentage of GNP stayed within a narrow range of 2.2 to 3.0 percent; between 1980 and 1987 (the latest year for which data are available), imports as a percentage of Japanese manufacturing declined from 11.4 to 10.4 percent.[30] U.S. imports of manufactured goods as a percentage of GNP rose from about 3.5 percent in 1980 to about 6.5 percent in 1988.[31] Using a different means of calculation, the 1989 report of the U.S. Advisory Committee for Trade

---

Table 9.3 **Ratio of Imports to Gross Domestic Product**
(percent)

	1956	1970	1986
Japan	12.3	9.3	6.5
United States	3.3	4.2	9.2
West Germany	14.1	16.2	21.4

SOURCE: International Monetary Fund, *International Financial Statistics Supplement on Trade Statistics,* 1988; 1956 and 1986 were the earliest and most current years, respectively, for which import penetration data are available.

---

*GDP equals gross national product less factor income flows from abroad and factor income flows to other countries, mainly repatriated profits from overseas corporate subsidiaries.

Policy and Negotiations demonstrated the same trend, made more dramatic by a comparison with the upward trends for the United States and West Germany (see table 9.4). Japan's unusually low marginal propensity to import appears also in the anomaly of a small *absolute* decrease in manufactured goods imports in 1985, despite a healthy increase of 6.4 percent in nominal GNP between 1985 and 1984.

Another Japanese foreign trade peculiarity is an unusually low rate of intra-industry trade, a measure of a country's imports and exports of similar manufactured products. Because of increasing product differentiation, specialization, and economies of scale, most industrialized countries experience extensive two-way trade in different models or types of such goods as cars, electronics, chemicals, machinery, and office equipment. Japan's index is dramatically below average (by about one-half), and Japan is the only major industrialized country demonstrating no increase in such trade. In addition, Japanese exports tend to cluster in industrial sectors with exceptionally low levels of intra-industry trade. "When Japan chooses to engage in major exports of a product, it imports very little."[32] Thus, products accounting for large percentages of Japan's total exports correlate closely with those amassing large trade surpluses. Japan's "pattern of behavior is seriously at odds with all the expectations generated by intra-industry theory," concludes Edward Lincoln in a study published by the Brookings Institution.[33] Another Brookings analyst, Robert Lawrence, has made similar arguments based on an econometric model; in 1987, he found that Japanese imports of manufactured goods were about 40 percent lower than expected. If Japan traded like other countries, he concluded, it "would have considerably more intra-industry trade."[34]

A final statistical indication of unusual trade patterns is the notable

---

Table 9.4   Import Ratios in Manufacturing
(imports as a percentage of apparent consumption)

	United States	West Germany	Japan
Imports from:			
World			
1975	7.0	24.3	4.9
1986	13.8	37.2	4.4
OECD			
1975	4.9	20.5	2.9
1986	9.3	30.6	2.6
Developing countries			
1975	2.1	2.6	1.8
1986	4.2	4.4	1.8

SOURCE: "Analysis of the U.S.–Japan Trade Problem," Report of the Advisory Committee for Trade Policy and Negotiations, February 1989.

difference in the adjustments between U.S. trade with Japan on the one hand and with the European Community (EC) on the other, subsequent to the downturn in the dollar's exchange rate in early 1985. The overvalued dollar caused a universal deterioration in the U.S. trade account, and its subsequent depreciation led to a significant improvement in the U.S. position as of 1989 with all but one of its major trading partners. After peaking at a deficit of $23 billion in 1986, the U.S. balance with the EC countries fell to a deficit of $9.2 billion in 1988 and then rebounded to a surplus of $1.2 billion for 1989.[35] The deficit with West Germany fell by almost one-half between 1987 and 1989, reflecting a sharp increase in U.S. exports and a modest absolute decrease in imports. The deficit with Japan peaked at $56.3 billion in 1987 and remained stuck at $50 billion for the next two years.

OPEN DOOR, CLOSED SOCIETY

The centuries-old struggle against foreign influences explains a major paradox in Japan's trade position: continuing evidence that Japan is the world's most difficult market for exporters of manufactured goods, despite an absence of formal import barriers. No one disagrees that the Japanese heavily protected their markets through the early 1960s; controversy arises over the extent to which the markets truly opened with extensive liberalization over the subsequent twenty years. The argument recited here is that Japan's market is not yet open "wide" to imports of processed raw materials or relatively sophisticated manufactured goods.

Successful sales efforts by Japanese subsidiaries of foreign companies are not the same as an open door to manufactures imports. Nor are recently increasing exports in "mature" technologies and labor-intensive products comparable to observing imports capture and maintaining a significant market share in advanced, high-tech industries that have been targeted for nurturing. The latter events seldom occur in Japan.

The liberalization process that phased out many import barriers has been peculiarly Japanese and predominantly a public relations effort to assuage U.S. anger about lack of market access. Import liberalization neither emanated from domestic political pressures by Japanese consumers nor economic guidance from Japanese economists committed to free trade and genuinely open markets. Removal of import barriers on a given product generally has come after, not before, Japanese producers become internationally competitive. Until domestic producers become ready to fend off foreign competition, the Japanese government finds ways to reinstate disappearing barriers by other means. The rotating restrictions on cigarettes were described in chapter 2. A more important example is the countermeasures taken after the decontrol of computers in 1976: on the eve of implementing the computer liberalization measures, the Japanese government announced that it would continue to "cherish" the domestic industry's "independence and future growth" and "will keep an eye on movements in the computer market so that liberalization will not adversely affect domestic producers nor produce confusion" (officialdom's code word for excessive price competition from imports). The government subsequently increased its contribution to R&D in the computer sector and initiated administrative guidance to tighten buy-Japan procurement practices by all official agencies and government-owned corporations.[36] Translation: Japan was going to practice "fair" trade, not free trade, retaining an informally controlled import market for computers at least until domestic producers achieved world-class competitive status.

Japan is second to no other country in the limited results of removing overt import barriers. Statutory changes do not always change the ingrained Japanese cultural attitude toward purchasing priorities, first to buy from a fellow member of a business group, or *keiretsu*, second to buy from a Japanese company. Imports are a last recourse, acceptable only if no comparable Japanese-made product is available. This hierarchy would explain why, even after the Japanese government implemented all reforms requested by the U.S. government with regard to, for example, baseball bats (see chapter 2), U.S. export sales remained all but nonexistent. A study of foreign-owned companies in Australia found the purchasing behavior of Japanese subsidiaries there similarly distinct from those of other countries. The Japanese subsidiaries "are tightly controlled by the respective parent company, procure their equipment mainly in Japan, and own and operate mainly Japanese machinery."[37]

For all the hoopla about Japan's increased imports, at least three layers of import protection remain, with the result that market shares for most technologically significant foreign-made goods at best linger at low rates and at worst tumble to near zero when at least approximate Japanese-made equivalents enter the market.

The formal barriers of the first layer are similar to those of other countries, protecting politically sensitive agricultural and industrial sectors. A second layer of indirect, or historical, barriers emanates from business and social practices. They include the distribution system, putting long-standing personal relationships above increase in profit margin from opting for cheaper goods from a new supplier, the asymmetrical interests of trading companies in exporting rather than importing manufactured goods that compete with domestic production, the almost 300 legal cartels, and more—all peculiar to the Japanese system, at least in intensity. This layer creates obstacles to all new entrants to the market, be they Japanese or foreign, although the problems are the most severe for the latter.

The third layer might be termed attitudinal, and once again is something unique to Japan: the majority of Japanese government officials and business executives apparently still have an unshakable feeling it is undesirable, even unnatural, to import goods that can be produced in Japan at anything like the same price or quality.

A metaphorical chrysanthemum curtain remains. Less a matter of formal statutes than attitudes, relationships, and non-verbal communication, the curtain makes life difficult to impossible for foreign interlopers in advanced industrial sectors deemed important to the future of the Japanese economy. The following details should put to rest the opposing argument that the Japanese market today can be called open.

So many formal trade barriers remain that Japan retains the dubious honor of having the most pages devoted to it in the annual survey of foreign trade barriers produced by the Office of the U.S. Trade Representative. In 1990, the U.S. government's negotiating agenda for increased foreign markets was again dominated by Japan and included such important sectors as telecommunications equipment, supercomputers, semiconductors, construction, and intellectual property rights (patent and trademark laws). Low tariffs on raw materials combined with high tariffs on many processed goods create a high effective tariff discriminating against processed raw materials, like wood and wood products as opposed to logs. Although all countries sin in the agricultural sector, Japan's trade barriers on rice, citrus fruits, and meat cause the loss of billions of dollars annually in potential U.S. exports.

Important nontariff barriers also remain. Japanese government procurement policies discriminate against imports in targeted industries. A bilateral agreement in 1987 notwithstanding, the Japanese government and publicly funded universities still do not buy U.S.–made supercomputers, even though the latter have an 80 percent world market share. U.S. makers of communication satellites have a similarly poor record with the Japanese government. Much-touted internationalization did not prevent the Japanese from trying in 1987 to limit Motorola's exports of its highly competitive cellular car phones. Besides discriminatory regulatory burdens (such as foreign cellular phone companies having to sign up customers before being granted a license), the telecommunications ministry originally permitted Motorola to sell its equipment only in the western part of Japan, reserving the lucrative Tokyo and Nagoya markets for a Japanese competitor.

The notoriously convoluted standards and product-testing requirements have been eased. Japanese customs agents no longer look like trade soldiers, though the zeal they once brought to their mission of keeping out impure, unsafe, and unwanted imports is still commented on. A container of pineapples from the Philippines was rejected because the name of the fruit was incorrectly spelled with a hyphen separating pine and apple.[38] U.S. companies often were unable to discover what ingredients and specifications were acceptable and unacceptable in Japan. U.S. makers of cosmetics and data communications machinery were merely told yes or no as to whether their products could enter, and the Japanese government refused to disclose the criteria on which the rejections were based.

A Japanese citizen ran into difficulties in early 1982 when he tried to import two Mercedes-Benz luxury cars from Germany. Customs officials at Narita Airport told him the first-aid kits and fire extinguishers in the cars did not comply with government drug laws and high-pressure-gas control regulations. When these officials refused to open the first-aid kits to see that no illegal drugs were present, the would-be importer was so outraged that he became the first Japanese to file a complaint with the Office of the Trade Ombudsman.[39]

Another example of Japanese extremism in customs regulation is the case of the business representative of a U.S. food products manufacturer who had asked his home office to ship him some newly designed salad dressing bottles to show potential Japanese buyers. Japanese customs officials refused to allow the shipment to enter, since the bottles contained salad dressing that had not received import approval under Japan's food sanitation law. Since the representative was interested only in the bottles themselves, he offered to pour out the contents in the presence of customs inspectors, but the offer was rejected, and the entire shipment was returned to the United States.[40]

Also in 1982, after a U.S. manufacturer of soft drink dispensers had been selling its product in Japan for ten years, the Japanese Ministry of Health and Welfare changed health standards in such a way that only one Japanese manufacturer met the new requirements. A request for a reconsideration of the changes was rejected by the ministry. The Trade Ombudsman "solved" this case by sending the U.S. company's representative back to the same Health and Welfare Ministry bureaucrat who originally had refused to respond to the complaint. In this second meeting, the Japanese official said: "I told you the last time that we are not going to change this and if you keep complaining to the Ombudsman, not only will we not change the regulations, but we will make you take all your installed dispensers out of Japan."[41] Given the power of senior Japanese bureaucrats, this threat could not be dismissed as a bluff.

As recently as 1989, a U.S. company encountered a bizarre rejection of its bid to export wood treated with a fire-resistant coating that foams on contact with flames. Japanese product standards require that wood withstand exposure to fire for a minimum (unspecified) time period. The new product was unable to meet the standard because it was too good: by so quickly extinguishing the flames applied to it, the coated wood failed to demonstrate that it could withstand fire for the required minimum length of time.[42]

The Japanese government could increase U.S. exports by bringing domestic policies, which presently act as de facto nontariff trade barriers, into conformity with those in the West. Patents are routinely taken out by Japanese companies on *projected* inventions or technologies that have not yet been perfected. Trademarks owned by foreign companies can be registered in Japan under some circumstances by local companies. The Japanese government often demands precise technical plans before granting import approval to new products, arousing suspicions by U.S. companies that proprietary information is leaked to favored domestic companies.

A major impediment to imports is Japan's convoluted distribution system, which places an inordinate number of pitfalls in the path of foreign exporters. One law restricts construction of the large discount and chain stores that are more amenable to carrying competitively priced imported goods than the traditional retail outlets—small mom and pop stores typically beholden to one Japanese producer or distributor. Small electronics stores usually handle a single brand; some intermediate distributors provide financing to small retailers in return for control of their inventory.

The current lax state of antitrust enforcement is another important, albeit indirect import barrier. Japanese industrial policy encourages cartel behavior at both ends of the spectrum: sunrise industries targeted for growth and sunset industries that have agreed to participate in rationalization efforts to consolidate domestic production.

The soda ash cartel has been the most publicized example to date of grand collusion between the private sector and government to protect an inefficient Japanese industry from the fate experienced by so many U.S. import-impacted industries. The violation of Japan's antitrust laws were so egregious in this case that in 1983, the Japan Fair Trade Commission (JFTC) issued a cease and desist order that relieved, though it did not eliminate, discrimination against U.S. exporters of this product, a chemical used in various manufacturing processes. Prior to 1983, lower U.S. prices were entirely negated by a comprehensive market-fixing scheme. In addition to consulting with each other on domestic production levels and prices in the Japan Soda Ash Industry Association, the major Japanese producers of soda ash were all members of a *keiretsu* and thus linked to the major trading companies who handled virtually all imports of the product. Five Japanese trading companies controlled imports; each one was specifically assigned to one of five U.S. exporters of soda ash. Each of the latter five had an informal quota of 12,000 tons annually, and collectively their exports of 60,000 tons accounted for only about 5 percent of Japanese consumption at that time. All of the imported soda ash was (and still is) purchased directly from trading companies by the major Japanese soda ash producers and resold domestically at prevailing local prices. All five trading companies earned the same annual profits, even though they did not necessarily import the same volume of the chemical.[43] All of the imported soda ash was mandated for delivery to the same dock, owned by the Japanese Soda Ash Industry Association. When U.S. producers of the chemical tried to expand sales by selling more product to their assigned trading company or directly to Japanese users, they were rebuffed because "delicate relationships" would be upset.[44] Prior to its filing a complaint with the JFTC, the U.S. government sought MITI's good offices to aid the U.S. industry's export efforts. True to form, MITI officially reported that it could find no evidence of collusion. The problem was alleged to rest in misunderstandings between buyers and sellers.

After a decade of relentless pressure and publicity, U.S. soda ash shipments more than quadrupled; in the late 1980s, U.S. market share exceeded 20 percent before leveling off. Efforts to bypass the chrysanthemum curtain by using a Japanese trading company (Sumitomo) with no soda ash producers in its group slowed after the company was pressured to limit imports. In an apparent effort to cover all bases, a MITI vice-minister subsequently informed the head of the U.S. soda ash exporters association that, with the Japanese industry operating at low capacity, imports from the U.S. had gone far enough. The bottom line in this situation, wrote Clyde Prestowitz, was:

> To Americans nurtured on the pure market concepts of antitrust,
> Japanese practice seems unfair and protectionist. But in Japan it
> is part of not breaking your neighbor's rice bowl. There is a sense
> of mutual obligation and a duty to help those in trouble.[45]

Japan's industrial structure is another element in the business practices that comprise the second layer of import barriers, and it involves more than abstractions like loyalty and continuity. The problem here for exporters is mainly the propensity of member companies of a *keiretsu* to acquire goods and services from one another. Furthermore, the trading companies in the groups are reluctant to import any industrial goods that might impose sales losses on fellow manufacturing members.

The tight bonds within the Japanese business community might be less daunting to internationally competitive foreign companies if it were not for the sheer expense of setting up a business presence in Japan. The costs of land acquisition and Western-style housing for U.S. executives can be so astronomical that a perfectly rational business decision may well be that the uphill effort to crack the still tightly bound, inward-looking Japanese society is just not cost-effective. Furthermore, the prospect of continuous and long after-hours drinking and eating with prospective customers may cause U.S. businesspeople with families to find a tour of duty in Japan personally undesirable.

The third, or attitudinal, layer of import barriers is partially the outgrowth of unconscious Japanese behavior and partially the reflection of out-and-out dirty tricks. Foreigners may be ignorant of more intangible forms of discrimination or doubtful of its significance in a nominally free-market economy. To be sure, beyond a certain, unquantifiable point, most Japanese businesspeople, in most circumstances, will indeed buy better, cheaper foreign goods even if it means abandoning a local supplier; if this were not the case, Japanese home markets would not have needed tariff or nontariff protection. Furthermore, the attitudinal problem exporters meet is mainly on the government and corporate levels, not among individual consumers.

There is significant evidence that for most Japanese, the concept of internationalization does not include unlimited foreign competition. Certain activities may be totally off-limits for foreigners, especially at the local level. The absence of local production of a new product or technology seems to be taken as a sign of weakness or oversight. When overseas manufacturers come up with something new, the Japanese feel challenged to replicate and improve on it domestically—perhaps an instinctive reflex in a country that has traditionally acted to minimize its dependence on the outside world and wanted to absorb foreign things strictly on its own terms.

Importing important, advanced manufactured goods is viewed as a temporary inconvenience. This attitude, together with Japan's supposedly across-the-board excellence in process technology, makes it the foremost "disappearing market" in the world. Once a roughly comparable domestically produced version of a foreign innovation comes to market, imports of that product can dry up overnight. For example, Japanese orders for the U.S.–made 8080-type microprocessor quickly dropped to zero in late 1979, when adequate supplies of Japanese-made equivalents became available;[46] worldwide, sales of this chip showed a much slower rate of descent.

One does not need to be a revisionist to conclude that it is more than a coincidence that the foreign market share in Japan for a number of high-tech capital goods remains clustered at ten percent. A dry, sober minded, meticulously documented study of the Japanese distribution system prepared by the professional staff of the U.S. International Trade Commission made one of the rare public references to the usually muted suspicion that Japanese trading companies follow an informal "10 and 20 rule." The latter allegedly limits foreign suppliers' shares of the Japanese market for a given product to about 10 percent unless they have a 20 percent or greater price advantage over domestic competitors.[47]

In what other country would a local distributor for imported goods bristle at an exporter's plans to increase its local market share? Yet, when the Japanese distributor of European telecommunications equipment was told of plans to try to double market share to 20 percent, he expressed surprise. Despite the prospect of higher earnings for himself, he argued to the manufacturer that they had done well to achieve the 10 percent share they had, and he spelled out the difficulties of going further. (He did not refer to the rumored unofficial allocation of 10 to 15 percent market share for imports of the product.)[48] The same telecommunications corporation lost a sale to a Japanese bank because—the bank later admitted—it favored the bid from a Japanese company that the bank several years before had helped go public. The local distributor for a U.S. sporting goods company fought tooth and nail against the company's plan to increase its market share in Japan through price reductions, claiming that such actions would "disrupt the marketplace" (again, that buzzword for avoiding gloves-off price competition within the Japanese market).[49]

Additional circumstantial evidence of an unwritten Japanese allocation of a small, fixed market share for foreign goods is the unchanging 10 percent penetration ratio for imported semiconductors prior to the 1986 agreement. The U.S. share of the Japanese telecommunications equipment market remained between 2 and 3 percent throughout the late 1980s.[50] A Siemens–Corning Glass joint venture in optical fiber has about half of the world market outside Japan, but after sixteen years of effort in Japan, the market share there remains minor.[51] Similarly, the success of U.S. semiconductor companies selling chips to Japanese automakers is a tiny fraction of its performance in all other automobile-manufacturing markets. Some of the Japanese explanations for this failure are ludicrous, such as that Japanese automobiles are smaller than U.S. models and therefore (fingernail-sized) U.S. chips might not fit in them; or that Tokyo-based Japanese executives have had trouble reaching the Nagoya-based Japanese auto parts firms on the telephone.[52] (If true, this is indirect evidence that Motorola's excluded cellular phones are needed in that once denied market.)

Japanese defense of the domestic market for the high-purity silicon from which semiconductors are made induced the Union Carbide Company to file an antitrust suit in U.S. federal court in 1988. It alleges major Japanese buyers conspired to regularly exchange business data and form a buyer's cartel that not only restricted the price paid in Japan for high-purity polysilicon, but imposed a 40 percent market share ceiling on foreign suppliers.[53] Unsubstantiated stories in other product and service sectors about meetings among Japanese competitors to plan common strategy and allocate market share to imports seem plausible, given the experiences of foreign exporters.

Pressures can also be applied *after* orders for foreign goods have been made. All Nippon Airways was criticized by MITI as recently as 1988 for ordering U.S.–made jet engines instead of doing the patriotic thing and buying the engines from an international consortium that included Japanese firms.[54] Pressures against imports are often less benign. That the market share allocated foreigners can be zero was suggested by the experience in the late 1980s of the Japanese affiliate of a U.S. land development and construction company. A rural building project was halted when subcontractors begged off after being warned by major regional contractors that the latter would never again hire them if they went ahead with the job for the U.S. company. Efforts by the same company to build its own headquarters building met an identical fate: intimidated subcontractors forced the company to work with the *dango,* the entrenched construction cartel.[55]

Japanese distributors or wholesalers interested in adding imports to their sales lines often are threatened with a shutoff of supply or with demands by Japanese manufacturers and distributors for immediate payment. Japan's largest agricultural cooperative threatened to withhold subsidy payments if farmers purchased foreign feed or fertilizer. The Mitsubishi Bank threatened in early 1989 to quadruple its transfer account commission if American Express and Nomura Securities consummated their planned joint effort for a new credit card.[56] The difficulty encountered by American Express in its early efforts to establish its credit card in Japan affords a classic example of the often extraordinary ways business is done in that country. Among other things, the standards-setting Japanese card association refused membership to American Express because it opposed the U.S. company's practice of returning copies of signed receipts to cardholders.[57]

The Playtex Corporation has been shut out in its efforts to export brassieres and pantyhose to Japan by threats from the Japanese industry leader (Wacoal) to pull out its line from any retailer selling Playtex merchandise.[58] A former American businessman in Japan told the author that potential customers for imported lemons would not buy his cheaper product because they knew that their suppliers would tell them "if you don't need my lemons, then you don't need my grapes, melons, etc." Similar threats from suppliers to potential importers of specialized steel products have been reported.

The supposedly toothless MITI continues to pursue "controlled competition" to protect the business establishment. Hoping to ensure that the mainstream market remains in local hands, the government actively encourages foreign manufacturers to concentrate on specified niches, such as the low-price end of the consumer market (especially labor-intensive or low-tech goods) and the luxury market where high markups and snob appeal assure limited sales volume. One MITI official boasted—or let slip—to a visiting U.S. scholar the protocol for imposing administrative guidance on a Japanese construction company that was importing so much Korean cement that local companies were complaining. Among the contingencies presented to the company in an effort to help make it see that its own interests lay in cooling its purchases of imported cement were: it could face major problems getting contracts for government-financed construction; it might find its corporate tax returns more closely examined; and it might be shut out of any future MITI support programs for the industry.[59] This seems an updated version of the widely publicized and successful MITI effort in the mid-1970s to utilize administrative guidance to flatten an unwanted growth spurt in imported ski boots.

If the trade complaint filed with the U.S. government in early 1990 by the Allied-Signal Corporation is accurate, the ability of the Japanese system to squelch high-tech exports to Japan continues unabated even without overt trade barriers. Allied-Signal's efforts over many years testify that a foreign company is no match for a Japanese ministry that decides to target an industry for domestic development. Amorphous metals, first developed in the 1970s by Allied-Signal, have an enormous array of potential commercial applications in reducing energy loss in electrical devices such as power lines. Despite sales success in the United States and other foreign markets, Allied-Signal got nowhere either exporting to or producing in the Japanese market. MITI's tactics appear to be simple: encouraging would-be domestic producers and potential customers to wait while the government attacks on the patent front. As a result of delays of up to twelve years on patent applications, Allied-Signal's protection expires in 1993 in Japan (the exclusionary period starts when a patent application is filed, not granted). Meanwhile, through the publicly owned Japanese Research and Development Corporation (JDRC), MITI has organized a thirty-four-company group to develop an indigenous amorphous metals industry. Membership entails "a commitment to refrain from making any exclusive move with outsiders for introducing 'amorphous' technology" into Japan, and a joint venture between Allied-Signal and Nippon Steel fell through in 1981 because of opposition by the JDRC. Allied-Signal also claims that the Tokyo Electric Power Company, Japan's biggest public utility, admitted that its strategy was to postpone purchases of amorphous metals until after the expiration of Allied-Signal's patents.[60]

It does not appear that Allied-Signal was lazy or inefficient in its efforts to sell amorphous metals in Japan. Early on, it reached an agreement with the Mitsui Group to market the metals and later build a local plant. The quality and cost-effectiveness of its product were demonstrated to numerous Japanese companies. Its resident representative in Japan, Dr. Ryusuke Hasegawa, was not only a Cal Tech Ph.D. with numerous publications on amorphous metals, but born and raised in Japan before emigrating to the U.S. He could hardly be accused of not understanding the language or local customs. When he asked why his sales efforts were being rejected, he often was given an unusually blunt answer: "You're destroying our harmony. Everything was harmonious until you came along."[61]

A definitive list of barriers, restraints, and miscellaneous interferences limiting the access of specific foreign manufactured goods to the Japanese market would be long enough to make a book by itself. The letters of complaint sent by U.S. companies to the Commerce Department (obtained by a colleague of the author under the Freedom of Information Act) reveal a wide range of problems encountered in exporting to Japan. A leading producer and exporter of airport baggage handling equipment, for example, learned that a Japanese competitor had picked up a large Haneda Airport contract awarded without price competition. The letter of complaint included this revealing quotation from Nissho-Iwai, the trading company with which the U.S. company had contracted to enter the Japanese market: "Frankly speaking, we still have difficulty selling the high-quality, less-expensive foreign made products for Japanese public projects."[62]

All in all, it seems fair to conclude that something funny is going on in the market behind the chrysanthemum curtain. Market access for many goods has not significantly improved despite countless liberalization programs, yen revaluation, rapid Japanese GNP growth, and competent, dedicated efforts by U.S. business to sell in the Japanese market. Few formal barriers remain to the establishment of subsidiaries in Japan by foreign companies, but foreign direct investment accounts for only 1 percent of Japan's national assets as compared to 17 percent in West Germany.[63] The door may be officially open, but the society is still closed to full-scale competition in favored sectors.

A GLOBAL CHORUS OF CRITICISM

Japan does not have a trade problem with the United States alone; it has a trade problem with the world. The complaints voiced by European countries and the developing countries in Asia are similar to those of the United States. The disdainful Japanese responses to these complaints have a familiar ring: "try harder to export to our market, and accept the fact that our outpouring of manufactured goods exports reflects our harder work and our lack of raw materials."

It is difficult to believe that the rest of the world is wrong and the Japanese are right. More likely, Japan's trade relations are out of step with the countries of North America, Western Europe, and elsewhere in Asia, triggering the following policy responses:

- The larger European countries have imposed "voluntary" export restraints on Japan at least as extensively as those arranged by the United States. Milder European antitrust laws have enabled them to force Japanese cutbacks in such goods as steel, ships, automobiles, numerous consumer electronics products, ball bearings, and machine tools without any formal resort to the equivalent of an escape clause (safeguards) investigation.

- To reduce its $3.4 billion bilateral deficit with Japan in 1981, Taiwan in July 1982 temporarily banned more than 1,500 Japanese-made consumer items.

- The Republic of Korea, in its 1982–83 Annual Trade Plan, included measures to diversify the market for several imported products and reduce the severe Korean trade imbalance with one unnamed country.

European and Asian laments about Japanese markets are difficult to distinguish from U.S. complaints, and these countries respond with equal cynicism to Japanese protestations that their market is easily accessible for those who work to master its intricacies. In 1982, the Europeans became so incensed over market access problems they initiated an extraordinary complaint in the GATT. It alleged that Japan's import practices as a whole were so out of step with everyone else's that the country failed to comply with its international trade obligations, that is, it systematically violated the spirit of the GATT. The West German foreign minister told the German-Japanese Society in January 1982 that he rejected the notion that Japan's greater dependence on imported raw materials explained its low level of imports of manufactured goods. He suggested instead, "Japan is still not fully integrated into the world market in regard to industrial products."[64]

The Commission of the European Community, "like Japan's other partners," continues to press Japan to reduce its export dependency in favor of an economy relying more heavily on domestic demand, "with all the structural reforms, market liberalization and internationalization which this requires."[65] Lingering European dissatisfaction with Japan is summarized in a communiqué issued by the commission after its annual High Level Consultations with Japan in November 1989:

> The Commission pointed to structural phenomena of the Japanese economy as a factor contributing to the persistence of the trade deficit. It acknowledged that cultural differences do exist, and that the present economic structure of Japan had grown over time and could not be changed overnight. However, belonging to a market-oriented world economy implied the need for participants to have certain minimum features in common. . . . In the meanwhile, Japanese economic agents should behave in such a way as to prevent tension over the continuing Japanese trade surpluses to surface again in Europe.[66]

A significant upturn in European exports to Japan during the past decade has not obviated public criticism, which reached a zenith with the famous leaked memo lamenting that the Japanese were workaholics living in houses scarcely better than rabbit hutches. Europeans say the rate of change in Japan is still not fast enough; an unofficial postmortem of a high-level European Community–Japan meeting in July 1987 grudgingly noted "For once, the Commission's representative was able to report . . . that the picture *was not entirely gloomy* (emphasis added)."[67]

European anger with Japan about foreign direct investment may exceed that of the United States, even though the basic themes are identical. Japanese direct investment in Europe is often derided as consisting mainly of screwdriver plants with little value-added or local content, simply assembling imported Japanese goods to circumvent import barriers. Noting that foreign direct investment *in* Japan "can be essential to the penetration of the Japanese market," Europeans complain that an "unfavourable climate" for such investment has created a 15 to 1 ratio between Japanese direct investment in Europe and European direct investment in Japan.[68]

A major international trend in the 1980s was the emergence of the so-called newly industrialized countries or economies (NICs, or NIEs) of east Asia: South Korea, Taiwan, Singapore, and Hong Kong. Their rapidly expanding exports of increasingly sophisticated manufactured goods have been spawned by combining advanced technology; market-oriented economic policies; and a skilled, low-paid labor force. Their exports to the United States nearly tripled between 1982 and 1989, when U.S. imports from the four NICs of $63 billion were about 60 percent more than the total for U.S. exports to them ($39 billion).[69] As shown in table 9.5, the relatively large bilateral trade surpluses of each of the four NICs with the United States are in sharp contrast to their large deficits with Japan. More recently, Japanese imports from these countries have increased, but not much more than the comparable percentage rates of import growth by the United States, which started from a much higher base. U.S. government officials have repeatedly claimed that even in the late 1980s, the United States was taking more than 50 percent of all developing countries' exports of manufactured goods, compared to only 9 percent for Japan (and 26 percent for the European Community).[70]

It is unsurprising, therefore, that other Asian economies criticize market access in Japan. NIC denunciation of Japanese import practices cannot be shrugged off as racism or the sour grapes of inept, nonchalant exporters. The "export platforms" of East Asia can hardly be dismissed as unable to understand the Asian business mentality or as being geographically distant from Japan. The anecdotal evidence that South Korea, Taiwan, Singapore,

Table 9.5 U.S. and Japanese Trade with the Asian NICs
(millions of U.S. dollars)

	U.S. Bilateral Trade					
	Exports to		Imports from		Balance with NICs	
	1982	1988	1982	1988	1982	1988
Hong Kong	$2,453	$ 5,691	$5,895	$10,810	$ −3,442	$ −5,119
South Korea	5,529	11,290	6,011	21,209	−482	−9,919
Singapore	3,214	5,770	2,274	8,226	+940	−2,456
Taiwan	4,367	12,131	9,587	26,256	−5,220	−14,125

	Japanese Bilateral Trade					
	Exports to		Imports from		Balance with NICs	
	1982	1988	1982	1988	1982	1988
Hong Kong	$4,707	$11,708	$ 621	$ 2,111	$ +4,086	$ +9,597
South Korea	4,869	15,442	3,270	11,827	+1,599	+3,615
Singapore	4,357	8,312	1,821	2,338	+2,536	+5,974
Taiwan	4,244	14,357	2,438	8,739	+1,806	+5,618

SOURCE: International Monetary Fund, *Direction of Trade Statistics Yearbook, 1989.*

and Hong Kong share the difficulties of Western countries trying to sell in Japan demonstrates again that the critical variable in U.S.–Japanese relations is the Japanese import sector, not the U.S. export sector.

A December 1981 report of the Asian trade mission of the House Ways and Means Committee, covering Hong Kong, Singapore, Malaysia, and Thailand, found "Without exception, leaders in these countries said Japan was an unfair trader, that trade was a one-way street, and that the Japanese simply do not want to import."[71] The report then quoted from a speech delivered in Tokyo by a Singapore trade official:

> In 1980, the export price of refrigerators from Singapore was only 46 per cent of the price that they are retailing for in Tokyo, but we are not able to sell a single refrigerator to Japan. Similarly, the export price of our vacuum cleaners was only 42 per cent of the retail price in Tokyo, and we also were unable to sell a single one in the Japanese market. Our color TV sets cost only 40 per cent of the retail price in Tokyo, but we only were able to sell about 400 sets here. The same story goes for clothing, footwear and other manufactured goods.[72]

The Singapore Department of Trade put the problem in context with this overview:

> Commercial practices, many unique only to Japan, had severely inhibited the ability of companies wishing to enlarge their share of the market. For example, it is virtually impossible to sell to Japan without having an affiliate company doing the marketing and distribution. . . . The structure of Japan's distribution network is a major impediment to our exporters gaining a bigger share of the market. The distribution network is so complex that the imported product becomes very expensive by the time it reaches the consumer.[73]

The Hong Kong Department of Trade argued in the mid-1980s that "the Japanese testing and certification procedures are generally considered as a non-tariff barrier to exports to Japan."[74] In a 1989 interview with the author, a Hong Kong trade official suggested that market access improved only after the appreciation of the yen in 1985 made clear to the Japanese the diminishing future in domestic production of the labor-intensive goods in which Hong Kong specializes. Prior to reading this handwriting on the wall, the official said, the Japanese had a bad "attitude problem" towards imports: they looked first to their own manufacturers, and Japanese trading companies abroad took little interest in buying manufactured goods to export back to Japan. Hong Kong factories found few Japanese interested in importing, except for an occasional department store wanting something cheap on a one-time basis to sell as a loss leader. The Japanese market operated in a "unique" manner, the official said, and his government's complaints about import barriers had absolutely no effect.

An article in a Taiwanese magazine complained of Japanese insensitivity to Taiwan's economic problems. Expressing understanding of Japan's economic position and appreciation of its high-quality goods, the author denounced Japan's trade policies: the overriding fact was "the Japanese want to sell as much as they can and buy as little as possible." They want to keep the home market largely to themselves. The author went on:

> If a product can be made in Japan, it is, and the Japanese people must pay through the nose to buy it. The Japanese have been clever in concealing this. They look up innocent-eyed and say their market is "open to all." If anyone knows the Japanese market, our traders do. And almost to a man, they attest that it is nearly impossible to do business in most of the Japanese market. All the regulations favor Japanese products, no matter how inefficiently these are produced.
>
> All of this is far from new. Our government has been appealing to the Japanese for years to give us a better chance. The Japanese smile, say they will and do nothing. Trade talks are held year after year, and then the deficit goes up again. . . .[75]

South Korea has the largest economy of the NICs and is closest geographically to Japan. But relations between the two countries are complicated by Japan's occupation of Korea earlier this century and Japan's view of South Korea as its greatest contemporary competitive threat in many industrial sectors. Japan's supposedly open door often slams shut on South Korean exports. In the mid-1980s, when it was running surpluses with virtually all of its other trading partners, South Korea ran a deficit with Japan and urged the Japanese to relax discriminatory import barriers so that they could transfer increased export earnings into additional imports from the increasingly protectionist United States.

Japanese trade officials, arriving in Seoul in late 1984, just days after the first deliveries of South Korean exports of cement, demanded informal, "voluntary" export restraint, even though the shipment in question amounted to a miniscule 0.3 percent of Japanese cement consumption. When South Korean officials refused, all outstanding orders from Japanese wholesalers were "abruptly and mysteriously cancelled."[76] The South Korean government received a lesson in Japanese Catch-22 logic when it filed a complaint in Tokyo in support of a South Korean cosmetics company forbidden to export to Japan. The Japanese government brushed off the complaint, noting that cosmetics can be imported only by holders of import permits and complaints from would-be exporters cannot be investigated until a competent Japanese importer is identified.[77]

If Japan is just as open and market oriented as other countries, it must come as news to Hyundai, the South Korean automaker. In the late 1980s, after completing marketing surveys and financial arrangements, Hyundai developed a dealer network and generated sales at the six-figure level in the far-away United States within a matter of months. At the end of the decade, the company had yet to make plans to tackle the Japanese market. The only recorded exports by Hyundai to Japan thus far have been 150 special Olympics edition cars shipped in 1988.[78] The market may not be formally closed, but there are still no regular exports of South Korean cars to Japan.

A final instance of the evasive Japanese import market involves South Korean exports of steel. According to a report by the House Ways and Means Subcommittee on trade, South Korea exported 89 million pounds of steel sheets and plates to nearby Japan in 1978 and sent 1,179 million pounds across the Pacific to the United States.[79] While the subcommittee had "no concrete answers" on the reasons for this and other export disparities, such as those regarding apparel and radios, there are three possible explanations: (1) a relatively inefficient U.S. industry, (2) the practice of Japanese steel companies licensing technology to South Korean companies on the specific condition that any steel produced as a result will *not* be exported back to Japan, and (3) harassment tactics such as following trucks leaving Japanese ports loaded with incoming shipments of South Korean steel—observation tactics presumably designed to identify local buyers of the foreign-made steel.[80] It would be fascinating to know whether those vigilantes were aggressive salesmen from a Japanese steel producer or "enforcers" from MITI preparing for an administrative guidance assignment.

In conclusion, table 9.6 shows the relative importance of the Japanese and U.S. markets for all of South Korea's major exports of manufactured goods. A larger or even comparable percentage in any product category for Japan, a country far closer to South Korea than the United States, is unusual. The rule of thumb is clear—even the NICs have had limited success in penetrating Japan's formal and informal trade barriers.

BEWARE THE EXPORT JUGGERNAUT

Nothing in modern economic history compares with the volume of Japanese manufactured goods exported to the United States over the past three decades, nor with the devastation they caused. It can be argued the United States has dangerously mortgaged its economic future by allowing itself to be a dumping ground for the insatiable Japanese appetite for export maximization, with a resulting decimation of domestic production and jobs in an ever-growing list of industries. It really does not matter whether the Japanese export machine is driven by a calculated drive to reduce the

Table 9.6 Markets for South Korean Exports, 1985

Sector	Exports to World (millions of U.S. dollars)	Share to U.S.	Share to Japan
Iron and steel	$1,825.3	34.07%	24.08%
—Primary forms	364.5	14.65	58.73
—Pipes and tubes	434.0	69.87	3.62
Metal manufactures	1,483.2	40.09	2.39
Non-electric machinery	1,127.4	51.32	7.45
—Aircraft engines	53.3	71.03	11.15
—Computers	24.2	89.71	1.01
—Statistical machinery	396.5	64.11	0.36
—Office machinery	159.4	62.64	14.46
—Mechanical handling equipment	97.2	52.82	0.62
Electrical machinery	3,613.6	52.91	10.09
—TV receivers	591.1	57.95	0.50
—Radios	499.9	50.03	2.42
—Telecommunications equipment	481.1	65.30	11.13
—Semiconductors, computers	1,136.9	54.07	12.22
Transportation equipment	6,282.5	15.04	5.47
—Passenger cars	518.8	0.39	0.13
—Ships	4,948.6	13.07	1.86
Clothing	4,452.6	51.21	13.65
Footwear	1,534.3	74.30	7.50
Miscellaneous manufactured goods	1,796.5	59.32	10.76

SOURCE: United Nations data from Peter Allegeier, "Korean Trade Policy in the Next Decade," *World Development,* January 1988. Reprinted with permission of Pergamon Press plc.

industrial United States to empty, boarded-up factories or merely is a by-product of economic efficiency and savage corporate quest for market share. The result is the same: severe costs to the U.S. economy.

The carnage is far from over. The basic industries overwhelmed by Japanese competition—consumer electronics, automobiles, steel, shipbuilding, motorcycles, and so forth—were merely the beginning. The high-tech sector is now reeling under the onslaught of Japanese competition. Without a viable high-technology sector, the United States will be forced to pay for the hundreds of billions of dollars worth of imported merchandise it uses through exports in agriculture and services. Presidential candidate Walter Mondale drew applause in 1982 by warning that future generations of Americans were being cheated by present U.S. trade policies. Our kids' future, he worried, "will consist of sweeping up around Japanese computers and spending a lifetime serving McDonald hamburgers."[81]

The Japanese insistence on joint development of a new generation of fighter support aircraft—the FSX—suggests aerospace has joined the long list of advanced technologies targeted for development in Japan. The list will continue to grow, with the traditional Japanese trade strategy applied to ever new technologies. Domestic Japanese production in these sectors will be encouraged while imports are minimized; later, economies of scale will be pursued by maximizing exports. A U.S. management consultant concluded:

> The strategic leverage provided the selected Japanese industries by the initial protection has been crucial. By now the evidence is overwhelming that real unit costs in an industry will decline—that is, that productivity will rise—systematically as experience accumulates with market growth. By denying U.S. companies access to Japan's rapidly expanding markets while simultaneously exploiting Japan's free access to the U.S. market, Japan, in case after case, has preempted the lion's share of the available market growth and all the cost productivity benefits that go with it.[82]

For the United States, the situation can be described as intolerable. As illustrated in table 9.7, the bilateral U.S. trade deficit in manufactures has increased seventeenfold since 1970. Japan would never allow the United States—or any other country—to do to it what it has done to U.S. industry. Aided by government policies, cultural factors, a psychological compulsion for industrial success, a distaste for industrial import dependence, and

Table 9.7   U.S. Trade with Japan in Manufactured Goods
(billions of dollars)

	1970	1975	1980	1985	1988	1989*
U.S. exports	2.0	3.2	8.6	12.4	20.7	26.9
U.S. imports	5.9	11.9	32.1	71.6	92.5	92.9
U.S. deficit	−3.9	−8.7	−23.5	−59.2	−71.8	−66.0

*Preliminary figures.

NOTE: Product classifications changed slightly in 1989.

SOURCES: U.S. Department of Commerce, *U.S. Trade Performance* (various issues); and Japan Economic Institute.

an indifference to profits in the short term, Japanese corporations have exploited and will continue to exploit U.S. markets with no regard for the consequences and costs to the U.S. economy or society. For the alarmists, the excellence, sincerity, and hard work associated with the Japanese export onslaught is less relevant than a marketing strategy that ruthlessly promotes production and export volume. In the words of the then-chairman of the now defunct American Motors Corporation, "Japan is the only country to launch an attack on our basic industries as a matter of national policy." The nature and the success of that attack arise from the "failure of the Japanese to play by the same rules as the rest of the international business community."[83]

One of the very few smoking guns to substantiate the charge of fanaticism in the Japanese export drive was the internal memorandum from Hitachi's U.S. operations that fell into the hands of U.S. trade officials. "The 10% Rule" has become a metaphor for Japanese disregard for profits, as the memo urged the Hitachi semiconductor sales force to "Quote 10% below competition; if they requote . . . bid 10% under again; the bidding stops when Hitachi wins." The sales force was also told to reduce their price quotes by 10% as many times as necessary: "Don't quit till you *win!*" U.S. distributors did not need to worry about profit margin because, as the memo also advised, Hitachi "guaranteed" a 25 percent profit margin for specified chip models.

A "low-tech" demonstration of the force of Japan's export drive was the fight for survival waged in 1982 by the last U.S.–owned producer of motorcycles, the Harley-Davidson Corporation. With less than 5 percent of the U.S. market left to it and imports of larger, heavyweight motorcycles rising sharply, the company successfully petitioned the U.S. government for relief from foreign competition under the escape clause provision, obtaining higher U.S. tariff rates on motorcycles with an engine displacement of more than 700 cc. The Japanese already have "95 percent of the motorcycle industry. You might think they were a little greedy going after the last five percent," Vaughn Beals, Harley-Davidson's chairman pleaded, and drew a sympathetic U.S. response.[84] Accusations that Harley-Davidson suffered from poor management at that time were ignored.

The sharp increase in exports of heavyweight Japanese-built motorcycles to the U.S. market did not appear to be the result of a conscious desire by the Japanese industry to destroy its last U.S. competitor. The primary factor seems to have been a no-holds-barred battle for increased U.S. market share between the Honda and Yamaha corporations. When the latter decided to challenge the dominant position of the former, Honda responded like a wounded tiger. The first casualty of the marketing barrage, price cutting, and increased inventories by the Japanese giants was the sole survivor of the once-flourishing U.S. motorcycle industry. Faced with the probable demise of Harley-Davidson, Americans were not interested in *why* the Japanese were moving toward total ownership of the U.S. market.

Large Japanese companies also seek market domination by other means than market share, such as direct investment in the United States. Promising jobs, tax revenues, and even exports, the Japanese direct investment can be accused of constituting a modern-day Trojan horse, which may lead to a dual economy as new, state-of-the-art Japanese-owned factories follow their familiar practice of seeking long-term market share through superior manufacturing technology regardless of short-term profits. Waves of new Japanese direct investment may thus prove even more traumatic to surviving U.S. industries than Japanese exports. The best current example of this fear is the proliferation of investment in the United States by Japanese automakers. When planned production lines reach full capacity in the mid-1990s, there is every likelihood of a major domestic automobile production glut, after which Japan's market share—imports plus local production—for new car sales in the United States could approach 40 percent and transform Detroit's Big Three into the Big Two. There will continue to be a U.S. automobile industry, notes a U.S. business school professor, "It's just that the owners will be different."[85]

CONCLUSION

The country that is the most aggressive exporter, and the most constrained importer, of manufactured goods in the world must expect frequent and emotionally charged criticism. While some complaints may be unjustified or exaggerated, Japan's growing global economic power means that its import policies need to be like Caesar's wife—above suspicion—if it wants to be treated like other countries with major trade surpluses such as West Germany. Critics of Japan still have ample reason to characterize Japanese trade behavior as operating on a double standard between minimal willingness to accept foreign competition within their home market and maximum determination that the rest of the world is a proper outlet for a virtually unlimited torrent of Japanese exports. The available data point in the direction of a lack of full reciprocity by a country still not playing the trade game on an entirely fair basis, even after an unprecedented initiation of unilateral liberalization.

The criticism and accusations presented in this chapter probably will meet less doubt among knowledgeable Japanese readers than among Americans. The United States is a legalistic society, and despite the well-documented prima facie case against Japan, there is a paucity of "smoking guns." Americans would like to see a mass of clear evidence that some kind of conspiracy is at work in Japan, especially if the drastic option of deviating from a liberal trade policy is being considered. Informal collusion is intrinsic to the Japanese system, but there is no master conspiracy, no file cabinets overflowing with incriminating memoranda documenting systematic market perversion and proving the existence of Japan, Inc. (The Japanese don't need written directives to enforce the broad programs and goals espoused by their power hierarchy.)

Defenders of Japan are not yet willing to admit that the cultural-economic system of Japan operates differently from those of other democratic, capitalist countries. Some of these people are free-market ideologues. Some are not fully informed about the Japanese system. Some are paid representatives of Japanese interests. The important thing is that fewer and fewer dispassionate observers can sift through the analytic and statistical data without realizing that the Japanese economic drive and trade policies emanate from a national sense of self-identity that is unique in its nature and its motivational impulses. Foreign jealousy is certainly a factor. But there is ample justification for the rest of the world generating complaints faster than Japan can generate excuses about its compatibility with the interests of its trading partners.

CHAPTER 10

Synthesizing the Argument: The Inefficient and the Insensitive

A plague on both your houses.

> —Mercutio, in Shakespeare's *Romeo and Juliet*

When two men fight, both should be punished.

> —Traditional Japanese saying

The extremist with a fixed mind-set will have rejected one of the two previous chapters out of hand and embraced the other as a guide to total understanding of the U.S.–Japanese trade relationship. For the rest of us, the situation is messier, the subject being riddled with subjective value judgments, ambiguities, and paradoxes, with a paucity of scientifically demonstrable cause-and-effect relationships. The often explosive U.S.–Japanese economic relationship often is a classic example of perceptions defining reality and politics superseding economics.

In this chapter I will offer a balanced, objective synthesis of the underlying realities and ambivalences of what arguably has become the world's most important bilateral relationship. The purpose is not to side with one country over the other. A hypothetical "conviction" of the guilty party might have been entertaining and brought things to a precise ending. However, such an approach is not intellectually sound. Neither Japan nor the United States has monopolized wisdom, virtue, and logic any more than either country has monopolized absurdity, deception, and hyperbole. Neither deserves unqualified blame, but neither warrants unqualified praise.

Two distinct manifestations of bilateral trade frictions can be distinguished. The first is Japan's unequalled record of export expansion in a continuous sequence of increasingly sophisticated industrial products. In this case, the Japanese deserve far more praise than condemnation. As will be noted below, Japanese companies played rough and occasionally resorted to unfair trade practices, mainly dumping, to establish market share.

But by and large, export success was a reflection of their superiority in process technology, in management's ability to take long-term time horizons, and in constructive government policies that often are more deserving of adaptation than of denunciation.

The second manifestation of trade frictions is Japan's formal and informal barriers that have made life hell for foreign exporters, even those who expended effort and patience and who, in effect, did everything right. One should not overlook the inadequacies of American industry in general and its export sagacity in particular. Nevertheless, it is a whitewash of Japan's import-inhospitable market and nationalistic mentality to suggest that American complaints were merely the anguished cries of an established, but graying economic power under siege from an aggressive newcomer who previously was little more than a U.S. protectorate.

Regrettably, the focus of the debate over the last 20 years—the bilateral trade balance—has deflected attention from two far more important issues: (1) the ability of Japan to achieve international competitiveness in almost any industry so targeted, and (2) the refusal of Japan to offer opportunities to American businesses to export to Japan in a manner that reciprocates the opportunities afforded to Japanese companies in the U.S. market.

DIFFERENT INPUTS/DIFFERENT OUTPUTS

To evaluate who did what to whom and why, we might start with the question originally posed in chapter 1: What exactly has been the problem between the two countries since 1969? The short answer is a mismatch of policies and attitudes. One country's industrial sector, though deliberately cordoned off from external competition, outperformed that of the other to the extent that painful adjustments were inflicted on the second country over a short period of time. One country possessed exceptional economic and social advantages in its carefully scripted, determined pursuit of international leverage and respectability through industrial strength. Pursuing export maximization and import minimization, this country ignored the costs of its zealousness to itself and its trading partners.

The second country was uncommitted, unwilling, and unable to match this dedication to industrial growth or to use its political leverage to force the first to import significantly more manufactured goods and processed raw materials. The second country also was unmindful of the costs to itself of its zeal to play the game according to its own interpretation of the rules.

Japan was insensitive.

The United States was inefficient.

Japan sought to maximize internal harmony, but ignored the need to seek harmony with its foreign trading partners.

The United States committed itself to the political goal of keeping at least one military step ahead of the Soviets, but ignored the cost of falling behind the Japanese in industrial competitiveness. These inconsistencies in the priorities of the two countries continue to shape bilateral trade relations.

The Japanese economic system has not conformed to Western norms hitherto dominant in international commercial competition. The United States and other countries have failed to rise to the occasion and ameliorate the twin problems of Japan's unusual export and import propensities.

For two decades, the essence of the problem has been that a large, powerful market-oriented economy that sets a low priority on foreign trade can be quite *un*successful competing against the industrial sector of a smaller, but talented, capitalist country where government and business cooperate in a determined approach to foreign trade policy. The story of economic relations between Japan and the United States is one of extremes: one of the world's most open economies and societies, committed to the traditional theory of liberal trade, must compete against one of the world's most closed economies and societies, committed to an inspired form of infant industry protection that methodically induces competitive advantage. The story of bilateral relations is also one of strange phenomena above and beyond those disussed in the previous chapter: Japan, for example, with few formal import barriers to steel, still has an import penetration ratio—imports as a percentage of total consumption—less than half that of the United States, a country that has protected its steel industry from import competition since the late 1960s. Another example is the apparent rejection of an offer of *free* sparkplugs to at least one major Japanese automaker by a U.S. company anxious to prove the reliability of its product in Japanese cars.

Bilateral economic relations have been a kind of morality play illustrating a myriad operational differences in two economies that share the same basic disciplines of the capitalist system. The intensity of conflict rose as the bilateral relationship expanded from a political and military arrangement in which there was a clearly recognized junior and senior status for the partners into a struggle for global industrial supremacy. The conflicts have seemingly fed on themselves, generating inappropriate analyses and responses. Myopia about the arithmetic of the bilateral disequilibrium has derailed efforts to remedy what is a systemic—not arithmetic—problem. This myopia also has given false credence to the assertion that since bilateral trade balances are far less relevant than multilateral balances, U.S. pressures on Japan have been a classic case of overreaction, little more than a rallying point for special interest groups unable to compete. In fact, few U.S. senior officials or business executives have suggested any need for perfect balance, and few have absolved the United States from considerable blame as a cause of the bilateral imbalance. Debating how big an arithmetic imbalance is acceptable is an exercise in futility.

Bilateral trade balances can matter. They take on political importance when one country perceives that the other is gaining advantage by violating the perceived rules of the trade game. They are important economically when discussed in terms of the *causes* of a major disequilibrium. Since Japan is the number one foreign competitor to U.S. industry, reasons for and costs of structural imbalance between the two are of major importance. The sheltering of "sunrise" Japanese industries through a closed market inflicts real handicaps on U.S. competitors. To the extent that U.S. high-tech companies are deprived of reciprocal access to the world's second-largest market, even a bilateral U.S. surplus (presumably based on raw materials) ought not to be considered satisfactory.

When all traditional methods of eliminating a bilateral trade disequilibrium fail over an extended period of time, it is economically significant. When the bilateral deficit reflects an inability of essentially all the exporting industries in the deficit country to achieve market share in the surplus country to a degree comparable to that obtained in other countries, it is economically significant. When the Japanese try to rewrite the law of comparative advantage by claiming they have an across-the-board relative efficiency in the entire manufacturing sector, it is economically significant—not so much as fact as for evidencing the different Japanese concept of trade. When a single bilateral trade deficit remains virtually unchanged while almost all others are improving, thereby becoming a sizeable and growing percentage of the total deficit, it is economically significant.

Japan is neither conspirator nor innocent victim of jealous racists. It is a very different society and economy from the United States. For good reason, Japan has never been successful in persuading the United States, or the rest of the world, that its concepts of the contribution of economic policy to national security and of the contribution of trade policy to economic objectives were equivalent to those practiced among the other industrialized countries. For Japan, economic strength is essential to the larger goal of cultural self-preservation and to the more specific goal of allowing foreign intrusions only on Japan's terms. For Japan, free markets are not an end in themselves. Industrial strength is not chance blessings bestowed by the invisible hand and is too important to be left to fate.

The contemporary cowboy and samurai economies exhibit many important cultural differences that overshadow their similarities in number and importance. Like people everywhere, both Americans and Japanese respond to an established reward system. But their reward systems are dissimilar: The Japanese economy is run mainly for the benefit of producers, while the U.S. economy is run mainly for the benefit of consumers. Japanese workers are supposed to give of themselves, to demonstrate unquestioning loyalty and dedication to their employer. U.S. workers take for granted putting self-interest first, demonstrating maximum loyalty to themselves in the process of extracting maximum financial rewards from their employer. Japanese companies are concerned with making quality goods and achieving the largest possible market share, while U.S. companies look for immediate profits.

The samurai society saves, it cooperates, and it glorifies exports. The cowboy society consumes, it believes in strength through an adversarial process between government and business, and it luxuriates in imports. The samurai society judges proper economic behavior normatively by respect for an intricate web of interpersonal loyalties and obligations. The cowboy society judges proper economic behavior quantitatively, responding to the best price or best offer case by case, believing in an ever-expanding frontier of opportunity for individual self-enhancement. Japan equates industrial strength and self-sufficiency with national security, while the United States equates military strength with national security. "It is only a slight exaggeration to say that the Japanese will accept higher factor costs for essentially the same reasons that the United States will overpay for its defense systems. It makes each feel more secure."[1] The two countries maintain disparate foreign relations objectives that, ironically, have been simultaneously achieved: the United States has successfully minimized straying from its liberal trade beliefs while maximizing its short-term consumption; Japan has successfully minimized foreign intrusion in its economy while maximizing both exports and global market shares of its big industrial companies. Mutual contentment with results may be the best explanation of the systemic imbalance that now has persisted for more than two decades. The United States successfully pursued an international political policy of containing the spread of communism. Japan successfully followed an international commercial policy of spreading exports. Consequently, both countries achieved their respective global priorities.

The Japanese recognized that the best, perhaps the only, means of restoring full economic vigor and dignity was organization—patterns of cooperation that complemented the talents of the Japanese people. Society at large, the national government, and industrial corporations effectively imbued the Japanese character with a commitment to economic recovery that emphasized harmony and foresight. Policies, programs, hard work, and guile were incorporated into a drive to do whatever was necessary to develop international industries as quickly as possible.

Americans in the early 1960s recognized neither the long-term Japanese challenge nor any need to set industrial competitiveness as a top national priority. Society as a whole, government, unions, and corporations were organized to serve individual needs. Organization was used to redistribute existing wealth among interest groups rather than create new wealth for society as a whole. Through 1989, the pursuit of self-interest worked reasonably well in competing against foreign countries—with the exception of Japan.

Neither Japan nor the United States deals well with the systemic changes in the international trading system that emerged in the 1960s. Japan opted for the politics of sincerity and the economics of shallow public relations gestures. The United States adopted the politics of intimidation and the economics of complacency instead of meeting the problem head on. The persistence and intensity of the frictions between the two suggest that a disequilibrium in trade relations existed throughout the period reviewed, although there are no data to permit precise measurements. The United States, like other countries, judged Japan's international behavior in the 1969–89 period as unacceptable. Even if Japan's counterarguments to U.S. complaints had been economically flawless, public opinion in the United States still would have perceived an inequitable relationship in the intolerable discomfort of U.S. companies and workers. As E. H. Carr noted more than forty years ago, "Economic forces are in fact political forces. . . . The science of economics presupposes a given political order, and cannot be profitably studied in isolation from politics."[2]

The United States suffered a genuine disequilibrium because most Americans perceived its existence. Popular opinion and government decree define the condition, not econometric analysis. Economics aside, a political disequilibrium emerged in an international system where political forces are dominant over economic forces. Japan's rising bilateral surplus ignited pressures for adjustments in the form of increased U.S. exports and more moderate Japanese shipments. Economic arguments in Japan's defense could not dismiss political priorities in the United States or excuse the nonmarket element of Japan's economic strengths. In addition, no one could guarantee that an open-ended deterioration in U.S. industrial competitiveness would not have serious implications for the future of the U.S. economy.

A relatively inefficient country operating in the international economy inevitably must pay the price for its lack of competitiveness. Aside from questions of domestic economic rejuvenation, there is a choice that must be made between: (1) deflationary macroeconomic policies that lead to rising unemployment, (2) import restrictions that subsidize relatively inefficient industries, and (3) a depreciating currency. The unique U.S. ability to pay for its imports of real economic resources by foreigners increasing their dollar holdings reduced but did not eliminate the burdens imposed by Japan's superior competitiveness in the industrial sector.

As nature abhors a vacuum, political economy cannot accept a disequilibrium. U.S. dissatisfaction with Japan's export exuberance and import inhospitality was inevitable. Ad hoc export restraints, floating exchange rates, Japanese import liberalization, U.S. export promotion all had in common the failure to eliminate the perceived disequilibrium. The "internationalization" of Japan's economy was viewed by the United States and other countries as being unacceptably slow at best, and possibly illusory. Japan's hunger for world leadership in key industries was perceived by many Americans as an obsession that could not be reproduced in the U.S. system and thus threatened U.S. status and power.

Right and wrong become secondary intellectual constructs in this situation. Until the perceived structural competitive gap is deemed to be narrowing, the U.S. political system will likely continue invective and protectionist threats against Japanese products. Japan's resistance to altering its economic priorities encouraged incessant U.S. pressures for changes in Japanese trade policies. U.S. demands, however, constituted a decidedly inadequate adjustment mechanism. Both countries groped for an effective means of accommodating Japanese export "overachieving" to the inability of the United States to rise adequately to the commercial challenge. Adequate response was still not forthcoming at the onset of the 1990s.

A communication gap born from cultural difference was only part of the problem. Comprehension of the other country's needs, goals, and motives, as well as the legitimacy of its complaints, would not necessarily have sufficed to produce a harmonious bilateral economic relationship. Understanding is not the same as acceptance, and the Japanese would not have accepted a greater presence of U.S. manufactured-goods imports or foreign direct investment, even if they understood fully U.S. sentiment regarding bilateral strains after 1969. Japan would not have delayed achievement of domestic economic goals or changed broader societal practices to accommodate U.S. demands; internationalization was, and is, resisted in Japan because it poses a threat to the unique cultural base of Japan's economy. Insular feelings have not disappeared even in an age of economic interdependence. Nor would the United States have accepted the costs of diminished internal production and jobs associated with Japan's increased commercial competitiveness, no matter how well it understood Japanese practices and sentiment. The United States would not have played by the economics textbook even if it perceived that Japan's strength rested entirely on fair practices that could be emulated in the United States. The primary focus in any circumstance would have been self-protection in the quickest manner possible. Mutual lack of understanding and poor communications only compounded a basic economic dilemma.

Japan and the United States deserve each other's scorn. The Japanese have demonstrated remarkable insensitivity, putting themselves in a fool's paradise. They thought the rest of the world would welcome their becoming the world's principal generator of internationally traded manufactured goods and would support the insularity of their economic system. Americans have demonstrated remarkable unresponsiveness. They, too, opted for a false security, interpreting Japan's economic success as based on temporary factors, unfair trade practices, and cultural idiosyncrasies. They, too, were foolish in believing the Japanese would be touched with compassion for faltering U.S. industries. In short, Japan failed to consider the problem from other countries viewpoints, while the United States contented itself with simplistic excuses for its economic shortcomings vis-à-vis Japan. The cumulative impact of disparate economic ideologies, economic priorities, and cultural patterns has been a communication gap of monumental proportions. Despite the extent and frequency of bilateral talks on economic matters, the two countries understood each other only slightly better at the onset of the 1990s than they did twenty years previously. Most Americans cannot yet grasp the limited applicability in Japan of Western-style thinking. Most Japanese cannot fully believe that some of their corporations utilized dirty tricks to limit market access to certain foreign-made manufactured goods or accept the argument that there is more to Japan's trade successes than hard work on their part and Western decadence.

THE UNITED STATES'S WORST ENEMY: THE UNITED STATES

The poor record of the United States in effectively competing with Japanese industry is self-inflicted to a significant degree. The absence of a tangible, self-evident crisis has fostered a U.S. government willingness to rely more on rhetoric than meaningful action, even as foreign competition intensifies and the cost of shortcomings in economic policies and performance rises ever higher. The United States could afford lax industrial efforts and pursuit of international political-military priorities only as long as it maintained technological superiority.

Japan is not so much an enemy as a mirror image of U.S. industrial and foreign trade weaknesses. More than any other country, Japan introduced an obsolescence into U.S. international economic policies, the nature and significance of which is still foolishly minimized in the United States. The U.S. industrial machine was built on markets that changed only slowly and used relatively simple assembly systems conducive to mass production. The Japanese mastered today's new industrial reality of exploiting rapidly changing, information-intensive technologies involving complex assembly operations, dependent on skilled employees and teamwork, and enhanced by product differentiation and sophisticated global marketing operations.

The decline in the competitiveness of U.S. companies was inevitable in mature industries where current technology is disseminated on a worldwide basis. Unfortunately, the problem was magnified by two factors. The most important was the compression of this trend into a relatively short time period. The second factor was the rapid, broadly based success of one foreign competitor: Japan. The burdens of dislocations and adjustment would have been considerably easier if any of the following contingencies had materialized:

1. Japan's resurgence had not been so quick;

2. More U.S. business executives had geared up to fight the new war of international competition instead of being content to seek import protection;

3. The "nonindustrial" policy emanating from Washington had been better thought out; or

4. Greater access to the Japanese market had existed.

The United States lacked the will, not the capacity, to respond more effectively to the Japanese industrial surge. At least three specific reasons explain the U.S. failure to respond in kind, as it had so often done before in its history, to a new challenge:

1. It did not perceive the need; U.S. overconfidence about the power of its economic prowess dominated thinking in the early post-World War II era.

2. It did not know how; the Japanese challenge was unprecedented, unforeseen, unquantifiable, and underestimated.

3. It could not; national security, domestic social priorities, the short-term time horizons of business executives, and lack of social cohesion precluded any effort to emulate Japanese economic goals and policies.

Over the span of two decades, most U.S. observers attributed Japan's success to unfair advantages (cheap labor, minimal military expenditures, etc.) and unfair practices (dumping, etc.). Furthermore, the eclipse of the Japanese economic miracle has been forecast with boring repetition, be it because of a lack of creativeness or impending decadence in the form of increased leisure and spending. It is only relatively recently that a grudging acceptance has spread that Japanese goods are successful in the American market mainly because they perform better, are more advanced, are cheaper, or some combination thereof. Nevertheless, no credence is given by most opinion makers and decision makers that the University of Tokyo school of thought extolling certain forms of industrial policy as well as pragmatic trade policy could run roughshod over the University of Chicago school of thought extolling markets free of government involvement and free trade.

U.S. economic ideology and economic priorities will not change until political leaders galvanize or respond to a popular consensus that further erosions in the U.S. standard of living and global position are unacceptable and that it would be cost-effective to reduce increases in consumption and to introduce more effective business practices and government policies. The U.S. political system is not primed for taking quick, decisive action on an issue that is as abstract, distant, and confusing as is the external threat to the country's future economic well-being. Paralysis was what was to be expected—and what occurred. An increasing number of Americans express concern that their children will be left to service the spiraling national debt, without improvements in their standard of living. Amidst record peacetime economic expansion, the American people, in effect, have conspired with their government in the use of smoke and mirrors to reduce the published size of the federal budget deficit. As long as mercantilistic countries like Japan exchange their real economic resources for dollars and then return most of them to the United States, the emperor can thrive without clothes.

Prominent on the list of Washington's deficiencies in economic policy is failure to deal with inadequate productivity increases. During the 1980s, as shown in figure 10.1, the United States had the lowest average annual percentage increases in productivity of any major industrial country. This is not a new trend. In the 1960s, the average annual percentage increase in U.S. productivity in manufacturing was 3.5 percent, compared with 8.8 percent in Japan and 4.5 percent, on average, in the Group of Seven industrial countries; in the 1970s, these figures were 3.0, 5.3, and 3.3 percent, respectively.[3] This long-standing acceptance of below average productivity increases has heavily burdened U.S. global industrial competitiveness. Japan is not to be damned for being above average.

Nor is it Japan's fault that the U.S. public—at least until the recent thaw in the cold war—was willing to pay phenomenal sums to protect itself from communists and to pay more than $500 million apiece for Stealth bombers. Nor is it Japan's fault that Americans have refused to mobilize the financial resources (a euphemism for raising taxes) to pay for a better educational system, meaningful attention to substance abuse (a scourge whose total cost to the United States is well above $100 billion annually), the rebuilding of its decaying transportation infrastructure, or crime-free streets. It is not Japan's fault that U.S. political leaders cling to the obsolete belief that spending on military hardware stimulates advances in commercial technology, when the reverse is increasingly true, or that they limit government-business cooperation to production of spy satellites of mind-boggling technical capabilities, space-age weapons, and a flourishing agri-

**Figure 10.1 Worker Productivity
(Average Annual Percent Change in Output
per Person, 1980–1988)**

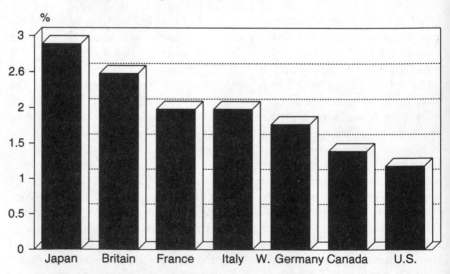

SOURCES: *Washington Post* and British Information Services.

culture sector, rejecting such cooperation in commercial technology (because the government cannot and should not pick winners and losers).

Japan did not impose short-term thinking on U.S. managers or conspire to fascinate the U.S. economy with financing mergers, acquisitions, and leveraged buy-outs with the mountain of appropriately named junk bonds that require everything to go right for them to be able to repay debt on schedule. Japan does not need to apologize for the fact that a readership poll published in *Consumer Reports* magazine in April 1990 found that Japanese cars had widened their quality advantage over U.S. automakers; nor need it apologize for producing twenty-eight of thirty-one models receiving the highest quality rating, while all but one (a Jaguar) of the thirty-three worst were American.[4] The Japanese did not create the conditions that made the term brain-dead appropriate to categorize the potency of contemporary political creativity in Washington.

All these are home-grown failings. The political columnist George Will did not overstate the situation when he wrote in early 1990, "not since the 1920s have Americans looked less to the national government for leadership, or believed less that what it does matters to their lives." President George Bush's first year in office, he added, "illustrates—in a sense is—the echoing emptiness at the core of contemporary politics. Its intellectual and moral flaccidity reflect . . . the sagging of America deeper into a peripheral role abroad and self-indulgence at home."[5] The economic result of political drift will be pockets of private wealth amidst deteriorating public goods and sagging industrial competitiveness. Aided by deregulation and changes in tax law, a handful of hungry capitalists propelled themselves on a self-indulgent, often speculative or law-breaking money-making binge in the 1980s, and much energy will need to be expended in the 1990s to clean up the mess they left. The average citizen has seen the American dream becoming so elusive that an unprecedented revolt—to *increase* government revenues—is emerging in some areas to preserve public services.

The U.S. government quickly recognized, understood, and responded to Soviet challenges in military and space competition, but has been largely oblivious to appreciating the extent of Japan's use of industrial growth and trade relations to achieve national goals. American history and ideology contains blind spots that dismiss the possibility that the free market is not necessarily the ultimate model of economic organization and that other societies might transcend individual greed in favor of a dedicated, brilliantly conceived collective effort to realize societal goals centered on industrial growth.

An evaluation of the U.S. economic performance leads to the conclusion that the United States was much less prepared than Japan for the inevitability of change. The result of economic failures has been the transference of the inevitable adjustment process to the political sector, as exemplified by repetitious demands on Japan for "voluntary" export restraint agreements. U.S. trade policy is, and always will be, vulnerable to political pressures for short-term remedies in the form of import barriers.

The bottom line is that import protectionism in the United States has not been, is not, and never will be an optimal response to more efficient competition. If the United States does not pay more attention to preparing itself for the future, it will be living in the past. Living standards will regress. Restricted import competition will cause further domestic industrial decay, thereby necessitating still more protectionism. Uniquely competitive dynamics within the Japanese economic system exempted Japan, at least in the 1969–89 period, from these widely experienced results of protectionism.

Ironically, independent-minded Americans seem more anxious to adopt Japanese practices—teamwork, quality control, better labor-management relations, more accommodating government economic policies, and so forth—than vice versa. To its credit, the United States has been a leading advocate of economic changes in Japan that should benefit Japanese consumers as well as U.S. producers. Progress has been slow, but it is likely there would have been none at all if opening up to the outside world had been left entirely in the hands of the ruling Japanese Liberal Democratic party. It is no exaggeration to say that since the 1960s, unrelenting U.S. government pressures have been tantamount to the most effective opposition party in Japan.

Since the 1970s, U.S. economic performance vis-à-vis Japan has been stuck between the rock of domestic inadequacies and the hard place of a trading partner with different priorities. Improving the bilateral performance is not an either/or proposition. An economically sound U.S. response to Japan's competitive threat requires *both* an internal and an external dimension. Japan's attitudes toward the relative desirability of exporting and importing represent a real problem for the United States, and only Japan can change them. Structural weaknesses in U.S. industrial and technological efforts are U.S. problems of major importance, the correction of which must come from within.

JAPAN'S WORST ENEMY: JAPAN

Japan seems determined to dominate every important sector of advanced commercial technology. The Japanese are not unique in this ambition, but they are unique in the competence and success with which they pursue it. In Japan's case, competence begins with insecurity about an unpredictable and undependable outside world, continues with a chain of cultural factors, and culminates with superb intellect. If extremism in the pursuit of economic power were not a vice, there would be few grounds for criticizing the Japanese.

The Japanese have no master plan for economic conquest. No documents or credible witnesses suggest any nationwide (as opposed to corporate or industry-wide) conspiracy. But the Japanese do have a national purpose of cultural self-preservation, and in the post–World War II period, global industrial power and technological innovation have become synonymous in Japan with national security. The entire nation was and still is mobilized to achieve economic goals. Any let up in the quest for world-class status in advanced industry is unacceptable. It is feared that larger, though slower witted, foreigners will dominate if Japan ever becomes content to rest on its laurels or to behave like a Western country. Since the late nineteenth century, the Japanese people have been inspired like few others to great levels of accomplishment. Such social psychology would appear to be easier in a racially homogeneous country where a single word *(gaijin)* means both "outsider" and "foreigner," and another *(chigaimasu)* both "to be wrong" and "to be different." So, too, consensus would appear easier to achieve in a country where a high school educator can tell his students that "The purpose of . . . education . . . isn't to develop your personalities. The purpose is to enable you to conform to society."[6]

This socio-psychological explanation might be criticized as extreme, extraneous, or simplistic. But it does explain the humorless fanaticism and ruthless efficiency by which Japanese industry, since the 1950s, systematically went about the twin tasks of surpassing its more relaxed, less organized foreign competition and limiting the access for foreign manufactured goods to Japan's home market. The cultural approach also explains why even the brightest, most accomplished people of this major economic power can be so insular that they have not yet been active candidates for top positions in the international civil service of global economic institutions.

The tenets of sociology and psychology have been used by noted U.S. scholars to analyze Japanese economic behavior. Peter Drucker popularized the term "adversarial trader" for Japan:

> Competitive trade aims at creating a customer. Adversarial trade
> aims at dominating an industry. . . . Competitive trade is fighting
> a battle. Adversarial trade aims at winning the war by destroying
> the enemy's army and its capacity to fight.[7]

Arthur Schlesinger, Jr. accused Japan of being "even more mystical [and] humorless in its hypernationalist traditions than Germany and far more scornful of other countries."[8] Charles H. Ferguson has spoken of Japan's "technoeconomic Prussianism."[9]

The assertion that Japanese economic performance illustrates the student outperforming its teacher may be flattering to the U.S. ego, but does not accurately reflect the way history, culture, and psychology affect an economy. The Japanese prefer control and manipulation to the vagaries of the invisible hand of the market place, industrial domination to consumer satisfaction. Japan opens markets to imports because of foreign pressure, not because it wants trade to flow freely. (The downside of letting in foreigners who won't necessarily follow the rule of what's best for Japan was empirically demonstrated in early 1990, when several days of computer-driven program trading in stocks by foreign securities firms was cited as a major cause of wild swings in prices on the Tokyo stock market.)

The difficulty in exporting to Japan has been discussed in detail. Increasingly, the efforts are paying off in realizing the rewards of selling in Japan's large, affluent market. It is no longer uncommonly difficult to export most consumer goods to Japan, in part because Japanese consumers no longer avoid purchasing imports; nor is it uncommonly difficult for most foreign companies or individual entrepreneurs to set up a business in Japan and successfully sell goods and services. Problems are increasingly confined to the exporting of high-tech goods to Japan. Even when the market is legally open, it can be impenetrable. This is especially true for products that threaten targeted industries; for products produced within the *keiretsu*; for products made by reliable subcontractors; or for products that would be sold in retail outlets controlled by Japanese producers. It is true, to some extent, that their businesspeople prefer dealing with fellow Japanese suppliers because they better understand the society's premium on trust, dependability, and mutual obligations and also because their presence in the Japanese market is usually seen as being more permanent than ephemeral foreigners. This preference for dealing with other Japanese partly reflects the fact that foreigners have gotten a late start, having been systematically excluded from business activity in Japan throughout all of the immediate postwar period. It is therefore too soon to remove the stigma of anti-import bias from most Japanese companies.

Success with high-tech goods depends on meeting most or all of the following criteria: the exporter having a unique, high-quality product that is new to Japan but not threatening the success of a targeted industry, making a major marketing commitment or involving one of the small start-up Japanese companies that are taking on established powers like NTT, and on the U.S. government having expressed specific intent to watch out for possible Japanese dirty tricks. Thus, Motorola can export a large volume of pagers and cellular telephones. Given enough of a price and performance edge in a very competitive sector, even imports of high-tech goods will prevail—at least temporarily. If the Japanese economic system was a thoroughly rigged conspiracy, manipulated by an all-knowing, all-powerful bureaucracy, formal import barriers would never have been necessary. At some point in any capitalist system, the survival of the company must come first; in such cases Japanese purchasing agents can be expected to override the traditions of supporting a targeted industry and of preserving personal relationships and buy imports. The Japanese attitudinal disinclination to go with imports is conceptually a non-tariff barrier, but in practice it works like a tariff: with a big enough price advantage, an import can circumvent the obstacles. Nevertheless, runaway success for exporters of high-tech goods to Japan is like beating the odds in gambling; it happens, but not very often.

In some cases, initiating or expanding exports to Japan is an all but impossible task. Problems exemplified by advanced telecommunications equipment and amorphous metals in chapter 9 show that most Japanese view nurturing domestic industry as far more important than any benefit of competitive imports saturating an existing or even a *potential* market. In such cases, foreigners are fighting the Japanese notion that when it comes to targeted industries, importing instead of buying domestically will hurt the long-term health of the Japanese economy. In all too many cases, exporters of high-tech goods are fighting an economic version of guerrilla warfare, chasing fleeting, or even invisible, images rather than fixed targets. Only about Japan could it be said that it was theoretically possible that the end of all remaining direct and indirect overt trade barriers would produce only a nominal reduction in the trade surplus. In other words, it may be that the import liberalization process will never be a significant force for change, even when completed.

Despite the dubious distinction of having by no means exhausted their direct and indirect import barriers after three decades of nonstop efforts, the Japanese could be expected to exhibit more candor about the effects of their remaining import-retarding practices. U.S. government negotiators are likely to be offered, in order, the following sequence of excuses by the Japanese government concerning market access:

1. "We are not doing it";

2. "There is no GATT violation";

3. "There is something wrong with the price or quality of the U.S. good being offered in the Japanese market";

4. "There has not been adequate testing of the new technology"; and

5. "Since the problem is possibly of limited proportions, let's talk at length [and hopefully your short American attention span will cause the complaint to fade out with time]."

Only cultural factors can explain why the Japanese continue to venerate a large trade surplus long after they have achieved a strong industrial base and massive holdings of foreign exchange reserves. An entire country avidly and persistently pursuing a net exchange of massive amounts of real economic resources for paper money is inconsistent with economic theory as taught in the United States. Economically, it would make far more sense for Japan to invest its earnings in the lagging Japanese infrastructure (housing, roads, recreation facilities) or in developing countries in the third world. Instead, most Japanese capital is channeled into speculative purchases of land and stocks at home and into the already affluent, overconsuming United States. There is nothing inherently wrong with an affluent country with a high savings rate and a genuinely liberal trade policy financing a chronic current account surplus with a net capital outflow to less advanced countries; this is what the United States should be doing now, just as it did in the 1950s and early 1960s. The problem with Japan doing it is the lingering doubts about market access for imports and the direction of its capital outflows.

If some cultural traits have contributed to an excessive Japanese embrace of mercantilism, positive cultural traits and common sense have contributed to Japan's admirable competitiveness. To a large extent, there are no deep secrets behind this; there are no mysterious "black boxes." Success has come to the Japanese, at least in part, because cultural factors have encouraged them to venerate the spiritual rewards of hard work, to have long-term time horizons, to emphasize the advantages of teamwork and collective responsibilities over personal aggrandizement, to be sticklers for detail, to welcome the opportunity to serve well, and to have a kind of inspired insecurity that has let them turn weakness into strength time and time again.

Beyond cultural factors, "applied" intelligence is an important, continuing cause of Japan's competitive success. Asked recently to explain the long business success of a friend in Washington who heads a private firm that analyzes public policy, I came up with the following list: tolerate nothing short of the highest quality service to clients; anticipate and address clients' evolving needs; keep after staff to improve the product no matter how well the firm is doing; view competing firms with a visceral fear that they are out to take away everything that you personally hold dear; and instill long-term loyalty in employees by convincing them that they will profit as the firm does. As I spoke, I realized these were the standards of successful Japanese management, an observation in fact neither coincidental nor shocking. Good management is good management. It is based on universal truths, not cultural virtues monopolized by the Japanese. Their intellectual understanding of how to achieve what is really important in the manufacturing process, not culture per se, has been the "first among equals" responsible for Japan's important innovations in process technology.

Japan's success in attaining international industrial competitiveness is truly impressive. The level of this success should not be underestimated, nor should the reasons for it be denigrated. Even if the Japanese import barriers are as bad as the harshest critic suggests, it cannot be denied that Japanese industry has been an extraordinarily successful exporter because it consistently produces goods more efficiently and at higher levels of quality. It is impossible to quantify precisely how efficient the Japanese really are internationally, but the following three examples suggest that they often are without peer. First is the breadth of Japan's world-class industrial status: in 1988, in microelectronics and telecommunications equipment, Japan was in first place for global export market share; second place in computers, machine tools, and robotics; and third in scientific and precision equipment.[10] Motor vehicles provide a second example; despite paying a hefty 25 percent tariff on light (mainly pickup) trucks exported to the United States (a legacy of U.S. trade retaliation in the sixties against the European Community) and despite yen revaluation, Japanese producers still sold hundreds of thousands of pickup trucks annually in the United States during the eighties.[11]

The third example of Japanese competitiveness classically illustrates the quick and effective Japanese response to adversity. Faced with an international price disadvantage associated with yen appreciation in the mid-eighties, Japanese industrial companies expended little energy bemoaning their fate, but sprang into a search for new methods of cutting production costs to protect their overseas market share. A measure of their success is that it is now conventional wisdom that the larger, more efficient Japanese industries could still break even if the yen rose to an exchange rate of 100 to the dollar. Reduced production costs, offshore sourcing, foreign direct investment, and better marketing have led many analysts to conclude that the larger Japanese companies have made themselves independent of any foreseeable appreciation of the yen against the dollar. The means were an awesome ability to minimize production costs, not dirty tricks.

In producing and exporting greater quantities of cheaper and better manufactured goods, the Japanese outthought, outworked, outsmarted, outflanked, and outran most of their U.S. and other foreign competition. They were among the first in the modern world economy to determine (1) that comparative advantage was not a given, and (2) that the government could successfully coax the private sector into industrial achievements that seemed economically impractical, if not impossible. The Japanese anticipated and initiated change in industrial production better than anyone else in the 1969–89 period. They combined national goals and commitment by society with private industry's brilliant mastery of the production process. Conversely, when it came to the issue of equity in providing reciprocal market access to foreigners, the Japanese anticipated and initiated change less than anyone else.

Any Western evaluation of the Japanese phenomenon must recognize the limits inherent in the Western intellect in understanding Japanese behavior. The incessant energy of this culture remains an enigma. Another unsolved mystery is Japan's ability to turn some basic concepts of Western economic theory on their heads. Some of the world's most competitive industrial sectors emerged from a most unlikely environment. Cartels were encouraged, the volume of competition frequently was calibrated by government dictates, and foreign competition was prevented from pushing aside an emerging industry. A U.S. policy approach that ignored antitrust enforcement and violated liberal trade principles undoubtedly would have produced a disastrous, rather than a merely inadequate, U.S. economic performance.

The explosive growth in Japanese industrial strength is partially an outgrowth of governmental policies that emerged relatively recently in Japan's long history. The acceptance of a role for government in the management of the economy has long been greater in Japan than in the United States, but not until after World War II was the optimal balance between official guidance and private initiative perfected. The Japanese realized that government policy could join land, labor, and capital in creating comparative advantage. The fact of the matter is that investment and risk taking were encouraged in certain sectors as could not have been done under pure market conditions. Japan's macroeconomic and industrial policies successfully introduced a rich atmosphere of encouragement and safety to venturesome Japanese industrialists. The elite bureaucratic corps that staffed Japan's postwar economic ministries excelled in several respects. It exploited the population's respect for authority, hierarchy, and status. It had a vision of where Japan should be heading. It created a stable, uninterrupted policy environment that nurtured the emergence of a new breed of viciously competitive companies.

The continuity and predictability of Japan's growth-promoting economic policies stand in stark contrast to the measures followed by recent U.S. presidents, Congress, and leaders of the Federal Reserve Board. This is not necessarily praise for Japan and criticism for the United States. Each had valid, responsible, and attainable objectives. The Japanese pursued economic strength, while the United States opted to maximize consumption in the short term and defend the noncommunist world from the Soviet threat. Each fostered institutional arrangements and policies that encouraged successful pursuit of these diverse goals.

Although MITI has done many things in pursuit of the goals of economic growth, it was not responsible for teaching large corporations an export strategy that rewrote the international commercial textbooks. Business executives learned how to operate in the modern international marketplace better than anyone else. One of the unexplainable talents of the Japanese has been their uncanny ability, despite their different traditions and attitudes, to crack the code of Western consumers' preference.

A question must be posed: was Japan's high-speed pursuit of its perceived economic destiny worth the costs? The continuous reelection of the Liberal Democratic party in free elections suggests that the majority of Japanese would answer this question in the affirmative. From the West's perspective, the cost-benefit ratio looks less favorable. Environmental concerns, from pollution to urban crowding, have been sacrificed to the overly revered god of economic growth. Any government in North America or Western Europe that asked its citizens to make the sacrifices demanded of the Japanese people would not have survived for long. Most Japanese were so preoccupied with domestic goals that they ignored the costs of adjustment they were imposing on other countries. The political determination by the United States, among others, that Japan's trade position was out of step with the rest of the world dominated all economic arguments. Even today, only a relatively small, elite minority of Japanese accept the need for major changes in their country's insular view of international economic relations; and they think this way not because of an innate love of internationalism, but because they correctly perceived how Japan's interests must be served in the future.

By the late seventies, Japan's naïveté was a heavy burden on bilateral relations with the United States and most other countries. Only Japanese observers and foreign economists viewed Japan's willingness to cover the earth with the output of its industrial efficiency as a virtue. Only Japanese could feel that promises to its trading partners of additional market access at unspecified times in the future were sufficient payment of dues for an international economic superpower. The Japanese are not being penalized for hard work, but for mistakenly supposing trading partners would not really insist on operating commercial relations on a foundation of reciprocity. The Japanese government believed U.S. demands for increased market access could be handled by conciliatory gestures of good faith, but such efforts were bound to be rejected as meaningless or disingenuous by those seeking specific objectives rather than symbolism.

The inward-looking pattern of Japanese thought has exaggerated and prolonged the difficult issue of integrating this unique economy into the international system. The Japanese, in the period under review, never demonstrated any comprehension of a basic principle of international trading relations: that it is not enough to be superb in the production of manufactured goods. Japan never accepted the fact that its trade success was a nail sticking up so far that, inevitably, it would be hammered down by deficit countries. The extremes of its trade performance left Japan with virtually no reserves of goodwill with which to defend itself against either fair or unfair foreign complaints and demands.

All praise and criticism of Japan needs to be tempered by the realization that its trading policies are changing relatively rapidly. On the positive side, the Japanese market continues to open wider. Another positive change that can be anticipated is that the "critical mass" factor will change Japanese attitudes, that is, the proliferation of overseas travel by Japanese will educate them about what a pro-consumer market looks like, and the rising numbers of children of businesspeople stationed overseas who are returning to Japanese schools should reduce the long-standing prejudice and suspicion about students educated abroad. At the margin, attitudes toward work habits and imports will be different among generations born into relative affluence. Japan has an excellent record of dealing with its problems, and foreign perceptions that it still is not playing the trade game fairly is a genuine problem for the Japanese.

The insecurity that incites the Japanese to excel in all important industrial technologies seems no more likely than ever before to subside. The linchpin of Japan's system—the alliances within industry and between it and the government—are unlikely to loosen. Ironically, a change induced by increasing Japanese imports of manufactured goods will be, other things being equal, an increase in exports: economic theory teaches that a country's restrictions on imports have the eventual effect of imposing restraints on its exports. In Japan's case, its unusually low propensity to import manufactured goods encouraged protectionist trade policies in foreign countries, deprived trading partners (outside of the United States) of additional foreign exchange which could have been used to purchase additional Japanese goods, and at times, because of large, growing Japanese trade surpluses, tended to cause yen appreciation relative to the dollar.

Until Japan can convince its trading partners it has broadened its self-centered commercial agenda, foreigners will continue to measure their access to Japan's market by its barriers rather than its claims of an open market. Until Japan qualifies for the image accorded West Germany, that is, as a country pursuing common objectives and seeking economic integration with its major trading partners, the Japanese will be viewed skeptically by other countries as suspicious outsiders with nationalistic intentions.

PRIORITIES FOR THE FUTURE

Where do the two economies go from here? Trade frictions and confrontations show no sign of ending; they may well intensify. Neither of the two systemic problems spawned by the bilateral policy and attitudinal mismatch has been solved: a declining U.S. competitiveness that encourages Japanese exports or the inhospitable Japanese climate that discourages imports of manufactured goods, especially in the high-tech sector. Reciprocity is a concept easier said than achieved. Even, as the nineties start, the latest Japanese market-opening measures generate excessive media optimism that they will restore trade harmony. Regrettably, the extent to which expectations of conflict resolution rise after the latest round of negotiations seems inversely proportional to the observers' comprehension of the thirty-year history of Japanese liberalization.

Opening the Japanese market is vital, and efforts to accomplish this end must continue. But the likelihood increases that the most important problem for the future is the continued inability of U.S. industry to remain competitive with its Japanese competition, particularly in the critical high-tech sector. Growing evidence suggests Japan's leadership in production skills and its emerging leadership in advanced technology may accelerate rather than narrow in the 1990s and into the next century. The improved manufacturing efforts of many U.S. companies and the continuing U.S. lead in basic science are no guarantees for staying neck and neck with a rapidly moving target as committed and talented as Japan. And the remedy for this deficiency is to be found within the United States, not in Japan.

Although we can never definitively know what the future holds, a prudent country gives careful thought to the possibility that adversity lurks just over the horizon and prepares remedial policy initiatives to hopefully forestall it. It is tempting to think things have gone so well for Japan for so long that the odds favor future difficulties, thereby diminishing the need for new U.S. policies. Some argue concerns about continuing U.S. decline are too pessimistic, simplistic extrapolations of past trends. Consider the following angst:

> We see a foreign challenger breaking down the political and psychological framework of our societies. We are witnessing the prelude to our own historical bankruptcy. . . . This war—and it is a war—is being fought not with dollars, or oil, or steel, or even with modern machines. It is being fought with creative imagination and organizational talent.[12]

This sounds like contemporary high anxiety about the Japanese menace. In fact, the passage is from *The American Challenge,* J.-J. Servan-Schreiber's widely discussed warning in the late sixties that Europe's industry was doomed to fall under U.S. domination. In retrospect, it was an exaggerated fear. The ebb and flow of economic fortune found a happier medium.

Yet, it may be well to heed the warning of Professor Paul Kennedy, the unofficial laureate of fallen great powers:

> If a nation becomes so indebted that it loses its credit-worthiness; if its manufacturing base shrinks so much that it cannot produce goods (for example, microchips) needed for its own industry and its defense forces; if its currency has less and less value on international exchanges; if it devotes too much of its national resources to consumption and defense spending, at the cost of long-term investment; if it produces fewer and fewer engineers and more and more lawyers and dentists and stock jobbers, then sooner or later all that is going to have serious *impacts* upon the wealth and strength of the nation. If that is "economic determinism," so be it. It sounds more like common sense to me.[13]

I must emphasize Kennedy's important caveat that the *causes* of such trends are neither irreversible or inevitable. The bottom line in forecasting the future of U.S.–Japanese trade relations, therefore, is first, assessing the likelihood that the adverse trends in U.S. international industrial performance since 1970 will improve, and second, assessing the probable costs if they do not.

These assessments will be made in the pessimistic chapter that follows. Its central premise is that we can no longer take for granted that, even if

Japan genuinely adopts a consensus that more manufactured imports are in its own national interest, U.S. industrial competitiveness, relative to Japan and third countries, will be sufficient to trigger a large, sustained upsurge in U.S. exports to Japan. The U.S. industrial sector seems unlikely to shine in the truest measure of competitiveness: the magnitude of incremental exports if Japan opened its mind as well as its rules.

CHAPTER 11

Bowing to the Opposition—The Costs of Second Place in Industrial Supremacy

> It is an iron law of history that power passes from debtor to creditor.
>
> —Senator Daniel Patrick Moynihan

In how many industries and technologies must the Japanese surpass their U.S. counterparts before the critical mass of public and governmental opinion sits up, takes notice, and demands remedial action? As of 1990, all but a few of Japan's targeted industries had either put their U.S. counterpart on the defensive (as in semiconductors) or assumed a role of undisputed global dominance (consumer electronics). Exceptions like aircraft and pharmaceuticals aside, in virtually no case has a Japanese effort in an industry involving complex assembly or volume production failed to become a world-class competitor. A prudent economic policy agenda for the United States would begin with thinking the "economically unthinkable," namely the possibility that the Japanese industrial development model as a whole is superior overall to the *current* U.S. model in terms of physical output. It would be more prudent for U.S. economic policy to accept this worst case assumption than to continue blissfully in the increasingly dubious belief that the tried and true U.S. system for generating industrial strength is so good and so appropriate to the U.S. psyche that, even without improvement, it will continue to prove itself superior to any known alternative.

It would also seem prudent to discard two decades of wishful thinking that, for one reason or another, the Japanese miracle has peaked and reservoirs of U.S. dynamism will assure a triumphant comeback. Accumulating data on the bilateral economic relationship undermines this notion. When something is not working well, it needs to be fixed. The Soviet Union, for example, has radically redefined how it calculates its national security interests and decided to put economic concerns above imposing an increasingly ineffectual ideology on its own people as well as its former East European satellites. Even though there is *no* parallel between the degree of Soviet and U.S. economic problems, the United States would be well advised to question the growing domestic and external costs of turning a blind eye to the apparently accelerating momentum of relative Japanese industrial competitiveness. Industrial competitiveness is increasingly the determinant of both a country's standard of living and its international political stature, a trend accelerating in a global system no longer centered around military competition between two superpowers. Thus, the potential descent of the United States into second-class industrial and technological status comes at a particularly inopportune time.

The theme of this chapter is the increasing risk and potential cost for the United States of accepting the arguments of the naïve, the free-market ideologues, and the "Japologists" that U.S. industrial and trade performances are satisfactory. Events and trends plainly contradict the argument that Japan is just another capitalist economy nearing its peak of power, whose trade surpluses can be neutralized through market-opening measures and an improved U.S. effort at exporting.

My theme that a further decline in U.S. industrial competitiveness could be damaging and dangerous is rooted in what might be termed enlightened nationalism. Even if unappealing, there is nothing necessarily wrong or dangerous about the prospect of a continuing relative decline in international economic and political power and influence for the United States. Perhaps the world would be better off with a "pax consortium" managed on a trilateral basis by Japan, Europe, and the United States. Perhaps Japanese leadership would have more to offer the post–cold war international system than a tired political-economic superpower that may have overstayed its time as global hegemon, even though it "won" the cold war.

Perhaps not.

THE OMINOUS TREND IN U.S. COMPETITIVENESS

Projections in economics and politics rest on assumptions. The core assumption in this analysis is that the trend of international competitiveness is still moving against the United States and in favor of Japan, and the measurable past decline in relative U.S. industrial strength vis-à-vis Japan is far more likely to continue than to end. Indeed, the gap is likely to widen. This core assumption does not ignore mitigating circumstances and adjustments. It recognizes the United States faces escalating competition from a unifying Europe and from East Asia, but not necessarily at the cutting edges of technology. It also recognizes continuing U.S. strengths: the seemingly bottomless pool of creative entrepreneurs, the world's strongest basic science research, many innovative and magnificently managed companies, immigrants anxious to keep alive the American dream, and so forth. I further note that the U.S. foreign trade performance would be enhanced *statistically* by reductions in the federal budget deficit and in the value of the dollar (depreciation), by increased domestic saving rates, and by the inclusion of estimated sales in excess of $500 million annually by overseas subsidiaries of U.S. manufacturing corporations not counted in U.S. export data.

Still, there remain sufficient grounds for concern. The United States has fallen behind Japan in the industrial race and catching up will not be easy even when a full-fledged attempt is made. Patient Japanese tactics designed piece by piece to capture maximum market share in important industrial sectors will not be easily, quickly, or cheaply reversed. The rule of thumb in the high-tech sector is that it is cheap to buy market share early in the product cycle, expensive to buy it late in the cycle, and almost impossible to reclaim market share once it has been lost. The record of U.S. companies coming from behind to reclaim market share lost to the Japanese has been a sorry one, even with import restraints. Rightly or wrongly, U.S. companies have exhibited a comparative advantage in bailing out of a product line dominated by the Japanese; the next phase in maximizing current profits will be to avoid even entering a new product field where Japanese money is earmarked for R&D. An aggressive long-term strategy of counterattack will be needed to leapfrog Japan's current and future manufacturing and technological lead.

The forecast made here that the trend line is ominous does not put much weight in certain economic "red herrings" that exaggerate both sides of important issues relevant to U.S. competitive standing. It was natural, indeed inevitable, that the unusually dominant global economic and technological position the United States found itself in immediately after World War II would erode. But there is no reason to expect or welcome the recent propensity of U.S. industry to fall behind its foreign competitors in new product development and state-of-the-art technology and manufacturing processes. The United States is not deindustrializing in any basic way; despite the relative small increase in new jobs in manufacturing, that sector's share of GNP remains basically unchanged today from thirty or forty years ago. The *prospect* of deindustrialization must *not* be looked upon favorably. A shift to a wholly services-oriented economy is not desirable, and advocates of allowing American manufacturing to be displaced by imports from Japan and elsewhere have yet to demonstrate how the United States could pay the resulting swollen import bill solely through the exports of raw materials and services. Nor can they show that many high-paying service positions, such as industrial designers and engineers, would not gravitate to the new production centers. Shifting into a services economy is not the "third economic revolution." The United States did not abandon the agricultural sector in favor of the industrial sector in the early twentieth century; it applied so much capital to rich land that a small fraction of the total work force maintained agricultural production levels and price competitiveness.

Japan is changing in a way that provides more opportunities for profitable business activity by U.S. companies. Prophesies that Japanese economic strength will substantially dissipate from such causes as the decadence of the young, or increasing numbers of older Japanese traveling extensively overseas, or a lack of creativity making the Japanese good copiers but mediocre innovators are all based on wishful thinking and ignorance about Japan, not sound, relevant economic criteria. Japan's overall level of industrial competitiveness need not decline from the labor force taking a few more days of vacation or working a few less overtime hours. That working smart and efficiently is more important than long hours is demonstrated by the continuing industrial success of West Germany, the world's second-largest exporter (after the much larger United States) despite a shorter workweek and significantly more vacation days than either Japan or the United States (see table 11.1).

Manufacturing now accounts for less than one-fifth of the total U.S. work force, but the sector is not heading for oblivion except in the extremely unlikely event that the global economic order permanently and formally designates the United States as the consumer of last resort. Only such a bizarre arrangement could ensure foreigners financing in perpetuity a permanently growing, structural U.S. trade deficit by accepting an infinite supply of dollars, many of which have to be recycled back into the United States to maintain the disequilibrium game, as has in fact been the case since the early 1980s. Economists believe disequilibria cannot last indefinitely because either economic or political forces eventually correct or eliminate them. Consequently, the warning by Paul Volcker in 1985 (while chairman of the Federal Reserve Board) would seem to have far more long-term validity than the assertion, quoted on the first page of chapter 5, that the U.S. trade deficit is a mark of strength and success:

> Economic analysis and common sense coincide in telling us that the budgetary and trade deficits of the magnitude we are running are not sustainable indefinitely in a framework of growth and prosperity. They imply a dependence on foreign borrowing by the United States that, left unchecked, will sooner or later undermine

Table 11.1   International Working Hours in Manufacturing, 1987

	Total Hours Worked	Total National Holidays & Paid Vacation Days
Japan	2,168	28
United States	1,949	30
West Germany	1,642	41

SOURCE: Japanese Ministry of Labor.

the confidence in our economy essential to a strong currency and to prospects for lower interest rates.[1]

By the time the U.S. trade deficit disappears, the external debt accumulated to finance it may exceed $1 trillion, by far the largest in the history of the world. (By the end of 1989, the U.S. external debt had hit $664 billion). U.S. production of goods and services will need to grow large enough to meet most of future domestic demand *plus* sustain an export surplus to finance rising interest and principal repayments on this foreign debt already measured in tens of billions of dollars annually. Inevitably, a significant portion of the responsibility for balance of payments adjustment will fall on the U.S. manufacturing sector.

The key economic question is: At what level of productivity, technology, and quality control will the U.S. manufacturing sector perform in the 1990s and beyond relative to its major trading partners? The optimum solution is for U.S. industry to competitively produce a maximum quantity of sophisticated, high-value-added goods made by well-paid, but highly productive, highly skilled workers. This is the method by which the internal costs of balance of payments adjustment will be minimized. A distantly second-best option is for the United States to compete globally, as it did in the late 1980s, mainly through dollar depreciation (decreasing the local currency costs to foreigners of most U.S. exports, but increasing the costs of most imports to Americans) and declining real wages (in real terms, U.S. private sector wages dropped between 1973 and 1989), both of which reduced the country's standard of living. So far, the United States has mainly chosen not to compete more efficiently, but to accept a large trade deficit and finance it by unsustainably high levels of borrowing and selling off domestic assets, from companies to real estate. If one assumes the U.S. trade balance must move towards equilibrium, the economic question *how* that is to be achieved is far more important than the arithmetic question *how much* improvement is necessary.

If a country's terms of trade (the ratio of average export prices to average import prices) deteriorates, more real wealth must be exported to pay for imports and debt service. The composition of exports is at least as important to a country's economic well-being as their total dollar value. Should the United States be forced to rely mainly on cheap, low-tech manufactured goods and agricultural commodities for incremental exports in lieu of high-value-added goods, the resulting terms of trade deterioration will be steep and therefore very costly. The United States will pay a heavy price in reduced living standards—or become the first country to disprove two accepted economic maxims: (1) economic development cannot be achieved through exporting raw materials other than oil (this was at the heart of the less developed countries' collective demands in the 1970s for a New International Economic Order), and (2) low-wage countries are inherently poor.

The current trend of comparative U.S.–Japanese industrial strengths suggests that only a major effort to reverse competitive forces will allow the United States to retain competitiveness as defined by the President's Commission on Industrial Competitiveness: the degree to which a country can, under free and fair market conditions, produce goods and services that meet the test of global markets while simultaneously maintaining or expanding the real incomes of its citizens.[2] Reinvigorated U.S. competition is unlikely to come about through some natural adjustment or some currently emerging trend, either in Japan or the United States. Japanese and U.S. government studies agree Japan is either ahead of or gaining ground on the United States in product development in most of the important new technologies (see table 11.2). Absent a major reorientation of government policies and business strategies, the United States can expect to drop even further behind. Even U.S. strengths are at risk now that MITI has organized and supports two research consortia, Tron and Sigma, to correct Japanese weaknesses in microprocessors and software, respectively.

The long-standing Japanese ability to achieve higher levels of productivity growth and their more recent ability to forge ahead in advanced technologies suggest an uphill fight for the United States to achieve the kinds of increases in technological and manufacturing supremacy that produce higher real incomes, better living standards, and quality trade surpluses. The bottom line of this analysis is that the extent of arithmetic reduction in the multilateral—or bilateral—U.S. trade deficit is not necessarily more important than changes in product composition. The key issue for the overall social good of the United States appears to be the extent to which its high-tech industry continues to be bypassed by stronger Japanese competitors. The possibility of more dollar depreciation is not to be applauded, and possibilities such as more Japanese tourism in the United States or more rice exports to Japan are marginal in the larger scheme of things.

U.S. chauvinism notwithstanding, one could argue that there simply is nothing virtuous in the fact that declining relative U.S. industrial competitiveness is partially self-inflicted, the result of mistakes, short-sightedness, and inadequacies. Advocates of giving the Japanese a turn at the glories and heartaches of a global superpower cannot demonstrate the inherent desirability or logic of America's expensive obsession with short-term individual and corporate gratification. There is no escaping the longer-term need to respond domestically in a positive way to global economic change. *Acknowledging established Japanese virtues is one thing, prolonging correctable U.S. vices is quite another.*

Signs of U.S. indifference to turning around its sagging competitive fortunes are everywhere. Only the fall of Drexel Burnham Lambert, Inc. slowed the greedy economics of leveraged buyouts and outside acquisitions, both hostile and friendly. The stillbirth of the U.S. Memories semiconductor consortium (see page 65) suggests that preoccupation with short-term profits continues to cloud long-term judgment. Efforts to cor-

AREA OF RESEARCH	BASIC RESEARCH		ADVANCED DEVELOPMENT		PRODUCT MANUFACTURING/ENGINEERING	
	Japan's Position	Direction	Japan's Position	Direction	Japan's Position	Direction
Artificial intelligence	▬	▼	▬	■	▬	■
Automated factory assembly	•	■	✚	◄	✚	◄
Biotechnology	▬	■	•	◄	N.A.	N.A.
Compact-disk technology	▬	■	✚	◄	✚	◄
Computer design	▬	▼	•	◄	✚	◄
Computer integrated manufacturing	▬	◄	▬	◄	✚	▼
Computer software	▬	▼	▬	◄	✚	◄
Fiber optics	✚	◄	✚	◄	✚	◄
High-strength construction plastic	▬	◄	▬	◄	▬	◄
Integrated circuits	✚	◄	✚	◄	✚	◄
Mobile radio systems	✚	◄	•	◄	•	◄
Telecommunication networks	▬	▼	▬	■	▬	◄

Legend:
- ▬ behind   ▼ losing ground
- ✚ ahead   ◄ gaining ground
- • even   ■ holding constant

SOURCE: National Science Foundation data published in the *Wall Street Journal*, November 14, 1988. Reprinted by permission of the *Wall Street Journal* © 1988 Dow Jones & Company, Inc. All rights reserved.

rect the federal budget deficit have been confounded by political refusals to limit consumption or increase taxes. The worsening deficit in turn further constrains governmental funding for such vital determinants of industrial competitiveness as education, transportation infrastructure, and industrial R&D. Funding for foreign policy initiatives in Central America and Eastern Europe suffer similar constraints; hence, the recent effort by the Bush administration to encourage quick increases in Japanese foreign aid to those regions.

The United States economy is *not* suffering from that classic malady of great powers, overseas military overreach, but from the delusion that there is something noble in refusing short-term sacrifices in current consumption or personal enrichment and in refusing to pay for needed government services. One thing there is no shortage of in the United States is wishful thinking when it comes to the factors making the Japanese the low-cost producers in one industry after another as they eclipse the United States in one advanced technology after another. *None of the factors which collectively produced the systemic policy and priority mismatch identified in chapter 1 have shifted in favor of the United States.* Several are intensifying in favor of Japan. (One that might have helped, dollar depreciation, went in the opposite direction in early 1990, when the yen depreciated.) It is not enough that a few factors favorable to the United States are evident, e.g., most Americans are more aware of the problem of declining competitiveness and more manufacturing companies have successfully rejuvenated the means by which they design and assemble their products (often by replicating proven Japanese management innovations). The Japanese embrace of *kaizen,* continuous incremental improvements in the manufacturing process, means that Japanese industry must be viewed as a moving target, one that is not about to rest on its laurels. The cliche of having to run faster just to stand still is very relevant to the dilemma in which American industry finds itself. Its ability to run fast enough to keep from falling further behind cannot be taken for granted.

At least five major trends are tilting the odds further against the relative industrial competitiveness of the United States. The first trend is the continuing large growth in Japanese corporate investment in additional and more efficient plants and capital equipment. In 1988, the smaller Japanese economy surged ahead of the United States in *absolute* amounts of investment expenditures, an important barometer of industrial efficiency and capacity. The exact figure varies with the exchange rate used to convert yen to dollars, but by 1990, the annual differential approached $100 billion. The gap can be expected to widen, at least in the short run, according to ongoing investment surveys; a September 1989 survey by the Industrial Bank of Japan showed a 24 percent increase in plant and equipment investment by Japanese manufacturing firms in fiscal year 1989 (ending 31 March 1990), a growth rate about six times greater than overall GNP growth. At 24 percent of GNP, fixed investment (excluding housing) in Japan is just about twice as high as the comparable figure for the United States.

Japan's investment surge has been fueled by healthy profits, low borrowing costs, and corporate windfalls from investing in Japan's stock market and land booms. Even if these short-term factors abate, Japanese companies are likely to continue investing more money than their American counterparts, partly to diminish the threat from the increasingly efficient production of mature-technology, labor-intensive goods by the newly industrialized countries of Asia (and, in the future, perhaps Eastern Europe). The relentless Japanese concentration on upmarket, technology-intensive, high-value-added goods; the push to minimize production costs; and rapid product innovation all require extensive investment in new plant and equipment.

A second trend is the accelerating research and development outlays by Japanese companies. Nondefense R&D already is considerably higher (by almost 50 percent) than past U.S. outlays when expressed as a percentage of GNP. Industrial R&D outlays in Japan should surpass those of the United States in absolute amounts by the end of the century. Precise competitive implications for the two countries in the R&D race are all but impossible to calculate because of the lack of up-to-date data, differing distinctions between basic and applied research, and methodological problems of disaggregating absolute R&D figures for corporate, nondefense outlays specifically for manufacturing. As a rough comparison of absolute spending, estimated 1988 R&D outlays by U.S. industry for commercial purposes were $67 billion, with Japanese corporate R&D outlays in the same period estimated at $50 billion, most of which would go to applied research in civilian technology.[3]

Surveys of the literature reveal a familiar trend: Japanese companies are rapidly increasing their R&D outlays (which go mainly into nondefense sectors). Conversely, a National Science Foundation survey released in January 1990 calculated that in real terms, there would be little or no increase in U.S. corporate R&D for calendar years 1989 and 1990;[4] the sample on which this projection was based may have been biased by data from companies recently merged or acquired, activities that generally force cutbacks in R&D.

The third trend working against U.S. industry, a consequence of Japan's intensifying investment and R&D, is the widening Japanese lead in innovative production technology and shortened time for new-product innovation. Breakthroughs in flexible manufacturing and software for robotics will introduce a new generation of low-cost product customization techniques for mass production assembly lines. Kenneth Courtis, an economist working in Japan, has predicted that Japan is about to emerge as the "new product laboratory for the world." Recent innovations in process technology are only the beginning, he argues: "Soon we will see 'just-in-time development and design,' an even more sophisticated technique that will be lethal for less competitive systems."[5]

The fourth unfavorable trend for U.S. industrial competitiveness arises from the increasing cost advantages of Japan's industrial structure. Well-financed Japanese electronics conglomerates appear to be in the best position to handle the exploding costs of developing and manufacturing new generations of technology and to exploit the increasing interconnectedness of technologies within the data processing and telecommunications industries. These advantages already have been demonstrated by Japan's steady ratcheting up the so-called high-tech food chain, moving from one level of technological dominance to the next, often by the "termite" tactic of first gaining control of the production of key components of a system through very aggressive pricing.

In consumer electronics, the Japanese moved from domination of small-screen black and white televisions to large-screen sets, then from small-screen color televisions to large-screen sets to videocassette recorders and hand-held video cameras. It is quite natural, therefore, that the Japanese quickly moved in front in developing the potential blockbuster high-definition television (HDTV) technology. In a horizontal example of the chain, domination of consumer electronics, including audio equipment, bolstered the Japanese semiconductor industry with a booming domestic demand.

The food chain involves more than the consumer segment of electronics. Japan's growing dominance of semiconductor memory devices potentially will place it in a position to make major inroads in current U.S. leadership in logic chips. More R&D money is generated with volume sales of memory chips, and Japan's leverage in tight supply situations may lead some of its companies to link the availability of memory chips to a customer's purchase of logic chips as well. Potential domination of both segments of the semiconductor industry, along with existing leadership in high-tech components such as disk drives and flat screen displays, may already have placed Japan within reach of the pinnacle of the electronics food chain: computers. Alarmists in the U.S. semiconductor industry claim that in 1990, the U.S. computer industry is about where the U.S. semiconductor industry was in 1980—vulnerable to a steady loss in market share to increasingly powerful, aggressive Japanese competition.

Japanese strength in traditional computers, in turn, is a stepping-stone to domination of supercomputers. Consider the anxieties expressed in a 1988 report on U.S. supercomputer vulnerability prepared by the Institute of Electrical and Electronics Engineers:

> Supercomputers appear to represent only a next step in an ongoing process that is gaining momentum . . . Japan seeks a dominant position in the information industries—the computer and commu-

nications industries of the world. And it is well on the way to achieving that position. . . .

Once they were to achieve preeminence in supercomputers, the Japanese would have established themselves as the manufacturers of the most powerful computer systems, with supercomputers installed with the "Gold Chip" accounts of the world. They could then use that base and prestige to cement their move into the more lucrative market for commercial data processing systems. . . .

This continues the familiar, oft-repeated pattern. Japanese firms plan and act in accord with long-range strategic goals. When they achieve a technological advantage in one area, they use that advantage to ensure their advance into new areas.[6]

The fifth source of the forecast for U.S. competitiveness is existing Japanese advantage in developing new technology, even beyond the increased outlays for industrial R&D. With what might be dubbed the if-it-has-a-price-Japan-can-afford-to-buy-it syndrome, Japan for decades has treated U.S. technological innovation and basic science research as a kind of intellectual public works that could be drawn on freely. In recent years, some U.S. companies have wised up to the risks of licensing state of the art technology to their most dangerous competitors, but the economics of the high-tech sector has given the Japanese a new, often better entrée to innovative U.S. research and distribution rights: equity.

Japan is cash rich, with a strong currency, at a time when U.S. entrepreneurs need unprecedented amounts of capital. Secondhand equipment in a basement or garage is no longer adequate to produce and manufacture breakthroughs in commercially significant technologies. As discussed earlier, Japanese industrial giants can borrow at relatively low costs, and most have ample cash. The increasingly frequent result is Japanese investors displacing U.S. banks and venture capital firms in backing start-up high-tech companies with interesting new ideas and expensive overhead. Capital transfers by Japanese industrial companies usually involve equity participation and, therefore, a claim on whatever discoveries are made. The financial press reports a growing number of partial and total Japanese acquisitions of relatively new, privately held companies in state-of-the-art technologies. Venture Economics, Inc., a firm that tracks such deals reported "Cash-laden Japanese corporations are buying into some of the most attractive, small high-tech businesses in the U.S. And the pace of this activity is accelerating." The total dollar value of Japanese investment in U.S. high-tech venture businesses identified by this firm rose from $7 million in 1983, to $142 million in 1986, and then to $320 million during 1989.[7] More broadly, the Japanese spent an estimated $14 billion on corporate mergers and acquisitions in the United States in 1989.[8]

In some cases, the motive for acquisition seems to be the desire of Japanese high-tech firms to tap in to the most advanced scientific thinking in Silicon Valley; in others, to control supply of sophisticated components; and still others exemplify smokestack industries instantaneously diversifying in the high-tech sector. It may be premature to talk about a new form of technology diffusion, but more and more Japanese investors are making buy-in offers that U.S. high-tech entrepreneurs cannot refuse. Certainly it is not premature to argue that, with their money and dedication to detail, the Japanese are increasingly buying their way out of any perceived limitations on their own innovative capabilities. U.S. corporate and university brainpower is for sale, and the Japanese now can afford anything that has a price. Their traditional vacuum cleaner approach to sucking up new ideas from around the world has gained increased voltage and a larger nozzle.

A related buying effort is going on within Japan as a growing number of U.S. companies realize tremendous profits from selling their manufacturing or distribution operations in Japan to a Japanese company. Long-run possibilities for these U.S. companies maintaining or expanding their sales in the world's second-largest market are unclear, but they would appear to be diminished by their preference for taking the money and running over a serious long-term commitment to building market share. Disinvestment by U.S. companies, amounting to billions of dollars, may be another long-term, self-inflicted detriment to U.S. exports to Japan.

A second noncash advantage of the Japanese is that by temperament, they seem to possess strengths important to high-tech innovation, their creativity-stifling educational and laboratory management systems notwithstanding. The sheer complexity of many of tomorrow's new technologies favor group effort over the individual innovator. Superconductor development, for example, seems to require more a laborious examination of different combinations of existing materials that would have no resistance to electrical current, than creative, abstract imagination. The Japanese penchant for teamwork and close communication seems a distinct plus for research increasingly involving a fusion of several specialties, as in the new field of bioelectronics, bringing together biotechnology, computer and semiconductor design, and chemistry. The Japanese seldom let an existing weakness permanently stand in their way. They are not so convinced of the perfection of their system that they will be unable to modify educational and management policies to encourage greater creativity.

The Japanese may also possess a sixth factor, decisively setting future trends in their favor. Japan's enormous trade surpluses have yielded capital inflows that in turn helped create the situation at the end of the 1980s, where all ten of the world's ten largest banks (as measured by assets expressed in dollars) were Japanese. As yet, it is impossible to predict the results for industrial competition should Japan come to dominate the crucial commercial banking sector and then move on to dominate the investment banking sector and securities trading. That Japanese corporations would get preferential access to capital on a permanent basis under such circumstances is only hypothetical.

DECREASED ECONOMIC STRENGTH EQUALS
DECREASED SOVEREIGNTY

Redistribution of economic power between Japan and the United States and of political-military power between the United States and the Soviet Union suggest that international relations are entering yet another new era. It will not be an era magically freed of traditional resort to brute force by non-democracies seeking additional land, resources, or ideological conquests beyond their national borders. But the crisis triggered by Iraq's invasion of Kuwait is presumably the exception to the emerging rule that economic power is becoming an increasingly important credential to a nation-state's playing a sustained role of global superpower.

If the United States is to remain a bona fide "full service" superpower in the twenty-first century—it is perhaps the only country potentially able to do so—it cannot afford further deterioration in its *relative* economic strength. Because this assertion ties into a larger debate about the supposed decline of U.S. power, it may be best to begin with framing the assumptions for assessing the extent to which relative economic weakness can lead to relative international political weakness. I will *not* argue here that the United States has tripped headfirst down the slippery slope of absolute decline. Concerns over this scenario may be a self-negating prophecy. There is merit in the thesis that the more the United States frets over possible decline in its global power, the more likely it will be to take the necessary countermeasures to prevent the contingency from materializing.

The United States does not—yet—match the profile of global superpowers in previous centuries whose imperial overreach led to downfall. The likelihood of that fate befalling the United States has been diminished significantly with the growing prospects for declining real outlays for military expenditures following the sudden, dramatic cold war thaw; the civilian sector of the U.S. economy should be a net recipient of resources in the 1990s. A society's ability to renew itself through innovation and adaptation is another key factor in determining decline. From this perspective, the openness of its economy, society, and politics makes the United States "less likely to decline than any other major country."[9] Despite all of its problems, the United States continues to attract a torrent of foreign investment.

Predictions that Japan is in advanced stages of ascent to the status of global superpower are open to question on a number of accounts. First and foremost, it is not at all clear that Japan's political mainstream covets such a role. Nor has there has been a surge of compassion in Japan about the welfare of other peoples that would inspire a heretofore absent drive to spread a social or political ideology around the globe. A social philosophy celebrating the virtues of hard work, rigid self-discipline, self-sacrifice, and the ultra-uniqueness of the Japanese people would not seem to offer ideas that the rest of the world is anxiously waiting to embrace. Without the kind of global mission that burned in the spirits of first the British and second the Americans, Japan seems to lack an essential criterion for modern-day great-power leadership. Japan's dependency on the outside world for a significant percentage of its raw materials and fuel places another obstacle in the way of potential Japanese ambitions. Finally, ethnocentric Japan does not seem willing to make sacrifices in the pursuit of a vision for world order, such as making it easier for foreigners to earn yen and to transfer yen balances outside Japan.

None of these factors negate the probability that Japan will carve out a special niche in the emerging new international order, one in which money and technology matter more than weapons. In light of the changes taking place on the international political scene, Japan has no need to cultivate power in the historic sense. Its economic power alone all but guarantees it enduring influence, prestige, and behind-the-scenes deal-maker status that are probably more than adequate for a country that is not about to try again the military route to great-power status. Certainly Japan will want, and be able to command, global influence over the use of its overseas loans, investments, and foreign aid programs, as well as contributions to international economic organizations. For it is Japan, not the United States, whose gross overseas assets of $1.8 trillion at the end of 1989 made it the world's largest net creditor country (see figure 11.1). It is Japan that passed the United States in 1990 to become the world's largest disburser of foreign development assistance. Japanese government officials will be able to influence foreign countries, especially in Asia and Eastern Europe, with promises of large, quick financial packages. They also will be able to travel anywhere in the world, including the United States, and command respect by waving a briefcase bulging not only with loan capital, but also with advanced technology, foreign direct investment commitments, and promises of increased access to the burgeoning Japanese import market. The crinkling of money, not the rattling of missiles, will be the main symbol of great-power muscle-flexing in the post–cold war era.

In the long run, the United States will retain considerable global influence no matter what. Aside from the sheer size of its economy, the United States should continue producing a disproportionate share of the world's new scientific discoveries. On the military front, the virtual overnight build-up of American armed forces in Saudi Arabia in 1990 demonstrated the absolute need for U.S. leadership in any joint international response to military aggression. In the long run, the increasing strength of an economically surging Japan and a reunited Germany should make the counterbalance of U.S. overseas military presence in the Pacific and Europe more desirable than ever to a large number of countries.

U.S. influence ("soft" power) will continue to devolve from the more desirable elements of American culture. Many foreigners admire the United States for the moral example it sets at home in the defense of personal freedom and the encouragement of maximum individual potential for all residents.

**Figure 11.1   Net International Investment
(billions of dollars)**

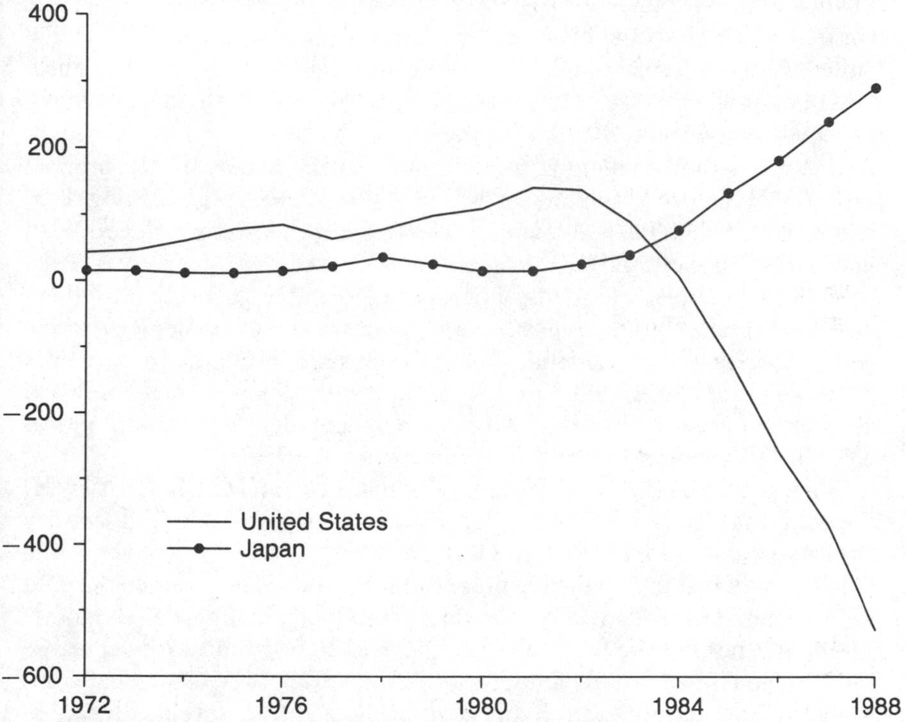

SOURCES: Bank of Japan, U.S. Department of Commerce,
and the Japan Economic Institute.

In the short term, however, a money-short U.S. government must tell the many countries in turnaround situations ("emerging democracies") to content themselves with U.S. advice or go to the more affluent West Europeans or Japanese for capital. Any net increases in U.S. government lending in regions such as Central America and Eastern Europe would tend to increase the federal budget deficit, setting in motion the series of events that starts with the need for additional U.S. capital inflows and ends with Japanese and other foreign financial institutions agreeing to lend.

To the extent one believes that Japanese economic influence is an adequate or preferable alternative to U.S. world leadership, declining U.S. leverage should present no serious problem. There is a contrary opinion, (far too sophisticated to be dismissed as chauvinism or racism) which worries that Japan's intense sense of uniqueness and tendency to keep the rest of the world at arm's length preclude its assuming the mantle of global leadership in the Western tradition. R. Taggart Murphy, a U.S. banker working in Japan, has argued "To turn sheer financial strength into leadership, a country must be able to think in global terms, to view itself as a world central banker, to sacrifice certain short-term gains to maintain stable financial and trading systems. Japan does not have this world view."[10] The bottom line is that Japan has assumed leadership of the world's financial sector but lacks a global sense of purpose, while the United States has a sense of mission it is increasingly less able to finance. "This uncoupling of financial power and global vision poses a dilemma— for Japan, the United States, and the world."[11]

Japan's steadily rising industrial competitiveness has direct implications for U.S. foreign policy, in at least two respects threatening U.S. independence of action and retention of global superpower privileges. With increasing U.S. dependence on Japan for advanced, high-tech goods used for both commercial and military purposes, Japan has superbly positioned itself to exploit the increasing ability of powerful technology-intensive industries to determine national status in international affairs. In the words of Japanese politician Shintaro Ishihara, a new age is dawning, when advances in high technology will be the main determinants of global strength, a situation that means Japan "will be superior."[12]

This argument feeds the gloomy conclusion of MIT'S Charles H. Ferguson that the tightening overlap between traditional national security concerns and industrial strength has produced a situation in which the United States "faces a challenge more fundamental than any since the cold war" began. If the United States fails to implement internal economic reform and perform better in its technological competition with Japan, he foresees the United States facing "severe tradeoffs between its global commitments and its domestic living standards."[13] More specifically, he is concerned about Japanese domination of semiconductors and computers. This kind of ascendancy in Japanese industrial power would constitute a "watershed in geopolitical relations. . . . For the first time, the U.S. no longer will dominate the crucial technologies needed for military power and future industrial development."[14]

The gravity of the problem posed by the potential for Japan's surpassing the U.S. in technological know-how is, once again, a function of what assumptions are made. One can argue that profit-seeking, export-oriented companies in a friendly country pose no significant threat of cutting off supplies to foreign customers. One can also argue that a superpower ought to operate from a worst case scenario, always minimizing dependence on foreigners for commodities critical to civilian or military production. The situation is somewhat analogous to individuals buying life insurance, despite the probability of its being a poor financial investment, because there is no guarantee that you are not going to die in the near future.

Advocates of the cautious approach to U.S. high-tech dependence received a bonanza from Ishihara in one of the most frequently quoted passages in the controversial book, *The Japan That Can Say No:*

It has come to the point that no matter how much [Americans] continue military expansion, if Japan stopped selling them the [semiconductor] chips, there would be nothing more they could do.

If, for example, Japan sold chips to the Soviet Union and stopped selling them to the U.S., this would upset the entire military balance. . . . The more technology advances, the more the U.S. and the Soviet Union will become dependent upon the initiative of the Japanese people. . . . Very soon now, the defense of America will become dependent upon supply sources abroad.[15]

These comments represent neither official policy nor a significant body of Japanese public opinion—at present. But who can guarantee that after another decade of non-stop complaints and demands from the United States, mainstream political thinking in Japan might not adopt this hard line approach? And who but the most trusting would be unable to foresee the possibility of vertically integrated Japanese semiconductor producers delaying the export of newly introduced, top-of-the-line chips to rival American computer makers? A congressional Office of Technology Assessment report quoted an NEC manager alluding to the disadvantages that the U.S. maker of supercomputers, Cray, faced by being forced to buy certain custom-made high-speed chips from his company, a rival maker of supercomputers. The report also noted instances of U.S. supercomputer companies being told that the highest performance memory and bipolar logic chips "were not yet available for export" from Japan although Japanese supercomputer systems incorporating them were available for export.[16]

If the trend line is as serious a threat to the real income level and external position of the United States as has been suggested, the liberal trading system may be very much at risk. The possible path to unrestrainable American frustration that triggers protectionist actions was vividly outlined by Sheridan Tatsuno, a specialist in Japanese high technology: "The signs are all around us. Japan has the money, the talent, the technologies, and the will." Their companies have already pulled ahead of the United States in a number of key sectors and are making a strong bid for superiority in many others. "By the mid-1990s Japan's technological prowess could overwhelm the West, and the political shock waves of losing one next-generation industry after another to Japan will be severe."[17]

The second threat further decline in relative U.S. competitiveness poses to U.S. independence of action and global leadership is the likelihood of perpetuating the country's continuing heavy dependence on imported capital—most of which comes from Japan—to offset the internal U.S. savings-investment disequilibrium. The United States became the world's biggest debtor country because of its uninterrupted need since the mid-1980s for net capital inflows in excess of $100 billion annually (a figure roughly corresponding in size to both the savings-investment imbalance and the current account deficit in the U.S. balance of payments). Japanese holdings of U.S. assets (corporations, real estate, stocks, bonds, government securities, and so forth) increased more than tenfold during the eighties. Whenever the federal government, state governments, or domestic corporations needed to borrow large sums quickly, Japanese lenders came immediately to mind. To the extent that foreign investors are reluctant to finance the U.S. savings shortfall, they must be enticed with higher interest rates that threaten recession, or with a cheaper, that is, depreciating, dollar, which can be inflationary.

Japan's position as chief external banker to the United States means that indirectly, Japanese consent will be required for any extended U.S. overseas military operation that requires incremental capital inflows to finance it. Already, the United States risks diminished ability to influence world events because, like any debtor, it is vulnerable to the withdrawal of kindnesses extended by creditor countries. Moral vision and a strong military remain important, but the additional need for economic strength to hold superpower status is becoming clearer. Worldwide projection and protection of national values is increasingly a function of a strong industrial base and technological leadership. "Economic strength is key to global influence and power" is the succinct way that the director of Central Intelligence, William Webster, put it.[18]

Ironically, the absence of any imminent threat of the United States launching a trade war with Japan lies in the very diminution of U.S. economic leverage against Japan. The balance of power in the executive branch remains in the hands of the soft-liners, in part because the powerful Treasury Department adamantly opposes behavior that might provoke Japanese retaliation in the financial sector. The financial community generally accepted estimates in the late 1980s and at the start of the new decade that dollar-rich Japanese investors were buying up to one-third of total new U.S. Treasury borrowings. This is sufficient presence that even rumors of Japanese indifference to an upcoming auction of Treasury bills or bonds temporarily boosted domestic interest rates, a trend that, if continued, could drag the U.S. economy into a recession. For the Treasury Department and the rest of the financial community, the worst nightmare is Japanese outrage with U.S. government trade actions provoking precipitous dumping of their existing portfolio of stocks and bonds—triggering immediate financial and economic chaos in the United States. This relatively recent loss of control over its domestic interest rates is tantamount to diminished sovereignty for the United States.

The reality of progressive displacement by Japan of industrial production in the United States is a third manifestation of lost leverage. As seen in the incident where the United States reversed the proposed sanctions on imports from the Toshiba Corporation (see page 160), U.S. companies, as well as consumers, could be hurt badly by discriminatory barriers to the increasing array of goods for which the United States is mainly or exclusively import dependent. The Office of the U.S. Trade Representative did not realize what a difficult task it had set for itself when it decided to subject only items produced domestically in significant amounts to retaliatory high tariffs in the wake of Japan's alleged noncompliance with the 1986 semiconductor agreement.

In a narrow, technical sense, the continuing U.S. current account (goods and services) deficit could be financed for many more years through recycled Japanese capital. The question must be asked, however, whether continued large U.S. trade deficits are politically sustainable in the context of an open, liberal trading order. At some point, incessant trade deficits of significant size will lead to the political decision that it is necessary for the United States to regain control of its economic destiny and to protect domestic producers from the onslaught of foreign competition. The means to this end would inevitably include mutually costly unilateral trade barriers against Japanese goods and an end to the open, liberal trade order. Restrictions on both U.S. foreign policy goals and the U.S. standard of living will tend to spread in proportion to U.S. weakness, that is, the growth of Japanese industrial strengths and capital resources relative to those of the United States. The trend that would ensue in political attitudes is perhaps best summed up by the prediction made in early 1990 by an unnamed U.S. senator: "In a couple of years, it will be as hard to be pro-Japanese in public as it was to be pro-Russian in the early 1950s."[19] If trends in bilateral trade relations continue on their present course, the prospects intensify for a negative-sum game where everyone loses.

CONCLUSION

The United States has a very good economic system—but one that no longer can be taken for granted as fully adequate to the task of staying even with its fast-charging, fiercely committed Japanese competition in the high-stakes race for high-tech supremacy. What can be taken for granted is that the international political influence, industrial base, and standard of living of the United States will seriously erode if Japan's established pattern of investing more and obtaining faster productivity growth than the United States continues into the next century.

Japan does pose a problem in the form of a large, affluent market that is not open to manufactures imports in the same sense as the U.S. market. But Japan has an even larger importance as the country posing the greatest challenge to the United States' economic and technological leadership. Large U.S. companies like IBM and AT&T are sufficiently concerned about Japan's becoming the sole commercial source of crucial electronics components that they are willing to share their most advanced technology with U.S. research and production consortia. A professional engineering association believes the U.S. presence in the supercomputer industry is at risk from Japan's strategic climb up the high-tech food chain. It is not wise for nonspecialists to scoff at such concerns.

Time and momentum are on Japan's side. The fundamentals that put it ahead in the international industrial race are still at work. Present trends work directly against U.S. competitiveness and indirectly against its standard of living and its international power base. If the United States assumes that the plodding Japanese eventually must falter before rugged Yankee entrepreneurialism and the free-market mechanism, the gap will only widen and the difficulty of catching up increase. This prognosis is *not* a "fantastic vision of the Japanese one day running America, having bankrupted half our companies and bought the other half."[20] It *is* a vision of a potentially undesirable, costly, and humbling second-place U.S. status in the increasingly critical industrial high-technology sector.

CHAPTER 12

Policy Initiatives for a More Balanced and Friendlier Partnership

Those who cannot learn from the past are condemned to repeat it.

—George Santayana

One step ahead is darkness.

—Traditional Japanese saying

All single-factor explanations of Japan's relative economic success are wrong. All single-factor explanations of the relatively unfavorable U.S. trade performance are wrong. All single-factor solutions are doomed to fail. There is no finish line in the international competitive race between Japan and the United States. A look into the future suggests that in the near term, the extremely important trade relationship between the two largest, strongest national economies will not change significantly. The factors leading to Japan's competitive edge and persistently large bilateral trade surpluses will not disappear. Japanese industries will continue producing high quality, competitively priced goods. Neither U.S. economic policies nor corporate strategies promise changes sufficient to alter the global competitiveness battle in the short to medium term. Policies and strategies may improve, but probably not fast enough to close the gap with the dynamic Japanese industrial sector that is itself rapidly improving.

If the basic hypothesis of this book is correct, we can expect the two governments to keep to superficial remedies to defuse current tensions, with no reform of underlying sources of the problem. The status quo means continuing the current disequilibrium in the relative ability of the two countries to sell in each other's market, thereby perpetuating the cycle of economic friction. Systemic economic problems do not correct themselves. More of the same is not enough. Real changes need to be made—but only after a careful examination of what the problem really is and what its proper remedies are.

ADDRESSING THE RIGHT PROBLEM

Defining the problem correctly is a critically important, but very difficult chore. If we define reality as "a collective hunch,"[1] the road to problem solving is immediately clouded by the presence of several widely-held hunches—no one of which accurately and totally captures the essence of the bilateral economic situation. Inaccurate, misleading, or simplistic assessments lead to recommendations of limited value or with undesirable, or even dangerous, effects. Given the increasing importance of the situation, the number of proposed remedies that should be avoided has grown as quickly as the problem itself.

Foremost among the inadequate assessments is the notion that the core of the problem is the bilateral deficit per se, and the solution is to eliminate the deficit, or at least limit it to some tolerable amount. But arbitrarily tying the value of Japan's total exports to the United States to its imports from the U.S. makes little sense—unless the bilateral trade problem boils down to U.S. job creation and some urgent need for the sense of equity that presumably would accompany symmetrical bilateral trade balance numbers. It does not. Furthermore, this approach would not likely contribute anything to improving industrial productivity, to assuring greater American efficiency and a higher standard of living, or to correcting the recent propensity of the United States to consume more than it can produce.

A second faulty diagnosis that would lead to costly or irrelevant corrective actions is the allegedly growing dangers of Japanese investment in the United States and the supposed need to restrict it. While national security considerations limit foreign ownership of some domestic assets, the problem with present foreign direct investment is mainly psychological. In economic terms, the issue is the factors that cause the rising investment by Japanese and other foreigners—mainly the U.S. need for capital inflows brought on by its trade deficit and inadequate savings. (A second reason is the periodic tendency for the trade imbalance to depreciate the dollar against the yen, thereby making corporate and real estate acquisitions in the U.S. relatively cheap in yen terms.)

Anyone who believes the cause of the problem is Japan's low defense expenditures as a percentage of its GNP is manipulating the statistics: the size of Japan's defense budget in absolute dollar terms is approximately the same as those of West Germany, France, and Great Britain (the figures vary depending on the exchange rate used). If present trends continue, Japan's defense budget soon will be the third largest in the world. A significantly larger Japanese military establishment might please some Americans, but would likely upset friendly countries in Asia more than the Soviets, and might eventually lead to Japan producing electronic weapons more advanced than those produced in the United States.

Other misdiagnoses are based on grossly oversimplified assertions, such as the allegations that the bilateral trade problem is a simple, unambiguous reflection of Japanese conspiracy or the anger of a fading, jealous, and racist country looking for a scapegoat to stand in for its failings. Those who insist on seeing the bilateral problem in unambiguous black and white terms exemplify the aphorism "If you aren't a little confused, you don't really understand the situation."

Yet another misguided solution based on oversimplified analysis is the creation of a Japan–U.S. free-trade agreement. Such an arrangement would work so overwhelmingly in favor of Japanese interests as to worsen existing problems. Since indirect and informal trade barriers, currently the chief Japanese impediment to imports, would hardly be affected by officially abolishing formal barriers, the United States would receive virtually nothing in exchange for disassembling its own protective mechanisms.

One must also beware the smiling faces who counsel the United States not to worry about its sagging competitive position simply because foreign trade has become a struggle between big companies, not countries. While there is no denying the growing influence of multinational companies, it is ludicrous to assert that they have outgrown national identity. Virtually all of their key decisions continue to be made in the home country. Increasing collaborations among large high-tech companies from different countries undoubtedly will further alter the course of international trade flows, but corporate marriages of convenience cannot be expected to diminish the desire or ability of Japanese companies to dominate their sector of the global market. Finally, those who argue that commercial squabbles should not be allowed to disrupt the political bonds between the two countries are ignorant of the changing components of national security. Passive trade policies run the risk of so seriously debilitating U.S. economic strength that in the end, they are likely to trigger far more serious tensions than anything experienced to date.

Throughout this book I have argued for an analysis of bilateral problems based on the policy and attitudinal mismatch described in chapter 1. This is not a widely held view, but it leads usefully to the determination that there are two distinct problems at work: (1) The current and prospective ability of Japanese industry as a whole to be more competitive than its U.S. counterparts in terms of production costs, technological leadership, product quality, product innovation, and customer service; and (2) continued problems of market access in Japan for a wide range of foreign-made manufactured goods.

Three major causes of the large bilateral trade deficit follow as being genuinely in need of being addressed and none of them is in the mutual economic or political interests of the two countries to allow to continue uncorrected. They are:

- Divergent macroeconomic conditions in the two countries which, among other things, produce too little savings in the

United States and too much in Japan, and lower capital costs in Japan.

- Superior Japanese production techniques and management strategies that have made the average Japanese manufacturing company more competitive than the average U.S. manufacturing company.

- A lack of reciprocity in market access, mainly due to the indirectly restrictive effects of Japanese business practices and residual negative attitudes towards high-tech imports by most Japanese companies and government officials.

Changing any of these factors will be an uphill battle, a task beyond normal market forces. As things are, the Japanese government will reluctantly and cautiously continue to modify its international trade behavior in a compromise between two conflicting forces: incessant foreign demands for more evenly balanced trade relations and the reluctance of its own population to change a winning economic formula or to allow fellow Japanese workers to be hurt for the sake of foreign companies. The reality that the rest of the world can produce virtually anything that Japan exports reinforces the notion that the country is vulnerable to retaliation against its exports. It cannot possibly win a trade war. Fear of trade wars, however, has not displaced the historic desire to minimize foreign interference. The opening of the market continues at a slow, deliberate pace of Japan's own choosing.

An insular mentality, developed over two millennia, will not change radically in the short run. The Japanese will continue to be perplexed and annoyed at an unappreciative, hostile, and relatively inefficient outside world. They will continue to be oblivious to the questionable aspects of their country's trade practices and indifferent to contributing more positively to the global growth and balance of payments processes. But Japan cannot escape accommodating U.S. and other foreign demands; the only issue is timing and magnitude. The Japanese elite seems to understand the consequences of having gotten too far in front in an international economic race, the rules of which were formulated by Western thought; but the United States should expect neither a major diminution in Japanese exports nor a sudden bonanza in Japanese imports. The relative competitive strength of Japan is not about to dissipate, nor is the government about to abandon its commitments to targeted industries. Japan's fear of contracting the advanced industrial countries' sickness of self-indulgence and inefficiency is unlikely to materialize. A gradual increase in the acceptance of more leisure time without guilt and an increased incidence of teenage rebellion are unlikely to realize the tiresome predictions of the demise of the Japanese economic miracle. The latter won't collapse because new generations of Japanese workers take a few extra days of vacation and spend more freely. The age-old sense of the unique Japanese self will probably triumph over "creeping decadence." Since the U.S. public is unlikely to revive the nineteenth-century Puritan work ethic, Japan will not seriously narrow the bilateral "hedonism gap" for several generations to come.

Import policy will continue to mix a conscious desire to buy more goods from abroad with unconscious attitudes and practices that frequently neutralize the new products or competitive advantages of foreign producers. As a successful international competitor, Japan will remain an outspoken advocate of liberal trade. It will denounce protectionism. It will continue to expend more energy than any other country to reduce formal import restrictions. The ability of these efforts to produce results was, is, and will be limited. Japanese trade patterns will still be dominated by a sense of economic insecurity and an instinct for understanding how to translate visions of industrial growth into economic reality. The United States will still restrict *exports* of state-of-the-art manufactured goods for national security reasons. The Japanese will still discourage *import* dependence in all important high-tech products for national security reasons. (A simple test of this argument is to monitor Japanese willingness to continue buying superior, competitively priced U.S. computer software products and military aircraft.) Result: persistence of a large Japanese trade surplus in manufactured goods, one that is consistent with national priorities.

Attacking unfair Japanese business practices and obstacles to reasonable export success in the Japanese market is a legitimate, necessary objective for U.S. trade policy. But it is being eclipsed as the priority means of correcting the bilateral trade imbalance by the need for internal changes in the United States that can only be effected by enhanced efforts by its business, government, and labor sectors. The advent of Reaganomics in 1981 led to a revolutionary shift in domestic economic policies, but only cosmetic changes in foreign trade policy. Reductions in government regulations and corporate tax rates were inadequate to close the gap with Japanese industry. The extraordinary international role of the dollar continues to shield the United States from the discipline, faced by every other country, of having to earn through exporting the foreign exchange necessary to pay for imports. Without easier access to cheaper capital, more efficient production techniques, and better educated workers, optimism seems unwarranted. The competitive battle is being lost mainly on the factory floor and only secondarily through Japan's adversarial trade practices. An end to trade disequilibrium and frictions presupposes a better performance by the United States, by way of more aggressive economic policies and undesired changes in the U.S. life-style, that is, harder work, more savings, and less consumption. Hoping for a decline in Japan's economic performance as the way to bridge the gulf is wishful thinking that, even if realized, would be undesirable in economic efficiency terms.

If the United States contents itself with ad hoc market-opening concessions by Japan, it will never accomplish anything more than the temporary calm that comes with papering over deeper problems. The distinction between making deals and solving a systemic problem has never been adequately articulated in bilateral trade negotiations, and this is the main reason that trade conflicts constantly reappear.

I offer the following proposals with humility. Their consistency with what I believe is the proper interpretation of the underlying dilemma of U.S.–Japanese trade relations and with good economic practices are insufficient reasons to assume a majority are likely to be quickly implemented. Some are politically sensitive, some are unconventional, and some are burdensome. Some will be opposed on grounds of economic ideology. All will run up against the lethargy in both countries that flows from the mutual belief that the burden of correction rests with the other. All attempt to confront the overwhelming desire in both countries to muddle through rather than make quick, radical policy changes that might bring bilateral trade into a sustainable equilibrium. Perhaps the most realistic goal I can have for these proposals is the stimulation of a new dialogue and perspective in addressing bilateral trade frictions.

Finally, all of the proposals are sensitive to the larger reality that the United States and Japan are operating in a *multilateral* context. Neither the international trading system nor the domestic economies of the two countries under consideration would be damaged by implementing the following proposals to resolve bilateral and internal problems.

TASKS FOR BOTH COUNTRIES

To begin with measures that should be undertaken by both countries:

1. A dramatic, all-encompassing step toward the resolution of the differentials in the two countries' internal and foreign trade performances would be achieved by one simple agreement: Japan and the United States should commit themselves to mutually enact the measures they requested of each other in the Structural Impediments Initiative negotiations. This detailed package designed to get the Japanese to ease up (lower retail prices, less business collusion, easier access to home buying, and so forth) and the Americans to tighten up (more savings, longer time horizons for management, improved educational system) is ready for implementation and requires only that both sides swallow their pride, accept a de facto diminution of sovereignty, and jointly implement the vast majority of each other's recommended reforms. Both would be better off economically.

2. Both countries need to more explicitly recognize their economies are so deeply intertwined that there is no rational alternative to mutual tolerance, continuous dialogue, and constructive action. They need to better appreciate that they share responsibility for this occasionally stormy marriage where divorce must be ruled out and friendship and accommodation

must be considered imperative. The bottom line here is the formidable task of managing interdependence.

3. Both countries should sponsor intensive, ongoing research by savvy, independent-thinking, private groups in both countries to fill in the gaps in knowledge in a number of contentious issues of importance. Examples of questions short on facts and long on emotion are the impact of targeting policies on Japan's willingness to import products of targeted industries, relative national strengths in key industrial technologies, the relative quality and performance of U.S. high-tech goods, the advantages of and need for additional U.S. government funding of manufacturing R&D, and the exact product composition of growing Japanese imports of manufactured goods from all countries.

4. Both governments should seek devices to assure conflict resolution at earlier stages. Early consultations on emerging issues would be more effective than continued reliance on reactive talks after the problem has been allowed to fester.

5. The government and business sectors in both countries should cooperate to minimize the false, unflattering stereotypes of the people in the other country that seem to be gaining more widespread acceptance. The growing image in the United States of the Japanese as conspiratorial economic animals incapable of making mistakes and the growing image in Japan of Americans as lazy, crime-prone, and undereducated has-beens are poisoning public opinion and public support of intelligent policy initiatives.

TASKS FOR JAPAN

Japan would contribute to the social welfare of the world by expanding its export volume of high-quality, low-cost manufactured goods. It could most easily do so by correcting the major flaw in what is otherwise an awesome export machine. The weakness, of course, is a set of cultural patterns, deliberate policies, and practices that create an extraordinarily inhospitable environment for importing a wide range of foreign-made manufactured goods that are made, or could be made in Japan.

The suggested course of action for Japan concentrates on the theme of making its market more receptive, in real terms, to imports. It would be absurd to offer advice to Japan on how to improve its industrial efficiency and production techniques. It seems redundant to restate obviously desirable internal changes: completion of Japan's import liberalization process, rationalization of its inefficient agricultural policies that would allow termination of agricultural quotas, and increased enjoyment of life outside of the workplace.

There is no point in seriously advocating what is at once the most effective and most impractical proposal for reducing Japan's relative industrial power: behaving in a less Japanese manner. Adoptions of a Western-style welfare state, interest group rivalries, and workers' putting self before group interests would do wonders in undermining Japan's indefatigable pursuit of international leadership in key industries. Nevertheless, asking the Japanese to reorient their value system primarily to accommodate the inadequacies of U.S. economic practices is just slightly more politically ludicrous than it is economically undesirable.

The following fifteen proposals are offered in the hope of pointing out actions in support of enlightened self-interest without going so far as to preach to the Japanese about how they should think and behave. Assuming they are genuinely sincere in wanting to respond to foreign complaints, the Japanese could still use some practical advice on carrying out two extraordinarily difficult tasks. Both of these efforts have already commenced: first, altering the system that for many decades has rewarded efforts to thwart imports and maximize exports, and second, loosening a system based on long-term business relationships that for many years excluded foreign businesspeople.

These not necessarily original proposals are advanced in the belief that, first and foremost, they would be in the best long-run economic interests of Japan and the international trading system. Their presumed benefits to U.S. exporters is a secondary consideration.

1. The Japanese establishment needs to reach a genuine consensus that the long-term welfare and national security of Japan depends more on the lasting friendship of the United States and other major trading partners than on the size (or product composition) of its trade surplus. This means rethinking the mercantilist theory that has dominated Japanese trade strategy since the end of World War II. A small first step has already been taken with the recent advent of very limited, very gentle arm-twisting of industrialists by MITI, warning of unacceptably costly foreign retaliation if the business sector does not make a greater effort to increase imports. A potentially important second step—symbolically and financially—is the proposed corporate tax incentive for incremental imports, a policy that should be made permanent and increased in magnitude as necessary.

2. As part of the above-mentioned reorientation of values, the Japanese government and business sectors should accept that world superiority and self-sufficiency in every major technology need not be vital national objectives. A "declaration of interdependence" should reflect a genuine willingness in a limited number of cases to rely on the comparative advantage of other countries, that is, imports, for meeting some Japanese needs. (The United States might reciprocate with a comparable declaration.)

3. An important first step in greater Japanese acceptance of interdependence would be a government-business consensus that the collusive apportionment of markets has outlived its usefulness and should be phased out—just as formal import barriers were. Suspiciously constant foreign market shares in targeted industries should become increasingly rare, while strict enforcement of the antitrust law should become more frequent.

4. Beginning with the educational curriculum for primary school children, the Japanese government and mass media should increase efforts to inform all Japanese that they are inextricably involved in a world order that is not necessarily hostile toward nor inferior to Japan. The Japanese should put their sense of uniqueness in a larger context, for all countries are unique. Insightful writers like Karel van Wolferen should not have grounds to argue that Japan is "In the world but not of it." The Japanese should realize they have caught up with the West—and there are measures of character and success other than market share and size of GNP.

5. The Japanese elite should minimize its holier-than-thou, exaggerated argumentation about the openness of the Japanese market and engage in a more useful dialogue about how to ameliorate some of the hard facts of economic life in Japan that limit imports even in the absence of formal barriers, such as the practice of members of business groups *(keiretsu)* to buy from one another and the difficulties encountered by foreign companies trying to establish manufacturing subsidiaries in Japan.

The Japanese should understand that there is some justification for Western accusations that their trading relationships with Japan have not been, and are not yet, fully equitable. It should be more widely realized in Japan that the Western pursuit of what the West regards as equity will continue without regard for what bilateral trade balances look like. The Japanese should better appreciate that many of their counterarguments and promises fall on deaf ears overseas, sometimes for good reasons. Westerners demand tangible results that can be observed and quantified.

The Japanese also need to understand that an increase in the publicity surrounding their capital outflows for foreign aid and overseas investment cannot be a political or economic substitute for genuinely increased access to the Japanese market for foreign-made goods.

6. Japan's government, business sector, and media should better articulate the political and economic obligations that accompany Japan's status as an international economic superpower. The Japanese people must learn that international economic leadership cannot stop with manufacturing efficiency and exaggerated assertions of comparative advantage in production of the vast majority of manufactured goods. Japan needs to begin making intellectual contributions toward improving the international trading order.

7. More Japanese citizens should familiarize themselves with the costs to other countries of their country's exports, the occasional use of dirty tricks by their companies to expand foreign sales or acquire proprietary foreign technology, and their government's occasional use of clandestine pressures to restrict competitive imports.

8. Japanese companies and public corporations should make long-term procurement needs known to foreign companies with the same lead times as those given to traditional suppliers; access to design data is essential for

producers of intermediate goods to bid successfully for contracts. Granting early access to such information only to favored Japanese subcontractors has been a major indirect trade barrier in the procurement process.

9. The Office of the Prime Minister should monitor and counter the often highly protectionist "domestic" ministries that have jurisdictions touching on key foreign trade issues, such as agriculture, health care, and telecommunications.

If the Japanese people are genuinely committed to increased imports, not just increased symbolism, the next six action proposals should be implemented, political difficulties notwithstanding:

10. Japan's general trading companies should realize it is not antipatriotic and it is acceptable business behavior to ship foreign goods to Japan. The gap between trading company zest for exporting and importing should be narrowed, again through a consensus that manufactured imports are something better than a necessary evil.

11. Imports should be shielded from the worst inefficiencies of the notorious distribution system. For example, the Japanese government should assist foreign companies that wish to set up their own distribution operations bypassing the current Byzantine system. Government policies should expedite the opening of stores, big or small, that are free of obligation to sell exclusively the output of only one Japanese company.

12. Japan's patent system should be altered to better protect foreign technology, mainly through quicker approval of applications and longer life for patents approved. Copyright laws also need to be strengthened to more adequately protect intellectual property rights.

13. More rational land policies to encourage additional housing at more affordable prices would significantly expand the buying power of Japanese consumers.

14. The Japanese should redirect to their home market some of their public relations energies and budgets designed to sell the U.S. public on the virtues of being able to freely purchase foreign goods. Such an inward-directed education effort might convince the dubious Japanese that the previous suggestions are mainly designed to benefit the Japanese consumer, not the U.S. exporter. Public relations campaigns should seek to dispel unjustified doubts about the quality of many U.S.–made goods.

15. The Japanese government should be prepared to impose an export tax in cases of distortions caused by a misalignment of exchange rates or where a foreign government has made clear that Japanese sales of a specific product have become excessive. The Japanese treasury might as well be enriched, rather than a foreign government that imposes higher import duties or a Japanese company that increases profit margins with quantitative export restraints. The main drawback is political: It is more convenient for the Japanese government to be able to point to an overseas restraint of Japanese exports rather than one imposed in Tokyo.

If, on the other hand, the majority of Japanese believe it inappropriate to make additional sacrifices of self-determination on behalf of an exaggerated, idealistic U.S. vision of a liberal international trading order, the country should make no further concessions. Japan is entitled to the beliefs that further foreign intrusions into its economy are not justified and that the international division of labor has bestowed it with a blank check to enjoy mammoth trade surpluses in manufactured goods. If this is the prevailing attitude, then Japan should announce these feelings in clear, unambiguous terms and hope that the costs of foreign retaliation will never become prohibitively expensive.

TASKS FOR THE UNITED STATES

The burden of effort to reduce the bilateral competitive imbalance now rests with the United States. It is the country with the trade deficit, the lagging capital formation and productivity increases, and the larger sense of aggrievement. The United States needs to catch up—quantitatively and qualitatively—with Japan's vigorous industrial strength and expansion. Neither unfulfilled promises, nor excuses, nor exaggerated fantasies about Japanese economic omnipotence are acceptable alternatives for needed changes in U.S. attitudes, policies, and performance. If a collective effort by government, business, and labor fail to initiate such changes, both the U.S. standard of living and its international influence will certainly decline.

The recommendations that follow are based on four assumptions. First, the United States has a lot to lose and little to gain from a continuation of its declining competitive position vis-à-vis Japanese industry. Far better the United States overestimate the internal and external economic problems facing it and respond with positive, appropriate countermeasures than underestimate the costs of inaction and see them increase down the road. Even if no Japanese challenge existed, the United States would be better off in the long run correcting the shortcomings in its industrial sector, governmental policies and organization, human resources, and capital formation.

Second, the proper path to economic reinvigoration for the United States is to reorder its priorities. The imperative of giving greater priority to enhanced U.S. industrial competitiveness means neither abandoning American economic ideology and institutions in favor of imitating Japan, nor clinging further to the belief that if in fact a problem exists, an unfettered free market will find the best solution. The federal government need not take a radically increased activist role in the management of the economy, but continuing blindly with the status quo could turn the current White House belief that it is "morning in America" to the need for "mourning for America."

The third assumption is that even for the United States, the term "national security" needs to be expanded to include industrial competitiveness. Finally, while changes in government policies are clearly necessary, they will not suffice to restore U.S. industrial competitiveness. A critical precondition is a sharp improvement in performance on the production line, for that is where the United States is losing much of the ground in the competitive battle. *The best pressure the United States can impose on Japan is enhanced private sector competitiveness, not official harangues.* The following proposals are offered in the hope of encouraging the nascent consensus that the United States must overcome its economic lethargy.

1. *Shuffling priorities.* Foreign trade and world competitiveness must be genuine (not lip service) national security policy imperatives in Washington, with all major domestic economic or foreign policy actions questioned for their potential impact on U.S. international commercial competitiveness. This shift in priorities needs to be supported by the same concentrated sense of national purpose and innovative thinking that characterized cold war efforts. U.S. public opinion, the political system, and business leaders must be galvanized into action, perhaps by an economic event equivalent to the early Soviet space successes—preferably not the disappearance of additional important U.S. industries. Americans might collectively visualize the potential consequences of a scenario like severe earthquakes destroying a significant percentage of Japanese production of strategically important goods not produced in the United States. Clearly, unthinking adherence to free-market philosophy in today's world of effective, dynamic industrial policies and astronomical high-tech new-product development costs may be damaging to a country's long-term national security.

2. *Fiscal policy reforms.* a. The federal budget deficit must be reduced significantly—without recourse to accounting tricks or the Social Security Trust Fund surplus to hide the real numbers. Moderate, steady reductions should produce a chain of highly desirable results, starting with, other things being equal, lowered interest rates as government demands on the private savings pool diminish and as the Federal Reserve Board eases monetary policy to offset more restrictive fiscal policy. Lowering the relatively high costs of capital would ease a major burden on U.S. industry. Reduction in U.S. domestic interest rates should also induce depreciation in the dollar, enhancing the competitiveness of U.S. goods in the world marketplace. A genuine reduction in the budget deficit would trigger an improvement in the U.S. balance of payments as the need for net capital inflows and the resultant current account (goods and services) deficit would gradually decline in tandem.

b. The serious mistake made in the 1980s of slashing income tax rates without other, compensating tax increases must be corrected. Additional revenues will be needed to reduce the budget deficit, because rising spending needs (the savings and loan bail-out, the war on drugs, the environment, and so forth) will swamp the so-called peace dividend. Needed revenue can be raised in the short term by increasing excise taxes on such "socially negative" goods as cigarettes, alcohol, environmental pollutants, and gasoline. Revenue can also be quickly raised by a *small* increase in the tax rates of the more affluent. The current 28 percent tax bracket could be raised by up to one-tenth, to 31 percent tops, without serious harm to equity or incentives to work and save. When making such a modification, congress should eliminate entirely the current anomaly in the tax law whereby the tax rate for the highest income levels (currently beginning at about $155,000 for joint returns) *declines* from what is in effect an upper-middle bracket of 33 percent to rejoin what is otherwise a lower-middle income tax rate of 28 percent. Instead, the tax bracket for upper incomes should *rise* from the current 28 percent to a 33 percent rate that would be applied exclusively to them. For the longer-term, serious study should be made for a more generalized consumption, or sales, tax.

c. Revenue-neutral tax changes should be implemented to encourage a longer time horizon for U.S. business executives. Taxes should minimize the encouragement of corporate debt. Strict limitations should be placed on deductions for interest payments on debt to maximize market consider-ations for mergers, acquisitions, and leveraged buy-outs. Obstacles should not be put in the way of outside efforts to displace inept management, but the high-yielding, high-risk junk bonds that have become the main instru-ment for corporate takeovers, unfriendly and otherwise, need not be subsi-dized or encouraged by unlimited tax write-offs for interest. Tax penalties, such as a special sales tax on sales of corporate assets acquired within twenty-four months, should be assessed to discourage corporate dismem-berment by raiders who immediately sell off pieces of a newly acquired corporation, either for profit or to finance the purchase of the remaining pieces. A revenue-producing measure that would encourage appreciation for longer-term corporate profits would impose an "in and out" tax on institutional investors (including the currently tax-exempt pension funds) whenever stocks are sold "very soon" after purchase.

Despite revenue loss, the capital gains tax on "socially useful" invest-ments should be sharply indexed by time to minimize taxes paid on profit-able sales of stocks held for at least two years. Tax breaks for senior managers whose income was tied to longer-term results would further encourage longer-term corporate earnings horizons. Corporate earnings reports could be shifted from a quarterly to a semiannual or annual sched-ule.

d. *Savings* should be encouraged by new tax incentives that would be paid for by further shifting taxation to consumption activities. One form of incentive would be restoration (at a higher level) of the now abandoned personal exemption on interest and dividends earned. Two other means of encouraging savings are enactment of President Bush's proposed Family Savings Accounts that would exempt from taxes the interest earned on nondeductible contributions to such accounts, and extension of "indexing" (to compensate for the effects of inflation) not just to capital gains, but also to interest earned on bonds and certificates of deposit.

e. Research and development by U.S. corporations should be more actively encouraged, for example, by the permanent enactment of credits on incremental R&D outlays, despite short-term tax revenue losses.

3. *Government assistance to business.* Steering a proper middle course between legitimate, positive governmental involvement and excessive, damaging government interference in the management of the economy will be no easy task, but the U.S. government must correct its present course of indifference. It needs to do more to stimulate investment, risk taking, innovation, improvements in process technology, and faster commercialization of basic research discoveries by the private sector—without encouraging excessive dependence on official funding, collusive business practices, or protectionism.

a. In lieu of the imprecise and politically controversial term "industrial policy," the U.S. government should adopt "selective industrial enhancement" efforts. The latter would close the strange gap in logic about the role of government in the economy: that public money and support can be efficiently harnessed in a wide array of sectors, including agriculture, housing, transportation, aerospace, medicine, and fisheries, but not in commercial industrial technology. A government that can manage the design and operation of spy satellites with breathtakingly sophisticated capabilities seemingly has the capacity to perform reasonably well in indirectly assisting in the development of promising new technologies with both commercial possibilities and at least some military applications (such as semiconductors, computers, composite materials, biotechnology, and telecommunications). Why should the United States government cling to the dogma—in the face of effective joint government-industry programs in Japan and persistently large U.S. trade deficits—that the absence of greater official participation is necessarily the optimal policy? It is a hypocritical stance, given the present ad hoc, random recourse to protectionist trade measures and subsidies.

b. Specifically, the U.S. government should increase funding to the corporate sector to *partially* defray the costs of generic research in manufacturing technology and the soaring expenses of developing new high-tech products (development costs of a new commercial jet now exceed $3 billion). Special consideration needs to be given to start-up ventures pursuing promising technologies deemed too risky for full private funding; the government could receive partial paybacks by sharing in whatever revenues accrued. Government funding programs should encourage new university research efforts to diversify away from the present heavy emphasis on pure science into commercial applications of technology. Such selective industrial enhancement efforts would equate to a fraction of the subsidies already being paid out to the agricultural and housing sectors, each of which averaged above $15 billion annually in the late 1980s.

No new agencies need be created: funding could be handled by modest increases in the research budgets of three existing entities, the Defense Advanced Research Projects Agency (DARPA), the National Science Foundation (NSF), and the National Institute of Standards and Technology (NIST). Their present budgets of approximately $1.3, $1.9, and $0.2 billion, respectively, would still be tiny in comparison with agricultural and housing subsidies even if their outlays to develop new industrial technology were tripled.

The charge to these three agencies would not be to "pick winners," but to build on DARPA's proven track record in successfully promoting long-term development of exotic new technologies. Even token financial support by experts at official agencies can enhance the credibility of a new product or process in the private capital markets sufficiently to unleash substantial private funding.

Checks and balances must be built into the selective industrial enhancement efforts. Appropriations should be insulated from the political process by giving trained professionals complete spending discretion subject to rigorous auditing by Congress's General Accounting Office. A high-level advisory group of engineers, scientists, and businesspeople could help identify important emerging technologies. To quiet critics, the incremental budget outlays for the funding agencies could be terminated after five years unless specifically extended by Congress.

c. New manufacturing sciences programs in the both the NSF and in the so-called national laboratories, whose agendas are still largely devoted to basic science and military research, respectively, could enhance the development of commercial technology.

d. The NSF-funded Japanese Technology Evaluation Program should receive additional funding to expand its scholarly efforts to review Japanese scientific and technical journals and published conference proceedings, translate articles, and to assess trends in Japanese R&D.

e. Additional encouragement and funding should be given to the Advanced Technology Program created in the NIST by the 1988 trade act to promote cooperation among industry, academic, and government researchers in developing new generic technologies.

f. The very modestly funded Regional Manufacturing Centers also created by the 1988 trade act should be upgraded in scope and budget to regional Centers of Excellence in Manufacturing. These would be jointly sponsored by government and business and presumably located on university campuses with both engineering and business schools; they would seek breakthroughs in process technology techniques, such as better integrating R&D, product design, and assembly line engineering. Both the centers and the Advanced Technology Program should pay specific attention to the needs of small- and intermediate-sized companies, as well as larger ones.

g. U.S. antitrust enforcement should not be significantly diluted, but it should be administered with closer attention to the changing nature of international competition, for example, broadly interpreting the National Cooperative Research Act of 1984 to ease collaborative R&D efforts among corporations. Exemptions for joint bidding by large U.S. companies on large foreign contracts should be made easier, as should collaborative efforts to save a domestic industry from intense import competition. In each of these circumstances, the Justice Department should issue quick, clear rulings on antitrust exemption petitions.

h. While research consortia among companies (such as SEMATECH) should not be actively discouraged by the Justice Department, they need not be overly encouraged by eager government funding. It depends on the particular case whether the sometimes enormous costs of "pre-competition" research is best shared by several companies in an industry. More generalized consortia, such as the National Center for Manufacturing Sciences, can have sufficient members to match up companies with limited but complementary abilities for developing a complex new technology. Research consortia are unlikely to effectively replace intense competition between companies in promoting commercial innovations once the preliminary research stage is over.

4. *Better business strategies and management practices.* No matter how much the government improves its macro- and microeconomic policies, the gap in competitiveness with Japan will not be closed without much better performance by manufacturers themselves. Washington can make only a limited contribution to reversing the competitive shortcomings of U.S. companies.

a. The great majority of U.S. companies need to improve their process technology in general and flexible manufacturing techniques and product differentiation in particular. U.S. business needs to shift its top concern from the short-term bottom line to improved production, product innovation, and after-sales service. U.S. manufacturers need to adopt a strategy that emphasizes the right way of cutting costs (simpler assembly of better designed products, more versatile assembly line machinery, just-in-time delivery), not the wrong way (a wholesale resort to robots, moving offshore for cheaper labor). U.S. industry needs to better realize that concentrating on the quantitative (as opposed to qualitative) size of capital expenditures and contenting themselves with modest increases in productivity simply are not sufficient to beat unabating Japanese competition.

b. While the Japanese system is neither universally applicable nor totally infallible, the U.S. business sector should better appreciate that many of the accomplishments of Japanese management, especially in process technology and continual improvements to the production line, arise from simple common sense, not cultural peculiarities, and are therefore fully applicable to the U.S. industrial sector.

c. U.S. business needs to reach a consensus on what kinds of internal and external policies it wants from Washington. The conflicting messages received by the executive and legislative branches from the splintered voices of business trade associations and coalitions should be replaced with a more cohesive lobbying agenda. The leadership of the National Association of Manufacturers, Business Roundtable, American Business Conference, Chamber of Commerce, and other key coalition groups should make a concerted effort to develop common diagnoses of problems and common remedies—that is, establish an informal, watered down version of Japan's master business coalition, the *Keidanren*.

One avenue for such an effort is the role provided for the business community in the Competitiveness Policy Council, created by the 1988 trade act, but not yet implemented. If the other major participants, government and labor, also were determined to make the Council work, it could become a major forum for developing a public consensus on proposals to correct U.S. international competitive weaknesses.

d. To remain competitive in the increasingly expensive high-tech sector, U.S. companies need to cooperate among themselves as well as with European counterparts to minimize costly product development overlap, expand their capital base, exploit economies of scale, and make the components acquisitions process more efficient. A middle ground between innovation-stifling collusion and vulnerability to the larger, well-capitalized, vertically integrated Japanese companies with superb manufacturing capabilities can be found by encouraging more equity tie-ins between established U.S. firms and start-up companies with exciting technologies, but limited capital.

e. U.S. manufacturers lacking subsidiaries or joint ventures in Japan need to look closer at the net advantages of producing in that often difficult market. Local manufacture seems to inspire greater confidence in quality control in Japanese customers, and it reduces difficulties such as meeting exacting delivery deadlines. The increase in "captive" imports by U.S. subsidiaries in Japan would probably produce the stimulus to U.S. exports as did extensive U.S. foreign direct investment in Western Europe.

f. The U.S. business sector should sponsor an appropriately scaled version of a "U.S. lobby" in Japan to articulate U.S. attitudes and goals more realistically and favorably than they are usually portrayed in the Japanese media; to encourage pro-consumer, pro-import movements; and to be an additional source of increased U.S. understanding of the inner workings of the Japanese market.

g. U.S. business must improve its inadequate commercializing of newly discovered technologies. Educational institutions and the Centers of Excellence in Manufacturing discussed earlier could assist in closing the curious and curable gap between strengths in basic science and weaknesses in applied technology.

h. U.S. business executives need to strengthen relations with suppliers and employees, paying more attention to both and treating the latter as valuable resources instead of replaceable inputs.

5. *Reorienting U.S. international trade policies.* a. The guiding theme

of U.S. trade policy toward Japan and all other countries should be maximization of the U.S. standard of living rather than quantitative trade balance targets or political rewards for favored interest groups. Improving the terms of trade (the ratio of overall export prices to import prices) and increasing the percentage of total exports composed of high-value-added goods should be the dominant goals of trade policy, not arithmetic equilibrium or currency depreciation.

b. Belief in the benefits of a free, open, global trading order should not obscure the need for a multilevel strategy going beyond the imperative of pressing other countries to practice liberal trade in the image of the United States. An effective strategy requires greater U.S. government support to domestic companies to develop and market new commercial technologies and the pragmatism to accept the notion that protectionist measures under certain circumstances can be cost-effective in the long run.

The administration should take a fresh look at the bilateral situation and try to establish a specific statement of what it still wants and needs from Japan. Representatives of government, business, labor, and academe should join in developing a national consensus as to how high a price the United States is willing to pay for greater access to Japan's markets. An extreme option would be to inform Japan that the United States had determined that its national interests dictate that it internationally dominate a few specifically delineated technologies, such as those with what economists call externalities, that is, they increase the competitiveness of other goods. The U.S. government could speak of retaliation if Japan targeted such industries in Japan for global powerhouse status, thereby indirectly protecting them from full import competition.

c. While U.S. trade policy must take cognizance of bilateral political relations and the contribution of U.S. industrial inadequacies, it should take as a given that allowing Japanese industries to operate from a protected home base is usually tantamount to a sentence of death or dismemberment for their U.S. counterparts. Whenever U.S. market share in Japan for advanced high-tech goods falls significantly below average U.S. global market share, the U.S. government should investigate for possible Japanese dirty tricks causing an unacceptable degree of import inhospitality. The U.S. government should make it clear that perversion of the market mechanism is unacceptable and retaliation can be counted on if a negotiated settlement cannot be reached. This must not be a bluff. While selective protectionism may be unpleasant in the short run, it can prevent even more costly long-run economic consequences, namely Japanese industry using high internal prices to undermine foreign competition through below fair value export prices. The history of U.S.–Japanese conflict management demonstrates very clearly that a credible threat and a specific demand are key to U.S. negotiating success.

d. "Results-oriented" trade strategy is extreme and should be limited to individual cases where traditional methods to enhance market access have failed. Demands for arithmetic results, that is, a certain level of exports by dollar amount or a minimum market share in Japan, should be made only for products deemed to be of extraordinary importance to American interests. The results-oriented approach is *not* appropriate on an across the board basis—unless one believes that the whole Japanese economy inevitably operates, or should be made to operate, by cartels.

e. If political and economic pressures to limit Japanese import competition are too intense to resist, the U.S. government should still categorically avoid anticompetitive agreements that give Japanese exporters a license to raise prices. Instead of restricting the inflow of Japanese goods through quantitative export restraints, the government should use the old, politically un-chic method of imposing higher tariffs. While in theory necessitating compensation elsewhere under the rules of the GATT, tariffs would allow the U.S. Treasury, rather than Japanese companies, to collect the economic rents (higher profit margins) associated with constraining supply.

f. The Structural Impediments Initiative dialogue should be continued until Japanese attitudes and business practices reduce their direct and indirect anti-import bias. The United States should be prepared to include these attitudes and practices as priority targets under the Super 301 provision.

g. U.S. antidumping law should be amended to authorize private suits for damages against foreign companies whose export pricing tactics seem so flagrant as to amount to predatory dumping intended to drive U.S. competitors out of business.

h. The United States should create a Department of Trade to consolidate the major trade-policy–related activities of the Commerce Department (mainly export controls and investigations of unfair foreign export practices) with the Office of the U.S. Trade Representative (USTR). A strong, clearly designated leader of trade policy is a prerequisite for the cohesive, pro-active policies needed by the United States. Multiple power centers encourage unimaginative, middle-of-the-road policies and invite outsiders to play off the ends against the middle. A single trade department would also diminish internal bureaucratic arguments and turf battles; it need not displace interagency consultations, but should lead them as the first among equals.

i. The senior professional staff dealing with Japan is inadequate, both in size and institutional memory. (There is currently only one full-time senior staff person dealing with Japan in the USTR.) Japanese-language ability should be considered a special skill justifying salary enhancements for career trade officials. A person with Japanese economics expertise should be regularly assigned as a senior officer on the National Security Council staff and/or any formal White House group coordinating economic policy. An important additional task for this staff is to monitor incremental export results—if any—of Japanese market-opening measures.

6. *Enhancing human resources.* The entire U.S. educational system needs infusions of new teaching methods, innovative curricula, additional money for teaching salaries and facilities, and increased commitments by both national and local governments. The abysmally low scores of U.S. students in standardized international science and math tests should formally be declared a national disgrace.

a. The granting of more engineering and science degrees to U.S. students should become a specific goal. Special federal funding should target improvements in the estimated 60,000 secondary math and science teachers at the secondary school level who are not fully qualified and to fill the estimated 1,300 engineering faculty positions vacant at the university level.[2]

b. Parents should be given flexibility to send their children to public schools demonstrating better records of learning achievement. The staffs of poorly run schools should be dismissed. Consideration should be given to a modest extension—perhaps two weeks—of the school year nationwide.

c. Business schools should shift attention from finance and marketing to production and engineering. Increased emphasis should be placed on the implications of the globalized marketplace.

d. Vocational training programs for recent high school graduates and the unemployed as well as experienced workers need to be expanded and improved, with joint funding by government and business. With the increasing sophistication of high-tech assembly operations, specialized training programs are essential to upgrade the manufacturing skills and literacy of the U.S. work force on a continuing basis. Such programs would also ease the transition for workers displaced by imports.

7. *Miscellaneous.* a. The United States should press Japan to substantially increase its "host nation support" (currently 40 percent), which defrays the costs of U.S. military facilities and locally hired personnel in Japan; the United States should stop urging Japan to expand the size and firepower of its self-defense forces, which seem more than adequate to Japanese defense needs.

b. The Foreign Agents Registration Act should be amended to assure a wider dissemination of information on payments by foreign sources to indirectly influence U.S. international economic policies. Employees of domestic subsidiaries of foreign companies as well as the lawyers, advisers, intellectuals, and others retained by foreign interests (but not considered "foreign agents") should make full disclosure to any public audience that their views on economic policy are given in the context of their being paid by foreign interests.

c. The White House should maintain an outside advisory team to provide a second opinion on the overall state of U.S. industrial competitiveness as well as on U.S.–Japanese relations in particular. This unofficial team should include persons whose views and philosophy differ from those of the president's senior advisers on international economics.

d. U.S. intelligence agencies should enhance their abilities to uncover evidence of secret, collusive Japanese corporate actions that discriminate against U.S. companies.

Neither the United States nor Japan will ever be able to escape the burden of rapid change in the international economy. The economic policy decision-making systems in both countries will face many new dilemmas. The one basic truth that will not change is that increased international economic interdependence is inescapable; the alternative is prohibitively costly economic nationalism. Japan and the United States will always need each other politically and economically. The global trading system cannot thrive in an atmosphere of hostile U.S.–Japanese relations.

Americans must respond further to the spreading realization that their economic size, political influence, and past accomplishments no longer necessarily assure them top status in an increasingly competitive global economy. Far too many people are prepared to agree with the fictional Japanese detective in the movie *Black Rain* who tells his U.S. counterpart "Music and movies are all America is good for. . . . We won the peace."[3] U.S. economic performance needs to revive in a way that proves him wrong.

The Japanese need to act further on their emerging realization that economic size and recent accomplishments have put them in the international economic spotlight. Given the inevitability of increased international economic interdependence, the increase in foreign influence on the operation of the Japanese economy seems an inevitable, and tolerable, price for benefits received from the global economic system. In 1857, the first U.S. consul to Japan, Townsend Harris, wrote in his journal that he doubted that "the opening of Japan to foreign influences [would] promote the general happiness of the people."[4] For 135 years, Harris's doubts have been correct. The Japanese people need to prove him wrong.

The implication of this book's hypothesis—that the Japanese are unlikely to truly open their markets in a legal, procedural, and attitudinal way, and that even if they did, the U.S. industrial sector is not sufficiently competitive to be guaranteed a significant increment in exports to that market—needs to be proven wrong, twice over.

Notes

CHAPTER 1

1. See, for example, "Americans Talk Security," *Wall Street Journal,* 17 October 1988; and the July 1989 poll in *Business Week,* 7 August 1989, p. 51.
2. Ronald Dore, *Taking Japan Seriously* (London: The Athlone Press, 1987), pp. 17–18.

CHAPTER 2

1. Lafcadio Hearn, *Japan–An Attempt at Interpretation* (New York: Grosset and Dunlap, 1904), p. 501.
2. Newspaper editorial quoted in William Newman, *America Encounters Japan* (Baltimore: Johns Hopkins University Press, 1963), p. 22.
3. Raymond Saulnier, "An Economist's Eye View of the World," *Fortune,* May 1962, p. 159.
4. Not-for-attribution interview with private sector trade attorney, October 1982.
5. See, for example, *Textile Organon* March 1971, p. 22; statistics are based on U.S. Department of Commerce import data.
6. The economic postscript of the textile battle is even more ironic than the overall economic irrelevance of imported Japanese textiles. Rising Japanese wages, an appreciating yen, and increased competition from the newly industrialized Asian countries rapidly cut into the ability of the Japanese textile industry to reach the limits of its bilateral export quota allocations. Had agreement not been reached in 1971, the market mechanism itself would soon have imposed a ceiling on Japanese exports.

    Yet another irony is that by 1973 Japan happily joined with the United States and Western Europe as an importer in negotiating the Multifiber Arrangement. Thanks to its participation in the MFA, Japan could alleviate its own fears of the "yellow peril," an upsurge in textiles produced by the cheap labor in less developed countries. Pressured by its own industry for relief from imports, the Japanese government actively participates in the textile restraint agreements established between LDC exporters and the industrial countries under the MFA framework.
7. An ironic footnote from the *New York Times,* 23 May 1972: Kakuei Tanaka, then minister of MITI, flatly declared that no further yen revaluation would occur and

in effect pledged his political future that the new program would achieve its goals. He said he "would hold himself administratively and politically accountable" for successfully implementing the seven-point program.

8. Memorandum written by the author in his capacity as chief economist of the council, 31 October 1972.

9. Calculated from U.S. Department of Commerce and International Monetary Fund data.

10. Masaru Yoshitomi, "Japan's Response to the Oil Crisis," *The Wheel Extended,* English edition (January–March 1982): 6.

11. Ronald I. Meltzer, "Color TV Sets and U.S.–Japanese Relations: Problems of Trade-Adjustment Policymaking," *ORBIS* 23 (Summer 1979): 421.

12. Clyde Prestowitz, Jr., *Trading Places: How We Allowed Japan to Take the Lead* (New York: Basic Books, 1988), p. 204.

13. Ibid., pp. 204–5.

14. For the full text of the joint statement by Minister Ushiba and Ambassador Strauss, see House Ways and Means Committee, *Task Force Report on United States–Japan Trade,* January, 1979, pp. 70–72.

15. Louis Kraar, "Japan Blows Smoke about U.S. Cigarettes," *Fortune,* 21 February 1983, p. 100.

16. *Yearbook of U.S.–Japan Economic Relations in 1980* (Washington, D.C.: Japan Economic Institute of America, 1981), pp. 61–62.

17. "High-Technology Gateway," *Business Week,* 9 August 1982, p. 42.

18. For a more detailed account of the automobile issue and settlement, see Stephen D. Cohen and Ronald I. Meltzer, *United States International Economic Policy in Action* (New York: Praeger, 1982), ch. 3.

19. See, for example, U.S. International Trade Commission, "A Review of Recent Developments in the U.S. Automobile Industry Including an Assessment of the Japanese Voluntary Restraint Agreements," February 1985; and Robert W. Crandall, "Import Quotas and the Automobile Industry: The Costs of Protection," *Brookings Review,* Summer 1984.

20. Phillip Agress, "U.S. Calls on Japan to Eliminate Import Barriers," *Business America,* 22 March 1982, p. 4.

21. Sources consulted for this and subsequent market-opening packages include the annual *Yearbook of U.S.–Japan Economic Relations,* 1982 through 1895 (Washington, D.C.: Japan Economic Institute of America); and the annual reports by the U.S. International Trade Commission, "Operation of the Trade Agreements Program," 1984 through 1988.

22. See, for example, Prestowitz, *Trading Places,* p. 229.

23. For a more detailed account of Congress's protectionist offensive and the administration's response, see the author's *The Making of U.S. International Economic Policy* (New York: Praeger, 1988), ch. 10.

24. James K. Jackson, "Japanese Investment in the United States," in *Japan–U.S. Relations,* Congressional Research Service, July 1989, p. 11.

25. U.S. Department of Commerce, *Survey of Current Business,* various issues.

CHAPTER 3

1. *Dynamic Random Access Memory Semiconductors of 256 Kilobits and Above from Japan,* U.S. International Trade Commission, Publication 1803, January 1986, p. 21.

2. Identical texts of the side letter were published in an American newsletter, *Inside U.S. Trade,* and in a Japanese magazine, *Bungei Shunju.*

3. Electronic Industries Association of Japan, "Statement on Semiconductors," 21 November 1988, p. 9.

4. U.S. Department of Commerce data (received by telephone from International Trade Administration official).

5. Not-for-attribution interview with former U.S. Trade Representative official, March 1989.

6. American Electronics Association, unpublished data.

7. Not-for-attribution interviews with current and former U.S. trade officials, Winter–Spring 1989.

8. Ibid.

9. See, for example, Kenneth Flamm, "Policy and Politics in the International Semiconductor Industry" (Presentation, 16 January 1989, to the SEMI ISS Seminar, Newport Beach, California.

10. Charles H. Ferguson, "Computers and the Coming of the U.S. Keiretsu," *Harvard Business Review* (July–August 1990): 66.

CHAPTER 4

1. The term "culture," as used here, encompasses (1) social and intellectual forms and (2) the totality of socially transmitted behavior patterns, beliefs, institutions, and all other products of human thought characteristic of a specific population group. (From *The American Heritage Dictionary of the English Language* (Boston: Houghton Mifflin, 1969).)

2. Daniel I. Okimoto, *Between MITI and the Market* (Stanford, Calif.: Stanford University Press, 1989), p. 237.

3. Mitsuyuki Masatsugu, *The Modern Samurai Society* (New York: AMACOM-American Management Associations, 1982), p. 9.

4. Karel Van Wolferen, *The Enigma of Japanese Power* (New York: Alfred A. Knopf, 1989), p. 3.

5. Edwin O. Reischauer, *The United States and Japan* (Cambridge, Mass.: Harvard University Press, 1965), p. 163.

6. Japanese business spent the equivalent of $14.2 billion on entertainment in 1980—more than the country budgeted for national defense (*Wall Street Journal,* 8 December 1981). More recent data from other sources suggest that in 1987–88 defense expenditures and estimated corporate entertaining expenditures were running about even at 4 trillion yen.

7. James Fallows, "The Japanese Difference," *Washington Post,* 5 February 1989, p. D1.

8. Van Wolferen, *Enigma of Japanese Power,* pp. 167–168.

9. James C. Abegglen and George Stalk, Jr., *Kaisha: The Japanese Corporation* (New York: Basic Books, 1985), p. 6.

10. Ronald Henkoff, "What Motorola Learns from Japan," *Fortune,* 24 April 1989, p. 168.

11. Abegglen and Stalk, *Kaisha,* p. 79.

12. Ibid., pp. 104–11.

13. Ibid., pp. 96–97.

14. Ramchandran Jaikumar, "Postindustrial Manufacturing," *Harvard Business Review* (November–December 1986): 72.

15. Ibid., p. 73.

16. House Committee on Science, Space, and Technology, Technology Policy Task Force, *Technology Policy and Its Effect on the National Economy,* December 1988, p. 214.

17. Van Wolferen, *Enigma of Japanese Power,* p. 171.

18. With 1967 as 100, the Japanese manufactured wholesale goods price index in 1984 stood at 203; the consumer price index in that same time had surged to 317. In all other major industrialized countries, the consumer and wholesale price indices increased by about the same amount during the same 1967–84 period; that is, there was minimal spread in their respective performances. (U.S. Department of Commerce, *International Economic Indicators,* March 1985.)

19. U.S. Department of Labor, "Hourly Compensation Costs for Production Workers," August 1989, p. 3.

20. Ibid., p. 1.

21. Organization for Economic Cooperation and Development, *OECD Economic Outlook,* December 1988, p. 177.

22. Laura D'Andrea Tyson and John Zysman, "Developmental Strategy and Innovation in Japan," in Chalmers Johnson, Laura D'Andrea Tyson and John Zysman, ed., *Politics and Productivity—How Japan's Development Strategy Works* (New York: Ballinger Publishers, 1989), p. 77.

23. Chalmers Johnson, *MITI and the Japanese Miracle* (Stanford, Calif.: Stanford University Press, 1982), p. 19.

24. Van Wolferen, *Enigma of Japanese Power,* p. 377.

25. Yoshihisa Ojima, Speech delivered to the OECD Industry Committee, June 1970. (Mimeo.)

26. Quoted in House Ways and Means Subcommittee on Trade, *Report on Trade Mission to Far East,* December 1981, p. 34.

27. Hiroya Ueno, "The Conception and Evaluation of Japanese Industrial Policy," in Kazuo Sato, ed., *Industry and Business in Japan* (White Plains, N.Y.: M.E. Sharpe, 1980), pp. 382–83, 396.

28. John Zysman and Stephen S. Cohen, *The Mercantilist Challenge to the Liberal International Trade Order,* (Washington, D.C.: Joint Economic Committee, 1982), pp. 16–17.

29. Van Wolferen, *Enigma of Japanese Power,* p. 376.

30. Kozo Yamamura, "Joint Research and Antitrust: Japanese vs. American Strategies," in Hugh Patrick, ed., *Japan's High Technology Industries* (Seattle: University of Washington Press, 1986), p. 205.

CHAPTER 5

1. *The Economist,* 19 August, 1989, p. 72.
2. Paul C. Roberts, "Economic Viewpoint," *Business Week,* 13 November 1989, p. 30.
3. Office of Management and Budget press release, 20 July 1989, p. 3.
4. Chalmers Johnson, *MITI and the Japanese Miracle* (Stanford Calif.: Stanford University Press, 1982), p. 19.
5. National Academy of Engineering, *The Technological Dimensions of International Competitiveness* (Washington, D.C., 1988), p. 37.
6. Ira C. Magaziner and Robert B. Reich, *Minding America's Business* (New York: Vintage Books, 1983), p. 200.
7. Murray L. Weidenbaum, *Business, Government, and the Public* (Englewood Cliffs, N.J.: Prentice-Hall, 1986), pp. 16, 24–26.
8. House Committee on Science, Space, and Technology, Technology Policy Task Force, *Technology Policy and Its Effect on the National Economy,* December 1988, p. 7.
9. Benjamin Friedman, quoted in *New York Times,* 22 October 1989, p. IV 3.
10. U.S. Treasury Department, press release, 12 September 1989, p.4.
11. The National Commission on Excellence in Education, *A Nation at Risk* April 1983, p. 7.
12. Bert Braddock, quoted in *Washington Post,* 24 October, 1982, p. A10.
13. *Washington Post,* 18 December, 1988, p. H5.
14. Stephen R. Hardis, quoted in *New York Times,* 30 October 1988, p. III 8.
15. Quoted in *Fortune,* 25 September 1989, p. 52.
16. Ibid.
17. MIT Commission on Industrial Productivity, *Made in America* (Cambridge, Mass.: MIT Press, 1989), pp. 8, 42.
18. Ibid., p. 166.
19. Stephen S. Cohen and John Zysman, "Puncture the Myths That Keep American Managers from Competing," *Harvard Business Review* (November–December 1988): 98.
20. "Stuck in Reverse," *New York Times Book Review,* 29 October 1989, p. 38; "Study Says Ford Leads in Efficiency," *New York Times,* 3 January 1990, p. D5.
21. MIT Commission, *Made in America,* p. 119.
22. "The Rival Japan Respects," *Business Week,* 13 November 1989, pp. 109, 118. For other examples of successful U.S. corporate emphasis on production technology, see "Beating Japan at Its Own Game," *New York Times,* 16 July 1989, p. III 1.

23. Eastman Kodak Company, *Meeting World Challenges: U.S. Manufacturing in the 1990s,* 1989 p. i.

CHAPTER 6

1. Masataka Kosaka, "The International Economic Policy of Japan," in Robert A. Scalapino, ed., *The Foreign Policy of Modern Japan* (Berkeley: University of California Press, 1977), p. 214.

2. Kyogoku Junichi, quoted in Kosaka, "International Economic Policy," p. 225.

3. *Washington Post,* 19 February 1989, p. H5.

4. Kiyoshi Kojima and Terutomo Ozawa, *Japan's General Trading Companies* (Paris: OECD, 1984), p. 71.

5. These and other measures discussed in Robert A. Flammang, *U.S. Programs That Impede U.S. Export Competitiveness: The Regulatory Environment* (Washington, D.C.: Georgetown University Center for Strategic and International Studies, 1980).

6. For more detail, see the author's *The Making of U.S. International Economic Policy* (New York: Praeger, 1988), ch. 10.

7. *The Economist,* 4 March 1989, p. 66.

8. Barry Bluestone and Bennett Harrison, *The Deindustrialization of America* (New York: Basic Books, 1982), p. 42.

9. "America's 50 Biggest Exporters," *Fortune,* 17 July 1989, p. 50.

10. U.S. Department of Commerce, *International Direct Investment: Global Trends and the U.S. Role,* 1988, pp. 31–32.

11. *U.S. Manufacturing Investment in Japan White Paper* (Tokyo: American Chamber of Commerce in Japan, 1980), p. 7.

12. U.S. Treasury Department, "Survey of G-7 Laws and Regulations on Foreign Direct Investment," 7 December 1988 (processed), p. 2.

13. *United States' Manufacturing Investment in Japan* (Tokyo: American Chamber of Commerce in Japan 1979), pp. v, vi.

14. Robert B. Reich, "The Quiet Path to Technological Preeminence," *Scientific American,* October 1989, p. 43.

15. John A. Alic, "Industrial Policy: Where Do We Go From Here?" (Paper presented at the Conference on Corporate Strategy and Structure: Japan and the USA, Chicago Council on Foreign Relations and the Johnson Foundation Racine, Wis., 30 April 1982), p. 18.

16. Clyde Prestowitz, Jr., *Trading Places: How We Allowed Japan to Take the Lead* (New York: Basic Books, 1988), p. 99.

CHAPTER 7

1. Philip H. Trezise, "The Realities of Japan–U.S. Economic Relations," *Pacific Community I* (April 1970): 359–60. The bulk of this article is still fully relevant to the bilateral trade situation in 1983.

2. Not-for-attribution interview, May 1971.

3. U.S. Congress, *Congressional Record,* 31 July 1978.

4. U.S.–Japan Trade Council, "Foreign Economic Legislation: A Year-End Review" (Washington, D.C.: U.S.–Japan Trade Council, December 4, 1979).

5. Clyde Prestowitz, Jr., *Trading Places: How We Allowed Japan to Take the Lead* (New York: Basic Books, 1988), p. 260.

6. Ibid., p. 281.

7. Advisory Committee for Trade Policy and Negotiations, "Analysis of the U.S.–Japan Trade Problem," February 1989 (processed), p. 112.

8. James Fallows, "The Japan Handlers," *Atlantic,* August 1987, p. 23.

9. Prestowitz, *Trading Places,* p. 259.

10. David Osborne, "Japan's Secret Agents," *New Republic,* 1 October 1984, p. 22.

11. Clyde Prestowitz, Jr., "Japan Talks Trade While America Sleeps," *New York Times,* 24 April 1988, p. III3.

12. Christopher Madison, "Is Japan Trying to Buy Washington or Just Do Business Capital Style?" *National Journal* 14 (October 1982): 1711.

13. "Japan's Clout in the U.S.," *Business Week,* 11 July 1988, p. 64.

14. See, for example, Clyde H. Farnsworth, "Japan's Loud Voice in Washington," *New York Times,* 10 December 1989, p. III1; and Pat Choate, "Money Talks: How Foreign Firms Buy U.S. Clout," *Washington Post,* 19 June 1988, p. C1.

15. Osborne, "Japan's Secret Agents," p. 20.

16. Robert Gray, "Yen at Work," *Regardies,* June 1989, p. 100.

17. Ibid.

18. House Judiciary Committee, *Restrictions on the Post-Employment Activities of Federal Officers and Employees,* Hearings, 4 May 1988, p. 77.

19. Osborne, "Japan's Secret Agents," p. 21.

20. David Osborne, "Lobbying for Japan Inc.," *New York Times Magazine,* 4 December 1983, p. 132.

21. *Business Week,* 11 July 1989, p. 69.

22. Kenneth J. Dillon, *Worlds in Collusion: The U.S. and Japan beyond the Year 2000* (U.S. State Department Foreign Service Institute, Center for the Study of Foreign Affairs, Paper No. 2, April 1989), p. 27.

23. "Sony Discussing Contribution to Reagan's Library," *New York Times,* 29 October 1989, p. I4.

24. "State Department Officer Hired by Japanese High-Tech Firm," *Washington Post,* 18 January 1990, p. C5.

25. Farnsworth, "Japan's Loud Voice," p. III1.

CHAPTER 8

1. Michael Blaker, "Japan, 1982: The End of Illusion?" *Washington Quarterly* 5 (Spring 1982):86.

2. *Washington Post,* 7 January 1990.

3. U.S. Treasury Department, "Report to Congress on International Economic and Exchange Rate Policy," October 1989.

4. "A Rising Tide of Protectionism," *Newsweek,* 30 May 1983, p. 27.

5. *New York Times,* 14 January 1990, p. III13.

6. *New York Times,* 18 January 1990, p. D8.

7. *Washington Post,* 23 April 1988, p. B1.

8. U.S. Department of Commerce, press release, 8 December 1981, pp. 4–5.

9. Toshikazu Maeda, "Japanese Perception of America: Evolution from Dependency to Maturity," in *U.S.–Japan Relations in the 1980's: Towards Burden Sharing* (Cambridge, Mass.: Harvard University Center for International Affairs, 1982), p. 24.

10. *Asahi Journal,* 26 March 1982, cited in Kent E. Calder, "Opening Japan," *Foreign Policy* 47 (Summer 1982): 29.

11. Hajime Ohta, "Recent U.S.–Japan Economic Relations: A Japanese View," (Washington, D.C.: U.S.–Japan Trade Council, 19 May 1979), p. 3.

12. Gary Saxonhouse, "The Micro- and Macroeconomics of Foreign Sales to Japan," in William Cline, ed., *Trade Policy in the 1980s* (Washington, D.C.: Institute for International Economics, 1983), p. 285.

13. Japan–United States Economic Relations Group, *Report of the Japan–United States Economic Relations Group,* January 1981, pp. 55–56.

14. Consulate of Japan at New York, *Twenty Questions and Answers on Japan–U.S. Relations,* 1982, p. 14.

15. Japan Economic Institute.

16. Despite occasional Japanese claims, the U.S. deficit with Japan is only slightly reduced when the comparison is calculated on the current account (which includes services) basis rather than the trade account.

17. "Japan, Weary of Barbs on Trade, Tells Americans Why They Trail," *New York Times,* 20 November 1989, p. A1.

18. "The U.S.–Japan Trade Imbalance: Causes and Remedies," Harvard Program on U.S.–Japan Relations, Occasional Paper 88-05, p. 54.

19. See reference to J.D. Powers and Associates "Satisfaction Index," *Wall Street Journal,* 21 December 1989, p. A17.

20. Brock Yates, "American Taste, Made in Japan," *Washington Post Magazine,* 3 September 1989, p. 29.

21. Akio Morita and Shintaro Ishihara, *The Japan That Can Say No* (Unofficial translation, no date, processed), pp. 8–10.

22. Ohta, "Recent U.S.–Japan Relations," p. 5.

23. See, for example, *New York Times,* 6 March 1988, p. iv 4.

24. See, for example, *New York Times Magazine,* 28 August 1988, p. 74.

25. *Wall Street Journal,* 19 November 1982, p. 33.

26. Quoted in Stephen Schlosstein, *Trade War* (New York: Congdon and Weed, 1984), p. 97.

27. *Washington Post,* 19 January 1986, p. C1.

28. "Report of the Study Group on a Japan–U.S. Free Trade Arrangement," June 1989, p. 12. Distributed by the Japanese Ministry of International Trade and Industry.

29. Carl J. Green, "Legal Protectionism in the United States and its Impact on United States–Japan Economic Relations," Appendix to the Report of the Japan–United States Economic Relations Group, p. 267.

30. Personal interview, June 1983.

31. Susan MacKnight, "Justice Department Looking into Sales of Japanese made 64K RAMS's," Japan Economic Institute report dated 6 August 1982, p. 2.

32. Economic Planning Agency of Japan, unpublished data.

33. Yung Chul Park and Won Am Park, "Changing Japanese Trade Patterns and the East Asian NICs" (National Bureau of Economic Research paper, 19 October 1989), p. 4.

34. Foreign Ministry of Japan.

CHAPTER 9

1. Ruth Benedict, *The Chrysanthemum and the Sword* (New York: Meridian Books, 1972), p. 1.

2. Henry Kissinger, *White House Years* (Boston: Little, Brown, 1979), pp. 321–22.

3. Quoted in James Fallows, "Containing Japan," *Atlantic,* May 1989, p. 48.

4. Senator John Danforth, press release, 13 January 1986, p. 1.

5. James C. Abegglen, "Narrow Self-Interest: Japan's Ultimate Vulnerability?" in Diane Tasca, ed., *U.S.–Japanese Economic Relations: Cooperation, Competition, and Confrontation* (New York: Pergamon, 1980), p. 27.

6. Dan Henderson, quoted in Bela Balassa and Marcus Noland, *Japan in the World Economy* (Washington, D.C.: Institute for International Economics, 1988), p. 215.

7. William Chapman, "Now the Japanese Are *Acting* As if They're Number One," *Washington Post,* 15 July 1984, p. B1.

8. Jared Taylor, *Shadows of the Rising Sun* (New York: William Morrow, 1983), p. 35.

9. Mitsuyuki Masatsugu, *The Modern Samurai Society* (New York: Amacom-American Management Associations, 1982), p. 91.

10. Hotta Masayoshi, quoted in Steven Schlossstein, *Trade War* (New York: Congdon and Weed, 1984), p. 104.

11. "Sony's Announcement on Columbia Bid Shows Japanese Curbs on Foreign Media," *Wall Street Journal,* 2 October 1989, p. A10

12. Senator John Heinz, press release, 10 July 1989, p. 3.

13. Karel van Wolferen, "The Japan Problem," *Foreign Affairs* (Winter 1986–87): 293.

14. Karel van Wolferen, *The Enigma of Japanese Power* (New York: Alfred A. Knopf, 1989), p. 420.

15. George Soros, "After Black Monday," *Foreign Policy* (Spring 1988): 77.

16. James Fallows, "Containing Japan," p. 51.

17. *Washington Post,* 12 June 1983, p. A1.

18. Alan W. Wolff, speech, 30 March 1989, p. 7.

19. "O.E.C.D. Calls on Tokyo To Lift Living Standards," *New York Times,* 27 December 1989, p. D2.

20. "Now Japan Is Feeling the Heat from the Gray Market," *Business Week,* 14 March 1988, p. 50.

21. *Japan Times,* 18 June 1986.

22. *Business Week,* 14 March 1988, p. 51.

23. "Japan's Oil Import Argument," *New York Times,* 21 January 1985, p. D10.

24. *The Economist,* 25 June 1988, p. 68.

25. "Japanese Film Exacerbates Trade Tensions," *Washington Post,* 9 April 1988, p. A14.

26. Van Wolferen, *Enigma of Japanese Power,* p. 53.

27. Joint Economic Committee, *Restoring International Balance: Japan's Trade and Investment Patterns,* Staff study, July 1988, p. 62.

28. Federal Reserve Bank of Chicago, "Chicago Fed Letter," October 1989, p. 3.

29. Sir John Harvey-Jones, quoted in *Japan Times,* 17 June 1986.

30. Edward J. Lincoln, *Japan's Unequal Trade* (Washington, D.C.: Brookings Institution, 1990), p. 103.

31. *The International Economy,* February/March, 1990, p. 49.

32. Lincoln, *Japan's Unequal Trade,* p. 60.

33. Ibid.

34. Robert Z. Lawrence, "Imports in Japan: Closed Markets or Minds?" *Brookings Papers on Economic Activity* 2:1987, p. 523.

35. Data for this and subsequent bilateral U.S. trade balances from U.S. Department of Commerce, "U.S. Foreign Trade Update," various issues.

36. House Ways and Means Committee, *High Technology and Japanese Industrial Policy: A Strategy for U.S. Policymakers,* October 1980, p. 13.

37. Mordechai E. Kreinin, "How Closed Is Japan's Market? Additional Evidence," *World Economy,* December 1988, p. 540.

38. *Financial Times,* 18 December 1984.

39. *London Sunday Times,* 21 February 1982.

40. Frank A. Weil and Norman D. Glick, "Japan—Is the Market Open? A View of the Japanese Market Drawn from U.S. Corporate Experience," *Law and Policy in International Business* 2, No. 3 (1979): 863.

41. Clyde V. Prestowitz, Jr., as quoted in *Japan Economic Survey,* December 1982, p. 9.

42. "Wood Products Enter the Trade Battle as U.S. Says Japan Frustrates Imports," *Wall Street Journal,* 15 June 1989, p. A10.

43. William V. Rapp, "Japan's Invisible Barriers to Trade," in *Fragile Interdependence* (Lexington, Mass.: Lexington Books, 1986), p. 28.

44. Ibid.

45. Clyde Prestowitz, Jr., *Trading Places: How We Allowed Japan to Take the Lead* (New York: Basic Books, 1988), p. 164.

46. U.S. Semiconductor Industry Association, *The Effect of Government Targeting on World Semiconductor Competition,* 1983 (processed), p. 82.

47. U.S. International Trade Commission, *Phase I: Japan's Distribution System and Options for Improving Its Access,* June, 1990 (processed), p. 36.

48. Not-for-attribution interview with European business representative, Tokyo, April 1989.

49. Not-for-attribution interview with U.S. government official, Tokyo, April 1989.

50. U.S. Department of Commerce, unpublished data.

51. Clyde Prestowitz, Jr., "Set Guidelines for Export Market Share," *New York Times,* 11 December 1988, p. III2.

52. Not-for-attribution interview with U.S. business representative, Tokyo, May 1989.

53. Complaint for Damages, filed in U.S. District Court for the Northern District of California, October 1988, p. 15.

54. Lincoln, *Japan's Unequal Trade,* p. 65.

55. Not-for-attribution interview with U.S. government official, Tokyo, April 1989.

56. American Chamber of Commerce in Japan, "Distribution Vision for the 1990's," no date, p. 6.

57. Not-for-attribution interview with former U.S. trade official, February 1989.

58. Robert C. Christopher, *Second to None—American Companies in Japan* (New York: Crown Publishers, 1986), p. 152.

59. Not-for-attribution interview, June 1989.

60. Section 301 Petition submitted by Allied-Signal Inc. to the Office of the U.S. Trade Representative, 5 March 1990, Volume I, pp. 20, 31, 45.

61. Fred Hiatt, "Hidden Wall: A Native Son Battles Japan's Trade Barriers," *Washington Post,* 23 June 1989, p. G1.

62. Letter from BAE Automated Systems, Inc. to the deputy assistant secretary of Commerce for Japan, 27 October 1988.

63. Richard Solomon, "U.S. and Japan: An Evolving Partnership" (U.S. Department of State text of speech to The Foreign Correspondents Club of Japan, 10 April 1990), p. 3.

64. Hans-Dietrich Genscher, "The Japanese Challenge," press release, 22 January 1982, p. 3.

65. "EEC-Japan Relations," European Community, unpublished memorandum, 2 June 1989, p. 1

66. "High Level Consultations—European Commission/Japan," European Community, press release, 10 November 1989, p. 1.

67. "European Report," 15 July 1987.

68. "EEC-Japan Relations," p. 7.

69. U.S. Department of Commerce, "U.S. Foreign Trade Update," February 1990.

70. See, for example, Carla Hills, "The United States, Japan and Trade Policy in the Twenty-First Century," Office of the U.S. Trade Representative press release, 13 October 1989, p. 7.

71. House Ways and Means Subcommittee on Trade, *Report on Trade Mission to Far East,* December 1981, p. 17.

72. Ibid., p. 18.

73. Balassa and Noland, *Japan in the World*, p. 236.

74. Ibid., p. 221.

75. "ROC Battles Trade Deficit with Japan," *Free China Review*, April 1982, p. 55.

76. "Symbiotic Relationship in Danger," *Financial Times*, 15 May 1985.

77. Balassa and Noland, *Japan in the World*, p. 218.

78. "Hyundai Touching All Bases as It Ponders Sales in Japan," *Automotive News*, 13 March 1989, p. 35.

79. House Ways and Means Subcommittee on Trade, *United States–Japan Trade Report*, September 1980, pp. 35–36.

80. Not-for-attribution interview with international trade lawyer, October 1982.

81. "Address by Walter F. Mondale," press release, 22 September 1982, p. 3.

82. William L. Givens, "The U.S. Can No Longer Afford Free Trade," *Business Week*, 22 November 1982, p. 15.

83. "Statement of American Motors Corporation," Testimony before the House Ways and Means Committee, 29 September 1982, p. 1.

84. "Survival's at Stake, Harley-Davidson Warns," *Denver Post*, 7 May 1983.

85. Vladimir Pucik, quoted in *Wall Street Journal*, 16 February 1990, p. 1.

CHAPTER 10

1. Richard J. Samuels, "Consuming for Production: Japanese National Security, Nuclear Fuel Procurement, and the National Economy," *International Organization* (Autumn 1989): 628.

2. Edward H. Carr, *The Twenty Years Crisis, 1919–1939* (New York: Harper and Row, 1964), pp. 116–17.

3. British Treasury ministry, "Economic Progress Report," April 1989, p. 1.

4. *Wall Street Journal*, 27 March 1990, p. B1.

5. *Washington Post*, 21 January 1990, p. B7.

6. *Wall Street Journal*, 9 January 1990, p. A10.

7. Peter F. Drucker, *The New Realities: In Government and Politics/In Economics and Business/In Society and World View* (New York: Harper and Row, 1988), pp. 129–30.

8. Arthur Schlesinger, Jr., "Our Problem Is Not Japan or Germany," *Wall Street Journal*, 22 December 1989, p. A6.

9. Charles H. Ferguson, "America's High-Tech Decline," *Foreign Policy* (Spring 1989): 125.

10. U.S. Central Intelligence Agency, "Handbook of Economic Statistics, 1989," p. 156.

11. Motor Vehicle Manufacturers Association of the United States, Inc.

12. J.-J. Servan-Schreiber, *The American Challenge* (New York: Atheneum, 1968), p. xiii.

13. Paul Kennedy, "A Guide to Misinterpreters," *New York Times*, 17 April 1988, p. IV27.

CHAPTER 11

1. Senate Foreign Relations Committee, *The United States in a Global Economy,* Hearings, February–March 1985, p. 5.

2. President's Commission on Industrial Competitiveness, *Global Competition: The New Reality,* 1985, p. 6.

3. National Science Foundation, "Science Resources Studies Highlights," memorandum, January 1990; and Japan Economic Institute, report No. 24A, 23 June 1989.

4. National Science Foundation, press release 90-4 (no date).

5. Kenneth S. Courtis, "Japan in Heisei 10: The Handwriting on the Wall," *Business Tokyo,* January 1990, p. 40.

6. Institute of Electrical and Electronics Engineers, "U.S. Supercomputer Vulnerability" (Report of the Scientific Supercomputer Subcommittee of the Committee on Communications and Information Policy, 8 August 1988), pp. 1, 7, 10.

7. "Corporate Venturing News," 4 May 1990, p. 1.

8. *New York Times,* 22 January 1990, p. D5.

9. Samuel Huntington, "The U.S.—Decline or Renewal?" *Foreign Affairs* (Winter 1988–89): 88–89.

10. R. Taggart Murphy, "Power without Purpose: The Crisis of Japan's Global Financial Dominance," *Harvard Business Review* (March–April 1989): 74.

11. Ibid., pp. 77–78.

12. Quoted in *Wall Street Journal,* 7 November 1989, p. A1.

13. Charles H. Ferguson, "America's High-Tech Decline," *Foreign Policy* (Spring 1989):139.

14. Quoted in *Forbes,* 9 February 1987, p. 76.

15. Akio Morita and Shintaro Ishihara, *The Japan That Can Say No* (Unofficial translation, no date, processed), pp. 3–4.

16. Congressional Office of Technology Assessment, *Making Things Better,* February 1990, p. 148.

17. Sheridan Tatsuno, *Created in Japan* (New York: Harper and Row, 1990), pp. 267–68.

18. William H. Webster, "The Role of Intelligence in a Changing World," (Remarks at the American University, 20 March 1990), p. 6.

19. Quoted in *The Economist,* 17 February 1990, p. 21.

20. Robert J. Samuelson, "Fears and Fantasies," *Newsweek,* 2 April 1990, p. 25.

CHAPTER 12

1. Jane Wagner, *A Search for Signs of Intelligent Life in the Universe* (New York: Harper and Row, 1986), p. 18.

2. National Science Foundation data quoted in "Picking up the Pace" (Report of the Council on Competitiveness, no date), p. 23.

3. Quoted in *New York Times,* 19 November 1989, p. II17.

4. Townsend Harris, *The Complete Journal of Townsend Harris* (Ruthland, Vt.: Charles Tuttle Company, 1959), p. 429.

Selected Bibliography

Abegglen, James C., and George Stalk, Jr. *Kaisha: The Japanese Corporation.* New York: Basic Books, 1985.

Ahearn, Raymond. *Japan: Prospects for Greater Market Openness.* Washington, D.C.: Congressional Research Service, 1989.

American Chamber of Commerce in Japan. *United States–Japan White Paper,* 1989. (The chamber is an excellent source of published trade and investment data by "resident" U.S. businesspeople.)

Balassa, Bela, and Marcus Noland, *Japan in the World Economy.* Washington, D.C.: Institute for International Economics, 1988.

Benedict, Ruth. *The Chrysanthemum and the Sword.* New York: Meridian Books, 1972.

Bergsten, C. Fred, and William Cline. *The United States–Japan Economic Problem.* Washington, D.C.: Institute for International Economics, 1985.

Christopher, Robert C. *The Japanese Mind: The Goliath Explained.* New York: Linden Press, 1983.

Cohen, Stephen D., and Ronald I. Meltzer. *United States International Economic Policy in Action.* New York: Praeger, 1982.

Cohen, Stephen S., and John Zysman. *Manufacturing Matters.* New York: Basic Books, 1987.

Destler, I. M., and Hideo Sato, eds. *Coping with U.S.–Japanese Economic Conflicts.* Lexington, Mass.: Lexington Books, 1982.

Destler, I. M., Haruhiro Fukui, and Hideo Sato. *The Textile Wrangle.* Ithaca N.Y.: Cornell University Press, 1979.

Dillon, Kenneth J. *Worlds in Collusion: the U.S. and Japan beyond the Year 2000.* U.S. State Department Foreign Service Institute, Center for the Study of Foreign Affairs, Paper No. 2, April 1989.

Dore, Ronald. *Flexible Rigidities.* London: The Athlone Press, 1986.

———. *Taking Japan Seriously.* London: The Athlone Press, 1987.

Fallows, James. "Containing Japan." *Atlantic,* May 1989.

———. "The Hard Life." *Atlantic,* March 1987.

———. "Playing by Different Rules." *Atlantic,* September 1987.

Ferguson, Charles H. "America's High-Tech Decline." *Foreign Policy,* Spring 1989.

General Accounting Office. *Industrial Policy: Case Studies in the Japanese Experience.* Washington, D.C.: Government Printing Office, October 1982.

———. *Industrial Policy: Japan's Flexible Approach.* Washington, D.C.: Government Printing Office, June 1982.

Gibney, Frank. *Japan, The Fragile Super Power.* New York: Meridian Books, 1979.

———. *Miracle by Design: The Real Reasons behind Japan's Economic Success.* New York: Times Books, 1982.

Haitani, Kanji. *The Japanese Economic System.* Lexington, Mass.: Lexington Books, 1976.

Hunsberger, Warren S. *Japan and the United States in World Trade.* New York: Harper and Row, 1964.

"Japan's Clout in the United States." *Business Week,* 11 July 1988.

Japan–United States Economic Relations Group. *Report of the Japan–United States Economic Relations Group.* January 1981.

Johnson, Chalmers. *MITI and the Japanese Miracle.* Stanford, Calif.: Stanford University Press, 1982.

Johnson, Chalmers, Laura D'Andrea Tyson, and John Zysman, eds. *Politics and Productivity—How Japan's Development Strategy Works.* New York: Ballinger Publishers, 1989.

Kaplan, Eugene J. *Japan: The Government-Business Relationship.* Washington, D.C.: U.S. Department of Commerce, 1972.

Lawrence, Robert Z. "Imports in Japan: Closed Markets or Minds?" *Brookings Papers on Economic Activity* 2:1987.

Lincoln, Edward J. *Japan's Unequal Trade.* Washington, D.C.: The Brookings Institution, 1990.

Lockwood, William W. *The Economic Development of Japan.* Princeton: Princeton University Press, 1968.

Magaziner, Ira C., and Thomas M. Hout. *Japanese Industrial Policy.* Policy Papers in International Affairs, Institute of International Studies, University of California, Berkeley, 1980.

Magaziner, Ira C., and Robert B. Reich. *Minding America's Business.* New York: Vintage Books, 1983.

Masatsugu, Mitsuyuki. *The Modern Samurai Society.* New York: AMACOM–American Management Associations, 1982.

MIT Commission on Industrial Productivity. *Made in America.* Cambridge, Mass.: MIT Press, 1989.

Morishima, Michio. *Why Has Japan 'Succeeded'?* Cambridge: Cambridge University Press, 1982.

Morita, Akio and Shintaro Ishihara. *The Japan That Can Say No.* Unofficial translation, no date.

Murphy, R. Taggart. "Power without Purpose: The Crisis of Japan's Global Financial Dominance." *Harvard Business Review* (March–April 1989): n.

Okimoto, Daniel. *Between MITI and the Market.* Stanford, Calif.: Stanford University Press, 1989.

Patrick, Hugh, ed. *Japan's High Technology Industries.* Seattle: University of Washington Press, 1986.

Prestowitz, Clyde, Jr. *Trading Places: How We Allowed Japan to Take the Lead.* New York: Basic Books, 1988.

Ozaki, Robert. *The Japanese: A Cultural Portrait.* Rutland, Vt.: Charles E. Tuttle Co., 1978.

Ramchandran, Jaikumar. "Postindustrial Manufacturing." Harvard Business Review (November–December 1986): n.

Reich, Robert. *The Next American Frontier.* New York: Times Books, 1983.

Reischauer, Edwin O. *Japan: The Story of a Nation.* New York: Alfred A. Knopf, 1976.

——. *The Japanese Today: Change and Continuity.* Cambridge, Mass.: Belknap Press, 1987.

——. *The United States and Japan.* Cambridge, Mass.: Harvard University Press, 1965.

Report of the Advisory Committee for Trade Policy and Negotiations. *"Analysis of the U.S.–Japan Trade Problem."* February 1989.

"The Rival Japan Respects." *Business Week,* 3 November 1989.

Schlossstein, Stephen. *Trade War.* New York: Congdon and Weed, 1984.

Tasca, Diane, ed. *U.S.–Japanese Economic Relations—Cooperation, Competition, and Confrontation.* New York: Pergamon Press, 1980.

Tatsuno, Sheridan. *Created in Japan.* New York: Harper and Row, 1990.

Taylor, Jared. *Shadows of the Rising Sun.* New York: William Morrow, 1983.

U.S. Congress. House Foreign Affairs Committee. *Developments in United States-Japan Economic Relations, May 1987.* Hearings of April–May, 1987.

——. *Government Decisionmaking in Japan: Implications for the United States.* 1982.

——. *United States Foreign Economic Policy Toward Japan.* Hearings of November, 1971.

——. *United States-Japan Relations.* Hearings of March–August, 1982.

U.S. Congress. House Ways and Means Committee. *High Technology and Japanese Industrial Policy: A Strategy for U.S. Policymakers.* Hearings of October, 1980.

——. *Report on Trade Mission to Far East.* December, 1981.

——. *Task Force Report on United States-Japan Trade.* January, 1979.

——. *United States-Japan Trade Relations.* Hearings of March–April, 1983.

——. *United States-Japan Trade Report.* September, 1980.

U.S. Congress. Joint Economic Committee. *Japan in United States Foreign Economic Policy.* November, 1961.

——. *Japan's Economy and Trade with the United States.* December, 1985.

——. *The Legacy of the Japanese Voluntary Export Restraints.* Hearings of June, 1985.

U.S. Congress. Senate Foreign Relations Committee. *U.S. Trade Relations with Japan.* Hearing of September, 1982.

U.S. Congress, Office of Technology Assessment. *Making Things Better—Competing in Manufacturing.* Washington, D.C.: Government Printing Office, 1990.

——. *Paying the Bill: Manufacturing and America's Trade Deficit.* Washington, D.C.: Government Printing Office, 1988.

Van Wolferen, Karel. *The Enigma of Japanese Power.* New York: Alfred A. Knopf, 1989.

Wilkinson, Endymion. *Misunderstanding: Europe versus Japan.* Tokyo: Chuo-koron-sha, 1979.

Index